# Learn OpenShift

Deploy, build, manage, and migrate applications with
OpenShift Origin 3.9

**Denis Zuev**
**Artemii Kropachev**
**Aleksey Usov**

**BIRMINGHAM - MUMBAI**

# Learn OpenShift

**Commissioning Editor:** Gebin George
**Acquisition Editor:** Shrilekha Inani
**Content Development Editor:** Ronn Kurien
**Technical Editor:** Prachi Sawant
**Copy Editor:** Safis Editing
**Project Coordinator:** Kinjal Bari
**Proofreader:** Safis Editing
**Indexer:** Mariammal Chettiyar
**Graphics:** Tom Scaria
**Production Coordinator:** Shraddha Falebhai

First published: July 2018

Production reference: 1270718

Published by Packt Publishing Ltd.
Livery Place
35 Livery Street
Birmingham
B3 2PB, UK.

ISBN 978-1-78899-232-9

www.packtpub.com

`mapt.io`

Mapt is an online digital library that gives you full access to over 5,000 books and videos, as well as industry leading tools to help you plan your personal development and advance your career. For more information, please visit our website.

# Why subscribe?

- Spend less time learning and more time coding with practical eBooks and Videos from over 4,000 industry professionals

- Improve your learning with Skill Plans built especially for you

- Get a free eBook or video every month

- Mapt is fully searchable

- Copy and paste, print, and bookmark content

# PacktPub.com

Did you know that Packt offers eBook versions of every book published, with PDF and ePub files available? You can upgrade to the eBook version at `www.PacktPub.com` and as a print book customer, you are entitled to a discount on the eBook copy. Get in touch with us at `service@packtpub.com` for more details.

At `www.PacktPub.com`, you can also read a collection of free technical articles, sign up for a range of free newsletters, and receive exclusive discounts and offers on Packt books and eBooks.

# Contributors

## About the authors

**Denis Zuev** is a worldwide IT expert with 10+ years' experience. Some people in the industry think that he is not human, and not without reason. His areas of expertise are networks, servers, storage, the cloud, containers, DevOps, SDN/NFV, automation, programming, and web development; you name it, he can do it. He is also known for his certification achievements. At the moment, he holds the following expert-level industry certifications: RHCI, RHCA.VI, 6xCCIE, 4xJNCIE, CCDE, HCIE, and VCIX-NV. He is a contractor and an instructor who works with top companies, including Cisco, Juniper, Red Hat, and ATT.

**Artemii Kropachev** is a worldwide IT expert and international consultant with more than 15 years' experience. He has trained, guided, and consulted hundreds of architects, engineers, developers, and IT experts around the world since 2001. His architect-level experience covers solution development, data centers, clouds, DevOps, middleware, and SDN/NFV solutions built on top of any Red Hat or open source technologies. He also possesses one of the highest Red Hat certification levels in the world – RHCA Level XIX.

**Aleksey Usov** has been working in the IT industry for more than 8 years, including in the position of infrastructure architect on projects of a national scale. He is also an expert in Linux with experience encompassing various cloud and automation technologies, including OpenShift, Kubernetes, OpenStack, and Puppet. At the time of writing, he holds the highest Red Hat certification level in CIS and Russia – RHCA Level XIV.

# Acknowledgments

Our personal gratitude to Oleg Babkin, Evgenii Dos, Roman Gorshunov, and Aleksandr Varlamov for all the help with this book. We would like to thank International Computer Concepts for Supermicro servers we used for most of the tests, and Li9 Technology Solutions for many ideas in this book. And of course, we would like to thank our families for their patience and support, without them this book would not be possible.

# About the reviewers

**Gopal Ramachandran** is a Red Hat-certified OpenShift expert, and advocate of DevOps and cloud-native technology. Originally from India, where he began his career as a developer, Gopal is now a long-term expat (since 2007) in the Netherlands. He works as a consultant at Devoteam, helping several large and small enterprises in Europe with their digital transformation journeys. He is actively engaged with the local tech community, and shares his thoughts via his Twitter handle @goposky.

**Roman Gorshunov** is an IT architect and engineer with over 13 years of experience in the industry, primarily focusing on infrastructure solutions running on Linux and UNIX systems for Telecoms. He is currently working on design and development of automated OpenStack on Kubernetes-resilient cloud deployment (OpenStack Helm) and CI/CD for the AT&T Network Cloud based on OpenStack Airship.

# Packt is searching for authors like you

If you're interested in becoming an author for Packt, please visit authors.packtpub.com and apply today. We have worked with thousands of developers and tech professionals, just like you, to help them share their insight with the global tech community. You can make a general application, apply for a specific hot topic that we are recruiting an author for, or submit your own idea.

# Table of Contents

**Preface**   1

**Chapter 1: Containers and Docker Overview**   9
  **Technical requirements**   10
  **Containers overview**   11
    Container features and advantages   11
      Efficient hardware resource consumption   12
      Application and service isolation   12
      Faster deployment   13
      Microservices architecture   13
      The stateless nature of containers   13
  **Docker container architecture**   13
    Docker architecture   14
    Docker's main components   14
    Linux containers   15
  **Understanding Docker images and layers**   16
    Container filesystem   16
    Docker storage drivers   17
    Container image layers   17
  **Docker registries**   18
    Public registry   19
    Private registry   19
    Accessing registries   19
  **Docker Hub overview**   19
  **Docker installation and configuration**   21
    Docker installation   21
    Docker configuration   23
  **Using the Docker command line**   23
    Using Docker man, help, info   24
  **Managing images using Docker CLI**   24
    Working with images   27
    Saving and loading images   29
    Uploading images to the Docker registry   30
  **Managing containers using Docker CLI**   32
    Docker ps and logs   33
    Executing commands inside a container   34
    Starting and stopping containers   34
    Docker port mapping   35
    Inspecting the Docker container   35
      Removing containers   36

**Using environment variables** 36
  Passing environment variables to a container 36
  Linking containers 38
**Using persistent storage** 41
**Creating a custom Docker image** 43
  Customizing images using docker commit 44
  Using Dockerfile build 46
  Using Docker history 47
  Dockerfile instructions 48
**Summary** 50
**Questions** 50
**Further reading** 52

**Chapter 2: Kubernetes Overview** 53
**Technical requirements** 54
**Container management systems overview** 54
**Kubernetes versus Docker Swarm** 55
**Kubernetes key concepts** 56
**Kubernetes installation and configuration** 61
**Working with kubectl** 63
  Getting help 64
  Using the kubectl get command 65
  Running Kubernetes pods 66
  Describing Kubernetes resources 68
  Editing Kubernetes resources 69
  Exposing Kubernetes services 69
  Using Kubernetes labels 70
  Deleting Kubernetes resources 71
  Kubernetes advanced resources 72
  Creating kubernetes services using YAML and JSON files 74
**Clearing the virtual environment** 75
**Kubernetes limitations** 76
**Summary** 77
**Questions** 77
**Further reading** 79

**Chapter 3: CRI-O Overview** 81
**Technical requirements** 81
**Container Runtime and Container Runtime Interface** 82
  CRI-O and Open Container Initiative 83
**How CRI-O works with Kubernetes** 84
**Installing and working with CRI-O** 85
  Stopping your virtual environment 87
**Summary** 88
**Questions** 88

Further reading                                                                89
**Chapter 4: OpenShift Overview**                                              91
  **Cloud technology landscape and the role of PaaS**                          91
  **OpenShift as an extension of Kubernetes**                                  93
  **Understanding OpenShift's business value**                                 94
  **OpenShift flavors**                                                        95
  **OpenShift architecture**                                                   96
  **Summary**                                                                  98
  **Questions**                                                                99
  **Further reading**                                                          100
**Chapter 5: Building an OpenShift Lab**                                       101
  **Technical requirements**                                                   101
  **Why use a development environment?**                                       102
  **Deployment variants**                                                      103
  **Working with oc cluster up**                                               103
    System requirements and prerequisites                                      103
    CentOS 7                                                                   104
    macOS                                                                      107
    Windows                                                                    110
    Accessing OpenShift through a web browser                                  112
  **Working with Minishift**                                                   114
  **Working with Vagrant**                                                     117
    Vagrant installation                                                       119
    Installing OpenShift with an all-in-one Vagrant box                        120
  **Summary**                                                                  121
  **Questions**                                                                121
  **Further reading**                                                          122
**Chapter 6: OpenShift Installation**                                          123
  **Technical requirements**                                                   123
  **Prerequisites**                                                            124
    Hardware requirements                                                      124
  **Overview of OpenShift installation methods**                               125
    RPM installation                                                           125
    Containerized installation                                                 125
    Deployment scenarios                                                       126
  **Environment preparation**                                                  128
    Docker                                                                     129
    SELinux                                                                    130
    Ansible installation                                                       130
    SSH access                                                                 131
  **Advanced installation**                                                    132
    OpenShift Ansible inventory                                                132

OpenShift Ansible playbooks                                         136
Installation                                                        137
Validation                                                          138
**Summary**                                                        140
**Questions**                                                      140
**Further reading**                                                141

**Chapter 7: Managing Persistent Storage**                         143
**Technical requirements**                                         144
**Persistent versus ephemeral storage**                            146
**The OpenShift persistent storage concept**                       146
Persistent Volumes                                                 147
Persistent Volume Claims                                           148
The storage life cycle in OpenShift                                148
**Storage backends comparison**                                    149
**Storage infrastructure setup**                                   150
Setting up NFS                                                     151
Installing NFS packages on the server and clients                  152
Configuring NFS exports on the server                              152
Starting and enabling the NFS service                              154
Verification                                                       154
Configuring GlusterFS shares                                       154
Installing packages                                                155
Configuring a brick and volume                                     156
Configuring iSCSI                                                  156
Client-side verification                                           158
NFS verification                                                   158
GlusterFS verification                                             159
iSCSI verification                                                 159
**Configuring Physical Volumes (PV)**                              160
Creating PVs for NFS shares                                        161
Creating a PV for the GlusterFS volume                             163
PV for iSCSI                                                       166
**Using persistent storage in pods**                               167
Requesting persistent volume                                       167
Binding a PVC to a particular PV                                   168
Using claims as volumes in pod definition                          170
Managing volumes through oc volume                                 172
Persistent data for a database container                           174
**Summary**                                                        176
**Questions**                                                      176
**Further reading**                                                177

**Chapter 8: Core OpenShift Concepts**                             179
**Managing projects in OpenShift**                                 179
**Managing users in OpenShift**                                    182

**Creating new applications in OpenShift**   184
**Managing pods in OpenShift**   186
**Managing services in OpenShift**   187
**Managing routes in OpenShift**   189
**Summary**   192
**Questions**   192
**Further reading**   193

**Chapter 9: Advanced OpenShift Concepts**   195
  **Technical requirements**   195
  **Tracking the version history of images using ImageStreams**   199
    Importing images   201
    Creating applications directly from Docker images   202
    Manually pushing images into the internal registry   203
  **Separating configuration from application code using ConfigMaps**   206
  **Controlling resource consumption using ResourceQuotas**   212
  **Controlling resource consumption using LimitRanges**   217
  **Creating complex stacks of applications with templates**   221
  **Autoscaling your application depending on CPU and RAM utilization**   230
    CPU-based autoscaling   231
    Memory-based autoscaling   235
  **Summary**   239
  **Questions**   239
  **Further reading**   241

**Chapter 10: Security in OpenShift**   243
  **Technical requirements**   243
  **Authentication**   247
    Users and identities   248
    Service accounts   255
    Identity providers   257
      AllowAll   258
      DenyAll   258
      HTPasswd   259
      LDAP   260
  **Authorization and role-based access control**   261
    Using built-in roles   262
    Creating custom roles   264
  **Admission controllers**   268
  **Security context constraints**   274
  **Storing sensitive data in OpenShift**   276
    What data is considered sensitive?   277
    Secrets   277
  **Summary**   285

**Questions**    285
**Further reading**    286

**Chapter 11: Managing OpenShift Networking**    287
  **Technical requirements**    288
  **Network topology in OpenShift**    291
    Tracing connectivity    292
  **SDN plugins**    297
    ovs-subnet plugin    298
    ovs-multitenant plugin    300
    ovs-networkpolicy plugin    306
  **Egress routers**    313
  **Static IPs for external project traffic**    313
  **Egress network policies**    314
  **DNS**    317
  **Summary**    323
  **Questions**    323
  **Further reading**    325

**Chapter 12: Deploying Simple Applications in OpenShift**    327
  **Technical requirements**    327
  **Manual application deployment**    329
    Creating a pod    330
    Creating a service    332
      Creating a service using oc expose    332
      Creating a service from a YAML definition    333
    Creating a route    334
      Creating a route by using oc expose    334
      Creating a route from a YAML definition    335
  **Using oc new-app**    336
    The oc new-app command    337
    Using oc new-app with default options    337
  **Advanced deployment**    339
    Deploying MariaDB    340
  **Summary**    342
  **Questions**    342
  **Further reading**    343

**Chapter 13: Deploying Multi-Tier Applications Using Templates**    345
  **Technical requirements**    345
  **OpenShift template overview**    347
    Template syntax    348
    Adding templates    350
    Displaying template parameters    350
    Processing a template    351

**Creating a custom template** 353
Developing YAML/JSON template definitions 353
Exporting existing resources as templates 355
Using the oc new-app -o command 356
**Using templates to deploy a multi-tier application** 357
The Gogs application template 358
Creating the Gogs application 358
**Summary** 361
**Questions** 361
**Further reading** 362

**Chapter 14: Building Application Images from Dockerfile** 363
**Technical requirements** 363
**Dockerfile development for OpenShift** 365
**Building an application from Dockerfile** 366
A simple Dockerfile build 368
**Dockerfile build customization** 370
**Summary** 374
**Questions** 374
**Further reading** 375

**Chapter 15: Building PHP Applications from Source Code** 377
**Technical requirements** 377
**PHP S2I** 379
**Building a simple PHP application** 381
**Understanding the PHP build process** 384
Starting a new build 387
**Summary** 388
**Questions** 389
**Further reading** 389

**Chapter 16: Building a Multi-Tier Application from Source Code** 391
**Technical requirements** 391
**Building a multi-tier application** 392
WordPress template 392
Building a WordPress application 393
**Summary** 398
**Questions** 398

**Chapter 17: CI/CD Pipelines in OpenShift** 399
**Technical requirements** 399
**CI/CD and CI/CD pipelines** 401
**Jenkins as CI/CD** 402
**Jenkins in OpenShift** 403
Creating Jenkins pipelines in OpenShift 404

Starting a Jenkins pipeline                                                408
Editing Jenkinsfile                                                        412
Managing pipeline execution                                                413
**Summary**                                                                415
**Questions**                                                              416
**Further reading**                                                        417
**Chapter 18: OpenShift HA Architecture Overview**                         419
**What is high availability?**                                             419
**HA in OpenShift**                                                        420
Virtual IPs                                                                422
IP failover                                                                423
OpenShift infrastructure nodes                                             425
OpenShift masters                                                          427
OpenShift etcd                                                             427
OpenShift nodes                                                            427
External storage for OpenShift persistent data                             428
**OpenShift backup and restore**                                           429
Etcd key-value store backup                                                429
OpenShift masters                                                          430
OpenShift nodes                                                            430
Persistent storage                                                         430
**Summary**                                                                431
**Questions**                                                              431
**Further reading**                                                        432
**Chapter 19: OpenShift HA Design for Single and Multiple DCs**            433
**OpenShift single-DC HA design**                                          434
OpenShift infrastructure nodes                                             434
OpenShift masters                                                          436
OpenShift nodes                                                            437
Etcd key-value store                                                       437
Persistent storage                                                         437
Physical placement consideration                                           437
Design considerations                                                      438
**OpenShift multi-DC HA design**                                           438
One OpenShift cluster across all data centers                              439
One OpenShift cluster per data center                                      440
Networking                                                                 442
Storage                                                                    444
Application deployment                                                     446
**Summary**                                                                446
**Questions**                                                              447
**Further reading**                                                        448
**Chapter 20: Network Design for OpenShift HA**                            449

**Common network topologies for OpenShift deployments**    449
   Data center networks    449
     Access layer switches    451
     Core layer switches    451
     Edge firewalls    452
     Load balancers    452
     Border routers    453
   Cloud networks    453
     SDN    454
     Security groups    455
     Load balancers    455
     Network Address Translation (NAT) gateways    455
**Commonly made mistakes while designing networks for OpenShift**    456
**General network requirements and design guidelines for OpenShift deployments**    456
**Summary**    457
**Questions**    457
**Further reading**    459

**Chapter 21: What is New in OpenShift 3.9?**    461
  **Major changes in OpenShift 3.9**    461
  **What to expect from the following OpenShift releases**    463
  **Summary**    465
  **Questions**    466
  **Further reading**    467

**Assessments**    469

**Other Books You May Enjoy**    475

**Index**    479

# Preface

OpenShift is an application management platform that leverages Docker as an isolated runtime for running applications and Kubernetes for container orchestration. First introduced on May 4, 2011, it drew heavily from Borg— a container orchestration solution developed by Google engineers for managing hundreds of thousands of containers. In September 2014, it was redesigned, with Docker and Kubernetes becoming its main building blocks, and, since then, it has seen a large number of improvements and a growing community of users and developers. At the time of writing, the most recent version of OpenShift is 3.9, which became generally available on March 28, 2018, with 3.10 under development. Release 3.9 was the next one after 3.7, so technically, it incorporates changes intended for 3.8 as well, and represents a significant step in its life cycle.

Relying on Docker, OpenShift brings the true power of containerization to businesses, allowing them to respond quickly to ever-increasing demand from customers, and to maintain a good reputation by supporting high-availability and multi-data center deployments out of the box. From a business perspective, OpenShift reduces the costs associated with your investment by 531% over five years, with average annual benefits of $1.29 million and a packback period of 8 months of payback period—more details can be found at `https://cdn2.hubspot.net/hubfs/4305976/s3-files/idc-business-value-of-openshift-snapshot.pdf`.

Developers will find OpenShift's self-service portal easy to use, providing quick access to all features and deployment strategies, supporting unmodified source code, as well as Docker images and Dockerfiles, allowing developers to concentrate on development instead of managing their environment. OpenShift can automate every aspect of your release management by relying on Jenkins pipelines and integration with SCM.

For operations, OpenShift provides automatic failover and recovery, as well as high-availability and scalability, meaning that operations teams can spend their time on more high-level tasks. It can also be integrated with various SDN technologies developed by vendors other that Red Hat. And the fact that it relies on well-known technologies makes the learning curve shallow.

From a security standpoint, OpenShift can be integrated with corporate identity management solutions for user management and role assignment. It can expose applications to corporate security infrastructure for granular access control and auditing, protect sensitive data used by your applications, and manage access between different applications.

Examples in this book are demonstrated on OpenShift Origin 3.9, but all of them are applicable to Red Hat OpenShift Container Platform™ as well due to their technical equivalence. The book is built in modular fashion, so if you feel that you are already familiar with certain topics, feel free to move on to another chapter.

# Who this book is for

This book is written for professionals who are new to OpenShift, but it also covers some advanced topics as well, such as CI/CD pipelines, high availability, and multi-data center setups. Readers do not require any background in Docker, Kubernetes, or OpenShift, although familiarity with the basic concepts will be beneficial. The book doesn't cover how to work with Linux though, so at least a year of previous experience with Linux is expected. The primary goal of this book is not so much about theoretical knowledge, as it is about hands-on experience, which is why we use a practical approach with virtual labs where possible. The book starts by introducing readers to the concept and benefits of containers in general, in order to get newcomers up to speed quickly, and then builds on that foundation to guide readers through the basic and advanced concepts of Kubernetes and OpenShift. The book finishes by providing readers with an architectural reference for a highly available multi-data center setup. Before we started working on this book, we realized that there is very little information available on how to deploy OpenShift in multiple data centers for high availability and fault tolerance. Due in no small part to that, we decided to pool our experience and collaborate on writing this book.

# What this book covers

Chapter 1, *Containers and Docker Overview*, discusses containers and how to use Docker to build images and run containers.

Chapter 2, *Kubernetes Overview*, explains how Kubernetes orchestrates Docker containers and how to work with its CLI.

Chapter 3, *CRI-O Overview*, presents CRI-O as a container runtime interface and explains its integration with Kubernetes.

Chapter 4, *OpenShift Overview*, explains the role of OpenShift as a PaaS and covers the flavors it is available in.

Chapter 5, *Building an OpenShift Lab*, shows how to set up your own virtual lab on OpenShift using several methods.

Chapter 6, *OpenShift Installation*, gives you hands-on experience of performing an advanced installation of OpenShift using Ansible.

Chapter 7, *Managing Persistent Storage*, shows you how OpenShift provides persistent storage to applications.

Chapter 8, *Core OpenShift Concepts*, walks you through the most important concepts and resources behind OpenShift.

Chapter 9, *Advanced OpenShift Concepts*, explores OpenShift's resources and explains how to manage them further.

Chapter 10, *Security in OpenShift*, depicts how OpenShift handles security on multiple levels.

Chapter 11, *Managing OpenShift Networking*, explores the use cases for each network configuration of a virtual network in OpenShift.

Chapter 12, *Deploying Simple Applications OpenShift*, shows you how to deploy a single-container application in OpenShift.

Chapter 13, *Deploying Multi-Tier Applications Using Templates*, walks you through the deployment of complex applications via templates.

Chapter 14, *Building Application Images from Dockerfile*, explains how to use OpenShift to build images from Dockerfiles.

Chapter 15, *Building PHP Applications from Source Code*, explains how to implement the Source-to-Image build strategy in OpenShift.

Chapter 16, *Building a Multi-Tier Application from Source Code*, shows how to deploy a multi-tier PHP application on OpenShift.

Chapter 17, *CI/CD Pipelines in OpenShift*, works through implementing CI/CD on OpenShift using Jenkins and Jenkinsfile.

Chapter 18, *OpenShift HA Architecture Overview*, shows how to bring high availability to various layers of your OpenShift cluster.

Chapter 19, *OpenShift HA Design for Single and Multiple DCs*, explains what it takes to build a geo-distributed OpenShift cluster.

Chapter 20, *Network Design for OpenShift HA*, explores the network devices and protocols required to build an HA OpenShift solution.

`Chapter 21`, *What is New in OpenShift 3.9?*, gives you an insight into the latest features of OpenShift 3.9 and explains why you might want to use it.

# To get the most out of this book

This books assumes that you have practical experience with Linux and open source, are comfortable working with a command-line interface (CLI), are familiar with text editors such as nano or vi/vim, and know how to use SSH to access running machines. Since OpenShift can only be installed on RHEL-derived Linux distributions, previous experience of RHEL/CentOS 7 is preferable, as opposed to Debian-based variants. Knowing about cloud technologies and containers will certainly be a plus, but is not required.

To ensure the smoothest experience, we recommend using a laptop or desktop with an adequate amount of RAM, as this is the most critical resource for OpenShift. You can see all requirements for your learning environment in the *Software Hardware List* section that is included in the GitHub repository. Using a system with less than 8 GB RAM may result in occasional failures during the installation of OpenShift and overall instability, which will be distracting, even though it will boost your troubleshooting skills.

Another important aspect concerns the DNS of your environment. Some network providers, such as Cox (`https://www.cox.com`), redirect requests for all non-existent domains (those that result in an NXDOMAIN response from upstream DNS) to a custom web page with partner search results. Normally, that is not a problem, but during the installation of OpenShift, it will manifest itself by failing the installation. This happens because local DNS lookup settings for your virtual machine and containers managed by OpenShift include several domains to contact in order before NXDOMAIN is returned to the client making the request, and the next one is tried only after the previous one has returned NXDOMAIN. So, when your provider intercepts such requests, it may return its own IP, which will result in the OpenShift installer trying to reach a certain service at that IP for a health check. As expected, the request will not be answered and the installation will fail. For Cox, this feature is called *Enhanced Error Results*, so we suggest you opt out of it on your account.

# Download the example code files

You can download the example code files for this book from your account at `www.packtpub.com`. If you purchased this book elsewhere, you can visit `www.packtpub.com/support` and register to have the files emailed directly to you.

You can download the code files by following these steps:

1. Log in or register at `www.packtpub.com`.
2. Select the **SUPPORT** tab.
3. Click on **Code Downloads & Errata**.
4. Enter the name of the book in the **Search** box and follow the onscreen instructions.

Once the file is downloaded, please make sure that you unzip or extract the folder using the latest version of:

- WinRAR/7-Zip for Windows
- Zipeg/iZip/UnRarX for Mac
- 7-Zip/PeaZip for Linux

The code bundle for the book is also hosted on GitHub at `https://github.com/PacktPublishing/Learn-OpenShift`. In case there's an update to the code, it will be updated on the existing GitHub repository.

We also have other code bundles from our rich catalog of books and videos available at `https://github.com/PacktPublishing/`. Check them out!

# Download the color images

We also provide a PDF file that has color images of the screenshots/diagrams used in this book. You can download it here: `https://www.packtpub.com/sites/default/files/downloads/LearnOpenShift_ColorImages.pdf`.

# Conventions used

There are a number of text conventions used throughout this book.

`CodeInText`: Indicates code words in text, database table names, folder names, filenames, file extensions, pathnames, dummy URLs, user input, and Twitter handles. Here is an example: "Let's assume that the template is stored locally as `wordpress.yaml`."

A block of code is set as follows:

```
...
node('nodejs') {
  stage('build') {
    openshiftBuild(buildConfig: 'nodejs-mongodb-example', showBuildLogs:
'true')
  }
```

When we wish to draw your attention to a particular part of a code block, the relevant lines or items are set in bold:

```
openshiftBuild(buildConfig: 'nodejs-mongodb-example',
showBuildLogs: 'true')
}
stage('approval') {
  input "Approve moving to deploy stage?"
}
stage('deploy') {
  openshiftDeploy(deploymentConfig: 'nodejs-mongodb-example')
}
```

Any command-line input or output is written as follows:

```
$ vagrant ssh
```

**Bold**: Indicates a new term, an important word, or words that you see onscreen. For example, words in menus or dialog boxes appear in the text like this. Here is an example: "Once you click on the **Log In** button, the following page is displayed."

Warnings or important notes appear like this.

Tips and tricks appear like this.

# Get in touch

Feedback from our readers is always welcome.

**General feedback**: Email feedback@packtpub.com and mention the book title in the subject of your message. If you have questions about any aspect of this book, please email us at questions@packtpub.com.

**Errata**: Although we have taken every care to ensure the accuracy of our content, mistakes do happen. If you have found a mistake in this book, we would be grateful if you would report this to us. Please visit www.packtpub.com/submit-errata, selecting your book, clicking on the Errata Submission Form link, and entering the details.

**Piracy**: If you come across any illegal copies of our works in any form on the Internet, we would be grateful if you would provide us with the location address or website name. Please contact us at copyright@packtpub.com with a link to the material.

**If you are interested in becoming an author**: If there is a topic that you have expertise in and you are interested in either writing or contributing to a book, please visit authors.packtpub.com.

# Reviews

Please leave a review. Once you have read and used this book, why not leave a review on the site that you purchased it from? Potential readers can then see and use your unbiased opinion to make purchase decisions, we at Packt can understand what you think about our products, and our authors can see your feedback on their book. Thank you!

For more information about Packt, please visit packtpub.com.

# 1
# Containers and Docker Overview

This book is much more than just the fundamentals of OpenShift. It's about the past, present, and the future of microservices and containers in general. In this book, we are going to cover OpenShift and its surroundings; this includes topics such as the fundamentals of containers, Docker basics, and studying sections where we will work with both Kubernetes and OpenShift in order to feel more comfortable with them.

During our OpenShift journey, we will walk you through all the main and most of the advanced components of OpenShift. We are going to cover OpenShift security and networking and also application development for OpenShift using the most popular and built-in OpenShift DevOps tools, such as CI/CD with Jenkins and **Source-to-Image** (**S2I**) in conjunction with GitHub.

We will also learn about the most critical part for every person who would like to actually implement OpenShift in their company—the design part. We are going to show you how to properly design and implement OpenShift, examining the most common mistakes made by those who have just started working with OpenShift.

The chapter is focused on container and Docker technologies. We will describe container concepts and Docker basics, from the architecture to low-level technologies. In this chapter, we will learn how to use Docker CLI and manage Docker containers and Docker images. A significant part of the chapter is focused on building and running Docker container images. As a part of the chapter, you are asked to develop a number of Dockerfiles and to containerize several applications.

In this chapter, we will look at the following:

- Containers overview
- Docker container architecture
- Understanding Docker images and layers
- Understanding Docker Hub and Docker registries
- Installing and configuring Docker software
- Using the Docker command line
- Managing images via Docker CLI
- Managing containers via Docker CLI
- Understanding the importance of environment variables inside Docker containers
- Managing persistent storage for Docker containers
- Building a custom Docker image

# Technical requirements

In this chapter, we are going to use the following technologies and software:

- Vagrant
- Bash Shell
- GitHub
- Docker
- Firefox (recommended) or any other browser

The Vagrant installation and all the code we use in this chapter are located on GitHub at `https://github.com/PacktPublishing/Learn-OpenShift`.

Instructions on how to install and configure Docker are provided in this chapter as we learn.

Bash Shell will be used as a part of your virtual environment based on CentOS 7.

Firefox or any other browser can be used to navigate through Docker Hub.

As a prerequisite, you will need a stable internet connection from your laptop.

# Containers overview

Traditionally, software applications were developed following a monolithic architecture approach, meaning all the services or components were locked to each other. You could not take out a part and replace it with something else. That approach changed over time and became the N-tier approach. The N-tier application approach is one step forward in container and microservices architecture.

The major drawbacks of the monolith architecture were its lack of reliability, scalability, and high availability. It was really hard to scale monolith applications due to their nature. The reliability of these applications was also questionable because you could rarely easily operate and upgrade these applications without any downtime. There was no way you could efficiently scale out monolith applications, meaning you could not just add another one, five, or ten applications back to back and let them coexist with each other.

We had monolith applications in the past, but then people and companies started thinking about application scalability, security, reliability, and **high availability** (**HA**). And that is what created N-tier design. The N-tier design is a standard application design like 3-tier web applications where we have a web tier, application tier, and database backend. It's pretty standard. Now it is all evolving into microservices. Why do we need them? The short answer is *for better numbers*. It's cheaper, much more scalable, and secure. Containerized applications bring you to a whole new level and this is where you can benefit from automation and DevOps.

Containers are a new generation of virtual machines. That brings software development to a whole new level. Containers are an isolated set of different rules and resources inside a single operating system. This means that containers can provide the same benefits as virtual machines but use far less CPU, memory, and storage. There are several popular container providers including LXC, Rockt, and Docker, which we are going to focus on this book.

# Container features and advantages

This architecture brings a lot of advantages to software development.

Some of the major advantages of containers are as follows:

- Efficient hardware resource consumption
- Application and service isolation
- Faster deployment

- Microservices architecture
- The stateless nature of containers

## Efficient hardware resource consumption

Whether you run containers natively on a bare-metal server or use virtualization techniques, using containers allows you to utilize resources (CPU, memory, and storage) in a better and much more efficient manner. In the case of a bare-metal server, containers allow you to run tens or even hundreds of the same or different containers, providing better resource utilization in comparison to usually one application running on a dedicated server. We have seen in the past that some server utilization at peak times is only 3%, which is a waste of resources. And if you are going to run several of the same or different applications on the same servers, they are going to conflict with each other. Even if they work, you are going to face a lot of problems during day-to-day operation and troubleshooting.

If you are going to isolate these applications by introducing popular virtualization techniques such as KVM, VMware, XEN, or Hyper-V, you will run into a different issue. There is going to be a lot of overhead because, in order to virtualize your app using any hypervisor, you will need to install an operating system on top of your hypervisor OS. This operating system needs CPU and memory to function. For example, each VM has its own kernel and kernel space associated with it. A perfectly tuned container platform can give you up to four times more containers in comparison to standard VMs. It may be insignificant when you have five or ten VMs, but when we talk hundreds or thousands, it makes a huge difference.

## Application and service isolation

Imagine a scenario where we have ten different applications hosted on the same server. Each application has a number of dependencies (such as packages, libraries, and so on). If you need to update an application, usually it involves updating the process and its dependencies. If you update all related dependencies, most likely it will affect the other application and services. It may cause these applications not to work properly. Sure, to a degree these issues are addressed by environment managers such as `virtualenv` for Python and `rbenv/rvm` for Ruby—and dependencies on shared libraries can be isolated via `LD_LIBRARY_PATH`—but what if you need different versions of the same package? Containers and virtualization solve that issue. Both VMs and containers provide environment isolation for your applications.

But, in comparison to bare-metal application deployment, container technology (for example, Docker) provides an efficient way to isolate applications, and other computer resources libraries from each other. It not only provides these applications with the ability to co-exist on the same OS, but also provides efficient security, which is a big must for every customer-facing and content-sensitive application. It allows you to update and patch your containerized applications independently of each other.

## Faster deployment

Using container images, discussed later in this book, allows us speed up container deployment. We are talking about seconds to completely restart a container versus minutes or tens of minutes with bare-metal servers and VMs. The main reason for this is that a container does not need to restart the whole OS, it just needs to restart the application itself.

## Microservices architecture

Containers bring application deployment to a whole new level by introducing microservices architecture. What it essentially means is that, if you have a monolith or N-tier application, it usually has many different services communicating with each other. Containerizing your services allows you to break down your application into multiple pieces and work with each of them independently. Let's say you have a standard application that consists of a web server, application, and database. You can probably put it on one or three different servers, three different VMs, or three simple containers, running each part of this application. All these options require a different amount of effort, time, and resources. Later in this book, you will see how simple it is to do using containers.

## The stateless nature of containers

Containers are stateless, which means that you can bring containers up and down, create or destroy them at any time, and this will not affect your application performance. That is one of the greatest features of containers. We are going to delve into this later in this book.

# Docker container architecture

Docker is one of the most popular application containerization technologies these days. So why do we want to use Docker if there are other container options available? Because collaboration and contribution are key in the era of open source, and Docker has made many different things that other technologies have not been able to in this area.

For example, Docker partnered with other container developers such as Red Hat, Google, and Canonical to jointly work on its components. Docker also contributed it's software container format and runtime to the Linux Foundation's open container project. Docker has made containers very easy to learn about and use.

# Docker architecture

As we mentioned already, Docker is the most popular container platform. It allows for creating, sharing, and running applications inside Docker containers. Docker separates running applications from the infrastructure. It allows you to speed up the application delivery process drastically. Docker also brings application development to an absolutely new level. In the diagram that follows, you can see a high-level overview of the Docker architecture:

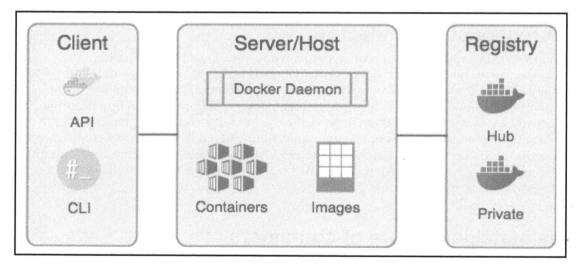

Docker architecture

Docker uses a client-server type of architecture:

- **Docker server**: This is a service running as a daemon in an operating system. This service is responsible for downloading, building, and running containers.
- **Docker client**: The CLI tool is responsible for communicating with Docker servers using the REST API.

# Docker's main components

Docker uses three main components:

- **Docker containers**: Isolated user-space environments running the same or different applications and sharing the same host OS. Containers are created from Docker images.
- **Docker images**: Docker templates that include application libraries and applications. Images are used to create containers and you can bring up containers immediately. You can create and update your own custom images as well as download build images from Docker's public registry.
- **Docker registries**: This is a images store. Docker registries can be public or private, meaning that you can work with images available over the internet or create your own registry for internal purposes. One popular public Docker registry is Docker Hub, discussed later in this chapter.

# Linux containers

As mentioned in the previous section, Docker containers are secured and isolated from each other. In Linux, Docker containers use several standard features of the Linux kernel. This includes:

- **Linux namespaces**: It is a feature of Linux kernel to isolate resources from each other. This allows one set of Linux processes to see one group of resources while allowing another set of Linux processes to see a different group of resources. There are several kinds of namespaces in Linux: **Mount (mnt)**, **Process ID (PID)**, **Network (net)**, **User ID (user)**, **Control group (cgroup)**, and **Interprocess Communication (IPC)**. The kernel can place specific system resources that are normally visible to all processes into a namespace. Inside a namespace, a process can see resources associated with other processes in the same namespace. You can associate a process or a group of processes with their own namespace or, if using network namespaces, you can even move a network interface to a network namespace. For example, two processes in two different mounted namespaces may have different views of what the mounted root file system is. Each container can be associated with a specific set of namespaces, and these namespaces are used inside these containers only.
- **Control groups (cgroups)**: These provide an effective mechanism for resource limitation. With cgroups, you can control and manage system resources per Linux process, increasing overall resource utilization efficiency. Cgroups allow Docker to control resource utilization per container.

- **SELinux**: **Security Enhanced Linux** (**SELinux**) is **mandatory access control** (**MAC**) used for granular system access, initially developed by the **National Security Agency** (**NSA**). It is an additional security layer for Debian and RHEL-based distributions like Red Hat Enterprise Linux, CentOS, and Fedora. Docker uses SELinux for two main reasons: host protection and to isolate containers from each other. Container processes run with limited access to the system resources using special SELinux rules.

The beauty of Docker is that it leverages the aforementioned low-level kernel technologies, but hides all complexity by providing an easy way to manage your containers.

# Understanding Docker images and layers

A Docker image is a read-only template used to build containers. An image consists of a number of layers that are combined into a single virtual filesystem accessible for Docker applications. This is achieved by using a special technique which combines multiple layers into a single view. Docker images are immutable, but you can add an extra layer and save them as a new image. Basically, you can add or change the Docker image content without changing these images directly. Docker images are the main way to ship, store, and deliver containerized applications. Containers are created using Docker images; if you do not have a Docker image, you need to download or build one.

## Container filesystem

The container filesystem, used for every Docker image, is represented as a list of read-only layers stacked on top of each other. These layers eventually form a base root filesystem for a container. In order to make it happen, different storage drivers are being used. All the changes to the filesystem of a running container are done to the top level image layer of a container. This layer is called a Container layer. What it basically means is that several containers may share access to the same underlying level of a Docker image, but write the changes locally and uniquely to each other. This process is shown in the following diagram:

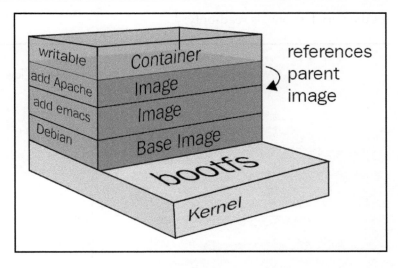

Docker layers

# Docker storage drivers

A Docker storage driver is the main component to enable and manage container images. Two main technologies are used for that—copy-on-write and stackable image layers. The storage driver is designed to handle the details of these layers so that they interact with each other. There are several drivers available. They do pretty much the same job, but each and every one of them does it differently. The most common storage drivers are AUFS, Overlay/Overlay2, Devicemapper, Btrfs, and ZFS. All storage drivers can be categorized into three different types:

| Storage driver category | Storage drivers |
|---|---|
| Union filesystems | AUFS, Overlay, Overlay2 |
| Snapshotting filesystems | Btrfs, ZFS |
| Copy-on-write block devices | Devicemapper |

# Container image layers

As previously mentioned, a Docker image contains a number of layers that are combined into a single filesystem using a storage driver. The layers (also called intermediate images) are generated when commands are executed during the Docker image build process. Usually, Docker images are created using a Dockerfile, the syntax of which will be described later. Each layer represents an instruction in the image's Dockerfile.

Each layer, except the very last one, is read-only:

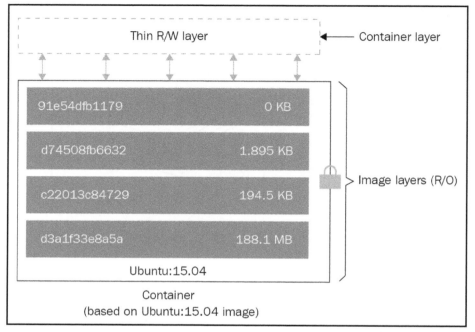

Docker image layers

A Docker image usually consists of several layers, stacked one on top of the other. The top layer has read-write permissions, and all the remaining layers have read-only permissions. This concept is very similar to the copy-on-write technology. So, when you run a container from the image, all the changes are done to this top writable layer.

# Docker registries

As mentioned earlier, a Docker image is a way to deliver applications. You can create a Docker image and share it with other users using a public/private registry service. A registry is a stateless, highly scalable server-side application which you can use to store and download Docker images. Docker registry is an open source project, under the permissive Apache license. Once the image is available on a Docker registry service, another user can download it by pulling the image and can use this image to create new Docker images or run containers from this image.

Docker supports several types of docker registry:

- Public registry
- Private registry

# Public registry

You can start a container from an image stored in a public registry. By default, the Docker daemon looks for and downloads Docker images from Docker Hub, which is a public registry provided by Docker. However, many vendors add their own public registries to the Docker configuration at installation time. For example, Red Hat has its own *proven and blessed* public Docker registry which you can use to pull Docker images and to build containers.

# Private registry

Some organization or specific teams don't want to share their custom container images with everyone for a reason. They still need a service to share Docker images, but just for internal usage. In that case, a private registry service can be useful. A private registry can be installed and configured as a service on a dedicated server or a virtual machine inside your network.

You can easily install a private Docker registry by running a Docker container from a public registry image. The private Docker registry installation process is no different from running a regular Docker container with additional options.

# Accessing registries

A Docker registry is accessed via the Docker daemon service using a Docker client. The Docker command line uses a RESTful API to request process execution from the daemon. Most of these commands are translated into HTTP requests and may be transmitted using `curl`.

The process of using Docker registries is shown in the following section.

A developer can create a Docker image and put it into a private or public registry. Once the image is uploaded, it can be immediately used to run containers or build other images.

# Docker Hub overview

Docker Hub is a cloud-based registry service that allows you to build your images and test them, push these images, and link to Docker cloud so you can deploy images on your hosts. Docker Hub provides a centralized resource for container image discovery, distribution and change management, user and team collaboration, and workflow automation throughout the development pipeline.

Docker Hub is the public registry managed by the Docker project, and it hosts a large set of container images, including those provided by major open source projects, such as MySQL, Nginx, Apache, and so on, as well as customized container images developed by the community.

Docker Hub provides some of the following features:

- **Image repositories**: You can find and download images managed by other Docker Hub users. You can also push or pull images from private image libraries you have access to.
- **Automated builds**: You can automatically create new images when you make changes to a source code repository.
- **Webhooks**: The action trigger that allows you to automate builds when there is a push to a repository.
- **Organizations**: The ability to create groups and manage access to image repositories.

In order to start working with Docker Hub, you need to log in to Docker Hub using a Docker ID. If you do not have one, you can create your Docker ID by following the simple registration process. It is completely free. The link to create your Docker ID if you do not have one is `https://hub.docker.com/`.

You can search for and pull Docker images from Docker Hub without logging in; however, to push images you must log in. Docker Hub gives you the ability to create public and private repositories. Public repositories will be publicly available for anyone and private repositories will be restricted to a set of users of organizations.

Docker Hub contains a number of official repositories. These are public, certified repositories from different vendors and Docker contributors. It includes vendors like Red Hat, Canonical, and Oracle.

# Docker installation and configuration

Docker software is available in two editions: **Community Edition** (**CE**) and **Enterprise Edition** (**EE**).

**Docker CE** is a good point from which to start learning Docker and using containerized applications. It is available on different platforms and operating systems. Docker CE comes with an installer so you can start working with containers immediately. Docker CE is integrated and optimized for infrastructure so you can maintain a native app experience while getting started with Docker.

**Docker Enterprise Edition** (**EE**) is a **Container-as-a-Service** (**CaaS**) platform for IT that manages and secures diverse applications across disparate infrastructures, both on-premises and in a cloud. In other words, Docker EE is similar to Docker CE in that it is supported by Docker Inc.

Docker software supports a number of platforms and operating systems. The packages are available for most popular operating systems such as Red Hat Enterprise Linux, Fedora Linux, CentOS, Ubuntu Linux, Debian Linux, macOS, and Microsoft Windows.

# Docker installation

The Docker installation process is dependent on the particular operating system. In most cases, it is well described on the official Docker portal—`https://docs.docker.com/install/`. As a part of this book, we will be working with Docker software on CentOS 7.x. Docker installation and configuration on other platforms is not part of this book. If you still need to install Docker on another operating system, just visit the official Docker web portal.

Usually, the Docker node installation process looks like this:

1. Installation and configuration of an operating system
2. Docker packages installation
3. Configuring Docker settings
4. Running the Docker service

We assume that our readers have sufficient knowledge to install and configure a CentOS-based **virtual machine** (**VM**) or bare-metal host. If you do not know how to use Vagrant, please follow the guidelines at `https://www.vagrantup.com/intro/getting-started/`.

 Once you properly install Vagrant on your system, just run `vagrant init centos/7` followed by `vagrant up`. You can verify whether vagrant is up with the `vagrant status` command, and finally you can `ssh` into VM by using `vagrant ssh` command.

Since Docker is supported on even the most popular OSes, you have an option to install Docker directly on your desktop OS. We advise you to either use Vagrant or any other virtualization provider such as VMware or KVM, because we have done all the tests inside the virtual environment on CentOS 7. If you still want to install Docker on your desktop OS, follow the link: `https://docs.docker.com/install/`.

Docker CE is available on CentOS 7 with standard repositories. The installation process is focused on the `docker` package installation:

```
# yum install docker -y
...
output truncated for brevity
...
Installed:
docker.x86_64 2:1.12.6-71.git3e8e77d.el7.centos.1
Dependency Installed:
...
output truncated for brevity
...
```

Once the installation is completed, you need to run the Docker daemon to be able to manage your containers and images. On RHEL7 and CentOS 7, this just means starting the Docker service like so:

```
# systemctl start docker
# systemctl enable docker
Created symlink from /etc/systemd/system/multi-
user.target.wants/docker.service to /usr/lib/systemd/system/docker.service.
```

You can verify that your Docker daemon works properly by showing Docker information provided by the `docker info` command:

```
# docker info
Containers: 0
Running: 0
```

```
Paused: 0
Stopped: 0
Images: 0
...
output truncated for brevity
...
Registries: docker.io (secure)
```

# Docker configuration

Docker daemon configuration is managed by the Docker configuration file
(/etc/docker/daemon.json) and Docker daemon startup options are usually controlled
by the systemd unit named Docker. On Red Hat-based operating systems, some
configuration options are available at /etc/sysconfig/docker and
/etc/sysconfig/docker-storage. Modification of the mentioned file will allow you to
change Docker parameters such as the UNIX socket path, listen on TCP sockets, registry
configuration, storage backends, and so on.

# Using the Docker command line

In order to start using Docker CLI, you need to configure and bring up a Vagrant VM. If
you are using macOS, the configuration process using Vagrant will look like this:

```
$ mkdir vagrant; cd vagrant
$ cat Vagrantfile
Vagrant.configure(2) do |config|
 config.vm.box = "centos/7"
 config.vm.hostname = 'node1.example.com'
 config.vm.network "private_network", type: "dhcp"
 config.vm.provision "shell", inline: "groupadd docker; usermod -aG docker
vagrant; yum install docker -y; systemctl enable docker; systemctl start
docker"
end
$ vagrant up
$ vagrant ssh
```

# Using Docker man, help, info

The Docker daemon listens on `unix:///var/run/docker.sock` but you can bind Docker to another host/port or a Unix socket. The Docker client (the `docker` utility) uses the Docker API to interact with the Docker daemon.

The Docker client supports dozens of commands, each with numerous options, so an attempt to list them all would just result in a copy of the CLI reference from the official documentation. Instead, we will provide you with the most useful subsets of commands to get you up and running.

You can always check available man pages for all Docker sub-commands using:

```
$ man -k docker
```

You will be able to see a list of man pages for Docker and all the sub-commands available:

```
$ man docker
$ man docker-info
$ man Dockerfile
```

Another way to get information regarding a command is to use `docker COMMAND --help`:

```
# docker info --help
Usage: docker info
Display system-wide information
--help               Print usage
```

The `docker` utility allows you to manage container infrastructure. All sub-commands can be grouped as follows:

| Activity type | Related subcommands |
|---|---|
| Managing images | `search, pull, push, rmi, images, tag, export, import, load, save` |
| Managing containers | `run, exec, ps, kill, stop, start` |
| Building custom images | `build, commit` |
| Information gathering | `info, inspect` |

# Managing images using Docker CLI

The first step in running and using a container on your server or laptop is to search and pull a Docker image from the Docker registry using the `docker search` command.

Let's search for the web server container. The command to do so is:

```
$ docker search httpd
NAME DESCRIPTION STARS OFFICIAL AUTOMATED
httpd ... 1569 [OK]
hypriot/rpi-busybox-httpd ... 40
centos/httpd 15 [OK]
centos/httpd-24-centos7 ... 9
```

Alternatively, we can go to `https://hub.docker.com/` and type `httpd` in the search window. It will give us something similar to the `docker search httpd` results:

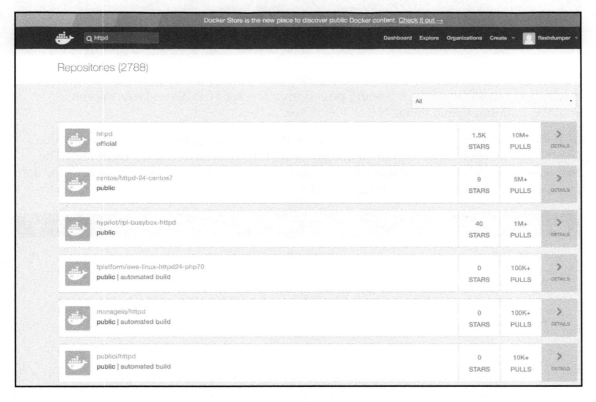

Docker Hub search results

Once the container image is found, we can pull this image from the Docker registry in order to start working with it. To pull a container image to your host, you need to use the `docker pull` command:

```
$ docker pull httpd
```

The output of the preceding command is as follows:

```
Using default tag: latest
latest: Pulling from library/httpd
4176fe04cefe: Pull complete
d6c01cf91b98: Pull complete
b7066921647a: Pull complete
643378aaba88: Pull complete
3c51f6dc6a3b: Pull complete
4f25e420c4cc: Pull complete
ccdbe37da15c: Pull complete
Digest: sha256:6e61d60e4142ea44e8e69b22f1e739d89e1dc8a2764182d7eecc83a5bb31181e
Status: Downloaded newer image for httpd:latest
```

Note that Docker uses concepts from union filesystem layers to build Docker images. This is why you can see seven layers being pulled from Docker Hub. One stacks up onto another, building a final image.

By default, Docker will try to pull the image with the latest tag, but we can also download an older, more specific version of an image we are interested in using different tags. The best way to quickly find available tags is to go to https://hub.docker.com/, search for the specific image, and click on the image details:

Docker Hub image details

There we are able to see all the image tags available for us to pull from Docker Hub. There are ways to achieve the same goal using the `docker search` CLI command, which we are going to cover later in this book.

```
$ docker pull httpd:2.2.29
```

The output of the preceding code should look something like the following:

```
2.2.29: Pulling from library/httpd
4d2e9ae40c41: Pull complete
a3ed95caeb02: Pull complete
71da54557245: Pull complete
721128148697: Pull complete
bb02db57acca: Pull complete
973e8b763f43: Pull complete
9792a80ebd27: Pull complete
Digest: sha256:0a39699d267aaee04382c6b1b4fe2fc30737450fe8d4fabd88eee1a3e0016144
Status: Downloaded newer image for httpd:2.2.29
```

You may notice that the download time for the second image was significantly lower than for the first image. It happens because the first image we pulled (`docker:latest`) has most layers in common with the second image (`httpd:2.2.29`). So there is no need to download all the layers again. This is very useful and saves a lot of time in large environments.

# Working with images

Now we want to check the images available on our local server. To do this, we can use the `docker images` command:

```
$ docker images
```

The output of the preceding command will be as shown in the following screenshot:

```
REPOSITORY          TAG             IMAGE ID          CREATED           SIZE
httpd               latest          01154c38b473      13 days ago       177MB
httpd               2.2.29          78ef8a7db81a      2 years ago       153MB
```

If we downloaded a wrong image, we can always delete it from the local server by using the `docker rmi` command: **ReMove Image** (**RMI**). In our case, we have two versions of the same image, so we can specify a tag for the image we want to delete:

```
$ docker rmi httpd:2.2.29
```

The output of the preceding command will be as shown in the following screenshot:

```
Untagged: httpd:2.2.29
Untagged: httpd@sha256:0a39699d267aaee04382c6b1b4fe2fc30737450fe8d4fabd88eee1a3e0016144
Deleted: sha256:78ef8a7db81acde885e627ceafbc7f2d76a052b44d679b9c274a18bce85d5ccc
Deleted: sha256:5d5325c9e14025425b154bcd4b4c4092fddc0cf28095dec4fda01da336a03aa6
Deleted: sha256:c04125bb67950cffe237d960070d48c9b29a00b27fcb12513406ecf0ab80d32d
Deleted: sha256:5f9dca6732ab55daa3c354a6de5c0e651a7032ad3700a8c5f5f2b4daefb3b8ef
Deleted: sha256:7a9b5807179ca1a30644ad5f8d0ff89c9970f6e30ed8957e7758321eff7036e4
Deleted: sha256:55efd6082c88416ed5089a9f9347d3493264931c11934299da4a0d0fe4aa22fb
Deleted: sha256:41324ac66556b527c8824ad9144cd2639e9753e4e387efde49fd2838082864ca
Deleted: sha256:c2b6854195202c32627a0918233531678a7f53ba89cb10c8ede6acc9c5139ab3
Deleted: sha256:5f7c1bd0a29de2d99977a1476cdc8eb357080a4831e91342738a2587e54bd095
Deleted: sha256:386ab9d75eab80ae1eedf219c639be1f398997e1b0773ccb05d4d0bbb7ca86d2
Deleted: sha256:080cf2d8b7f3c25eea37c4393b6696f30eb0411290ebaedc6dda57f17b375ec2
Deleted: sha256:64f09aa49f80203adc402b131fc8736961031f2b4478b1c5245bcaec404fd354
Deleted: sha256:a5dd5b712a2ae1a4868cedf54e44b8a63c8fd35c9a75edf74d64c099a9278331
Deleted: sha256:e10e5ea91f007db418b284f4adc5f0b98f374d79ae52b9687b0d6d33865ffbcf
Deleted: sha256:c69ae1aa46985cbaf186b6354c61a1d2e0d6af47133db47bf04f0c6eb9c858e9
```

At this point, we have only one image left, which is `httpd:latest`:

```
$ docker images
```

The output of the preceding command will be as shown in the following screenshot:

| REPOSITORY | TAG | IMAGE ID | CREATED | SIZE |
| --- | --- | --- | --- | --- |
| httpd | latest | 01154c38b473 | 13 days ago | 177MB |

# Saving and loading images

The Docker CLI allows us to export and import Docker images and container layers using export/import or save/load Docker commands. The difference between save/load and export/import is that the first one works with images including metadata, but the export/import combination uses only container layers and doesn't include any image metadata information such as name, tags, and so on. In most cases, the save/load combination is more relevant and works properly for images without special needs. The `docker save` command packs the layers and metadata of all the chains required to build the image. You can then load this *saved* images chain into another Docker instance and create containers from these images.

The `docker export` will fetch the whole container, like a snapshot of a regular VM. It saves the OS, of course, but also any change a you made and any data file written during the container life. This one is more like a traditional backup:

```
$ docker save httpd -o httpd.tar

$ ls -l httpd.tar
```

```
-rw-------  1 dzuev  staff  186355712 Feb 28 17:55 httpd.tar
```

To load the image back from the file, we can use the `docker load` command. Before we do that, though, let's remove the httpd image from the local repository first:

```
$ docker rmi httpd:latest
```

The output of the preceding command will be as shown in the following screenshot:

```
Using default tag: latest
latest: Pulling from library/httpd
4176fe04cefe: Pull complete
d6c01cf91b98: Pull complete
b7066921647a: Pull complete
643378aaba88: Pull complete
3c51f6dc6a3b: Pull complete
4f25e420c4cc: Pull complete
ccdbe37da15c: Pull complete
Digest: sha256:6e61d60e4142ea44e8e69b22f1e739d89e1dc8a2764182d7eecc83a5bb31181e
Status: Downloaded newer image for httpd:latest
```

We verify that we do not have any images in the local repository:

```
$ docker images
REPOSITORY TAG IMAGE ID CREATED SIZE
```

Load the image file we previously saved with the `docker save` command. Like `docker export` and docker import, this command forms a pair with Docker save and thus is used for loading a saved container archive with all intermediate layers and metadata to the Docker cache:

```
$ docker load -i httpd.tar
```

The output of the preceding command will be as shown in the following screenshot:

```
dzuev-mac15:~ dzuev$ docker load -i httpd.tar
ffc4c11463ee: Loading layer [==================>]   129.3MB/129.3MB
a9681abc377f: Loading layer [==================>]   3.584kB/3.584kB
53cbc0080070: Loading layer [==================>]   2.56kB/2.56kB
400eca481024: Loading layer [==================>]   5.12kB/5.12kB
ca92f217a68e: Loading layer [==================>]   46.6MB/46.6MB
6702ee5815dd: Loading layer [==================>]   10.44MB/10.44MB
11d3a23fba24: Loading layer [==================>]   3.584kB/3.584kB
Loaded image: httpd:latest
```

Check the local docker images with `docker image` command:

```
$ docker images
```

The output of the preceding command will be as shown in the following screenshot:

| REPOSITORY | TAG | IMAGE ID | CREATED | SIZE |
|---|---|---|---|---|
| httpd | latest | 01154c38b473 | 13 days ago | 177MB |

# Uploading images to the Docker registry

Now we know how to search, pull, remove, save, load, and list available images. The last piece we are missing is how to push images back to Docker Hub or a private registry.

To upload an image to Docker Hub, we need to do a few tricks and follow these steps:

1. Log in to Docker Hub:

```
$ docker login
Username: #Enter your username here
Password: #Enter your password here
Login Succeeded
```

2. Copy the Docker image you want to push to a different path in the Docker repository on your server:

```
$ docker tag httpd:latest flashdumper/httpd:latest
```

Note that `flashdumper` is your Docker Hub username.

3. Finally, push the copied image back to Docker Hub:

```
$ docker push flashdumper/httpd:latest
```

The output of the preceding command will be as shown in the following screenshot:

```
The push refers to repository [docker.io/flashdumper/httpd]
11d3a23fba24: Mounted from library/httpd
6702ee5815dd: Mounted from library/httpd
ca92f217a68e: Mounted from library/httpd
400eca481024: Mounted from library/httpd
53cbc0080070: Mounted from library/httpd
a9681abc377f: Mounted from library/httpd
ffc4c11463ee: Mounted from library/httpd
latest: digest: sha256:6a457fe47eaa405ea173ca61d29c4367a593e8b092ed2e6c0fda0c77d801c485 size: 1780
```

Now the image is pushed to your Docker Hub and available for anyone to download.

```
$ docker search flashdumper/*
```

The output of the preceding command will be as shown in the following screenshot:

| NAME | DESCRIPTION | STARS | OFFICIAL | AUTOMATED |
|---|---|---|---|---|
| flashdumper/httpd | | 0 | | |

You can check the same result using a web browser. If you go to `https://hub.docker.com/` you should be able to see this `httpd` image available under your account:

Docker Hub account images

# Managing containers using Docker CLI

The next step is to actually run a container from the image we pulled from Docker Hub or a private registry in the previous chapter. We are going to use the `docker run` command to run a container. Before we do that, let's check if we have any containers running already by using the `docker ps` command:

```
$ docker ps
CONTAINER ID IMAGE COMMAND CREATED STATUS PORTS NAME
```

Run a container with the `docker run` command:

```
$ docker run httpd
```

The output of the preceding command will be as shown in the following screenshot:

```
AH00558: httpd: Could not reliably determine the server's fully qualified domain name, using 172.17.0.2. Set the 'ServerName' directive glob
ally to suppress this message
AH00558: httpd: Could not reliably determine the server's fully qualified domain name, using 172.17.0.2. Set the 'ServerName' directive glob
ally to suppress this message
[Thu Mar 01 02:49:53.773723 2018] [mpm_event:notice] [pid 1:tid 139825906345856] AH00489: Apache/2.4.29 (Unix) configured -- resuming normal
 operations
[Thu Mar 01 02:49:53.773841 2018] [core:notice] [pid 1:tid 139825906345856] AH00094: Command line: 'httpd -D FOREGROUND'
```

The container is running, but we cannot leave the terminal and continue working in the foreground. And the only way we can escape it is by sending a TERM signal (*Ctrl + C*) and killing it.

# Docker ps and logs

Run the `docker ps` command to show that there are no running containers:

```
$ docker ps
CONTAINER ID IMAGE COMMAND CREATED STATUS PORTS NAMES
```

Run `docker ps -a` to show both running and stopped containers:

```
$ docker ps -a
```

The output of the preceding command will be as shown in the following screenshot:

```
CONTAINER ID    IMAGE      COMMAND             CREATED           STATUS                      PORTS        NAMES
5e3820a43ffc    httpd      "httpd-foreground"  About a minute ago  Exited (0) About a minute ago            vigorous_fermat
```

There are a few things to note here. The `STATUS` field says that container `5e3820a43ffc` exited about one minute ago. In order to get container log information, we can use the `docker logs` command:

```
$ docker logs 5e3820a43ffc
```

The output of the preceding command will be as shown in the following screenshot:

```
AH00558: httpd: Could not reliably determine the server's fully qualified domain name, using 172.17.0.2. Set the 'ServerName' directive globally to suppress this message
AH00558: httpd: Could not reliably determine the server's fully qualified domain name, using 172.17.0.2. Set the 'ServerName' directive globally to suppress this message
[Thu Mar 01 02:51:58.612492 2018] [mpm_event:notice] [pid 1:tid 139874373552000] AH00489: Apache/2.4.29 (Unix) configured -- resuming normal operations
[Thu Mar 01 02:51:58.612605 2018] [core:notice] [pid 1:tid 139874373552000] AH00094: Command line: 'httpd -D FOREGROUND'
[Thu Mar 01 02:52:26.822026 2018] [mpm_event:notice] [pid 1:tid 139874373552000] AH00491: caught SIGTERM, shutting down
```

The last message says `caught SIGTERM, shutting down`. It happened after we pressed *Ctrl + C*. In order to run a container in background mode, we can use the `-d` option with the `docker run` command:

```
$ docker run -d httpd
5d549d4684c8e412baa5e30b20697b72593d87130d383c2273f83b5ceebc4af3
```

It generates a random ID, the first 12 characters of which are used for the container ID. Along with the generated ID, a random container name is also generated.

Run `docker ps` to verify the container ID, name, and status:

```
$ docker ps
```

The output of the preceding command will be as shown in the following screenshot:

| CONTAINER ID | IMAGE | COMMAND | CREATED | STATUS | PORTS | NAMES |
|---|---|---|---|---|---|---|
| 00f343906df3 | httpd | "httpd-foreground" | 19 seconds ago | Up 21 seconds | 80/tcp | epic_ramanujan |

# Executing commands inside a container

From the output, we can see that the container status is UP. Now we can execute some commands inside the container using the `docker exec` command with different options:

```
$ docker exec -i 00f343906df3 ls -l /
total 12
drwxr-xr-x. 2 root root 4096 Feb 15 04:18 bin
drwxr-xr-x. 2 root root 6 Nov 19 15:32 boot
drwxr-xr-x. 5 root root 360 Mar 6 21:17 dev
drwxr-xr-x. 42 root root 4096 Mar 6 21:17 etc
drwxr-xr-x. 2 root root 6 Nov 19 15:32 home
...
Output truncated for brevity
...
```

Option `-i` (`--interactive`) allows you to run a Docker without dropping inside the container. But we can easily override this behavior and enter this container by using `-i` and `-t` (`--tty`) options (or just `-it`):

```
$ docker exec -it 00f343906df3 /bin/bash
root@00f343906df3:/usr/local/apache2#
```

We should fall into container bash CLI. From here, we can execute other general Linux commands. This trick is very useful for troubleshooting. To exit the container console, just type `exit` or press *Ctrl + D*.

# Starting and stopping containers

We can also stop and start running containers by running `docker stop` and `docker start` commands:

Enter the following command to stop the container:

```
$ docker stop 00f343906df3
00f343906df3
```

Enter the following command to start the container:

```
$ docker start 00f343906df3
00f343906df3
```

# Docker port mapping

In order to actually benefit from the container, we need to make it publicly accessible from the outside. This is where we will need to use the –p option with a few arguments while running the docker run command:

```
$ docker run –d –p 8080:80 httpd
3b1150b5034329cd9e70f90ee21531b8b1ab1d4a85141fd3a362cd40db80e193
```

Option –p maps container port 80 to your server port 8080. Verify that you have a httpd container exposed and a web server running:

```
$ curl localhost:8080
<html><body><h1>It works!</h1></body></html>
```

# Inspecting the Docker container

While the container is running, we can inspect its parameters by using the docker inspect command. The output is provided in JSON format and it gives us a very comprehensive output:

```
$ docker inspect 00f343906df3
[
    {
        "Id":
"00f343906df3f26c24e02cd61d6a37bbc36106b3b0372073673c2983cb6f",
        . . .
        output truncated for brevity
        . . .
    }
]
```

## Removing containers

In order to delete a container, you can use the `docker rm` command. If the container you want to delete is running, you can stop and delete it or use the `-f` option and it will do the job:

```
$ docker rm 3b1150b50343
Error response from daemon: You cannot remove a running container
3b1150b5034329cd9e70f90ee21531b8b1ab1d4a85141fd3a362cd40db80e193. Stop the
container before attempting removal or force remove
```

Let's try using `-f` option.

```
$ docker rm  -f 3b1150b50343
```

Another trick you can use to delete all containers, both stopped and running, is the following command:

```
$ docker rm -f $(docker ps -qa)
830a42f2e727
00f343906df3
5e3820a43ffc
419e7ce2567e
```

Verify that all the containers are deleted:

```
$ docker ps  -a
CONTAINER ID IMAGE COMMAND CREATED STATUS PORTS NAMES
```

# Using environment variables

Due to the dynamic and stateless nature of containers, applications cannot rely on either fixed IP addresses or DNS hostnames while communicating with middleware and other application services. Docker lets you store data such as configuration settings, encryption keys, and external resource addresses in environment variables.

## Passing environment variables to a container

At runtime, environment variables are exposed to the application inside the container. You can set environment variables in a service's containers with the *environment* key, just like with `docker run -e VARIABLE=VALUE`. You can also pass environment variables from your shell straight through to a service's containers with the environment key by not giving them a value, just like with `docker run -e VARIABLE`.

Environment variables are used to set specific application parameters, like IP addresses, for a server to connect the database server address with login credentials.

Some container startup scripts use environment variables to perform the initial configuration of an application.

For example, a `mariadb` image is created to use several environment variables to start a container and create users/databases at the start time. This image uses the following important parameters, among others:

| Parameter | Description |
| --- | --- |
| `MYSQL_ROOT_PASSWORD` | This variable is mandatory and specifies the password that will be set for the MariaDB `root` superuser account. |
| `MYSQL_DATABASE` | This variable is optional and allows you to specify the name of a database to be created on image startup. If a user/password was supplied (parameters in the row below) then that user will be granted superuser access (corresponding to `GRANT ALL`) to this database. |
| `MYSQL_USER` and `MYSQL_PASSWORD` | These variables are optional and used in conjunction to create a new user and to set that user's password. This user will be granted superuser permissions for the database specified by the `MYSQL_DATABASE` variable. Both variables are required for a user to be created. |

First, we can try to pull and start a `mariadb` container without specifying the password/user/database-related information. It will fail since the image expects the parameters. In this example, we are starting a container in the foreground to be able to see all error messages:

```
$ docker pull mariadb
latest: Pulling from docker.io/library/mariadb
    ...
    output truncated for brevity
    ...
Digest:
sha256:d5f0bc88ba397233677ff75b7b1de693d5e84527ecf2b4f59adebf8d0bcac3c4
```

Now try to run `mariadb` container without any options and arguments.

```
$ docker run mariadb
error: database is uninitialized and password option is not specified
You need to specify one of MYSQL_ROOT_PASSWORD, MYSQL_ALLOW_EMPTY_PASSWORD
and MYSQL_RANDOM_ROOT_PASSWORD
```

The `docker run` command failed because the MariaDB image initial startup script was not able to find the required variables. This script expects us to have at least the MariaDB root password to start a database server. Let's try to start a database container again by providing all required variables:

```
$ docker run -d --name mariadb -e MYSQL_ROOT_PASSWORD=password -e
MYSQL_DATABASE=example -e MYSQL_USER=example_user -e
MYSQL_PASSWORD=password mariadb
721dc752ed0929dbac4d8666741b15e1f371aefa664e497477b417fcafee06ce
```

Run the `docker ps` command to verify that the container is up and running:

```
$ docker ps
CONTAINER ID IMAGE COMMAND CREATED STATUS PORTS NAMES
721dc752ed09 mariadb "docker-entrypoint.sh" 10 seconds ago Up 9 seconds
3306/tcp mariadb
```

The container was created successfully. Run the verification command to check that `example_user` has access to the `example` database:

```
$ docker exec -it mariadb mysql -uexample_user -ppassword example -e "show
databases;"
+--------------------+
| Database           |
+--------------------+
| example            |
| information_schema |
+--------------------+
```

The startup script created a user named `example_user` with the password `password` as we specified in the environment variables. It also configured a password for the root user. The full list of MariaDB image variables you can specify is located at `https://hub.docker.com/_/mariadb/`.

# Linking containers

Environment variables adjust settings for a single container. The same approach can be used to start a multi-tier application where one container or application works alongside the other:

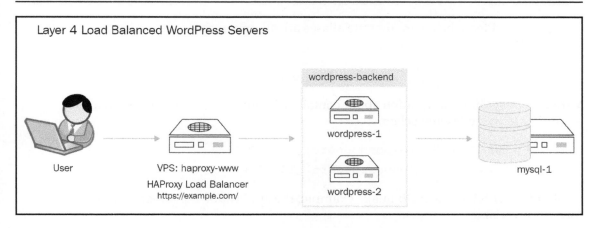

Layer 4 Load Balanced WordPress Servers

Multi-tier application example

In a multi-tier application, both the application server container and database server container may need to share variables such as database login credentials. Of course, we can pass all database connectivity settings to the application container using environment variables. It is very easy to make a mistake while passing multiple -e options to the docker run command, and it is very time-consuming, not to mention that it is very ineffective. Another option is to use container IP addresses to establish connections. We can gather IP address information using docker inspect but it will be difficult to track this information in a multi-container environment.

This means that using environment variables is just not enough to build multi-tier applications where containers depend on each other.

Docker has a featured called *linked containers* to solve this problem. It automatically copies all environment variables from one container to another. Additionally, by linking containers, we can define environment variables based on the other container's IP address and exposed ports.

Using linked containers is done by simply adding the --link container:alias option to the docker run command. For example, the following command links to a container named MariaDB using the DB alias:

```
$ docker run --link mariadb:db --name my_application  httpd
```

The new my_application container will then get all variables defined from the linked container mariadb. Those variable names are prefixed by DB_ENV_ so as not to conflict with the new container's own environment variables.

Please be aware that the aliases are all uppercase.

Variables providing information about container IP addresses and ports are named according to the following scheme:

- {ALIAS}_PORT_{exposed-port}_TCP_ADDR
- {ALIAS}_PORT_{exposed-port}_TCP_PORT

Continuing with the MariaDB image example, the application container would get the following variables:

- DB_PORT_3306_TCP_ADDR
- DB_PORT_3306_TCP_PORT

If the linked container exposes multiple ports, each of them generates a set of environment variables.

Let's take an example. We will be creating a WordPress container which needs access to a database server. This integration will require shared database access credentials. The first step in creating this application is to create a database server:

```
$ docker rm -f $(docker ps -qa)
$ docker run -d --name mariadb -e MYSQL_ROOT_PASSWORD=wordpress -e
MYSQL_DATABASE=wordpress -e MYSQL_USER=wordpress -e MYSQL_PASSWORD=password
mariadb
221462288bc578511154fe79411de002e05f08642b63a72bc7a8f16f7102e52b
```

The next step is to run a WordPress container. In that command, we will link the wordpress container with the mariadb container:

```
$ docker run -d --name wordpress --link mariadb:mysql -p 8080:80 wordpress
Unable to find image 'wordpress:latest' locally
Trying to pull repository docker.io/library/wordpress ...
latest: Pulling from docker.io/library/wordpress
...
output truncated for brevity
...
Digest:
sha256:670e4156377063df1a02f036354c52722de0348d46222ba30ef6a925c24cd46a
1f69aec1cb88d273de499ca7ab1f52131a87103d865e4d64a7cf5ab7b430983a
```

Let's check container environments with the `docker exec` command:

```
$ docker exec -it wordpress env|grep -i mysql
MYSQL_PORT=tcp://172.17.0.2:3306
MYSQL_PORT_3306_TCP=tcp://172.17.0.2:3306
MYSQL_PORT_3306_TCP_ADDR=172.17.0.2
MYSQL_PORT_3306_TCP_PORT=3306
MYSQL_PORT_3306_TCP_PROTO=tcp
...
output truncated for brevity
...
```

> You can see all these variables because the WordPress container startup script handles the `mysql` link. We can see here that the link set a number of `MYSQL_ENV` and `MYSQL_PORT` variables, which are used by the WordPress startup script.

# Using persistent storage

In the previous sections, we saw that containers can be created and deleted easily. But when a container is deleted, all the data associated with that container disappears too. That is why a lot of people refer to containers as a stateless architecture. But we can change this behavior and keep all the data by using persistent volumes. In order to enable persistent storage for a Docker container, we need to use the `-v` option, which binds the container filesystem to the host filesystem that runs that container.

In the next example, we will create a MariaDB container with persistent storage in the `/mnt/data` folder on the host. Then, we delete the MariaDB container and recreate it again using the same persistent storage.

First, remove all previously created containers:

```
$ docker rm -f $(docker ps -aq)
```

We have to prepare persistent storage on the node before we begin. Be aware that we need to give read/write permissions to the persistent storage directory. The MariaDB application works with a MySQL user with *UID=999* inside the container. Also, it is important to mention that the special SE Linux security context `svirt_sandbox_file_t` is required. This can be achieved using the following commands:

```
# mkdir /mnt/data
# chown 999:999 /mnt/data
# chcon -Rt svirt_sandbox_file_t /mnt/data
```

The next step is to create the container running the MariaDB service:

```
$ docker run -d -v /mnt/data:/var/lib/mysql --name mariadb -e
MYSQL_ROOT_PASSWORD=password mariadb
41139532924ef461420fbcaaa473d3030d10f853e1c98b6731840b0932973309
```

Run the docker ps command:

```
$ docker ps
CONTAINER ID IMAGE COMMAND CREATED STATUS PORTS NAMES
41139532924e mariadb "docker-entrypoint.sh" 4 seconds ago Up 3 seconds
3306/tcp mariadb
```

Create a new database and verify the existence of this new DB:

```
$ docker exec -it mariadb mysql -uroot -ppassword -e "create database
persistent;"

$ docker exec -it mariadb mysql -uroot -ppassword -e "show databases;"
+--------------------+
| Database           |
+--------------------+
| information_schema |
| mysql              |
| performance_schema |
| persistent         |
+--------------------+
```

Verify that there is new data in the /mnt/data directory created by the mariadb container. This is how we make the data persistent:

```
$ ls -l /mnt/data/
drwx------. 2 polkitd ssh_keys 4096 Mar 6 16:18 mysql
drwx------. 2 polkitd ssh_keys 20 Mar 6 16:18 performance_schema
drwx------. 2 polkitd ssh_keys 20 Mar 6 16:23 persistent
...
output truncated for brevity
...
```

Delete the mariadb container and verify that all files will be kept:

```
$ docker rm -f mariadb
mariadb

$ ls -l /mnt/data/
drwx------. 2 polkitd ssh_keys 4096 Mar 6 16:18 mysql
drwx------. 2 polkitd ssh_keys 20 Mar 6 16:18 performance_schema
drwx------. 2 polkitd ssh_keys 20 Mar 6 16:23 persistent
```

```
. . .
output truncated for brevity
. . .
```

We are going to rerun the container and verify whether the previously created database *persistent* survived container removal and creation:

```
$ docker run -d -v /mnt/data:/var/lib/mysql --name mariadb mariadb
c12292f089ccbe294cf3b9a80b9eb44e33c1493570415109effa7f397579b235
```

As you can see, the database with the name `persistent` is still here.

Remove all the containers before you proceed to the next section:

```
$ docker rm -f $(docker ps -aq)
```

# Creating a custom Docker image

The Docker community has Docker images for most popular software applications. These include, for example, images for web servers (Apache, Nginx, and so on), enterprise application platforms (JBoss EAP, Tomcat), images with programming languages (Perl, PHP, Python), and so on.

In most cases, you do not need to build your own Docker images to run standard software. But if you have a business need that requires having a custom application, you probably need to create your own Docker image.

There are a number of ways to create a new docker image:

- **Commit**: Creating a Docker image from a running container. Docker allows you to *convert* a working container to a Docker image using the `docker commit` command. This means that image layers will be stored as a separate docker image. This approach is the easiest way to create a new image.
- **Import/Export**: This is similar to the first one but uses another Docker command. Running container layers will be saved to a filesystem using docker export and then the image will be recreated using docker import. We do not recommend this method for creating a new image since the first one is simpler.

- **Dockerfile**: Building a Docker image using a Dockerfile. Dockerfile is a plain text file that contains a number of steps sometimes called instructions. These instructions can run a particular command inside a container or copy files to a container. A user can initiate a build process using Dockerfile and the Docker daemon will run all instructions in the Dockerfile in a temporary container. Then this container is converted to a docker image. This is the most common way to create a new docker image. Building custom docker images from Dockerfile will be described in details in a later chapter.
- **From scratch**: Building a base Docker image. In the two previous methods, Docker images are created using Docker images, and these docker images were created from a base Docker image. You cannot modify this base image unless you create one yourself. If you want to know what is inside your image, you might want to create a base image instead. There are two ways to do so:
  - Create a base image layer using the `tar` command.
  - Use special Dockerfile instructions (from scratch). Both methods will be described in later chapters.

# Customizing images using docker commit

The general recommendation is that all Docker images should be built from a Dockerfile to create clean and proper image layers without unwanted temporary and log files, despite the fact that some vendors deliver their Docker images without an available Dockerfile . If there is a need to modify that existing image, you can use the standard `docker commit` functionality to convert an existing container to a new image.

As an example, we will try to modify our existing httpd container and make an image from it.

First, we need to get the httpd image:

```
$ docker pull httpd
Using default tag: latest
Trying to pull repository docker.io/library/httpd ...
latest: Pulling from docker.io/library/httpd
...
output truncated for brevity
...
Digest:
sha256:6e61d60e4142ea44e8e69b22f1e739d89e1dc8a2764182d7eecc83a5bb31181e
```

Next, we need a container to be running. That container will be used as a template for a future image

```
$ docker run -d --name httpd httpd
c725209cf0f89612dba981c9bed1f42ac3281f59e5489d41487938aed1e47641
```

Now we can connect to the container and modify its layers. As an example, we will update index.html:

```
$ docker exec -it httpd /bin/sh
# echo "This is a custom image" > htdocs/index.html
# exit
```

Let's see the changes we made using the docker diff command. This command shows you all files that were modified from the original image. The output looks like this:

```
$ docker diff httpd
C /usr
C /usr/local
C /usr/local/apache2
C /usr/local/apache2/htdocs
C /usr/local/apache2/htdocs/index.html
...
output truncated for brevity
...
```

The following table shows the file states of the docker diff command:

| Symbol | Description |
|--------|-------------|
| A | A file or directory was added |
| D | A file or directory was deleted |
| C | A file or directory was changed |

In our case, docker diff httpd command shows that index.html was changed.

Create a new image from the running container:

```
$ docker commit httpd custom_image
sha256:ffd3a523f9848776d65de8302253de9dc78e4948a792569ee46fad5c099312f6
```

Verify that the new image has been created:

```
$ docker images
REPOSITORY TAG IMAGE ID CREATED SIZE
custom_image latest ffd3a523f984 3 seconds ago 177.4 MB
docker.io/httpd latest 01154c38b473 2 weeks ago 177.4 MB
```

The final step is to verify that the image works properly:

```
$ docker run -d --name custom_httpd -p 80:8080 custom_image
78fc5731d62e5a6377a7de152c0ba25d350603e6d97fa26967e06a82c8257e71

$ curl localhost:8080
This is a custom image
```

# Using Dockerfile build

Usually, those who use Docker containers expect to have a high-level of automation, and the `docker commit` command is difficult to automate. Luckily, Docker can build images automatically by reading instructions from a special file usually called a Dockerfile. A Dockerfile is a text document that contains all the commands a user can call on the command line to assemble an image. Using docker build, users can create an automated build that executes several command-line instructions in succession. On CentOS 7, you can learn a lot more using the Dockerfile built-in documentation page `man Dockerfile`.

A Dockerfile has a number of instructions that help Docker to build an image according to your requirements. Here is a Dockerfile example, which allows us to achieve the same result as in the previous section:

```
$ cat Dockerfile
FROM httpd
RUN echo "This is a custom image" > /usr/local/apache2/htdocs/index.html
```

Once this Dockerfile is created, we can build a custom image using the `docker build` command:

```
$ docker build -t custom_image2 .
Sending build context to Docker daemon 2.048 kB
Step 1 : FROM httpd
 ---> 01154c38b473
Step 2 : RUN echo "This is a custom image" >
/usr/local/apache2/htdocs/index.html
 ---> Using cache
 ---> 6b9be8efcb3a
Successfully built 6b9be8efcb3a
```

Please note that the . at the end of the first line is important as it specifies the working directory. Alternatively, you can use ./ or even $(pwd). So the full commands are going to be:

```
docker build -t custom_image2 .
```
or

```
docker build -t custom_image2 ./
```
or

```
docker build -t custom_image2 $(pwd)
```

```
$ docker images
REPOSITORY TAG IMAGE ID CREATED SIZE
custom_image2 latest 6b9be8efcb3a 2 minutes ago 177.4 MB
custom_image latest ffd3a523f984 19 minutes ago 177.4 MB
docker.io/httpd latest 01154c38b473 2 weeks ago 177.4 MB
```

# Using Docker history

We can check the history of image modifications using docker history:

```
$ docker history custom_image2
IMAGE CREATED CREATED BY SIZE COMMENT
6b9be8efcb3a 21 hours ago /bin/sh -c echo "This is a custom image" > /u 23
B
01154c38b473 2 weeks ago /bin/sh -c #(nop) CMD ["httpd-foreground"] 0 B
...
output truncated for brevity
...
```

Note that a new layer, 6b9be8efcb3a, is added. This is where we change the content of the index.html file in comparison to the original httpd image.

# Dockerfile instructions

Some Dockerfile instructions are shown in the table:

| Instruction | Description and examples |
|---|---|
| `FROM image[:tag]` | It sets the base image used in the build process.<br>Examples:<br>FROM httpd<br>FROM httpd:2.2 |
| `RUN <command>`<br>`<parameters>` | The RUN instruction executes any commands in a new layer on top of the current image and commits the results.<br>Examples:<br>RUN `yum install -y httpd &&\`<br>`echo "custom answer" >/var/www/html/index.html` |
| `RUN ["command",`<br>`"param1",`<br>`"param2"]` | This is the same as the last one but in Docker format. |
| `COPY <src> <dst>` | The COPY instruction copies new files from `<src>` and adds them to the filesystem of the container at the path `<dest>`. The `<src>` must be the path to a file or directory relative to the source directory that is being built (the context of the build) or a remote file URL.<br>Examples:<br>COPY `index.html /var/www/html/index.html` |
| `ENTRYPOINT`<br>`["executable",`<br>`"param1",`<br>`"param2"]` | An ENTRYPOINT helps you configure a container that can be run as an executable. When you specify an ENTRYPOINT, the whole container runs as if it were only that executable.<br>Examples:<br>ENTRYPOINT `["/usr/sbin/httpd","-D","FOREGROUND"]`<br>In most cases the default value of ENTRYPOINT is `/bin/sh -c`, which means that CMD will be interpreted as a command to run |
| `EXPOSE <port>` | This instruction informs a Docker daemon that an application will be listening on this port at runtime. This is not very useful when working with standalone Docker containers because port publishing is performed via the `-p` argument of the CLI, but it is used by OpenShift when creating a service for a new application deployed from a Docker image and by Docker itself when exporting default environment variables inside a container. |

| CMD ["executable", "param1", "param2"] | Provides arguments to an ENTRYPOINT command and can be overridden at runtime with the docker run command. Example: CMD ["/usr/sbin/httpd","-D","FOREGROUND"] |
|---|---|

When the docker build command is run, Docker reads the provided Dockerfile from top to bottom, creating a separate layer for every instruction and placing it in the internal cache. If an instruction from Dockerfile is updated, it invalidates the respective caching layer and every subsequent one, forcing Docker to rebuild them when the docker build command is run again. Therefore, it's more effective to place the most malleable instructions at the end of Dockerfile, so that the number of invalidated layers is minimized and cache usage is maximized. For example, suppose we have a Dockerfile with the following contents:

```
$ cat Dockerfile
FROM centos:latest
RUN yum -y update
RUN yum -y install nginx, mariadb, php5, php5-mysql
RUN yum -y install httpd
CMD ["nginx", "-g", "daemon off;"]
```

In the example, if you choose to use MySQL instead of MariaDB, the layer created by the second RUN command, as well as the third one, will be invalidated, which for complex images means a noticeably longer build process.

Consider the following example. Docker includes images for minimal OSes. These base images can be used to build custom images on top of them. In the example, we will be using a CentOS 7 base image to create a web server container from scratch:

1. First, we need to create a project directory:

   ```
   $ mkdir custom_project; cd custom_project
   ```

   Then, we create a Dockerfile with the following content:

   ```
   $ cat Dockerfile
   FROM centos:7
   RUN yum install httpd -y
   COPY index.html /var/www/html/index.html
   ENTRYPOINT ["/usr/sbin/httpd","-D","FOREGROUND"]
   ```

2. Create the index.html file:

   ```
   $ echo "A new cool image" > index.html
   ```

3.  Build the image using `docker build`:

```
$ docker build -t new_httpd_image .
Sending build context to Docker daemon 3.072 kB
...
output truncated for brevity
...
Successfully built 4f2f77cd3026
```

4.  Finally, we can check that the new image exists and has all the required image layers:

```
$ docker history new_httpd_image
IMAGE CREATED CREATED BY SIZE COMMENT
4f2f77cd3026 20 hours ago /bin/sh -c #(nop) ENTRYPOINT
["/usr/sbin/htt 0 B
8f6eaacaae3c 20 hours ago /bin/sh -c #(nop) COPY
file:318d7f73d4297ec33 17 B
e19d80cc688a 20 hours ago /bin/sh -c yum install httpd -y 129 MB
...
output truncated for brevity
...
```

 The top three layers are the instructions we added in the Dockerfile.

# Summary

In this chapter, we have discussed container architecture, worked with Docker images and containers, examined different Docker registries, learned how to manage persistent storage for containers, and finally looked at how to build a Docker image with Dockerfile. All these skills will be required in `Chapter 3`, *CRI-O Overview*, where we start working with Kubernetes. Kubernetes is an essential and critical OpenShift component. It all works like a snowball: Docker skills are required by Kubernetes, and Kubernetes skills are required by Openshift.

In the next chapter, we are going to work with Kubernetes. Kubernetes is an industry-standard orchestration layer for Docker containers. This is where you are going to install and run some basic Docker containers using Kubernetes.

# Questions

1. What are the three main Docker components? choose one:
    1. Docker Container, Docker Image, Docker Registry
    2. Docker Hub, Docker Image, Docker Registry
    3. Docker Runtime, Docker Image, Docker Hub
    4. Docker Container, Docker Image, Docker Hub

2. Choose two valid registry types:
    1. Personal Registry
    2. Private Registry
    3. Public Registry
    4. Security Registry

3. The main purpose of Docker Persistent Storage is to make sure that an application data is saved if a container dies:
    1. True
    2. False

4. What Linux feature controls resource limitations for a Docker container? choose one:
    1. Cgroups
    2. Namespaces
    3. SELinux
    4. chroot

5. What commands can be used to build a custom image from a Dockerfile? choose two:
    1. docker build -t new_httpd_image .
    2. docker build -t new_httpd_image .\
    3. docker build -t new_httpd_image ($pwd)
    4. docker build -t new_httpd_image ./

6. The `docker commit` command saves Docker images to an upstream repository:
    1. True
    2. False

# Further reading

Since we are covering the very basics of Docker containers, you may be interested in diving into specific topics. Here's a list of links that may be helpful to look through to learn more about Docker and containers in general:

- **Docker overview**: https://docs.docker.com/engine/docker-overview/
- **Docker CLI**: https://docs.docker.com/engine/reference/commandline/cli/
- **Docker Storage**: https://docs.docker.com/storage/volumes/
- **Docker storage drivers**: https://docs.docker.com/storage/storagedriver/select-storage-driver/

# Kubernetes Overview 2

In the previous chapter, we discussed container architecture, worked with Docker images and containers, took a look at different Docker registries, learned how to manage persistent storage for containers, and finally, learned how to build our own Docker image with Dockerfile. All these skills will be required in `Chapter 3`, *CRI-O Overview*, where we start working with Kubernetes. Kubernetes is an essential and critical OpenShift component. It all works like a snowball: Docker skills are required by Kubernetes, and Kubernetes skills are required by OpenShift.

Container management in a distributed environment is difficult, but not with Kubernetes. This brief introduction to Kubernetes will give you an idea of what Kubernetes is and how it works. In this chapter, you will learn how to install and configure a Kubernetes cluster using a simplified method. We will also explain the container management basics, including some theories regarding pods, services, and routes. We will show you how to deploy an application in a Kubernetes cluster.

 Since, in our lab environment, we have only one Kubernetes node, we are going to use the Kubernetes cluster and Minikube VM terms interchangeably in this chapter.

In this chapter, we will look at the following:

- Container management systems overview
- The difference between Kubernetes and Docker Swarm
- Kubernetes key concepts
- Kubernetes installation and configuration
- Working with kubectl
- Clearing the virtual environment
- Kubernetes limitations

# Technical requirements

In this chapter, we are going to use the following technologies and software:

- Minikube
- Bash Shell
- GitHub
- Kubernetes
- Docker
- Firefox

You will be required to install Minikube on your laptop or any other virtual environment you are going to use. All the instructions for installing Minikube can be found at `https://kubernetes.io/docs/tasks/tools/install-minikube/`.

All the code for this chapter is located on GitHub at `https://github.com/PacktPublishing/Learn-OpenShift`.

Bash Shell will be used as a part of your virtual environment.

Firefox or any other browser can be used to navigate through Docker Hub.

# Container management systems overview

Containers offer unmatched benefits in terms of density, deployment speed, and scalability in comparison to virtualization. But containers by themselves are not enough to match all the requirements of today's business, which expects the infrastructure to be adaptable to dynamic challenges. It is quite simple to start and manage a couple dozen containers, but things get complicated when the number climbs to hundreds, which is very common for large workloads. This is where **Container Orchestration Engines** (**COE**) come in. They bring true power to containers, offering various mechanisms to deploy, destroy, and scale multiple containers rapidly.

There are multiple container management solutions available, with the most popular being Kubernetes and Docker Swarm:

- **Kubernetes**: First released in July 2015, Kubernetes comes directly from Borg—a cluster management and job scheduling system developed by Google. Kubernetes was also developed by Google engineers; in fact, many developers who previously worked on Borg later moved to working on Kubernetes. Like Docker, it is written in Go, the language also designed and implemented by Google in 2007. It's built around the concept of resources—complex API entities that serve as an interface to the underlying mechanisms and serialized in YAML or JSON. All software components run on two types of machine: masters and nodes. Masters perform management, dispatching, and synchronization functions, while nodes provide a runtime environment for running containers.
- **Docker Swarm**: Docker Swarm is a native container orchestration solution provided by the Docker project. It has many features that Kubernetes provides, but does this using different mechanisms and can be used to quickly deploy a single service or even a stack of services on worker nodes. Swarm Cluster consists of two types of node: managers and workers. Managers control the placement of containers, which are referred to as *tasks* in Swarm terminology, and workers do the heavy lifting of running containers.

# Kubernetes versus Docker Swarm

Kubernetes and Docker Swarm are the most commonly used orchestration frameworks. They provide a similar set of capabilities and essentially solve the same problem—management containers in an unsafe and highly dynamic environment. While some of their features overlap, there are also significant differences and the choice of system depends on many factors, such as the number of containers, availability requirements, and team expertise, to name a few.

The table provides an insight into the most important differences:

| Kubernetes | Docker Swarm |
| --- | --- |
| A separate modular design project that has its own dependencies. | Native container orchestration solution available out of the box. |
| Relatively steep learning curve due to new concepts and complex architecture. | Easy to get started; uses familiar terminology; more lightweight. |

| | |
|---|---|
| A pod is a minimal unit of deployment which represents a group of containers. Integration with other applications is accomplished via services that in this case represent a consistent `IP:port` pair. | Application deployed in containers as services across an entire cluster or a subset of workers using labels. |
| Auto-scaling is supported via deployments/replication controllers by specifying a desired number of pods. Dynamic auto-scaling that takes CPU utilization into account is provided by the `HorizontalPodAutoscaler` resource. | Auto-scaling is not supported out of the box; manual scaling is still possible. |
| A persistence storage layer is separated into two components, PVs and PVCs, which are dynamically bound together on request and can be used to implement shared storage. | Storage volumes are mounted directly into containers. |
| New masters can join an existing cluster, but promotion/demotion of a node is not supported. | Worker nodes can be easily promoted to managers and vice versa. |
| Services are assigned unique DNS names based on the projects they were created in and their names, so each service can reach any other in the same namespace by using its name without domains. | Each service is registered in an internal DNS with the name based solely on the name of the service itself. |

# Kubernetes key concepts

Like any complex system, a Kubernetes cluster can be viewed from multiple perspectives. From the infrastructure perspective, it comprises two sets of nodes; they can be bare-metal servers as well as VMs:

- **Masters**:

    This type of node is responsible for cluster management, network allocation, quota enforcement, synchronization, and communication. Master nodes act as the main point of contact for clients—be it actual people or some external system. In the simplest setup, there can be only one master, but highly available clusters require at least two to prevent common fail situations. The most important service that masters run is the API.

- **Nodes**:

  Nodes do the actual work of hosting Docker containers. More specifically, nodes provide a runtime environment for running pods, which are described later in this book. These servers run the kubelet service to manage pods:

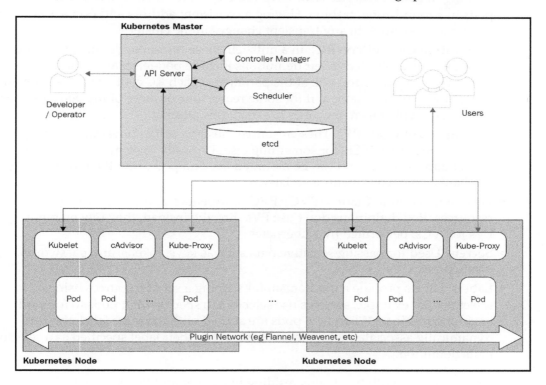

Kubernetes architecture

Logically, the Kubernetes API provides a number of resources that allow you to use various mechanisms provided by Kubernetes while abstracting some low-level implementation details. These resources can be defined in either YAML or JSON format. Here are some of them:

- **Namespaces**: These resources serve the purpose of separating organizational units of users and their projects in a multitenant environment. Moreover, they are used for more fine-grained access control and quota enforcement. Almost all Kubernetes resources, except Volumes and Namespaces themselves, are namespaced, which means their names must be unique in any given namespace.

- **Pods**: Pods represent a collection of containers and each pod serves as a basic management unit in Kubernetes. All containers in a pod share the same storage volumes and network.
- **Services**: They represent an interface between clients and the actual application running in pods. A service is an `IP:port` pair which forwards traffic to backend pods in a round-robin fashion. Having a consistent address and port saves clients having to keep up with any transient changes in the cluster.
- **Replication Controllers** (**RC**): In a nutshell, these resources define how many pods must be replicated. Their definitions include pod templates that describe pods to be launched, and one of the parameters each RC contains is the number of replicas to be maintained. If for some reason one or more of the pods go down, Kubernetes will launch new ones to satisfy this number.
- **Persistent Volumes** (**PV**): These resources abstract actual physical storage systems, be it NFS, iSCSI, or something else. Typically, they are created by a cluster administrator and can be mounted inside a pod using the PVC binding mechanism, which is mentioned later.
- **Persistent Volume Claims** (**PVC**): PVC represents a request for storage resources. Pod definitions don't use PVs directly; instead, they rely on binding PVs to PVCs, performed by Kubernetes.
- **Secrets**: Used for passing sensitive data such as keys, tokens, and passwords inside pods.
- **Labels**: Labels provide a mechanism for scoping a set of resources using selectors. For example, services use selectors to specify what pods to forward incoming traffic to. When new pods are started with the same label, they are dynamically associated with the service that has their label specified as a selector in its definition.

Here is a sample scenario with two teams residing in Denver and Phoenix, with separate namespaces. Selectors, labels, and a number of replicas are specified using the same notation as in actual YAML definitions of services, pods, and replication controllers, respectively:

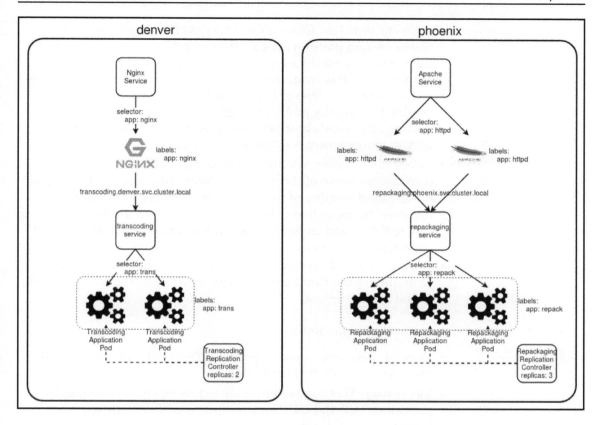

Kubernetes resources

From a service point of view, Kubernetes can be represented as a set of interacting services:

- These services typically run on masters:
    - `etcd`: This is a distributed key-value configuration store that holds all metadata and cluster resources. Due to its quorum model, you are advised to run an uneven number of etcd nodes, starting from three in a highly available setup.
    - `kube-apiserver`: Service that exposes the Kubernetes API to clients. Its stateless nature enables it to be deployed in a highly available configuration by scaling horizontally.

- `kube-scheduler`: Component that governs the placement of newly created pods on nodes. This procedure takes into account such factors as hardware/policy limitations, data locality, and affinity rules. It is worth noting that from the cluster point of view, masters are no different from any other node and thus can be eligible for running pods, although best practices suggest not putting additional strain on master nodes and dedicating them only to management functions.
- `kube-controller-manager`: The component that runs various controllers—some of them are replication controllers that maintain the required number of running pods, node controllers for discovering nodes that went down, a volume controller for binding PVs to PVCs, and an endpoints controller that binds services and pods together.
- `cloud-controller-manager`: Service that provides integration with underlying cloud providers, such as DigitalOcean and Oracle Cloud Infrastructure.

- These services typically run on nodes:

  - **kubelet**: This service uses a pod specification to manage its pods and conduct periodic health checks.
  - **kubeproxy**: This component implements service abstraction by providing TCP and UDP forwarding capabilities across a set of backend pods.
  - **Container runtime environment**: This component is represented in Kubernetes by an underlying container technology. At the time of writing, Kubernetes supports docker and rkt as runtimes:

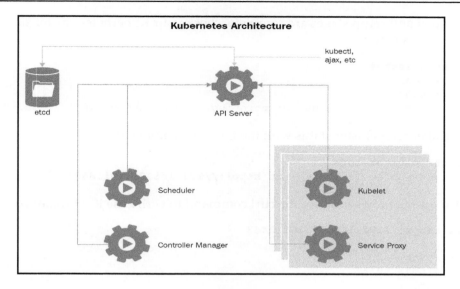

Kubernetes services

# Kubernetes installation and configuration

In this chapter, you will install Minikube—a simple single-node Kubernetes cluster. While not suitable for any production-grade workload, it is a useful tool to learn the basics of cluster management quickly. Although it supports several drivers for VM providers, in this tutorial we will use the KVM2 driver since KVM virtualization is available even in a base Linux environment.

The easiest method is to go to https://kubernetes.io/docs/getting-started-guides/ minikube/ and install Minikube on your favorite OS. Then go to https://kubernetes.io/ docs/tasks/tools/install-kubectl/ and install kubectl. kubectl is a CLI command to manage Kubernetes. Once you are done, it is time to start Minikube:

```
$ minikube start
Starting local Kubernetes v1.9.0 cluster...
Starting VM...
Downloading Minikube ISO
...
<output omitted>
...
Kubectl is now configured to use the cluster.
Loading cached images from config file.
```

Once download and setup stages are complete, check your Kubernetes cluster status with the `minikube` command:

```
$ minikube status
minikube: Running
cluster: Running
kubectl: Correctly Configured: pointing to minikube-vm at 192.168.99.101
```

Check the Kubernetes cluster status with the `kubectl` command:

```
$ kubectl cluster-info
Kubernetes master is running at https://192.168.99.101:8443
```

We can also open a browser or use the curl command to verify the Kubernetes API:

```
$ curl https://192.168.99.101:8443
{
"kind": "Status",
"apiVersion": "v1",
"metadata": {
},
"status": "Failure",
"message": "Unauthorized",
"reason": "Unauthorized",
"code": 401
}
```

There is a nice dashboard that comes with Kubernetes's nice-looking GUI, available on port 30000 via HTTP (for example, `http://192.168.99.100:30000/`). You can open your browser using the same IP we used for cluster verification:

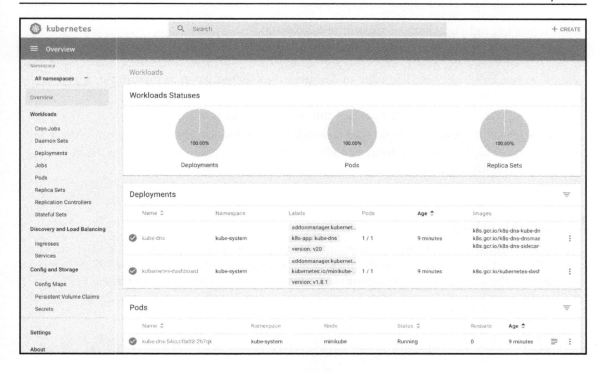

Kubernetes GUI

At this moment, there is not much to look at, as our simple cluster has only one node, one service, and three default namespaces. This is one way to manage Kubernetes, but to be able to effectively use all its features and troubleshoot issues, you need to get comfortable with using CLI, which is what the next section is about.

# Working with kubectl

Kubectl is a command-line interface for managing a Kubernetes cluster and its resources. In this section, you will learn about the most common commands and their use cases.

The syntax for all the commands follows this convention:

```
$ kubectl <COMMAND> <RESOURCE_TYPE> <RESOURCE_NAME> <OPTIONS>
```

Commands in angle brackets <> mean the following:

- `COMMAND`: An action to be executed against one or more resources.
- `RESOURCE_TYPE`: The type of resource to be acted upon, for example, a pod or service.
- `RESOURCE_NAME`: The name of the resource(s) to manage.
- `OPTIONS`: Various flags used to modify the behavior of kubectl commands. They have higher priority than default values and environment variables, thus overriding them.

# Getting help

kubectl has hundreds of different subcommands, options, and arguments. Luckily, kubectl has really good help options. The first one is man pages. If you are using macOS or Linux, you can run the `man-f kubectl` command to check kubectl-related man pages:

```
$ man -f kubectl
kubectl(1) - kubectl controls the Kubernetes cluster manager
kubectl-alpha(1), kubectl alpha(1) - Commands for features in alpha
kubectl-alpha-diff(1), kubectl alpha diff(1) - Diff different versions of
configurations
...
<output omitted>
...
```

If for some reason you do not have man pages available on your system, you can just run the `kubectl` command without any options or arguments. It will show you a list of available subcommands:

```
$ kubectl
kubectl controls the Kubernetes cluster manager.
Find more information at https://github.com/kubernetes/kubernetes.
Basic Commands (Beginner):
  create Create a resource from a file or from stdin.
  expose Take a replication controller, service, deployment or pod and
expose it as a new Kubernetes Service
...
<output omitted>
...
Basic Commands (Intermediate):
 get Display one or many resources
 explain Documentation of resources
...
<output omitted>
```

```
...
Use "kubectl <command> --help" for more information about a given command.
Use "kubectl options" for a list of global command-line options (applies to
all commands)
```

The next step is to check the list of available resources by
running `kubectl <command>` or `kubectl <command> --help` commands, for example,
`kubectl get`:

```
$ kubectl get
  * all
  * certificatesigningrequests (aka 'csr')
  * clusterrolebindings
...
<output omitted>
...
Use "kubectl explain <resource>" for a detailed description of that
resource (e.g. kubectl explain pods).
See 'kubectl get -h' for help and examples.
```

As you can see, you can also get `kubectl get` command examples by running `kubectl
get -h` and a detailed resource explanation by running `kubectl explain pods`. The
`kubectl` command is very easy to navigate and work with.

# Using the kubectl get command

The first essential command to run is `kubectl get nodes`. It gives us the number of
Kubernetes nodes available:

```
$ kubectl get nodes
NAME       STATUS   ROLES    AGE   VERSION
minikube   Ready    <none>   2h    v1.9.0
```

In our case, the number of nodes will be equal to one, since we are using one VM for our
practice. As we mentioned already, in order for different projects to coexist on the same or
different nodes, namespaces are used. You may guess that the command we should use is
`kubectl get namespaces`:

```
$ kubectl get namespaces
NAME          STATUS   AGE
default       Active   15h
kube-public   Active   15h
kube-system   Active   15h
```

It shows you that three default namespaces are available when you install Kubernetes with Minikube:

| Name | Description |
|------|-------------|
| default | The namespace where all resources without other namespaces are placed. It is used when the name of a namespace is not specified. |
| kube-public | Used for resources that must be publicly available even to unauthenticated users. |
| kube-system | As the name implies, it is used internally by Kubernetes itself for all system resources. |

The last main missing component here is pods; as previously mentioned, pods represent a collection of containers and a pod is a basic management unit in Kubernetes. In our case, pods are Docker containers. We do not have any running pods yet, which can be easily verified by kubectl get pods:

```
$ kubectl get pods
No resources found.
```

It says No resources found, all because the pod is a Kubernetes resource, similar to other resources we are going to cover in this book.

 Similarly to kubectl get pods, you can get the status of any other Kubernetes resource. We will discuss other Kubernetes resources later in this chapter.

# Running Kubernetes pods

As with Docker, we can run a Kubernetes pod with the kubectl run command. Let's start with a simple web server example:

```
$ kubectl run httpd --image=httpd
```

We can verify the result by getting a list of Kubernetes pods, by running the kubectl get pods command:

```
$ kubectl get pods
NAME                      READY     STATUS     RESTARTS     AGE
httpd-8576c89d7-qjd62     1/1       Running    0            6m
```

The first time you run this command, you will probably see that the Kubernetes pod status shows up as `ContainerCreating`. What is happening behind the scenes is that the Docker httpd image is being downloaded to Minikube VM. Be patient and give it some time to download the image. A few minutes later you should be able to see the container status is `Running`.

The `kubectl run` command does more than just download an image and run a container out of it. We are going to cover this later in this chapter.

The `8576c89d7-qjd62` part is generated automatically. We are going to discuss this later in this chapter.

Essentially, this pod is a Docker container inside our Minikube VM, and we can easily verify this. First, we need to ssh into Minikube VM with `minikube ssh`, and then run the `docker ps` command:

```
$ minikube ssh
$
$ docker ps
CONTAINER ID IMAGE COMMAND CREATED STATUS PORTS NAMES
c52c95f4d241 httpd "httpd -g 'daemon ..." 12 minutes ago Up 12 minutes
k8s_httpd-container_httpd_default_39531635-23f8-11e8-ab32-080027dcd199_0
...
<output omitted>
...
```

We can try to kill this httpd Docker container, but Kubernetes will automatically spawn the new one:

```
$ docker rm -f c52c95f4d241
```

Check the container status one more time:

```
$ docker ps
CONTAINER ID IMAGE COMMAND CREATED STATUS PORTS NAMES
5e5460e360b6 httpd "httpd -g 'daemon ..." 5 seconds ago Up 5 seconds
k8s_httpd-container_httpd_default_4f5e05df-2416-11e8-ab32-080027dcd199_0
$ exit
```

Note that the httpd container is still up, but with another ID. The initial ID was `c52c95f4d241` and it became `5e5460e360b6` (you will have other IDs). That is one of the benefits of Kubernetes: if one container dies, Kubernetes will bring in a new one automatically. We are going to discuss this in detail later in this chapter.

# Describing Kubernetes resources

We can quickly take a look at the internals of this pod by running the `kubectl describe` command:

```
$ kubectl describe pod httpd-8576c89d7-qjd62
Name: httpd
Namespace: default
Node: minikube/192.168.99.101
Start Time: Sat, 10 Mar 2018 00:01:33 -0700
Annotations: <none>
Status: Running
IP: 172.17.0.4
...
<output omitted>
...
```

It gives us enough information to efficiently locate the pod and do the proper troubleshooting when necessary. In our case, we can ssh to Minikube VM and run the curl command to check if the pod is running the web server properly.

 You may need to use another IP address for the `curl` command; in our case it is `172.17.0.4`, derived from the `kubectl describe` command output.

```
$ minikube ssh
$
$ curl 172.17.0.4
<html><body><h1>It works!</h1></body></html>
$ exit
```

 Note that this pod is accessible only inside the Kubernetes cluster. That is the reason why we need to log in to Minikube VM. If we try to access this address from our local PC, it will not work. We are going to discuss this in the following sections.

# Editing Kubernetes resources

We can also edit the properties of a running container with `kubectl edit pod httpd-8576c89d7-qjd62`. We are not going to change anything at this point, but you can try to change something before we delete the container. We are going to work with the edit command while working with OpenShift in further chapters.

> The `kubectl edit` command by default uses the vi editor. Learn how to use vi first if you are not familiar with this text editor, otherwise you might get into trouble.
>
> Another trick that you can do is to change the editor by running `export EDITOR=nano`, where nano is your favorite text editor.

Similarly, you can edit any other Kubernetes resources. We will discuss other Kubernetes resources later in this chapter.

# Exposing Kubernetes services

When we run a pod using the `kubectl run` command, this pod is accessible only inside Kubernetes. In most of cases, we would want this pod to be accessible from the outside as well. This is where the `kubectl expose` command comes in handy. Let's create the httpd pod one more time and then expose it to the outside world:

```
$ kubectl run httpd --image=httpd
```

```
$ kubectl get pods
NAME READY STATUS RESTARTS AGE
httpd-66c6df655-8h5f4 1/1 Running 0 27m
```

Now let's use the `kubectl expose` command and expose the httpd web server to the outside of Kubernetes:

```
$ kubectl expose pod httpd-66c6df655-8h5f4 --port=80 --name=httpd-exposed -
-type=NodePort
```

While using the `kubectl expose` command, we specify several options:

- `port`: Pod (Docker container) port that we are going to expose to the outside of the Kubernetes cluster.
- `name`: Kubernetes service name.
- `type`: Kubernetes service type. NodePort uses Kubernetes Node IP.

The command to get a list of exposed Kubernetes services is `kubectl get services`:

```
$ kubectl get services
NAME           TYPE        CLUSTER-IP      EXTERNAL-IP    PORT(S)       AGE
kubernetes     ClusterIP   10.96.0.1       <none>         443/TCP       1d
httpd-exposed  NodePort    10.110.40.149   <none>         80:31395/TCP  3s
```

Note that port `80` was mapped to dynamic port `31395` on the Minikube VM. The port is dynamically chosen in the range `30000–32767`.

Also, there is a `ClusterIP` field with the IP address `10.110.40.149` allocated for the `httpd-expose` service. Do not pay attention to this at the moment; we are going to discuss this later in the book.

Finally, use `curl` to check if the httpd server is available from the outside of the Kubernetes cluster:

```
$ curl 192.168.99.101:31395
<html><body><h1>It works!</h1></body></html>
```

If you open this link in your web browser, you should see `It works!` on the web page.

# Using Kubernetes labels

When you have an application that consists of one pod and one service, there is no problem operating these resources. But when your application grows, or you have tens or hundreds of projects, pods, services and other Kubernetes resources, it will get harder to operate and effectively troubleshoot Kubernetes. This is where we can use the Kubernetes labels we mentioned earlier in this chapter. We are going to run a couple more Kubernetes pods using labels:

```
$ kubectl run httpd1 --image=httpd --labels="app=httpd-demo1"
$ kubectl run httpd2 --image=httpd --labels="app=httpd-demo2"
```

Check the Kubernetes pods we have at the moment:

```
$ kubectl get pods
NAME READY STATUS RESTARTS AGE
httpd-8576c89d7-qjd62 1/1 Running 0 17m
httpd1-c9f7d7fd9-rn2nz 1/1 Running 0 21s
httpd2-5b4ff5cf57-9llkn 1/1 Running 0 15s
```

Now, imagine you have at least 10 or more pods. In order to efficiently filter out this output, we can use the −l option:

```
$ kubectl get pods -l="app=httpd-demo2"
NAME                        READY        STATUS       RESTARTS     AGE
httpd2-5b4ff5cf57-9llkn 1/1              Running      0            2m
```

 Filtering out output with Kubernetes labels is not the only use case. Labels are also used alongside selectors. You can get more information on both topics using the Kubernetes official documentation at https://kubernetes.io/docs/concepts/overview/working-with-objects/labels/.

# Deleting Kubernetes resources

If we've done something wrong with the pod, or it may have broken for some reason, there is a simple way to delete a pod using the kubectl delete pod command:

```
$ kubectl delete pod httpd-8576c89d7-qjd62
pod "httpd-8576c89d7-qjd62" deleted
```

We can delete all pods using the −−all option:

```
$ kubectl delete pod --all
pod "httpd-8576c89d7-qjd62" deleted
pod "httpd1-c9f7d7fd9-rn2nz" deleted
pod "httpd2-5b4ff5cf57-vlhb4" deleted
```

 Note that if you run kubectl get pods, you will see all the containers running again. The reason for this is that, when we run the kubectl run command, it creates several different Kubernetes resources, which we are going to discuss in the following section.

We can delete Kubernetes resources by running kubectl delete all with the −l option:

```
$ kubectl delete all -l app=httpd-demo1
deployment "httpd1" deleted
pod "httpd1-c9f7d7fd9-d9w94" deleted

$ kubectl get pods
NAME READY STATUS RESTARTS AGE
httpd-8576c89d7-qjd62 1/1 Running 0 17m
httpd2-5b4ff5cf57-9llkn 1/1 Running 0 15s
```

This command will delete all Kubernetes with a `httpd-demo1` label only. The other two pods will be still available.

Alternatively, we can delete all Kubernetes resources we have created so far by running the `kubectl delete all --all` command:

```
$ kubectl delete all --all
deployment "httpd" deleted
deployment "httpd2" deleted
pod "httpd-8576c89d7-ktnwh" deleted
pod "httpd2-5b4ff5cf57-t58nd" deleted
service "kubernetes" deleted
service "nginx-exposed" deleted
```

# Kubernetes advanced resources

When we create an application with the `kubectl run` command, it takes care of several things. Let's create an httpd pod by running this command one more time and take a deeper look at what actually happens behind the scenes:

```
$ kubectl run httpd1 --image=httpd
```

We can take a look at the series of events that took place during this process by running the `kubectl get events` command. It shows you what Kubernetes did behind the scenes to launch this application. You will see quite a long list, which may seem confusing at first glance, but we can narrow it down by using the following command:

```
$ kubectl get events --sort-by=.metadata.creationTimestamp | tail -n 8
4s   4s   ... kubelet, minikube pulling image "httpd"
4s   4s   ... replicaset-controller Created pod: httpd1-6d8bb9cdf9-thlkg
4s   4s   ... default-scheduler Successfully assigned httpd1-6d8bb9cdf9-thlkg
to minikube
4s   4s   ... deployment-controller Scaled up replica set httpd1-6d8bb9cdf9 to
1
4s   4s   ... kubelet, minikube MountVolume.SetUp succeeded for volume
"default-token-dpzmw"
2s   2s   ... kubelet, minikube Created container
2s   2s   ... kubelet, minikube Successfully pulled image "httpd"
2s   2s   ... kubelet, minikube Started container
```

 We are using the `kubectl get events` command with the `--sort-by=.metadata.creationTimestamp` option to sort our events by timestamp. If you execute this command without this option, events will be out of order.

We are mostly interested in the last two fields on every line. They are SOURCE and MESSAGE respectively. If we read from top to bottom in the series of events, we will see that one Kubernetes component tells the other component to create a pod with the name httpd1-6d8bb9cdf9-thlkg on Minikube VM, which finally happens. Let's describe some of those components:

- replicaset-controller: Sometimes we need more than one httpd pod up and running to handle all the load for the application. ReplicaSet makes sure that a certain number of pods are up and available. ReplicaSet is controlled by the Deployment controller.
- default-scheduler: Decides which node to run a specific pod on. In our case it is Minikube VM.
- deployment-controller: Defines the desired state for a Kubernetes resource. In our case, it is a state of httpd pod. The Deployment controller also instructs ReplicaSet to make sure that certain pods are running.

As already mentioned, the kubectl run command creates other Kubernetes resources including ReplicaSet and Deployment. We can verify that by running kubectl get replicaset and kubectl get deployment respectively:

```
$ kubectl get deploy
NAME DESIRED CURRENT UP-TO-DATE AVAILABLE AGE
httpd1 1 1 1 1 38m

$ kubectl get rs
NAME DESIRED CURRENT READY AGE
httpd1-6d8bb9cdf9 1 1 1 38m
```

We mentioned that Deployment controller defines how many instances of httpd pods run. By default, this number is 1. We can easily change this behavior and edit Deployment config with the kubectl edit deploy httpd1 command:

```
$ kubectl edit deploy httpd1
...
<output omitted>
...
spec:
 replicas: 1 # change this value to 3
...
<output omitted>
...
```

Once you have changed the replica value to 3, save the changes and exit edit mode. The Deployment controller will detect the changes in the config and instruct ReplicaSet to bring up two more `httpd` pods. Let's verify that:

```
$ kubectl get pods
NAME                      READY STATUS   RESTARTS    AGE
httpd1-6d8bb9cdf9-hqks6   1/1   Running  0           5s
httpd1-6d8bb9cdf9-thlkg   1/1   Running  0           48m
httpd1-6d8bb9cdf9-xwmmz   1/1   Running  0           5s
```

If we try to delete all the pods, ReplicaSet will run a new set of pods automatically. Let's see how it works one more time:

```
$ kubectl delete pods --all
pod "httpd1-6d8bb9cdf9-hqks6" deleted
pod "httpd1-6d8bb9cdf9-thlkg" deleted
pod "httpd1-6d8bb9cdf9-xwmmz" deleted

$ kubectl get pods
NAME READY STATUS RESTARTS AGE
httpd1-6d8bb9cdf9-7nx7k 1/1 Running 0 16s
httpd1-6d8bb9cdf9-gsxzp 1/1 Running 0 16s
httpd1-6d8bb9cdf9-skdn9 1/1 Running 0 16s
```

Delete all Kubernetes resources before we move on to the next section:

```
$ kubectl delete all --all
```

# Creating kubernetes services using YAML and JSON files

You can also create Kubernetes resources manually using YAML and JSON files. Let's go ahead and create a simple pod running a httpd web server using the `kubectl create` command. We will have to create a YAML-formatted file:

```
$ cat httpd-pod.yaml
apiVersion: v1
kind: Pod
metadata:
  name: httpd
  namespace: default
spec:
  containers:
  - name: httpd-container
    image: httpd
```

```
ports:
- containerPort: 80
```

 Reading YAML and JSON-formatted files is critical for Kubernetes and for later, in the OpenShift chapter. If you feel uncomfortable reading YAML or JSON files, read up on these subjects. Check the *Further reading* section for more information.

It may look a bit complicated and hard to understand, but as we move on in this book, you will see a lot of similarities between these YAML and JSON files.

 YAML configuration files are very structured and each resource is a set of keys and values. You can use the Kuberentes API documentation to find out what every parameter does: `https://kubernetes.io/docs/reference/generated/kubernetes-api/v1.9/`.

Create a pod using the `httpd-pod.yaml` file:

```
$ kubectl create -f httpd-pod.yaml

$ kubectl get all
NAME          READY      STATUS      RESTARTS     AGE
po/httpd      1/1        Running     0            25s

NAME             TYPE       CLUSTER-IP     EXTERNAL-IP  PORT(S)  AGE
svc/kubernetes   ClusterIP  10.96.0.1      <none>       443/TCP  56s
```

This command creates a pod named `httpd`; it does not create anything else. In larger deployments with heavy automation involved, this is the way to deploy Kubernetes resources, but this, of course, requires better Kubernetes skills.

Similarly, we can create other Kubernetes resources, including ReplicaSet, Deployment, and others.

# Clearing the virtual environment

Once you are done working with Kubernetes, you can easily stop the Minikube cluster by running the `minikube stop` command:

```
$ minikube stop
Stopping local Kubernetes cluster...
Machine stopped.
```

After that, you can delete the Minikube VM if you want by running the `minikube delete` command:

```
$ minikube delete
Deleting local Kubernetes cluster...
Machine deleted.
```

Verify that the Minikube cluster no longer exists:

```
$ minikube status
minikube:
cluster:
kubectl:
```

# Kubernetes limitations

Although it is a powerful orchestration engine, Kubernetes doesn't have the features that are commonly required by PaaS solutions such as OpenShift and others:

- **Security**:

  Kubernetes namespaces are provided mainly for the purpose of resource quota enforcement for different groups of users, but they do not provide any security constraints or authentication. For example, every user from every namespace can see all other namespaces and their resources.

- **Deployments**:

  Kubernetes provides the means to create a deployment from an image with a single command, but doesn't create a service for external clients.

- **SCM integration**:

  Kubernetes doesn't support integration with SCM via webhooks to facilitate deployment.

- **Builds**:

  Kubernetes doesn't provide advanced build modes such as **Source-to-Image** (**S2I**) and Custom Builder.

- **Authentication**:

  Support for advanced authentication schemes such as LDAP, Google, GitHub, Keystone, or Kerberos is achieved only through a webhook or authenticating proxy.

- **CI/CD**:

  Kubernetes has no integrated application life cycle support, which makes it difficult to integrate it into a corporate software delivery framework.

All these limitations will be addressed in the OpenShift sections in subsequent chapters.

# Summary

In this chapter, we have briefly discussed Kubernetes concepts and the Kubernetes architecture, and the main difference between Kubernetes and Docker Swarm. We installed Kubernetes using Minikube, which is a very easy-to-use CLI tool with which to set up a Kubernetes lab environment. Then we used the `kubectl` command to perform various tasks such as running, editing, describing, and deleting Kubernetes pods and other Kubernetes resources. Finally, we finished by listing the main Kubernetes limitations, which we are going to address later in this book.

In the next chapter, we are going to work with CRI-O, which is a universal container runtime interface that allows Kubernetes to provide support for different container platforms.

# Questions

1. What are the two Node types used by Kubernetes?:
     1. Node
     2. Minikube
     3. Vagrant
     4. Master

2. Which container platforms are supported by Kuberntes? choose two:
    1. Docker
    2. OpenShift
    3. Rkt
    4. Minishift

3. In Kubernetes, a pod is a minimal unit of deployment which represents a group of containers:
    1. True
    2. False

4. What are the main two Kubernetes services running on a Kubernetes Node? choose two:
    1. etcd
    2. kubelet
    3. kube-proxy
    4. kube-node
    5. kube-apiserver

5. What are acceptable file formats for creating Kubernetes resources with the `kubectl create -f` command? choose two:
    1. JSON
    2. Jinja2
    3. CSV
    4. YANG
    5. YAML

6. Kubernetes has a built-in CI/CD toolset to improve corporate software delivery frameworks:
    1. True
    2. False

# Further reading

Since we are covering the very basics of Docker containers, you may be interested in diving into specific topics. Here's a list of links that may be helpful to look through to learn more about Docker and containers in general:

- **Kubernetes concepts**: https://kubernetes.io/docs/concepts/
- **Kubernetes CLI**: https://kubernetes.io/docs/reference/generated/kubectl/kubectl/
- **Kubernetes installation**: https://kubernetes.io/docs/setup/pick-right-solution/
- **Kubernetes cheat sheet**: https://kubernetes.io/docs/reference/kubectl/cheatsheet/
- **Kubernetes API overview**: https://v1-9.docs.kubernetes.io/docs/reference/generated/kubernetes-api/v1.9/
- **YAML wiki page**: https://en.wikipedia.org/wiki/YAML
- **YAML syntax check**: http://www.yamllint.com/
- **JSON Wiki page**: https://en.wikipedia.org/wiki/JSON
- **JSON syntax check**: https://jsonlint.com/

# 3
# CRI-O Overview

In the previous chapter, we briefly discussed Kubernetes concepts and the Kubernetes architecture, and the main differences between Kubernetes and Docker Swarm.

The goal of this chapter is to give you a basic understanding of an alternative container runtime technology for Kubernetes—CRI-O. This chapter provides a basic understanding of the Container Runtime Interface, Open Container Initiative, and CRI-O, and describes how to manage containers using that technology.

After reading this chapter, you will have a solid understanding of the following topics:

- The Container Runtime Interface and Open Container Initiative
- How CRI-O works with Kubernetes
- Installing and working with CRI-O

## Technical requirements

In this chapter, we are going to use the following technologies and software:

- Minikube
- Bash Shell
- GitHub
- Kubernetes
- Docker
- Firefox

You will be required to install Minikube on your laptop or any other virtual environment you are going to use. All the instructions for installing Minikube can be found at `https://kubernetes.io/docs/tasks/tools/install-minikube/`.

Bash Shell will be used as part of your virtual environment.

Firefox or any other browser can be used to navigate through Docker Hub.

# Container Runtime and Container Runtime Interface

Before we start with CRI-O, we need talk about the basics. The best place to start will be container runtimes. We already know what containers, Docker, and Kubeknetes are. But how does this all work on a low level? The following diagram illustrates a high-level overview of the communications between Kubernetes and containers:

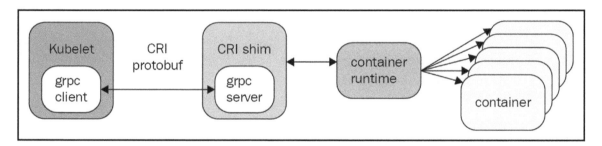

Kubernetes-to-container communications

As you can see, it is not just Kubernetes talking to the container directly. There are two additional layers in the diagram. Let's discuss why we actually need them:

- **Container Runtime**: Each and every container technology, such as Docker, Rkt, or Windows Containers, has its own runtime. In short, Container Runtime is a set of scripts and software tools to run and maintain the work of a container.
- **Container Runtime Interface (CRI)**: As the name implies, CRI is an interface, or a shim layer between Kubernetes and Container Runtime, if you like.

You may ask yourself, *Why do I need CRI? Why can't Kubernetes talk directly to Container Runtime?*. Imagine that Kubernetes and Container Runtime are a manager and an employee that speak English. No issues here. But imagine that there's a new employee—he's an expert in his field and has been contracted by an organization, so now they have to work with each other. However, this new employee speaks only Russian. Now we have a problem. Now, we need to start adding more and more employees speaking languages other than English. You can see where I'm going. In our case, we have a few solutions to this problem:

1. The manager has to learn a new language every time there is a new employee speaking a new language
2. An employee has to learn English
3. Hire an interpreter for every language that new employees speak
4. Hire an interpreter that speaks a universal language

Try to answer this question—what are the most efficient options out of the four that have been listed? I hope it makes sense that option 4 is the most efficient one. For the same reason, CRI and then CRI-O was born. Following the preceding analogy, CRI is option 3 and CRI-O is option 4 in the preceding example.

# CRI-O and Open Container Initiative

Kubernetes initially worked with Docker only, but some time later Rkt by CoreOS came into the picture and they wanted to be supported by Kubernetes as well. Therefore, you have to develop a CRI for every additional Container Runtime. Nowadays, different container technologies are often introduced. This solution is not really scalable and adds a lot of complexity and instability to the whole solution.

That is how CRI-O was brought into the picture. CRI-O stands for **OCI-compliant Container Runtime Interface**, and OCI stands for **Open Container Initiative**. The Open Container Initiative is an Open Source community project that designs open standards for Linux Containers. This is what allows Kubernetes to use any other OCI-compliant Container Runtime to run pods.

# How CRI-O works with Kubernetes

When you want to start or stop a container with Kubernetes, Kubernetes talks to CRI-O, and CRI-O talks to an OCI-compliant container runtime such as runc for Docker to start a container. CRI-O can also pull OCI-compliant container images and manage them on a disk. Good news for Container Developers—they do not need to work with CRI-O directly, as Kubernetes handles that automatically. But it is important to understand the concept and overall architecture:

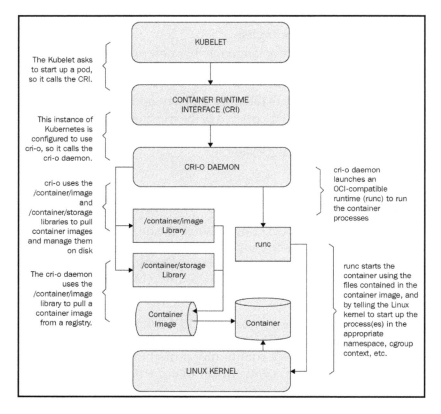

CRI-O architecture

To sum this up, there are a few things to note before we go to the hands-on part and install CRI-O in our lab:

- Kubernetes is configured to talk to CRI-O to launch a new Pod in a container environment

- CRI-O pulls the OCI-compliant Container Image, if necessary, from a registry and manages it locally
- CRI-O talks to OCI-compliant Container Runtime (`runc`, by default) to run it on a Kubernetes Node
- Container Runtime starts the container from a container image that's talking to a Linux Kernel
- Linux Kernel starts Container Processes such as an inappropriate namespace, group, context, and so on

- Each container is monitored and logged by a separate process controlled by Linux Kernel
- The networking part for containers is controlled by a **Container Network Interface** (**CNI**) that can be used by CRI-O as well

# Installing and working with CRI-O

It's time to get hands-on with CRI-O. We are not going to explore CRI-O in depth, but rather show you how to bring up a development environment with CRI-O configured with some basic functionality.

 At the time of writing, CRI-O is still under development. Therefore, the setup instructions in your case might be a bit different and you will need to refer to the official Minikube documentation.

In order to start Kubernetes with CRI-O as a Container Runtime Interface, we are going to use Minikube with an additional `--container-runtime crio` option:

```
$ minikube start --container-runtime crio
Starting local Kubernetes v1.9.0 cluster...
...
<output omitted>
...
Loading cached images from config file.
```

Check Minikube's status and make sure that it is up and running:

```
$ minikube status
minikube: Running
cluster: Running
kubectl:  Correctly Configured: pointing to minikube-vm at 192.168.99.106
```

It looks pretty standard, but if we take a look at the Minikube logs, we will see that Minikube is initializing CRI-O Runtime:

```
$ minikube logs | grep cri-o
Jul 08 21:11:36 minikube localkube[3098]: I0708 21:11:36.333484 3098
kuberuntime_manager.go:186] Container runtime cri-o initialized, version:
1.8.4, apiVersion: v1alpha1
```

Let's create a pod using a Docker image with the `kubectl run` command:

```
$ kubectl run httpd --image=docker.io/httpd
deployment "httpd" created
```

We need to specify a full path to a Docker image since CRI-O is a universal Runtime Interface and it does not know whether we want to use Docker or any other container technology registry.

Wait for a minute or so while Kubernetes Note downloads the `httpd` image and then verify that we have a httpd pod up and running:

```
$ kubectl get pods
NAME                    READY STATUS RESTARTS  AGE
httpd-7dcb9bd6c4-x5dhm 1/1    Running 0        4m
```

Again, from this point of view, it looks pretty standard, but if we run the `kubectl describe` command, we will see that the container ID starts with `cri-o://`:

```
$ kubectl describe pods/httpd-7dcb9bd6c4-x5dhm
Name: httpd-7dcb9bd6c4-x5dhm
...
<output omitted>
...
IP: 10.1.0.4
Container ID: crio://3f2c2826318f1526bdb9710050a29b5d4a3de78d61e0...
Image: docker.io/httpd
...
<output omitted>
...
```

At this point, this shows us that Kubernetes is using the CRI-O runtime interface. This means that Kubernetes is talking to CRI-O. CRI-O (the crio daemon, to be specific) is handling the image pulling and container creating processes. Let's verify this by running the `docker images` and `docker ps` commands inside the Minikube VM:

```
$ minikube ssh docker images
REPOSITORY TAG IMAGE ID CREATED SIZE
```

```
gcr.io/k8s-minikube/storage-provisioner v1.8.0 4689081edb10 4 months ago
80.8MB
```

```
$ minikube ssh docker ps
CONTAINER ID IMAGE COMMAND CREATED STATUS PORTS NAMES
```

As you can see, there are no images or containers named httpd. We mentioned earlier that CRI-O is using runc Container Runtime behind the scenes. To help us further with the verification process, we are going to use the runc command inside the Minikube VM. runc is a CLI command for running containers packaged according to the OCI format. The syntax of the runc command is very similar to the docker command we used in Chapter 1, *Containers and Docker Overview*.

```
$ minikube ssh "sudo runc ps \
3f2c2826318f1526bdb9710050a29b5d4a3de78d61e07ac9d83cedb9827c62e4"
UID PID PPID C STIME TTY TIME CMD
root 5746 5695 0 02:39 ? 00:00:00 httpd -DFOREGROUND
daemon 5788 5746 0 02:39 ? 00:00:00 httpd -DFOREGROUND
daemon 5792 5746 0 02:39 ? 00:00:00 httpd -DFOREGROUND
daemon 5793 5746 0 02:39 ? 00:00:00 httpd -DFOREGROUND
```

Note that 3f2c2826318f1526bdb9710050a29b5d4a3de78d61e07ac9d83cedb98 27c62e4 is the container ID from the kubectl describe pods/httpd-7dcb9bd6c4-x5dhm command we ran previously.

# Stopping your virtual environment

Before you move on to the next chapter, bring down your virtual environment:

```
$ minikube stop
Stopping local Kubernetes cluster...
Machine stopped.
```

And delete the Minikube VM:

```
$ minikube delete
Deleting local Kubernetes cluster...
Machine deleted.
```

# Summary

In this chapter, we briefly covered the Container Runtime and Container Runtime Interface basics, followed by what CRI-O is and how it works. Finally, we installed the Kubernetes cluster with CRI-O as a Container Runtime Interface and ran a few simple commands to verify that Kubernetes was working through CRI-O.

In the next chapter, we are going to talk about the OpenShift architecture, different OpenShift flavors, and OpenShift in general. We will also look at a comparison between OpenShift and Kubernetes so that you have an understanding of why we actually need OpenShift and what is so unique about it.

# Questions

1. Which of the following Kubernetes kubelet services directly communicates with in order to run a pod? choose 1:
    1. OCI
    2. CRI
    3. Docker
    4. Linux kernel

2. What container technologies are supported by CRI-O? choose 2:
    1. Docker
    2. Minishift
    3. Rkt
    4. Minikube

3. Originally, CRI-O was designed to work with the Kubernetes Container Management Platform:
    1. True
    2. False

4. What is the command to verify the CRI-O Container ID? choose 1:
    1. kubectl describe pods/httpd
    2. kubectl show pods/httpd
    3. docker ps
    4. docker images

5. Which two statements are true about CRI-O? choose 2:
    1. CRI-O talks directly to Linux Kernel
    2. CRI-O talks directly to Container Runtime
    3. CRI-O is OCI-compliant
    4. CRI-O is the only Container Runtime Interface available for Kubernetes

6. CRI-O uses the runc Container Runtime by default:
    1. True
    2. False

# Further reading

There is not a lot of information on the internet about CRI-O in comparison to other technologies. Here are a number of links if you are interested in learning more about CRI-O:

- **The CRI-O project's website**: http://cri-o.io/
- **CRI-O blog**: https://medium.com/cri-o
- **CRI-O GitHub repository**: https://github.com/kubernetes-incubator/cri-o
- **OCI website**: https://www.opencontainers.org/
- **CRI-O dashboard on Trello**: https://trello.com/b/xMCopwZm/containers

# OpenShift Overview 4

In the previous chapter, we briefly covered Container Runtime and Container Runtime Interface basics, followed by what CRI-O is and how it works. Finally, we installed a Kubernetes cluster with CRI-O as a Container Runtime Interface and ran a few simple commands to verify that Kubernetes was working through CRI-O.

This chapter is focused on giving a brief description of OpenShift as a **Platform as a Service (PaaS)** Solution. We will describe **Infrastructure as a Service (IaaS)** and PaaS clouds. As a part of the PaaS cloud descriptions, we will provide a basic explanation of OpenShift's business value. In this chapter, you will also learn about OpenShift's technical components and available OpenShift variants.

After reading this chapter, you will have learned about the following:

- Cloud technology landscape and the role of PaaS
- OpenShift as an extension of Kubernetes
- OpenShift business value
- OpenShift flavors
- OpenShift architecture

# Cloud technology landscape and the role of PaaS

Today, any business expects automation to be a cornerstone of success. Traditional approaches are too slow when it comes to delivering innovation at the pace at which the business ecosystem changes. This is one of the main reasons why many businesses are moving towards automation and DevOps.

If we take a look at evolving software delivery technologies, we can easily see that old-generation applications were installed first directly on bare metal, and then on virtual machines. And with time, these companies started using different IaaS cloud platforms. The reason is very obvious—the IaaS platform allows us to bring automation to the next level using cloud orchestration tools and exposed APIs. The way IaaS automation does this on an infrastructure level is that it simplifies virtual networking, storage, and virtual servers. To use IaaS platforms, we still need to install and configure applications and it is usually a time-consuming process. Imagine that there is a need to install and configure a PHP-based application from scratch each and every time you develop a new feature and test it. It takes a lot of time even with automation tools.

PaaS is the next generation of platforms to deliver applications in a quick and automated manner in production. With PaaS, the application delivering process looks very simple—there is no need to install and configure an application platform for web servers, databases, and so on. It is provided by the platform itself, OpenShift in our case. This means that you just need to upload your application code and database structures; the rest of it will be taken care of by PaaS:

The following diagram shows the difference between hosting applications on bare-metal, IaaS, and PaaS platforms:

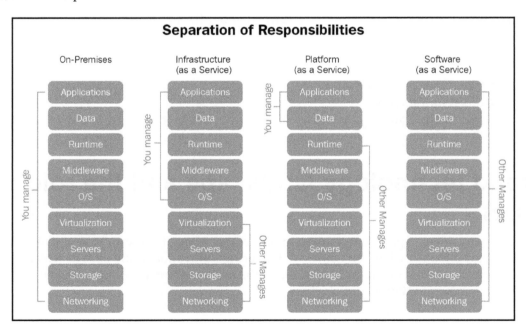

IaaS, PaaS, and SaaS cloud comparison

# OpenShift as an extension of Kubernetes

In previous chapters, we looked at how Kubernetes can simplify the management of Docker containers and take care of container deployment. Kubernetes brings additional value to container management across multiple nodes, which is very important in modern highly available and distributed infrastructure. Despite all the advantages Kubernetes has, it has drawbacks, and most of them are rectified by OpenShift.

OpenShift is a PaaS offering from Red Hat that natively integrates Docker and Kubernetes to create a powerful container cluster management and orchestration system. OpenShift encompasses the architecture, processes, platforms, and services needed to empower developers and operations teams. OpenShift increases reliability across all environments and meets all customer requirements while reducing infrastructure costs.

OpenShift leverages Kubernetes as a container management platform and adds several new important components and capabilities. Some of them are:

- Self-service Portal and Service Catalog
- Build and application deployment automation
- Built-in registry service
- Extended application routing

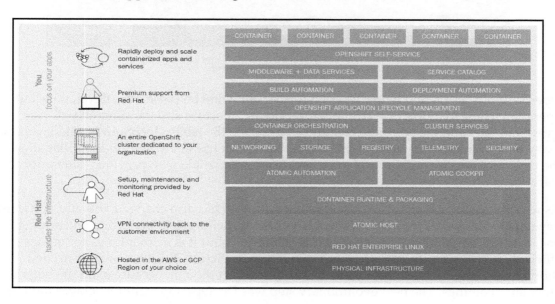

OpenShift services

# Understanding OpenShift's business value

N-tier design is a standard application design like a three-tier web app with web, application, and database tiers. This design slowly evolved into the microservice architecture. The microservice architecture influences the industry and forces many companies to embrace this new trend and make it a new standard. The microservice architecture is much cheaper, scalable, and more secure compared to the monolithic and N-tier architectures. That is why containerized applications bring you to a whole new level:

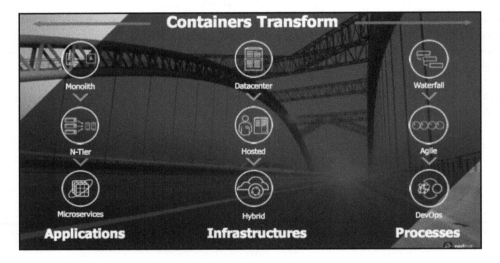

Application, Infrastructure, and Software development evolution

OpenShift pushes these boundaries even further, allowing both software developers and operation teams to utilize powerful microservice architecture and the simplicity of OpenShift GUI and the additional features it brings to the table. OpenShift is where you can really benefit from automation and DevOps. OpenShift has many built-in tools that allow the new microservice architecture to be backward-compatible with previous-generation software.

As we mentioned, the software development approach has also changed; initially, software developers followed a waterfall approach, polishing their apps to perfection and adding one feature after another, making sure it was bug-free. But it is neither time, nor money-efficient. That is why an agile approach came into the picture. Business owners needed shorted software development cycles. It was not perfect though, because of all the bugs and other shortcomings. The next evolutionary step was DevOps. OpenShift leverages modern DevOps processes and makes them simpler and more efficient.

# OpenShift flavors

OpenShift for production comes in several variants:

- OpenShift Origin
- OpenShift Container Platform
- OpenShift Online
- OpenShift Dedicated

As with other products under the Red Hat umbrella, OpenShift has an upstream project called **OpenShift Origin**. The OpenShift Origin homepage is available at `http://openshift.org`. It has a number of installation methods, including the installation of a development environment on a local developer machine.

**Red Hat OpenShift Container Platform** is a production-ready build of OpenShift Origin with all Red Hat production advantages including official support, certification, and so on. OpenShift Container Platform integrates with Red Hat Enterprise Linux and is tested via Red Hat's QA process in order to offer a stable, supportable product for customers who want to have their own private or on-site cloud. An enterprise might get updates every six months, maintaining stabilization across minor updates. OpenShift Container Platform allows for building a private or public PaaS cloud on your infrastructure.

**Red Hat OpenShift Online** is a multi-tenant public cloud managed by Red Hat. OpenShift Online can be a good choice for companies that want to start working with OpenShift but don't want to have their own on-premise infrastructure. This platform allows for hosting a small application for free.

**Red Hat OpenShift Dedicated** is a single-tenant container application platform hosted on **Amazon Web Services** (**AWS**) or Google Cloud Platform and managed by Red Hat. It allows application development teams to quickly build, deploy, and scale traditional and cloud-native applications. OpenShift Dedicated is built on Red Hat Enterprise Linux, Docker container technology, and Google Kubernetes for orchestration and management. It securely connects to your data center so you can implement a flexible, hybrid cloud IT strategy with minimal infrastructure and operating expenses. It can be a good choice for companies who don't want to share the platform with other companies.

# OpenShift architecture

The OpenShift Container platform is both simple and complex when it comes to OpenShift components and overall architecture. It is complex in that it involves a lot of components interconnected with each other, but OpenShift is simple in the sense that all its components work independently of each other, and work seamlessly if something fails:

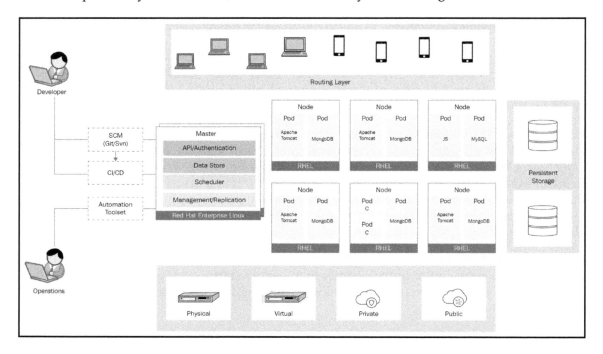

OpenShift components

OpenShift and Kubernetes have most architecture components in common, such as:

- OpenShift masters
- OpenShift nodes
- Etcd as a key-value store

Components that are unique to OpenShift are:

- Router as ingress traffic control
- OpenShift Internal Registry

The following diagram describes the OpenShift container platform from an architectural point of view:

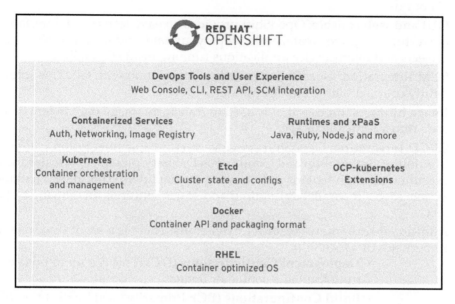

OpenShift architecture

OpenShift is built on top of Docker and Kubernetes, sometimes referred to as Kubernetes++. In addition to the Docker and Kubernetes solution, OpenShift brings additional capabilities and features required to provide a stable and production-ready PaaS platform. These new capabilities and features are:

- **Authentication**: OpenShift has several built-in authentication methods to allow granular access to OpenShift projects:
  - Local authentication
  - LDAP authentication
  - Request header authentication
  - Keystone authentication
  - GitHub authentication
- **Multi-tenancy**: OpenShift's powerful functionalities allow granular multi-user and multi-project access control, a must-have feature for medium and large organizations that allows collaboration and access control for different groups.

- **Internal Image Registry**: OpenShift uses an internal registry to store images in OpenShift that are ready to be deployed on OpenShift nodes. It is also used for S2I builds.
- **GUI and web console**: OpenShift provides an easy-to-use web interface, powerful enough to create, build, deploy, update, and troubleshoot OpenShift projects and microservice applications running inside OpenShift.
- **SCM Integration**: OpenShift has built-in integration with Git. This solution is tightly coupled with an image builder.
- **Image builders**: Process that is used to transform image parameters or source code into a runnable image.
- **CI/CD Integration**: OpenShift provides very flexible integration with Jenkins for Continuous Integration and Continuous Delivery pipelines. It scales the pipeline execution through Jenkins provisioning in containers. This allows Jenkins to run as many jobs in parallel as required and scales solutions on demand out of the box.
- **Additional Kubernetes resource extensions**: There is a set of resources added to Kubernetes by OpenShift:
    - **Deployment Configurations (DC)**: This is a set of pods created from the same container image.
    - **Build Configurations (BC)**: Primarily used by S2I to build an image from source code in Git.
    - **Routes**: DNS hostname service used by the OpenShift router as an ingress point for OpenShift applications,
- **REST API**: In addition to the Kubernetes API, Openshift provides its own API interface to leverage all the features of automation and seamless integration with external platforms, other automation frameworks, and DevOps solutions.

# Summary

In this chapter, we discussed, briefly, the difference between IaaS and PaaS solutions. We also talked about OpenShift as part of a PaaS solution. We provided a basic explanation of OpenShift's business value and the main OpenShift components, and talked about OpenShift in general.

In the next chapter, we are going to work with OpenShift and learn different ways to bring about an OpenShift development environment using the most popular methods and tools.

# Questions

1. OpenShift is one of the following cloud platforms:
    1. IaaS
    2. PaaS
    3. MaaS
    4. SaaS

2. Which two OpenShift flavors can be installed on-premise inside your data center? choose 2:
    1. OpenShift Origin
    2. OpenShift Dedicated
    3. OpenShift Enterprise
    4. OpenShift Offline

3. OpenShift uses its own container management platform to orchestrate and control container deployment:
    1. True
    2. False

4. Which of the following is NOT a new feature added by OpenShift in comparison to Kubernetes? choose one:
    1. SCM integration
    2. GUI and web console
    3. Multi-tenancy
    4. Persistent storage

5. Wich two components are unique to OpenShift in comparison to Kubernetes? choose two:
    1. Router as an ingress traffic control
    2. OpenShift Internal Registry
    3. OpenShift Master
    4. OpenShift Node

6. OpenShift provides an additional REST API in addition to the Kubernetes API:
    1. True
    2. False

# Further reading

The OpenShift development life cycle is every 3 months, which means that, every 3 months, new features are added. This implies that, by the time this book is published, OpenShift might be a bit different. So, it is highly important to keep track of these changes. Here is a list of links including further reading:

- **OpenShift general documentation**: https://docs.openshift.com/index.html
- **OpenShift Origin documentation web page**: https://docs.openshift.org/
- **OpenShift GitHub project**: https://github.com/openshift/

# 5
# Building an OpenShift Lab

In the previous chapter, we briefly discussed the differences between IaaS and PaaS solutions. We also discussed OpenShift as a part of the PaaS solution. We provided a basic explanation of OpenShift's business value and the main OpenShift components.

Some OpenShift users don't want to spend time deploying and configuring the OpenShift development or evaluation environment. However, they may need the environment to perform day to day operations. In this chapter, we are going to show you how to quickly set up a ready-to-use development environment on most popular desktop operating systems, using the most popular approaches.

We will cover the following topics in this chapter:

- Why use a development environment?
- Deployment variants
- Working with oc cluster up
- Working with Minishift
- Working with Vagrant

## Technical requirements

To successfully perform the labs in this chapter, you will need the following:

- One of the following desktop operating systems:
  - macOS
  - Linux (CentOS 7)
  - Windows
- Bash for Linux or macOS
- Brew package manager for macOS
- VirtualBox

- Virtualization support
- Docker for macOS/Linux/Windows
- The OpenShift client utility

You will also be asked to download and install some dependencies and binaries.

# Why use a development environment?

As we mentioned in the previous chapter, OpenShift is an application delivery platform that can simplify day to day duties for infrastructure engineers and development teams. If a company's software delivery strategy is aligned with containers, OpenShift can significantly help to reduce production time.

Every platform has a community. It is an ecosystem around the platform that helps to improve the platform's functionality, aligns the platform with end user needs, and so on. OpenShift has a community that includes some important members that use the platform: software developers, QA specialists, system administrators, IT architects, and so on. It is very important for OpenShift to extend its community and involve new team members and customers. To achieve this, all team members should have access to the OpenShift environment; depending on their roles, specialists will perform software development, testing, and software delivery. Not every software developer or QA team member will be able to set OpenShift up from scratch, and that is the main reason they seek an easy way to start working with OpenShift.

The OpenShift development environment can be created easily and doesn't require significant effort. Usually, this environment is located on a local PC and doesn't have a large capacity.

There are a number of benefits in having an easy-to-use development environment:

- **OpenShift evaluation**: Sometimes, users want to understand how OpenShift is aligned with their needs. They may have no experience with OpenShift, and may want to touch it on a real system. For most technical people, marketing presentations/demonstrations don't mean anything. A fast and easy deployment process for the development environment can help.
- **A quick environment for developers/QAs**: Developers usually don't want to get too involved with deploying an environment. A fast method for deploying OpenShift can save some effort, allowing them to focus on primary activities (such as software development and testing).

# Deployment variants

There are several ways to set up and start a development environment. Usually, the development environment is run on a workstation, and it is important to cover the most popular workstation operating systems. In the next section, we will describe several ways to quickly deploy OpenShift on workstations on different platforms. The most popular desktops are Windows, macOS, and Linux.

> Please be aware that a development environment is not equal to a production environment, due to capacity, scalability, and security limitations.

# Working with oc cluster up

The OpenShift client utility named `oc` can start a local OpenShift cluster, which includes all of the required services, such as an internal registry, a router, templates, and so on. This is one of the easiest ways to start a development environment. `oc cluster up` creates a default user and project, and once it is complete, it will allow you to use any commands to work with the OpenShift environment, such as `oc new-app`.

> This method provides a containerized OpenShift environment that can easily be run on a number of platforms.

# System requirements and prerequisites

The `oc cluster up` method supports Linux, macOS, and Windows-based workstations. By default, the method requires an environment with a Docker machine installed. However, the command can create a Docker machine by itself. The following table shows the available deployment scenarios:

| Operating system | Docker implementation |
|---|---|
| Linux | Default docker daemon for OS |
| macOS | Docker for macOS |
| macOS | Docker Toolbox |
| Windows | Docker for Windows |
| Windows | Docker Toolbox |

# CentOS 7

 This method can also be used on Fedora or RHEL based hosts.

The deployment process involves several steps:

1. Install Docker
2. Configure an insecure registry
3. Allow ports on the firewall
4. Download the OpenShift client utility
5. Start a cluster

Let's study these steps in detail:

1. **Docker installation**: This doesn't involve anything special, and was described in previous chapters. The following commands must be run under the root account:

   ```
   $ sudo -i
   # sudo yum -y install docker
   # systemctl enable docker
   ```

2. **Configuring an insecure registry**: This is required to be able to use an internal Docker registry, which comes with OpenShift installation. If this is not configured, oc cluster up will fail.

   To allow for an insecure OpenShift registry, run the following commands under the root user:

   ```
   # cat << EOF >/etc/docker/daemon.json
   {
      "insecure-registries": [
        "172.30.0.0/16"
      ]
   }
   EOF

   # systemctl start docker
   ```

This requires restarting the Docker daemon so as to apply the new configuration.

3. **Configuring the firewall**: The default firewall configuration doesn't enable all of the ports required for an OpenShift cluster. You need to adjust the settings using `firewall-cmd`:

| Port | Description |
|------|-------------|
| 8443/tcp | API port |
| 53/udp | DND |
| 8053/udp | Internal DNS |

This can be achieved through the following snippet:

```
# firewall-cmd --permanent --new-zone dockerc
# firewall-cmd --permanent --zone dockerc --add-source
172.17.0.0/16
# firewall-cmd --permanent --zone dockerc --add-port 8443/tcp
# firewall-cmd --permanent --zone dockerc --add-port 53/udp
# firewall-cmd --permanent --zone dockerc --add-port 8053/udp
# firewall-cmd --reload
```

In most cases, the firewall is not an issue in the development environment, and can be stopped with `systemctl stop firewalld` and `systemctl disable firewalld`.

You can determine the network address of Docker by running `docker network inspect -f "{{range .IPAM.Config }}{{ .Subnet }}{{end}}" bridge`.

4. **Downloading the oc utility**: The OpenShift client utility named `oc` is available in standard repositories; however, it is possible to download the utility from `https://github.com/openshift/origin/releases`. We would recommend using the standard CentOS repositories:

```
# yum -y install centos-release-openshift-origin39
# yum -y install origin-clients
```

We omitted the output of the commands. It is expected that these commands will install a number of dependencies.

5. **Starting an OpenShift cluster**: Once all of the prerequisites are met, you will be able to start the cluster by running `oc cluster up`. The command will download all of the required Docker images from public repositories, and then run all of the required containers:

```
# oc cluster up --version=v3.9.0
Starting OpenShift using openshift/origin:v3.9.0 ...
...
output truncated for brevity
...
OpenShift server started.

The server is accessible via web console at:
    https://127.0.0.1:8443

You are logged in as:
    User: developer
    Password: <any value>

To login as administrator:
    oc login -u system:admin
```

In the preceding example, we statically bound the version of the OpenShift cluster to `v3.9.0`. In most cases, you don't have to specify a version. So, you just need `oc cluster up` without any arguments.

As you can see, `oc cluster up` deployed a ready-to-use, one-node OpenShift environment.

By default, this OpenShift environment was configured to listen on the loopback interface (`127.0.0.1`). This means that you may connect to the cluster using `https://127.0.0.1:8443`. This behavior can be changed by adding special parameters, such as `--public-hostname=`. A full list of available options can be shown by using the following command:

```
# oc cluster up --help
```

6. **Verification**: Once the cluster has deployed, you can verify that it is ready to use. The default OpenShift configuration points you to an unprivileged user, named `developer`. You may raise your permissions by using the following commands:

```
# oc login -u system:admin
Logged into "https://127.0.0.1:8443" as "system:admin" using
existing credentials.

You have access to the following projects and can switch
between them with 'oc project <projectname>':

    default
    kube-public
    kube-system
  * myproject
    openshift
    openshift-infra
    openshift-node

Using project "myproject".
```

Once you have admin access rights, you can verify the node configuration with `oc get node`:

```
# oc get node
NAME        STATUS   AGE     VERSION
localhost   Ready    9m      v1.7.6+a08f5eeb62
```

7. **Shutting down**: Once an `oc cluster up` environment has deployed, it can be shut down with `oc cluster down`.

# macOS

The installation and configuration process for macOS is very similar to that for Linux. It assumes that Docker for macOS is being used. The deployment process involves the following:

- Docker for macOS installation and configuration
- Installation of `openshift-cli` and required packages
- Starting a cluster

The `oc cluster up` command requires Docker to be installed on your system, because essentially, it creates a Docker container and runs OpenShift inside that Docker container. It is a very elegant and clean solution.

The Docker for macOS installation process is described at the official portal: `https://docs.docker.com/docker-for-mac`.

Once the Docker service is running, you need to configure the insecure registry (`172.30.0.0/16`). From the Docker menu in the toolbar, you need to select the **Preferences** menu and click on the **Daemon** icon. In the **Basic** tab of the configuration dialog, click on the **+** icon under **Insecure registries** and add the following new entry: `172.30.0.0/16`:

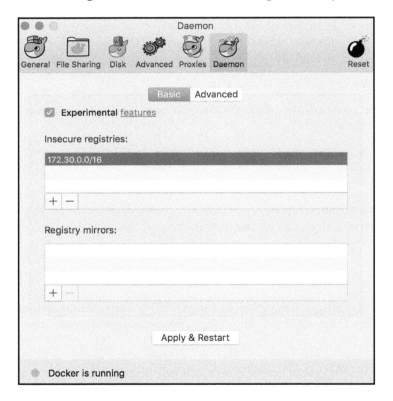

When finished, click on **Apply & Restart**.

Once the Docker service is configured, we need to install all the required software and start the cluster using the following steps:

1. **OpenShift client installation**: Install the `socat` and `openshift-cli` packages on your system as follows:

   ```
   $ brew install openshift-cli socat --force
   ```

   If you do not have `brew` installed, find the installation process at `https://brew.sh/`.

2. **Starting and stopping the OpenShift cluster**: The cluster can be started just like it was in Linux:

   ```
   $ oc cluster up
   Starting OpenShift using
   registry.access.redhat.com/openshift3/ose:v3.7.23 ...
   OpenShift server started.

   The server is accessible via web console at:
   https://127.0.0.1:8443

   You are logged in as:
   User: developer
   Password: <any value>

   To login as administrator:
   oc login -u system:admin
   ```

   At the time of writing this book, `oc cluster up` on macOS didn't work for version 3.9. I would recommend you to temporarily use 3.7 version of the client utility.

   An installation verification can be performed by the OpenShift admin user, as follows:

   ```
   $ oc login -u system:admin
   Logged into "https://127.0.0.1:8443" as "system:admin" using
   existing credentials.

   You have access to the following projects and can switch between
   them with 'oc project <projectname>':

   default
   ```

```
kube-public
kube-system
* myproject
openshift
openshift-infra
openshift-node

Using project "myproject".
```

The Openshift cluster is up and ready for work. We may check the status of the cluster using the following command:

**$ oc get nodes**
```
NAME        STATUS AGE VERSION
localhost Ready 20h   v1.7.6+a08f5eeb62
```

The cluster can be stopped as follows:

**$ oc cluster down**

# Windows

The OpenShift environment can be deployed on Windows on a machine that supports Docker for Windows.

- **Docker for Windows installation and configuration**:

 The Docker for Windows installation process is described at `https://docs.docker.com/docker-for-windows`.

Once Docker is running, you will need to configure the insecure registry settings, as follows:

1. Right-click on the **Docker** icon in the notification area, and select **Settings**.
2. Click on **Docker Daemon** in the **Settings** dialog.

3. Edit the Docker daemon configuration by adding `172.30.0.0/16` to the `"insecure-registries"`: setting:

```
{
"registry-mirrors": [],
"insecure-registries": [ "172.30.0.0/16" ]
}
```

4. Click on **Apply**, and Docker will restart.

Once Docker service is configured, the OpenShift client `oc` can be installed as shown below. The example also shows how to start the cluster:

- **OpenShift client installation**: Download the Windows `oc.exe` binary from `https://github.com/openshift/origin/releases/download/v3.7.1/ openshift-origin-client-tools-v3.7.1-ab0f056-mac.zip,` and place it in `C:\Windows\system32` or another path folder.

  You can also download the latest code from `https://github.com/openshift/ origin/releases` under `Assets`.

- **Starting/stopping a cluster**: The Windows version of the OpenShift client is also able to start and stop the cluster, as follows:

  ```
  C:\> oc cluster up
  ```

  The Openshift cluster is up. You may want to check the status of the cluster using the following:

  ```
  C:\> oc get node
  NAME STATUS AGE
  origin Ready 1d
  ```

# Accessing OpenShift through a web browser

Whether you use `oc cluster up` or any other solution, when OpenShift is up and running, you can access it via a web browser. OpenShift is available on port `8443`, by default. In the case of `oc cluster up`, you can reach the OpenShift login page at `https://localhost:8443/`:

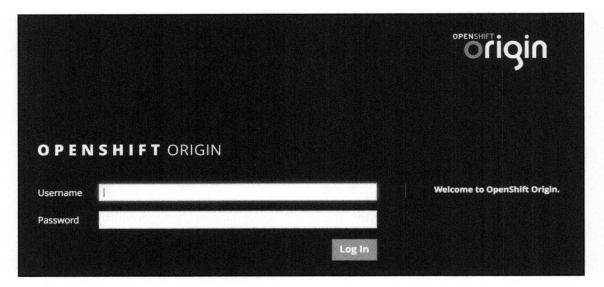

Use the developer login, with any password, to log in to OpenShift. We are going to work with the OpenShift web interface later in this book, while developing and running microservice applications.

Once you log in, you will be presented with the service catalog, which lets you to choose from available language runtimes:

*Project* in OpenShift extend the concept of namespaces from Kubernetes and serve as means of separating teams and individual users working with the same OpenShift cluster. Another term often used for projects is *tenant* (for example, in OpenStack). You can create projects from the web console by clicking on the Create Project button and specifying its name:

After the project is created, you can click on its name on the right side of the screen and you will be redirected to the project's overview page, from where you can create applications and other resources:

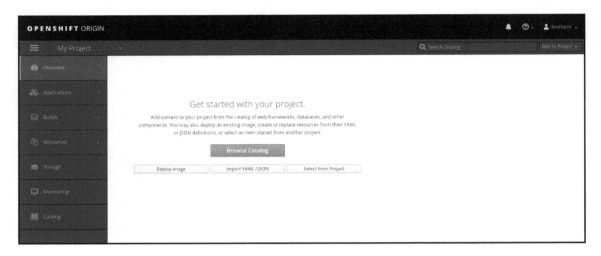

Just to give you the basic understanding of how to navigate through OpenShift web console, see the short guide below:

- **Applications** menu is used to access resources, directly responsible for your application, like **Deployments**, **Pods**, **Services**, **Stateful Sets**, and **Routes**
- **Builds** menu lets you manage configuration of **Builds** and build strategies, such as **Pipelines**, as well as **Images** used to build your application from source code
- **Resources** menu gives you access to other secondary resources that can be used by your application in advanced use cases, such as **Quotas**, **Config Maps**, **Secrets**, and **Other Resources**. You can also use this menu to view and manage **Membership** for your project
- **Storage** menu is used to request persistent storage by creating persistent storage claims
- **Monitoring** menu provides you with access to various metrics collected by OpenShift on CPU, RAM, and network bandwidth utilization (if you have metrics enabled), as well as **Events** going on in real time
- Finally, **Catalog** menu is a shortcut you can take to access service catalog directly from the project you are currently in without having to go back to the first page. This was introduced in OpenShift Origin 3.9.

# Working with Minishift

Minishift is another way to deploy OpenShift locally, by running a single-node OpenShift cluster inside a virtual machine. Recently, we showed you how to use Minikube to deploy a development environment for Kubernetes. Minishift uses the same approach, because it was developed by Kubernetes community as a continuation of Minikube, mentioned in the `Chapter 2`, *Kubernetes Overview*, so it uses the same command line syntax. Minishift deployment is supported on the Windows, macOS, and Linux operating systems. Minishift uses libmachine to provision a virtual machine, boot2docker as OS, and OpenShift Origin to run the cluster. Minishift requires a hypervisor to run the virtual machine containing OpenShift.

Depending on your host operating system, you have a choice between the following hypervisors:

| Operating system | Hypervisor | Platform |
|---|---|---|
| macOS | xhyve | VirtualBox |
| Linux | KVM | VirtualBox |
| Windows | Hyper-V | VirtualBox |

 `boot2docker` is a lightweight Linux distribution based on Tiny Core Linux, built specifically to run containers. The project is now deprecated.

Before you begin, you need to configure virtualization support (`https://docs.openshift.org/latest/minishift/getting-started/installing.html#install-prerequisites`) and install VirtualBox.

Then, you need to download the archive for your operating system from the Minishift releases page (`https://github.com/minishift/minishift/releases`) and unpack it. The `minishift` binary file from the archive needs to be copied to the OS's preferred location, and the location should be added to your `PATH` environment variable. Minishift will use the SSH binary found in the system `PATH` environment.

 On macOS, you can also use Homebrew Cask to install a stable version of Minishift:

```
$ brew cask install minishift
```

To update the binary, run the following command:

```
$ brew cask install --force minishif
```

If all of the prerequisites are met, you can start a cluster using `minishift start`.

```
$ minishift start --vm-driver=virtualbox
-- Starting profile 'minishift'
-- Checking if requested OpenShift version 'v3.7.1' is valid ... OK
...
output truncated for brevity
...
OpenShift server started.

The server is accessible via web console at:
    https://192.168.64.2:8443

You are logged in as:
    User: developer
    Password: <any value>

To login as administrator:
    oc login -u system:admin

-- Exporting of OpenShift images is occuring in background process
with pid 7123.
```

Once the deployment process is complete, you will be able to connect using the OpenShift client:

```
$ oc login -u system:admin
Logged into "https://192.168.64.2:8443" as "system:admin" using
existing credentials.

You have access to the following projects and can switch between
them with 'oc project <projectname>':

* default
kube-public
kube-system
myproject
openshift
openshift-infra
openshift-node

Using project "default".
```

You will need to install `oc client`, as well. You can refer to the previous sections in this chapter for the `oc client` installation procedure.

The OpenShift cluster is up. You may want to check its status using `oc get nodes` as it is shown in the following command:

```
$ oc get nodes
NAME        STATUS   AGE   VERSION
localhost Ready     20h   v1.7.6+a08f5eeb62
```

You can connect to the Minishift VM using `minishift ssh`. The Minishift cluster can be stopped with `minishift stop`.

Depending on the `oc client` and OpenShift versions, your output may vary.

To stop a Minishift environment and delete it, you can use `minishift stop` and `minishift delete`, as follows:

```
$ minishift stop
Stopping local OpenShift cluster...
Cluster stopped.
```

```
$ minishift delete
You are deleting the Minishift VM: 'minishift'. Do you want to continue
[y/N]?: y
Deleting the Minishift VM...
Minishift VM deleted.
```

# Working with Vagrant

This method allows for using an available Vagrant box, that has all the OpenShift software installed on a single VM.

Vagrant software allows for simplifying the deployment and the initial configuration of virtual machines, by using different underlying virtualization technologies. In most cases, a plain text file called `Vagrantfile` describes the parameters of the VM (such as the name, hostname, RAM, vCPUs, storage, and so on). Once `Vagrantfile` is ready, the Vagrant software can use it to create, stop, and destroy a VM.

The beauty of using Vagrant is that we can redeploy VMs as many times as we need to, and each time, we will have the same result:

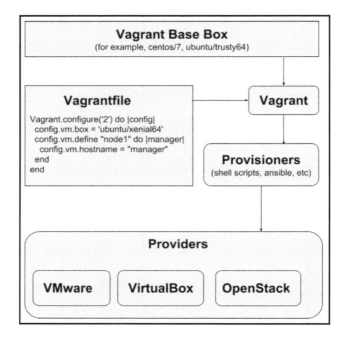

Vagrant architecture

Vagrant includes the following main components:

- **Vagrant software**: Automates virtual machine building and configuration. Has the vagrant CLI utility, available for different operating systems.
- **Box**: A TAR file that contains a virtual machine image, with metadata. Box files and their contained images are specific to each provider.
- **Provider**: The interface that allows Vagrant to communicate with different virtualization platforms. By default, it uses VirtualBox. Libvirt, KVM, OpenStack, and other providers are also available .
- **Vagrantfile**: A plain text file that contains the instructions for how to create virtual machines. The instructions are written using Ruby-based **Domain Specific Language** (**DSL**). Plain Ruby can also be used, for advanced use cases.

# Vagrant installation

The Vagrant instructions and the software to download are available at `https://www.vagrantup.com/docs/installation/`.

Just download the package for your OS, and then install it. Vagrant also requires a virtualization platform, like Vmware, KVM, VirtualBox, AWS, Hyper-V, or Docker. You will be required to install the appropriate virtualization platform, depending on your operating system.

**For macOS, install the following**:

1. Download the latest Vagrant software from the preceding link, and install it.
2. Download and install VirtualBox from `https://www.virtualbox.org/wiki/Downloads`.

**For CentOS, install the following**:

1. Download the latest Vagrant software from the preceding link, and install it.
2. Install `libvirt` drivers and `kvm`:

```
# yum install epel-release -y
# yum localinstall
https://releases.hashicorp.com/vagrant/1.9.5/vagrant_1.9.5_x86_64.r
pm
# yum install qemu libvirt libvirt-devel ruby-devel gcc qemu-kvm -y
# vagrant plugin install vagrant-libvirt
```

**For Windows install the following**:

1. Download the latest Vagrant software from the preceding link, and install it.
2. Download and install VirtualBox from `https://www.virtualbox.org/wiki/Downloads`.

Once you are done, verify that Vagrant is installed by checking the Vagrant software version:

```
$ vagrant --version
Vagrant 1.9.5
```

# Installing OpenShift with an all-in-one Vagrant box

Before introduction of Minishift in May 2017, users mostly relied on `openshift/origin-all-in-one` Vagrant all-in-one box. This method is not so popular, because the box hasn't been updated for almost 2 years and represents OpenShift Origin 1.3, which lacks in features, as well as in stability, so it's mostly of historical interest today. Even though it can still be used for testing purposes, we suggest you rely on `oc cluster up` and Minishift.

A Vagrant-based environment can be deployed as follows:

```
$ vagrant init openshift/origin-all-in-one
$ vagrant up
```

The preceding command will create the following `Vagrantfile`:

```
$ cat Vagrantfile
Vagrant.configure("2") do |config|
    config.vm.box = "openshift/origin-all-in-one"
end
```

Once the box has deployed, you can log in using `admin` and a password, as follows:

```
$ oc login
Server [https://localhost:8443]:
The server uses a certificate signed by an unknown authority.
You can bypass the certificate check, but any data you send to the server
could be intercepted by others.
Use insecure connections? (y/n): y

Authentication required for https://localhost:8443 (openshift)
Username: admin
Password: admin
Login successful.

You have access to the following projects and can switch between them with
'oc project <projectname>':

cockpit
* default
kube-system
openshift
openshift-infra

Using project "default".
Welcome! See 'oc help' to get started.
```

The OpenShift cluster is up. You may want to check the cluster status as shown in the following command:

```
$ oc get node
NAME STATUS AGE
origin Ready 1y
```

 Please keep in mind that the Vagrant box for this method is 2 years behind latest version of OpenShift, so if you want to see most recent features, we recommend using another option.

# Summary

In this chapter, we discussed how to create an OpenShift lab environment quickly and easily, using the most popular and simple methods: oc cluster up, Minishift, and Vagrant, on the CentOS 7, macOS, and Windows operating systems.

In the next chapter, you will learn about the hardware and software requirements of OpenShift Origin. You will get a basic understanding of OpenShift deployment scenarios and installation methods. Also, you will perform an advanced installation of OpenShift using Ansible, and you will learn about the various options to customize your setup with Ansible inventory.

# Questions

1. What is the main prerequisite for the oc cluster up solution? (Choose one):
    1. Docker
    2. Minishift
    3. Virtualbox
    4. Hyper-V

2. What port is used, by default, to reach the OpenShift management web page? choose one:
    1. 8443
    2. 443
    3. 8080
    4. 80

3. The `oc cluster up` command uses a VM to bring up the Openshift cluster:
   1. True
   2. False

4. What command is used to log in to Openshift via the CLI? choose one:
   1. oc login system:admin
   2. oc login -u system:admin
   3. oc login -u admin
   4. oc login admin

5. What are the commands to start and stop the OpenShift demo cluster with the `oc` command? choose one:
   1. oc cluster up
   2. oc cluster start
   3. oc cluster down
   4. oc cluster stop

6. The `minishift start` command uses a VM to bring up the Openshift Cluster:
   1. True
   2. False

# Further reading

Take a look at the following links, if you are interested in learning more or are facing some issues in your lab environment:

- **oc cluster up installation**: https://github.com/openshift/origin/blob/master/docs/cluster_up_down.md
- **Minishift installation**: https://docs.openshift.org/latest/minishift/getting-started/installing.html
- **Vagrant installation**: https://www.vagrantup.com/intro/getting-started/install.html
- **An alternative method to install the OpenShift cluster in a VM**: https://blog.openshift.com/openshift-developers-set-full-cluster-30-minutes/
- **4 ways to set up a development environment on OpenShift**: https://developers.redhat.com/blog/2016/10/11/four-creative-ways-to-create-an-openshiftkubernetes-dev-environment/

# OpenShift Installation

**6**

In the previous chapter, we discussed how to set up your OpenShift lab environment quickly and easily using the most popular and simple methods with `oc cluster up`, MiniShift, and Vagrant on CentOS7, macOS, and Windows operating systems.

In this chapter, you will learn about the hardware and software requirements of OpenShift Origin, and you will obtain a basic understanding of OpenShift deployment scenarios and installation methods. You will also be able to perform an advanced installation of OpenShift using Ansible and learn about various options to customize your setup with the Ansible inventory.

In this chapter, we will discuss the following topics:

- Prerequisites
- Overview of OpenShift installation methods
- Environment preparation
- Advanced installation

## Technical requirements

The learning environment for this chapter will be represented by a single virtual machine deployed through Vagrant on VirtualBox. You will need the following minimal configuration in order to support the environment:

| CPU | RAM, GiB | OS |
|-----|----------|-----|
| 2 cores with HT enabled | 6 | Fedora 26/CentOS 7/RHEL 7 |

The VM will be about 3 GB in size, so make sure that you have enough free space on your `/home` partition, or change the location of the directory where VirtualBox stores the VM's files in the **File | Preferences | General | Default Machine** folder.

The `Vagrantfile` that can be used for deploying our VM may look similar to the following:

```
$ cat Vagrantfile
Vagrant.configure("2") do |config|
  config.vm.box = "centos/7"
  config.vm.hostname = "openshift.example.com"
  config.vm.provider "virtualbox" do |v|
    v.memory = 4096
    v.cpus = 4
  end
  config.vm.network "private_network", ip: "172.24.0.11"
end
```

As all OpenShift services in this chapter will be deployed on a single VM, we will provide it with 4 vCPUs and 4 GiB RAM so that all processes have an adequate amount of resources to start with.
In order to be able to pull `centos/7` box, you will need Vagrant version 2.x.

# Prerequisites

In this chapter, we will focus on the Origin flavor of OpenShift, which is publicly accessible without any subscription. Like other OpenShift variants, Origin supports all features of commercial OpenShift versions that are provided by RedHat. OpenShift is a complex platform that consists of many components that interact and work together, with each having their own requirements, so before we start, we will have to satisfy them.

## Hardware requirements

Official OpenShift Origin documentation provides sufficient hardware requirements for different host types. They are summarized in the following table:

|          | Masters | Nodes | External etcd |
|----------|---------|-------|---------------|
| **vCPU** | 2       | 1     | 2             |
| **RAM, GiB** | 16  | 8     | 8             |

| Disk Storage/Partitioning, GB | /var: 40 /usr/local/bin: 1 /tmp: 1 | /var: 15 /usr/local/bin: 1 /tmp: 1 Docker storage backend: 15 | 20, SSD is recommended |
|---|---|---|---|
| **Network, GB/s** | 1 | 1 | 1 |

 The preceding information is not carved in stone and is only provided as a guideline. Hardware requirements for your particular installation are heavily influenced by such factors, as expected number of applications and workload. In fact, they may even be less strict.

# Overview of OpenShift installation methods

OpenShift Origin can be installed in several ways, depending on OS and requirements regarding availability, reliability, and scalability.

## RPM installation

This is the default method. It installs all required services as systemd units from RPM packages, and they are available on RHEL/CentOS/Fedora. We will focus on this method using the CentOS 7 Linux distribution in the upcoming sections so that you may get a better understanding of the mechanisms involved.

## Containerized installation

This is the only available method for Atomic Host OS. It installs OpenShift services in Docker containers, which provides an additional level of control. This method is preferable in an enterprise environment, as Atomic Host makes any dependency issues between packages a thing of the past and makes the host preparation process much easier, as Atomic Host provides a container-focused environment out of the box.

# Deployment scenarios

OpenShift Origin supports various models of deployment, which are listed as follows:

- **All in one**: Single master, single etcd, and single node installed on the same system.
- **Single master, single etcd, and multiple nodes**: This is the scenario we are going to focus on, as it is relatively simple to set up while providing relevant experience. Master and etcd will be installed on the same host.
- **Single master, multiple external etcd, and multiple nodes**: This scenario provides HA of etcd nodes by clustering. Multiple etcd nodes form quorum, which is why an odd number of nodes is advised.
- **Multiple masters, multiple external etcd, and multiple nodes**: This scenario provides native HA of API as well, which will be explored later in this book. Masters by themselves are stateless, which means that they don't require any synchronization mechanisms.

The following diagram illustrates an all-in-one installation:

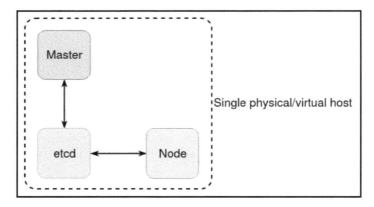

All-in-one

The following diagram shows a multi-node OpenShift installation with single master and etcd instances:

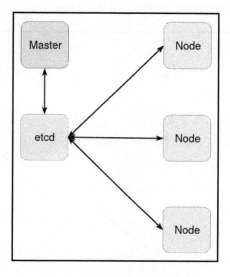

Single master, single etcd, and multiple nodes

The following diagram shows the installation scenario by using a multi-node cluster of etcd:

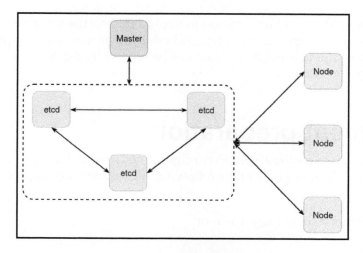

Single master, multiple etcd, and multiple nodes

In a production environment, redundancy and data durability are very important. The following diagram gives an example of a production OpenShift installation. The installation contains three master and three etcd services. All ingress traffic is load balanced:

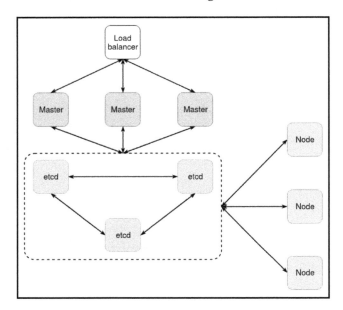

Multiple masters, multiple etcd, and multiple nodes

 Although it's not uncommon to deploy etcd on the same hosts as masters, they are independent entities and while the former require quorum in an HA setup, masters do not and can be separately deployed in practically any numbers.

# Environment preparation

For the RPM installation method, certain configurations need to be made before the installation begins. All commands in the following subsections are to be performed as the root.

First, start the vagrant VM and login as root:

```
$ vagrant up
Bringing machine 'default' up with 'virtualbox' provider...
...
<output omitted>
```

```
. . .
$ vagrant ssh
$ sudo -i
#
```

Before you do anything else, make sure that all hosts are up-to-date so that all features required by OpenShift are supported by the kernel and user-space libraries:

```
# yum -y update
...
<output omitted>
...
Complete!
# reboot
```

You will also need the following packages:

```
# yum -y install git docker epel-release
...
<output omitted>
...
Complete!
# yum -y install ansible
...
<output omitted>
...
Complete!
```

> We also installed the `epel-release` package that enables the EPEL repository needed for installing the latest version of Ansible, required by OpenShift 3.9.
> Generally speaking, you can install Ansible on any system, even on your laptop, and install OpenShift from there. But for the sake of simplicity we consolidate everything, including Ansible control functions, on a single VM.

# Docker

As with Kubernetes, Docker is relied on by OpenShift for providing a container runtime environment. Therefore, we will need to activate Docker on our OpenShift VM:

```
# systemctl start docker
# systemctl enable docker
Created symlink from /etc/systemd/system/multi-
user.target.wants/docker.service to /usr/lib/systemd/system/docker.service.
```

# SELinux

SELinux must be enabled on all OpenShift nodes, including masters, before running the installer. This is required for isolating container processes with special MLS labels.

Open the `/etc/selinux/config` file on the VM and make sure that the `SELINUX` and `SELINUXTYPE` parameters are set as follows:

```
$ cat /etc/selinux/config
# This file controls the state of SELinux on the system.
# SELINUX= can take one of these three values:
# enforcing - SELinux security policy is enforced.
# permissive - SELinux prints warnings instead of enforcing.
# disabled - No SELinux policy is loaded.
SELINUX=enforcing
# SELINUXTYPE= can take one of three two values:
# targeted - Targeted processes are protected,
# minimum - Modification of targeted policy. Only selected processes are
protected.
# mls - Multi Level Security protection.
SELINUXTYPE=targeted
```

SELinux should already be configured by default. You will need to reboot the VM to activate the changes if you made any.

Check to see if `SELINUX` is enabled:

```
# getenforce
Enforcing
```

# Ansible installation

Ansible is a configuration management and orchestration tool that's written in Python. OpenShift Origin installer is actually a collection of Ansible playbooks in YAML format that define what services must be installed and how they are to be configured.

Ansible playbooks are run from a single point, which is called a control machine in Ansible terminology. It can be any machine and in our demonstration of advanced installation, we will use the master as a control machine.

These packages are provided by the EPEL repository, which is already enabled out-of-the-box in our lab. If they weren't, you would have to install the `epel-release` package.

Next, clone the installation playbooks themselves from the Git repository:

```
# git clone https://github.com/openshift/openshift-ansible
Cloning into 'openshift-ansible'...
remote: Counting objects: 95983, done.
remote: Compressing objects: 100% (13/13), done.
remote: Total 95983 (delta 1), reused 6 (delta 0), pack-reused 95969
Receiving objects: 100% (95983/95983), 24.45 MiB | 972.00 KiB/s, done.
Resolving deltas: 100% (59281/59281), done.
# cd openshift-ansible
# git branch -r
...
<output omitted>
...
origin/release-3.9
...
<output omitted>
...
# git checkout release-3.9
Branch release-3.9 set up to track remote branch release-3.9 from origin.
Switched to a new branch 'release-3.9'
```

We switched specifically to the **3.9** release because the master branch actually tracks the development version.

# SSH access

Ansible connects to other systems over SSH protocol, so it requires an SSH key pair. In this section, we are going to ensure SSH access from the root account of our VM to the root account of the same VM. This can be accomplished with the following commands:

```
# ssh-keygen
Generating public/private rsa key pair.
Enter file in which to save the key (/root/.ssh/id_rsa):
Created directory '/root/.ssh'.
Enter passphrase (empty for no passphrase):
Enter same passphrase again:
Your identification has been saved in /root/.ssh/id_rsa.
Your public key has been saved in /root/.ssh/id_rsa.pub.
...
<output omitted>
...
# cat ~/.ssh/id_rsa.pub > ~/.ssh/authorized_keys
```

You can check whether access is indeed enabled by running the following commands:

```
# ssh 172.24.0.11
The authenticity of host '172.24.0.11 (172.24.0.11)' can't be established.
ECDSA key fingerprint is
SHA256:JX1N6Zt7136jH2cXzd0cwByvFTahuOj3NHYvcIjpG2A.
ECDSA key fingerprint is
MD5:9b:04:4a:89:5d:65:7a:b0:4b:02:62:fa:25:91:d3:05.
Are you sure you want to continue connecting (yes/no)? yes
Warning: Permanently added '172.24.0.11' (ECDSA) to the list of known
hosts.
[root@openshift ~]# logout
Connection to 172.24.0.11 closed.
```

# Advanced installation

Being able to start a small cluster in a matter of minutes with minimal effort is great, but what if you need more control over various features so that you get a fully functional cluster right after installation? The answer is advanced installation. As opposed to quick installation, it involves the following:

1. Creating an Ansible inventory file, containing all hosts spread over groups in accordance with the chosen deployment model, and variables customizing the installation for your environment
2. Running the Ansible playbook to install, configure, and start all OpenShift components, including internal registry, registry console, and router

## OpenShift Ansible inventory

A typical Ansible inventory is a text file that contains groups of hosts and their variables. In the case of OpenShift, there are specific sections that may be present depending on the deployment topology and other requirements. They are summarized in the following table:

| Section | Description | Required |
|---|---|---|
| masters | Hosts for installation of master services, notably API. Can be a single node for standalone deployment, or an odd number of hosts for an HA setup. | Yes |
| new_masters | Additional hosts for installation of master components when scaling an existing cluster up. | No |

| | | |
|---|---|---|
| nodes | Hosts for installation of node components, notably kubelet. Usually, there is more than one node, because best practice suggests designating at least one of the nodes as an infrastructure node to host such system services as registry and router.<br>This section must include all masters as well. | Yes |
| new_nodes | Additional hosts for the installation of node components when scaling an existing cluster up. | No |
| etcd | This section is specified only in the case of HA configuration with multiple external etcds. It may contain the same hosts as masters, but since masters and etcd have different system requirements, it is better to deploy them on separate machines. An odd number is suggested for a quorum. | Yes |
| nfs | The host for configuring NFS as a persistent storage backend for Ansible broker, internal registry, Hawkular metrics, and Elasticsearch logging. | No |
| lb | In the case of multiple masters, you will have to provide a point of contact for external clients, which will distribute traffic between master hosts. By placing a host in this section, you will instruct Ansible to install HAProxy on that host and configure it for load balancing and TLS/SSL passthrough. | No |
| glusterfs | Hosts for configuring GlusterFS as a persistent storage backend. | No |
| glusterfs_registry | Hosts for configuring GlusterFS as a persistent storage backend for the internal registry. | No |
| OSEv3:vars | This section contains global variables for configuring various aspects of OpenShift, such as authentication, registry placement, and so on. | Yes |
| OSEv3:children | This section lists all of the groups that are specified in the rest of the file. | Yes |

Ansible looks for specific variables to determine how various subsystems must be configured. The ones that we are going to use are listed in the following table. The full list of variables is available in the official documentation at `https://docs.openshift.org/latest/install_config/install/advanced_install.html`:

| Variable | Description |
|---|---|
| `openshift_node_labels` | Labels assigned to a particular node or to all nodes, depending on whether it is set for a node or globally in `OSEv3:vars`. You should have at least one node labeled as `{'region': 'infra'}`. |
| `openshift_schedulable` | Controls whether a node can be used to run pods. Masters are configured as unschedulable by default, but if you have no nodes labeled as infra, you must explicitly set it to true for at least one master, otherwise, pods for the registry and router will fail to start. |
| `ansible_ssh_user` | The user account used by Ansible to connect to hosts via SSH. |
| `openshift_master_identity_providers` | Authentication backends. By default, OpenShift uses `AllowAllPasswordIdentityProvider`, effectively accepting all credentials, which is insecure and unacceptable in enterprise environments. |
| `deployment_type` | OpenShift distribution to install. Acceptable values are `enterprise` for the Red Hat OpenShift Container Platform and `origin` for OpenShift Origin. |
| `openshit_master_default_subdomain` | The subdomain for exposed services. By default, it is `<namespace>.svc.cluster.local`. |

| | |
|---|---|
| openshift_disable_check | Prior to actual installation, Ansible runs a number of checks to make sure that the environment satisfies certain requirements, such as available memory, disk space, and so on. This is meant as a safeguard against poor resource planning, but can be excessive in proof-of-concepts installations, like ours. Since we do not need 8 GB of RAM, 40 GB of disk space for the master, and 15 GB for nodes in /var for a testing environment, these checks can be safely skipped. |
| openshift_clock_enabled | OpenShift hosts rely on timestamps for the correct propagation of updates through etcd, failover, and quorum, which is achieved by time synchronization through NTP. This setting controls whether the chronyd daemon must be activated. |

Summarizing the information given in the preceding tables, the inventory file's structure should resemble the following:

```
# cat /etc/ansible/hosts
...
<output omitted>
...
[masters]
172.24.0.11

[nodes]
172.24.0.11 openshift_node_labels="{'region': 'infra', 'zone': 'default'}"
openshift_schedulable=true

[etcd]
172.24.0.11

[OSEv3:vars]
openshift_deployment_type=origin
openshift_disable_check=memory_availability,disk_availability
openshift_ip=172.24.0.11
ansible_service_broker_install=false
openshift_master_cluster_hostname=172.24.0.11
openshift_master_cluster_public_hostname=172.24.0.11
openshift_hostname=172.24.0.11
openshift_public_hostname=172.24.0.11
```

```
[OSEv3:children]
masters
nodes
etcd
```

As we have only one node, we have to mark it as schedulable and belonging to `infra` region, so that registry, registry console, and router can be deployed. In production, you would usually dedicated masters to management and synchronization tasks, while leaving all the work of running containers to nodes, as well as have multiple nodes split up between different regions for availability..

# OpenShift Ansible playbooks

The OpenShift Ansible repository contains various playbooks for different tasks. Some of them are presented in the following table:

| Playbook | Description |
|---|---|
| `playbooks/prerequisites.yml` | Sets up prerequisites for the cluster deployment, such as subscribing hosts to Red Hat (in case of Red Hat Enterprise Linux), enabling repositories, and setting up firewall. |
| `playbooks/deploy_cluster.yml` | Performs a complete installation of OpenShift Origin by installing all required packages, configuring, and starting services. This is the playbook we will use in this chapter. |
| `playbooks/openshift-master/scaleup.yml` | Looks for the host group `new_masters` in the inventory and configures these hosts as new members of the cluster. After scaleup is complete, you must move these hosts to the group `masters` to prevent Ansible from treating them as new ones during the next run. |

| | |
|---|---|
| `playbooks/openshift-node/scaleup.yml` | Looks for the host group `new_nodes` in the inventory and configures these hosts as new members of the cluster. After scaleup is complete, you must move these hosts to the group `nodes` to prevent Ansible from treating them as new ones during the next run. |
| `playbooks/openshift-etcd/scaleup.yml` | Looks for the host group `new_etcd` in the inventory and configures these hosts as new members of the cluster. After scaleup is complete, you must move these hosts to the `etcd` group to prevent Ansible from treating them as new ones during the next run. |

Familiarity with Ansible is beneficial, but not required.

# Installation

At this point, we should have everything we need to begin the installation, so without further delay, let's get started by running the prerequisites playbook:

```
# ansible-playbook playbooks/prerequisites.yml
...
<output omitted>
...
PLAY RECAP
*****************************************************************************************
***********
172.24.0.11 : ok=65 changed=17 unreachable=0 failed=0
localhost   : ok=12 changed=0  unreachable=0 failed=0

INSTALLER STATUS
*****************************************************************************************
*****
Initialization : Complete (0:00:13)
...
<output omitted>
...
```

This playbook usually runs for a couple of minutes.

Finally, let's fire up the actual deployment:

```
# ansible-playbook playbooks/deploy_cluster.yml
...
<output omitted>
...
PLAY RECAP
*********************************************************************
***********
172.24.0.11 : ok=555 changed=234 unreachable=0 failed=0
localhost   : ok=13  changed=0   unreachable=0 failed=0

INSTALLER STATUS
*********************************************************************
*****
Initialization            : Complete (0:00:18)
Health Check              : Complete (0:01:12)
etcd Install              : Complete (0:00:50)
NFS Install               : Complete (0:00:17)
Master Install            : Complete (0:04:27)
Master Additional Install : Complete (0:00:29)
Node Install              : Complete (0:02:37)
Hosted Install            : Complete (0:02:21)
Web Console Install       : Complete (0:01:13)
Service Catalog Install   : Complete (0:01:23)
```

It is quite normal for this process to take 15-20 minutes, so you might as well use this time to skim through this book for basic operations to get you up and running faster.

# Validation

Once the installation has completed without any failures, you may perform basic sanity checks by querying the master API for installed nodes:

```
# oc get node
NAME          STATUS   ROLES           AGE    VERSION
172.24.0.11   Ready    compute,master  32m    v1.9.1+a0ce1bc657
```

As one would expect from the inventory, our single node acts both as master and node.

Another check you can run is to see if infrastructure components, like registry, registry console, and router were successfully deployed:

```
# oc get po -n default
NAME                        READY  STATUS    RESTARTS  AGE
docker-registry-1-8g89z     1/1    Running   0         42m
registry-console-1-2srg8    1/1    Running   0         42m
router-1-c6h95              1/1    Running   0         42m
```

 Infrastructure components of OpenShift reside in the `default` project/namespace.

You may also login to the web console at `https://172.24.0.11:8443`, where you will be prompted to accept a self-signed certificate, which you should do. You can use any credentials, as OpenShift accepts anyone by default, and you will see the following page:

Figure 1. OpenShift Service Catalog

The first thing users see when they log in to OpenShift is the Service Catalog, which presents them with various languages and runtimes they can use for deploying their applications. Technically, these are templates which you will get an in-depth understanding of in `Chapter 9`, *Advanced OpenShift Concepts* and in `Chapter 13`, *Deploying Multi-Tier Applications Using Templates*.

# Summary

In this chapter, you learned about various deployment scenarios of OpenShift Origin, as well as installation methods. You wrote an Ansible inventory file and used it to deploy a ready-to-use OpenShift Origin platform with an internal registry, registry console, and a router installed out-of-the-box.

In the following chapter, we are going to cover OpenShift core concepts such as creating new applications with OpenShift pods, services, routes, projects, and users. This will give you foundational skills, which will be enough for you to be able to run and manage your application container infrastructure in OpenShift.

# Questions

1. What sections of the Ansible inventory file are mandatory for OpenShift installation? choose two:
    1. masters
    2. nfs
    3. new_masters
    4. etcd

2. What label must be assigned to at least one node for successful deployment of a router and internal registry?
    1. infrastructure
    2. dedicated
    3. infra
    4. special

3. What Ansible playbook is being used to deploy the OpenShift cluster?
    1. playbooks/deploy_cluster.yml
    2. playbooks/byo/config.yml
    3. playbooks/prerequisites.yml
    4. playbooks/common/openshift-cluster/config.yml

# Further reading

Please see the following for further reading to accompany this chapter:

- **Hardware requirements**: `https://docs.openshift.org/latest/install_config/install/prerequisites.html`
- **Deployment scenarios**: `https://docs.openshift.org/latest/install_config/install/planning.html#installation-methods`
- **Advanced installation and variables reference**: `https://docs.openshift.org/latest/install_config/install/advanced_install.html`
- **OpenShit Installation and Configuration**: `https://access.redhat.com/documentation/en-us/openshift_container_platform/3.9/html-single/installation_and_configuration/#install-config-install-planning`

# Managing Persistent Storage

In the previous chapter, we described how to install an OpenShift cluster using an advanced installation method. The next step of the installation process is to make persistent storage available for OpenShift users. In Chapter 1, *Containers and Docker Overview*, we already how to use Docker persistent volumes. Usually, we do not need any for development or testing purposes, but it is not the case with production environments where we need to store persistent data in certain cases. In this chapter, we will describe the persistent storage concept regarding the OpenShift infrastructure. We will also explain the need for using persistent storage in a production environment. The focus of this chapter is all about configuring an infrastructure to support persistent storage. This includes the following storage types: NFS, GlusterFS, iSCSI, and more. Besides infrastructure preparations, this chapter covers how to leverage persistent storage in OpenShift using **Persistent Volumes (PVs)** and **Persistent Volume Claims (PVCs)**. Lastly, we will show you how to use persistent storage in your pods/applications that are deployed on OpenShift.

In this chapter, we will cover the following topics:

- Persistent versus ephemeral storage
- OpenShift persistent storage concept
- Storage backends comparison
- Storage infrastructure setup
- Configuring PVs
- Using persistent storage in Pods

# Technical requirements

The learning environment for this chapter consists of two VMs with the following characteristics:

| Hostname | RAM | vCPU | OS |
|---|---|---|---|
| openshift.example.com | 4GB | 2 | CentOS 7 |
| storage.example.com | 2GB | 1 | CentOS 7 |

These machines can be deployed anywhere (bare metal, VMware, OpenStack, AWS, and so on). However, for educational purposes, we recommend using the Vagrant + VirtualBox/libvirt configuration to simplify the process of deployment and re-deployment of our virtual environment.

We also assume that all servers are accessible via both FQDNs and short names. This requires configuring /etc/hosts records, which is shown as follows:

```
172.24.0.11 openshift.example.com openshift
172.24.0.12 storage.example.com storage
```

 The IPs must be the same as the ones that are specified in the following Vagrantfile. If you only want to use one machine for this lab, configure the /etc/hosts file to point both records to the same machine.

Lab environment deployment can be simplified by using the following Vagrantfile:

**$ cat Vagrantfile**

```
$lab_script = <<SCRIPT
cat <<EOF >> /etc/hosts
172.24.0.11 openshift.example.com openshift
172.24.0.12 storage.example.com storage
EOF
SCRIPT

$lab_openshift = <<SCRIPT
systemctl disable firewalld
systemctl stop firewalld
yum install -y epel-release git
yum install -y docker
cat << EOF >/etc/docker/daemon.json
{
  "insecure-registries": [
  "172.30.0.0/16"
```

```
    ]
  }
EOF
systemctl start docker
systemctl enable docker
yum -y install centos-release-openshift-origin39
yum -y install origin-clients
oc cluster up
SCRIPT

Vagrant.configure(2) do |config|
  config.vm.define "openshift" do |conf|
  conf.vm.box = "centos/7"
  conf.vm.hostname = 'openshift.example.com'
  conf.vm.network "private_network", ip: "172.24.0.11"
  conf.vm.provider "virtualbox" do |v|
  v.memory = 4096
  v.cpus = 2
  end
  conf.vm.provision "shell", inline: $lab_script
  conf.vm.provision "shell", inline: $lab_openshift
  end

  config.vm.define "storage" do |conf|
  conf.vm.box = "centos/7"
  conf.vm.hostname = 'storage.example.com'
  conf.vm.network "private_network", ip: "172.24.0.12"
  conf.vm.provider "virtualbox" do |v|
  v.memory = 2048
  v.cpus = 1
  end
  conf.vm.provision "shell", inline: $lab_script
  end
end
```

 It's not mandatory to use the same IPs that were used in the preceding code. What is important is that you point your /etc/hosts records to them.

# Persistent versus ephemeral storage

By default, OpenShift/Kubernetes containers don't store data persistently. We can start an application and OpenShift will start a new container from an immutable Docker image. It uses an ephemeral storage, which means that data is available until the container is deleted or rebuilt. If our application (and all related containers) has been rebuilt, all data will be lost. Still, this approach is fine for any stateless application. For example, it will work for a simple website that doesn't act as a portal and only provides information embedded into HTML/CSS. Another example would be a database used for development—usually, no one cares if data is lost.

Let's consider another example. Imagine that we need a database for a WordPress container. If we store database files on an ephemeral storage, we can lose all our data if the database container was rebuilt or deleted. We cannot allow our database files to be deleted or lost. OpenShift can rebuild our database container without any issues. It will give us a working instance of a database but without required databases/table structures and data in the tables. From the application's perspective, this means that all required information is lost. For these kinds of applications (stateful), we need a persistent storage that will be available even if the container crashed, was deleted, or was rebuilt.

Storage requirements (ephemeral versus persistent) are dependent on your particular use case.

# The OpenShift persistent storage concept

OpenShift uses the **Persistent Volume** (**PV**) concept to allow administrators to provide persistent storage for a cluster and then let developers request storage resources via **Persistent Volume Claims** (**PVC**). Thus, end users can request storage without having deep knowledge of the underlying storage infrastructure. At the same time, administrators can configure the underlying storage infrastructure and make it available to end users via the PV concept.

PV resources are shared across the OpenShift cluster since any of them can (if it is allowed) potentially be used by any users/projects. On the other hand, PVC resources are specific to a project (namespace) and they are usually created and used by end users, such as developers. Once PVC resources are created, OpenShift tries to find a suitable PV resource that matches specific criteria, like size requirements, access mode (RWO, ROX, RWX), and so on. If PV has been found to satisfy the request from the PVC, OpenShift binds that PV to our PVC. Once this is complete, PV cannot be bound to additional PVCs.

This concept is shown in the following screenshot:

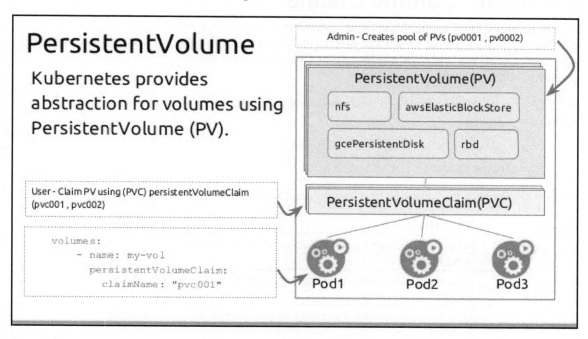

OpenShift Pod, PV, PVC, and the storage relationship

# Persistent Volumes

PVs are represented by a PersistentVolume OpenShift API object, which describes an existing piece of storage infrastructure like NFS share, GlusterFS volume, iSCSI target, a Ceph RBD device, and so on. It is assumed that the underlying storage component already exists and is ready to be consumed by the OpenShift cluster.

PVs have their own life cycle, which is independent of any pods that use PV.

High availability of storage in the infrastructure is left to the underlying storage provider.

# Persistent Volume Claims

As I mentioned previously, OpenShift users can request storage resources for their applications by means of PVCs that are defined by a `PersistentVolumeClaim` OpenShift API object. PVC represents a request made by an end user (usually developers). PVC consumes PV resources.

A PVC contains some important information regarding resources that are requested by applications/users:

- Size needed
- Access mode

There are several access modes that can be used in the OpenShift infrastructure:

| Mode | Description | Examples |
|------|-------------|----------|
| ReadOnlyMany | The volume can be mounted read-only by many nodes. | NFS in RO mode |
| ReadWriteOnce | The volume can be mounted as read-write by a single node. | iSCSI-based xfs, and so on |
| ReadWriteMany | The volume can be mounted as read-write by many nodes. | GlusterFS NFS |

Once a PVC resource is created, OpenShift has to find a suitable PV resource and bind it to the PVC. If the binding is successful, the PVC resource can be consumed by an application.

# The storage life cycle in OpenShift

The interaction between PV and PVC resources is comprised of several steps, which are shown in the following diagram:

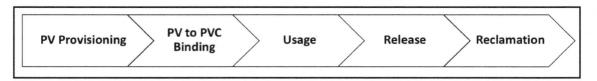

OpenShift: storage lifecycle

OpenShift cluster administrators can configure dynamic PV provisioning or configure PV resources in advance. Once a user has requested a storage resource using the PVC with specific size and access mode requirements, OpenShift looks for an available PV resource. The user always gets what they ask for, at least. In order to keep storage usage to a minimum, OpenShift binds the smallest PV that matches all criteria. A PVC remains unbound until a suitable PV is found. If there is a volume matching all criteria, OpenShift software binds them together. Starting from this step, storage can be used by pods. A pod consumes PVC resources as volumes.

OpenShift inspects the claim to find the bound volume and mounts that volume to the pod. For those volumes that support multiple access modes, the user specifies which mode is desired when using their claim as a volume in a pod.

Users can delete PVC objects, which allows reclamation of storage resources. If PVC is deleted, the volume is considered as *released* but is not yet immediately available to be bound to other claims. This requires that data stored on the volumes are handled according to the reclaim policy.

The reclaim policy defines the way OpenShift understands what to do with the volume after it is released. The following reclaim policies are supported:

| Policy | Description |
|--------|-------------|
| Retain | Allows manual reclamation of the resource for those volume plugins that support it. In this case, storage administrators should delete data manually. |
| Delete | Deletes both the PV object from the OpenShift Container Platform and the associated storage asset in external infrastructures, such as AWS EBS, GCE PD, or Cinder volume. |

# Storage backends comparison

OpenShift supports a number of persistent storage backends that work differently. Some of them support reads/writes from many clients (like NFS), while others support only one mount.

The following table contains a comparison of supported storage backends/plugins:

| Volume backend | ReadWriteOnce | ReadWriteMany | ReadOnlyMany |
|----------------|---------------|---------------|--------------|
| AWS EBS | Yes | | |
| Azure Disk | Yes | | |
| Ceph RBD | Yes | | Yes |
| Fibre Channel | Yes | | Yes |

| GCE Persistent Disk | Yes | | |
|---|---|---|---|
| GlusterFS | Yes | Yes | Yes |
| HostPath | Yes | | |
| iSCSI | Yes | | Yes |
| NFS (Network File System) | Yes | Yes | Yes |
| OpenStack Cinder | Yes | | |
| VMware vSphere | Yes | | |
| Local | Yes | | |

 `HostPath` allows you to mount persistent storage directly from the node your pod runs on and as such is not suitable for production usage. Please only use it for testing or development purposes.

There are two types of supported storage in an OpenShift cluster:

- Filesystem-based storage (like NFS, Gluster, and HostPath)
- Block-based storage (like iSCSI, OpenStack Cinder, and so on)

Docker containers need file system-based storage to use as a persistent volume. This means that OpenShift can use file system-based storage directly. OpenShift needs to create a file system on block storage before using it as a persistent volume. For example, if an iSCSI block device is provided, the cluster administrator has to define what file system will be created on the block device during the PV creation process.

# Storage infrastructure setup

Configuring the underlying storage infrastructure is usually a task for storage administrators. This requires a number of settings and design decisions so that you can achieve the expected level of durability, availability, and performance. This requires a significant knowledge of underlying resources, physical infrastructure, networking, and so on. Once the storage subsystem has been configured properly by storage administrators, OpenShift cluster administrators can leverage it to create PVs.

This book is about OpenShift administration, and thus the configuration of an underlying storage technology is out of its scope. However, we want to demonstrate how to perform the basic setup of storage infrastructure on Linux systems for NFS, GlusterFS, and iSCSI.

If you still need to set up a different kind of storage, please refer to the relevant documentation. For example, you may find some Ceph storage documentation at `https://ceph.com`; OpenStack Cinder documentation may be found on the project homepage at `openstack.org`.

We have chosen NFS and GlusterFS-based storage for a number of reasons:

- Both are file system-based storage solutions
- Both support the `ReadWriteMany` OpenShift access type
- Both can easily be configured on any OpenShift cluster nodes
- NFS is known to any Linux system administrator

We also want to demonstrate how to use block-based storage in the OpenShift cluster. We have chosen iSCSI-based storage as an example storage, as it is one of the easiest ways to go with block-based storage on Linux.

# Setting up NFS

The **Network File System** (**NFS**) is a client/server filesystem protocol that was originally developed by Sun Microsystems in 1984. NFS allows a user on a client computer (NFS client) to access files stored on the NFS server over a network, or even over the internet. The NFS server shares one or more NFS shares with a number of allowed NFS clients. NFS clients mount NFS shares as regular filesystems. No specific application settings are required since NFS is a POSIX compliant file system protocol. This is the main reason why NFS is very popular as a network storage solution. NFS is supported by Linux kernel by default and can be configured on any Linux-based server.

In this tutorial, we will use a standalone NFS server for providing persistent storage to applications that will be deployed on our OpenShift cluster.

The installation process that is described is for CentOS 7.

The NFS installation and configuration process involves several steps:

1. Installing NFS packages on the server and clients
2. Configuring NFS exports on the server
3. Starting and enabling the NFS service
4. Verification or mounting the NFS share(s) on clients

Before we begin, we need to deploy two machines, as described in the *Technical requirements* section. In this lab, we assume that machines were deployed as VMs using Vagrant.

Bring your Vagrant environment up and log in to `storage` VM:

```
$ vagtrant up
$ vagrant ssh storage
```

# Installing NFS packages on the server and clients

NFS packages need to be installed on the NFS server, as well as on all OpenShift nodes, as they will act as NFS clients. NFS libraries and binaries are provided by the `nfs-utils` package:

```
# yum install -y nfs-utils
...
<output omitted>
...
Updated:
  nfs-utils.x86_64 1:1.3.0-0.54.el7
Complete!
```

We will configure NFS services on storage.example.com. All configuration is done under the `root` account. You can use `sudo -i` command to switch to root.

# Configuring NFS exports on the server

This needs to be done on the server-side only. We are going to export several file systems under the `/exports` directory. The exports will only be accessible by OpenShift nodes.

OpenShift cluster runs Docker containers using random **User IDs** (**UIDs**). It is difficult to predict a UID to give proper NFS permissions, so we have to configure the following NFS settings to allow OpenShift to use NFS shares properly:

- A share should be owned by the `nfsnobody` user and group.
- A share should have `0700` access permissions.

- A share should be exported using the `all_squash` option. This will be described later in this topic.

1. Create the required directories and assign them to the proper permissions:

```
# mkdir -p /exports/{nfsvol1,nfsvol2,nfsvol3}
# chmod 0700 /exports/{nfsvol1,nfsvol2,nfsvol3}
# chown nfsnobody:nfsnobody /exports/{nfsvol1,nfsvol2,nfsvol3}
```

2. Configure the firewall:

```
# firewall-cmd --perm --add-service={nfs,mountd,rpc-bind}
success

# firewall-cmd --reload
success
```

This is not required on Vagrant box centos/7 since `firewalld` is disabled by default.

3. Create an NFS export by adding the following lines to `/etc/exports`:

```
# cat <<EOF > /etc/exports
/exports/nfsvol1 openshift.example.com(rw,sync,all_squash)
/exports/nfsvol2 openshift.example.com(rw,sync,all_squash)
/exports/nfsvol3 openshift.example.com(rw,sync,all_squash)
EOF
```

Instead of providing FQDNs, you may also specify IP addresses of the nodes. This will look like as shown in the following code:

```
# cat <<EOF > /etc/exports
/exports/nfsvol1 172.24.0.11(rw,sync,all_squash)
/exports/nfsvol2 172.24.0.11(rw,sync,all_squash)
/exports/nfsvol3 172.24.0.11(rw,sync,all_squash)
EOF
```

The `all_squash` NFS export option configures NFS to map all UIDs to the `nfsnobody` user ID.

# Starting and enabling the NFS service

We also need to enable and start nfs-server using the `systemctl` command. The following snippet shows how to enable and start all services required for NFS service:

```
# systemctl enable rpcbind nfs-server
Created symlink from /etc/systemd/system/multi-user.target.wants/nfs-
server.service to /usr/lib/systemd/system/nfs-server.service.
# systemctl start rpcbind nfs-server
```

# Verification

You may want to check that NFS share was exported properly. The following command will show all available exports:

```
# exportfs -v
/exports/nfsvol1
openshift.example.com(rw,sync,wdelay,hide,no_subtree_check,sec=sys,secure,r
oot_squash,all_squash)
/exports/nfsvol2
openshift.example.com(rw,sync,wdelay,hide,no_subtree_check,sec=sys,secure,r
oot_squash,all_squash)
/exports/nfsvol3
openshift.example.com(rw,sync,wdelay,hide,no_subtree_check,sec=sys,secure,r
oot_squash,all_squash)
```

# Configuring GlusterFS shares

GlusterFS is a free and scalable network file system that is suitable for data-intensive tasks, such as cloud storage and media streaming. GlusterFS creates a volume on top of one or more storage nodes using *bricks*. A brick represents a file system on a storage node. There are several types of GlusterFS volumes defined by the placement of data on bricks. More information can be found by following the links provided at the end of this chapter. In this chapter, we only need to have a basic knowledge of the following volume types:

| Type | Description |
|------|-------------|
| Distributed | All files are distributed between bricks/storage nodes. No redundancy is provided by this volume type. |
| Replicated | All files are replicated between two or more bricks. Thus, each file is stored on at least two bricks, which provides redundancy. |
| Striped | Each file is striped across several bricks. |

For this demonstration, we will set up a basic GlusterFS volume on a single storage node.

# Installing packages

First, we need to install the GlusterFS packages, which are located in a special GlusterFS repository. The `centos-release-gluster312` package configures the GlusterFS 3.12 repository. We need to install the `glusterfs-server` on the server side (`storage.example.com`) and the `glusterfs` package on the client side (`openshift.example.com`):

```
# yum install -y centos-release-gluster312
...
<output omitted>
...
# yum install -y glusterfs-server
...
<output omitted>
...
Dependency Installed:
 attr.x86_64 0:2.4.46-12.el7
 glusterfs.x86_64 0:3.12.6-1.el7
 glusterfs-api.x86_64 0:3.12.6-1.el7
 glusterfs-cli.x86_64 0:3.12.6-1.el7
 glusterfs-client-xlators.x86_64 0:3.12.6-1.el7
 glusterfs-fuse.x86_64 0:3.12.6-1.el7
 glusterfs-libs.x86_64 0:3.12.6-1.el7
 psmisc.x86_64 0:22.20-15.el7
 userspace-rcu.x86_64 0:0.10.0-3.el7

Complete!
```

Once the GlusterFS packages are installed, we need to start and enable the gluster management service—`glusterd`:

```
# systemctl enable glusterd
Created symlink from /etc/systemd/system/multi-
user.target.wants/glusterd.service to
/usr/lib/systemd/system/glusterd.service.
# systemctl start glusterd
```

## Configuring a brick and volume

The following steps of GlusterFS volume configuration require that we create a brick file system and the volume itself:

> For this lab, we will use the root file system to create a GlusterFS brick. This setup can only be used for test and development purposes and is not suitable for production usage. All GlusterFS production installations should use separate file systems for GlusterFS bricks, preferably located on separate physical block devices.

```
# mkdir /exports/gluster
# gluster volume create gvol1 storage.example.com:/exports/gluster force
volume create: gvol1: success: please start the volume to access data
```

The `force` option is required here since we are using the / file system to create glusterFS volume. If this isn't provided, you may see the following output:

```
# gluster volume create gvol1 storage.example.com:/exports/gluster
volume create: gvol1: failed: The brick
storage.example.com:/exports/gluster is being created in the root
partition. It is recommended that you don't use the system's root partition
for storage backend. Or use 'force' at the end of the command if you want
to override this behavior.
```

Now that we have created a volume, it is a good time to start it, making it available to clients:

```
# gluster volume start gvol1
volume start: gvol1: success
```

## Configuring iSCSI

The **internet Small Computer Systems Interface** (**iSCSI**) is a client/server protocol that provides block-level access to storage devices by carrying SCSI commands over a TCP/IP network. Since iSCSI uses the TCP/IP network, it can be used to transmit data over **local area networks** (**LANs**), **wide area networks** (**WANs**), and the internet, making location-independent data storage and retrieval possible. This protocol allows clients (*initiators)* to send SCSI commands to storage devices (*targets*) on remote servers. It is a **storage area network** (**SAN**) protocol. iSCSI allows clients to work with remote block devices and treat them as locally attached disks. There are a number of iSCSI target implementations (like stgtd, LIO target, and so on). As a part of this chapter, we will configure LIO target-based iSCSI storage.

The necessary steps to configure an iSCSI target on `storage.example.com` are outlined as follows:

1. Install the CLI tool:

   ```
   # yum install -y targetcli
   ```

2. Enable the `target` service:

   ```
   # systemctl enable target; systemctl start target
   ```

3. Configure the firewall:

   ```
   # firewall-cmd --permanent --add-port=3260/tcp
   # firewall-cmd --reload
   ```

4. Configure the iSCSI export using `targetcli`:

   ```
   # targetcli
   targetcli shell version 2.1.fb46
   Copyright 2011-2013 by Datera, Inc and others.
   For help on commands, type 'help'.

   /> /backstores/fileio create iscsivol1 /exports/iscsivol1.raw 1g
   Created fileio iscsivol1 with size 1073741824
   /> /iscsi create iqn.2018-04.com.example.storage:disk1
   Created target iqn.2018-04.com.example.storage:disk1.
   Created TPG 1.
   Global pref auto_add_default_portal=true
   Created default portal listening on all IPs (0.0.0.0), port 3260.
   /> cd iscsi/iqn.2018-04.com.example.storage:disk1/tpg1/
   /iscsi/iqn.20...ge:disk1/tpg1> luns/ create
   /backstores/fileio/iscsivol1
   Created LUN 0.
   /iscsi/iqn.20...ge:disk1/tpg1> set attribute authentication=0
   demo_mode_write_protect=0 generate_node_acls=1 cache_dynamic_acls=1
   Parameter generate_node_acls is now '1'.
   /iscsi/iqn.20...ge:disk1/tpg1> exit
   Global pref auto_save_on_exit=true
   Last 10 configs saved in /etc/target/backup.
   Configuration saved to /etc/target/saveconfig.json
   ```

All basic configuration options can be found in man `targetcli` under the *QUICKSTART* section. For educational purposes, the preceding example exports the iSCSI volume to any host. Please be aware that it is not a production-ready configuration. In production, you may only want to grant access to the target to certain hosts.

# Client-side verification

The followings topics will describe how to use NFS, Gluster, and iSCSI storage resources inside the OpenShift cluster. However, you can use previously configured resources manually as well. Before going to the next topic, we strongly recommend verifying that all your resources are configured properly by mounting them on the client side. In our case, the client is located on the `openshift.example.com` node. Let's log in to openshift node and switch to root account before we begin:

```
$ vagrant ssh openshift
Last login: Sun Jul 8 22:24:44 2018 from 10.0.2.2
[vagrant@openshift ~]$ sudo -i
```

# NFS verification

To verify that the NFS exports work properly, we need to mount them on the `openshift.example.com` node, which is shown in the following code. If all shares can be mounted without any issues, you can assume that that share was exported properly:

```
# yum install -y nfs-utils
...
<output omitted>
...
# showmount -e storage.example.com
Export list for storage.example.com:
/exports/nfsvol3 openshift.example.com
/exports/nfsvol2 openshift.example.com
/exports/nfsvol1 openshift.example.com
# mkdir /mnt/{nfsvol1,nfsvol2,nfsvol3}
# mount storage.example.com:/exports/nfsvol1 /mnt/nfsvol1
# mount storage.example.com:/exports/nfsvol2 /mnt/nfsvol2
# mount storage.example.com:/exports/nfsvol3 /mnt/nfsvol3
# df -h|grep nfsvol
storage.example.com:/exports/nfsvol1 38G 697M 37G 2% /mnt/nfsvol1
storage.example.com:/exports/nfsvol2 38G 697M 37G 2% /mnt/nfsvol2
storage.example.com:/exports/nfsvol3 38G 697M 37G 2% /mnt/nfsvol3
# umount /mnt/nfsvol1 /mnt/nfsvol2 /mnt/nfsvol3
```

 It's assumed that all required packages are already installed by running `yum install -y nfs-utils`.

# GlusterFS verification

The GlusterFS volume can be mounted manually by using the FUSE client. The verification procedure looks like this:

```
# yum install centos-release-gluster312 -y
# yum install glusterfs-fuse -y
# mkdir /mnt/gvol1
# mount -t glusterfs storage.example.com:/gvol1 /mnt/gvol1
```

Create a sample of persistent data to be used later:

```
# echo "Persistent data on GlusterFS" > /mnt/gvol1/index.html
```

 This storage will be used as web server root data storage.

Verify that mount point is available and then unmount the storage:

```
# df -h /mnt/gvol1/
Filesystem Size Used Avail Use% Mounted on
storage.example.com:/gvol1 38G 713M 37G 2% /mnt/gvol1
# umount /mnt/gvol1
```

# iSCSI verification

iSCSI verification assumes that an OpenShift node can access block storage devices. If everything goes well, you should see an additional disk at /proc/partitions. The iSCSI client utilities are provided by the iscsi-initiator-utils package. Once the package is installed, the iscsiadm utility can be used to scan the target for iSCSI exports:

```
# yum install -y iscsi-initiator-utils
...
<output omitted>
...
# iscsiadm --mode discoverydb --type sendtargets --portal
storage.example.com --discover
172.24.0.12:3260,1 iqn.2018-04.com.example.storage:disk1
# iscsiadm --mode node --login
Logging in to [iface: default, target:
iqn.2018-04.com.example.storage:disk1, portal: 172.24.0.12,3260] (multiple)
Login to [iface: default, target: iqn.2018-04.com.example.storage:disk1,
portal: 172.24.0.12,3260] successful.
# cat /proc/partitions
```

```
major minor #blocks name

    8  0 41943040 sda
    8  1 1024 sda1
    8  2 1048576 sda2
    8  3 40892416 sda3
  253  0 39288832 dm-0
  253  1 1572864 dm-1
    8 16 1048576 sdb
```

**# iscsiadm --mode node --logout**
```
Logging out of session [sid: 2, target:
iqn.2018-04.com.example.storage:disk1, portal: 172.24.0.12,3260]
Logout of [sid: 2, target: iqn.2018-04.com.example.storage:disk1, portal:
172.24.0.12,3260] successful.
```

**# iscsiadm --mode node -T iqn.2018-04.com.example.storage:disk1 --op delete**

You can also use the `lsblk` utility to discover block devices that are available in the system.

# Configuring Physical Volumes (PV)

As we mentioned previously, OpenShift cluster administrators can create PV resources for future usage by OpenShift users.

This topic assumes that the OpenShift environment is up and running on the `openshift.example.com` node. You may use `oc cluster up` or do an advanced OpenShift installation by using Ansible.

As we mentioned previously, only cluster administrators can configure PVs. So, before you begin the following labs, you have to switch to the admin account:

**# oc login -u system:admin**

We recommend creating a new project to perform this `persistent storage`-related lab:

**# oc new-project persistent-storage**

The client will automatically change the current project to the newly created one.

In the upcoming examples, we will create the following PVs:

| PV | Storage backend | Size |
|---|---|---|
| pv-nfsvol1 | NFS | 2 GiB |
| pv-gluster | GlusterFS | 3 GiB |
| pv-iscsi | iSCSI | 1 GiB |

# Creating PVs for NFS shares

The NFS-related `PersistentVolume` resource that was created by the OpenShift API can be defined using either a YAML or JSON notation and can be submitted to the API by using the `oc create` command. Previously, we set up several NFS exports on `storage.example.com`. Now, we need to create the appropriate PV resources for each of them.

The following example provides a file that can make NFS resources available for OpenShift clusters:

```
# cat pv-nfsvol1.yaml
apiVersion: v1
kind: PersistentVolume
metadata:
  name: pv-nfsvol1
spec:
  capacity:
    storage: 2Gi
  accessModes:
    - ReadWriteMany
  persistentVolumeReclaimPolicy: Retain
  nfs:
    path: /exports/nfsvol1
    server: storage.example.com
    readOnly: false
```

This file contains the following information:

- Persistent Volume name (pv_nfsvol1) in the `metadata` section
- Available capacity (2 GibiBytes)

- Supported access modes (ReadWriteMany)
- Storage reclaim policy (Retain)
- NFS export information (server address and path)

Once the file is created, we can make the resource available for the cluster by using the following command:

```
# oc create -f pv-nfsvol1.yaml
persistentvolume "pv-nfsvol1" created
```

The preceding command creates the appropriate OpenShift API resource. Please be aware that the resource is not mounted to pod yet, but is ready to be bound to a PVC.

 You may want to create two other definitions to abstract the rest of the NFS shares we created previously. The shares are located on `storage.example.com:/exports/nfsvol2` and `storage.example.com:/exports/nfsvol3`. Shares `/exports/nfsvol2` and `/exports/nfsvol3` will not be used.

As with any other OpenShift API resource, we can see its configuration by running the `describe` command:

```
# oc describe pv pv-nfsvol1
Name: pv-nfsvol1
Labels: <none>
Annotations: <none>
StorageClass:
Status: Available
Claim:
Reclaim Policy: Retain
Access Modes: RWX
Capacity: 2Gi
Message:
Source:
    Type: NFS (an NFS mount that lasts the lifetime of a pod)
    Server: storage.example.com
    Path: /exports/nfsvol1
    ReadOnly: false
Events: <none>
```

You can see our PV using the `oc get pv` command as follows:

```
# oc get pv | egrep "^NAME|^pv-"
NAME CAPACITY ACCESSMODES RECLAIMPOLICY STATUS CLAIM STORAGECLASS REASON
AGE
pv-nfsvol1 2Gi RWX Retain Available 37s
```

> `oc cluster up` creates a number of pre-defined PVs, which are named `pv0001` and `pv0100`. They are not shown in the preceding output.

# Creating a PV for the GlusterFS volume

GlusterFS is distributed by nature and is quite different from the previous NFS-based storage. OpenShift cluster needs to be aware of the underlying Gluster storage infrastructure so that any schedulable OpenShift node can mount a GlusterFS volume. Configuring a GlusterFS persistent volume involves the following:

- The `glusterfs-fuse` package being installed on every schedulable OpenShift node
- An existing GlusterFS storage in your underlying infrastructure
- A distinct list of servers (IP addresses) in the GlusterFS cluster to be defined as endpoints
- A service to persist the endpoints (optional)
- An existing Gluster volume to be referenced in the persistent volume object

First, we need to install the `glusterfs-fuse` package on our OpenShift nodes:

```
# yum install -y centos-release-gluster312
# yum install -y glusterfs-fuse
```

An endpoints' definition is intended to represent the GlusterFS cluster's servers as endpoints and as such includes the IP addresses of your Gluster servers. The port value can be any numeric value within the accepted range of ports (0 – 65535). Optionally, you can create a service that persists the endpoints.

The GlusterFS service is represented by a `Service` OpenShift API object, which is shown as follows:

```
# cat gluster-service.yaml
apiVersion: v1
kind: Service
metadata:
  name: glusterfs-cluster
spec:
  ports:
    - port: 1
```

Once this file is created, `glusterfs` endpoints can be created as regular API objects:

```
# oc create -f gluster-service.yaml
service "glusterfs-cluster" created
# oc get svc
NAME CLUSTER-IP EXTERNAL-IP PORT(S) AGE
glusterfs-cluster 172.30.193.29 <none> 1/TCP 3s
```

The GlusterFS endpoint's definition should contain information about all Gluster Storage nodes that are going to be used for data exchange. Our example only contains one node with an IP address of `172.24.0.12`. So, in order to create a Gluster endpoint definition file and create Gluster endpoints, run the following commands:

```
# cat gluster-endpoint.yaml
apiVersion: v1
kind: Endpoints
metadata:
  name: glusterfs-cluster
subsets:
  - addresses:
      - ip: 172.24.0.12
    ports:
      - port: 1

# oc create -f gluster-endpoint.yaml
endpoints "glusterfs-cluster" created

# oc get endpoints
NAME ENDPOINTS AGE
glusterfs-cluster 172.24.0.12:1 17s
```

Now, we are ready to create a PV which points to the Gluster volume we created previously:

```
# cat pv-gluster.yaml
apiVersion: v1
kind: PersistentVolume
metadata:
  name: pv-gluster
spec:
  capacity:
    storage: 3Gi
  accessModes:
    - ReadWriteMany
  glusterfs:
    endpoints: glusterfs-cluster
    path: gvol1
    readOnly: false
  persistentVolumeReclaimPolicy: Retain

# oc create -f pv-gluster.yaml
persistentvolume "pv-gluster" created
```

 We are using the `Retain` policy to demonstrate that the system administrator has to take care of data reclamation manually.

As we can see, the PV definition file for GlusterFS contains endpoints information and the volume's name.

Now, the following volumes should be available:

```
# oc get pv | egrep "^NAME|^pv-"
NAME CAPACITY ACCESSMODES RECLAIMPOLICY STATUS CLAIM STORAGECLASS REASON
AGE
pv-gluster 3Gi RWX Retain Available 2s
pv-nfsvol1 2Gi RWX Retain Available 2m
```

# PV for iSCSI

Unlike NFS or GlusterFS persistent volumes, iSCSI volumes can only be accessed from one client/pod at a time. This is a block-based persistent storage and we should provide the file system type we are going to use. In the following example, the `ext4` file system will be used:

```
# cat pv-iscsi.yaml
apiVersion: v1
kind: PersistentVolume
metadata:
  name: pv-iscsi
spec:
  capacity:
    storage: 1Gi
  accessModes:
    - ReadWriteOnce
  iscsi:
    targetPortal: storage.example.com
    iqn: iqn.2018-04.com.example.storage:disk1
    lun: 0
    fsType: 'ext4'
    readOnly: false
```

Let's create the volume:

```
# oc create -f pv-iscsi.yaml
persistentvolume "pv-iscsi" created
```

At the end of the lab, you should have at least three PVs, like the ones shown in the following code:

```
# oc get pv | egrep "^NAME|^pv-"
NAME CAPACITY ACCESSMODES RECLAIMPOLICY STATUS CLAIM STORAGECLASS REASON
AGE
pv-gluster 3Gi RWX Retain Available 1m
pv-iscsi   1Gi RWO Retain Available 6s
pv-nfsvol1 2Gi RWX Retain Available 3m
```

# Using persistent storage in pods

Previously, we created all required PV OpenShift API objects, which are provided by OpenStack cluster administrators. Now, we are going to show you how to use persistent storage in your applications. Any OpenShift users can request persistent volume through the PVC concept.

## Requesting persistent volume

Once the PV resource is available, any OpenShift user can create a PVC to request storage and later use that PVC to attach it as a volume to containers in pods.

 Upcoming examples don't have to be run under the `system:admin` account. Any unprivileged OpenShift user can request persistent volumes using PVC.

Users should create PVC definitions using either YAML or JSON syntax. The following example shows a claim that requests 1 GiB of persistent storage with `ReadWriteOnce` capabilities:

```
# cat pvc-db.yaml
apiVersion: v1
kind: PersistentVolumeClaim
metadata:
  name: pvc-db
spec:
  accessModes:
  - ReadWriteOnce
  resources:
    requests:
      storage: 1Gi
```

Now, we are able to create the corresponding API entity—PVC:

```
# oc create -f pvc-db.yaml
persistentvolumeclaim "pvc-db" created
```

We can verify the PVC status by using the `oc get pv` and `oc get pvc` commands. Both should show the status of PV/PVC:

```
# oc get pv | egrep "^NAME|^pv-"
NAME CAPACITY ACCESSMODES RECLAIMPOLICY STATUS CLAIM STORAGECLASS REASON
AGE
pv-gluster 3Gi RWX Retain Available 2m
pv-iscsi   1Gi RWO Retain Bound persistent-storage/pvc-db 1m
pv-nfsvol1 2Gi RWX Retain Available 4m

# oc get pvc
NAME STATUS VOLUME CAPACITY ACCESSMODES STORAGECLASS AGE
pvc-db Bound pv-iscsi 1Gi RWO 28s
```

In your particular case, PVC will be bound to the iSCSI-based physical volume, because it satisfies all requirements (`ReadWriteOnce` and `capacity`). `Bound` state means that OpenShift was able to find a proper physical volume to perform the binding process.

# Binding a PVC to a particular PV

Usually, users don't have to worry about underlying storage infrastructure. A user just needs to order required storage using PVC with the size and access mode specified. In some cases, there is a need to bind a PVC to a specific PV. Imagine the following scenario, where your storage infrastructure is complex and you need the storage for your database server to be as fast as possible. It would be good to place it on an SSD storage. In this case, storage administrators can provide you with either an FC or iSCSI-based volume that is backed by SSD drives. The OpenShift administrator may create a specific PV for future usage. On the user side, we will need to bind the newly created PVC to that specific PV. Static binding PVC to PV can be achieved by specifying the `volumeName` parameter under the `spec` section (`spec.volumeName`).

In our particular example, we have two remaining unbound volumes with the `ReadWriteMany` access type: `pv-gluster` and `pv-nfsvol1`. In the following example, we are going to perform their static binding.

Let's create a PVS definition for web server data:

```
# cat pvc-web.yaml
apiVersion: "v1"
kind: "PersistentVolumeClaim"
metadata:
  name: "pvc-web"
spec:
```

```
accessModes:
  - "ReadWriteMany"
resources:
  requests:
    storage: "1Gi"
volumeName: "pv-gluster"
```

Create the PVC from the previous definition and see if OpenShift found a matching PV for it:

```
# oc create -f pvc-web.yaml
persistentvolumeclaim "pvc-web" created
```

```
# oc get pv | egrep "^NAME|^pv-"
NAME CAPACITY ACCESSMODES RECLAIMPOLICY STATUS CLAIM STORAGECLASS REASON
AGE
pv-gluster 3Gi RWX Retain Bound persistent-storage/pvc-web 3m
pv-iscsi   1Gi RWO Retain Bound persistent-storage/pvc-db 2m
pv-nfsvol1 2Gi RWX Retain Available 5m
```

And lastly, we will request 100 MiB of data by using the following PVC:

```
# cat pvc-data.yaml
apiVersion: "v1"
kind: "PersistentVolumeClaim"
metadata:
  name: "pvc-data"
spec:
  accessModes:
    - "ReadWriteMany"
  resources:
    requests:
      storage: "100Mi"
```

```
# oc create -f pvc-data.yaml
persistentvolumeclaim "pvc-data" created
```

```
# oc get pv | egrep "^NAME|^pv-"
NAME CAPACITY ACCESSMODES RECLAIMPOLICY STATUS CLAIM STORAGECLASS REASON
AGE
pv-gluster 3Gi RWX Retain Bound persistent-storage/pvc-web 4m
pv-iscsi 1Gi RWO Retain Bound persistent-storage/pvc-db 2m
pv-nfsvol1 2Gi RWX Recycle Bound persistent-storage/pvc-data 6m
```

Notice that all PVSs are in the Bound state now.

# Using claims as volumes in pod definition

Previously, we requested a persistent storage by creating PVCs, and now we are going to create an application using corresponding PVCs, as they are now bound to PVs that are backed by real storage. OpenShift allows developers to create a `Pod` and use PVC as a volume. The following example shows how it can be used in order to create an Apache-based container:

```
# cat pod-webserver.yaml
apiVersion: v1
kind: Pod
metadata:
  name: mywebserverpod
  labels:
    name: webeserver
spec:
  containers:
    - name: webserver
      image: docker.io/centos/httpd
      ports:
        - name: web
          containerPort: 80
      volumeMounts:
        - name: volume-webroot
          mountPath: /var/www/html
  volumes:
    - name: volume-webroot
      persistentVolumeClaim:
        claimName: pvc-web
```

In the preceding code, we defined an Apache pod and configured it to attach persistent volume that was provided as part of our previous claim to `pvc-web` to its container. OpenShift will automatically find the bound PV and mount it to the container.

> The PVC named `pvc-web` is bound to the GlusterFS-based PV. This persistent storage implementation requires gluster endpoints and services to be defined in each namespace/project in OpenShift. So, before moving on to the next part of the lab, we will need to create these service and endpoints again by running the following commands:
>
> ```
> oc create -f gluster-service.yaml
> oc create -f gluster-endpoint.yaml:
> ```

```
# oc create -f pod-webserver.yaml
pod "mywebserverpod" created
```

We can display pod and volume-related information by using the following command:

```
# oc describe pod mywebserverpod | grep -A 4 Volumes:
Volumes:
  nfsvol:
    Type: PersistentVolumeClaim (a reference to a PersistentVolumeClaim in
the same namespace)
    ClaimName: pvc-web
    ReadOnly: false
```

If we connect to the container and try to create the `/var/www/index.html` file, it will reside in GlusterFS. We can verify that the GlusterFS volume was mounted on the node:

```
# df -h | grep gvol1
172.24.0.12:gvol1 38G 720M 37G 2%
/var/lib/origin/openshift.local.volumes/pods/e2ca34d3-4823-11e8-9445-525400
5f9478/volumes/kubernetes.io~glusterfs/pv-gluster
```

So, now the container has access to persistent data mounted at `/var/www/html`.

> Previously, we created an `index.html` file stored on GlusterFS storage. This means that our web server will automatically have access to all data on the GlusterFS volume `gvol1`.

Now, we can verify that the persistent data written earlier is accessible. First, we will need to get the cluster IP address of our web server:

```
# oc describe pod mywebserverpod | grep IP:
IP: 172.17.0.2
```

And secondly, try to reach it via `curl`:

```
# curl http://172.17.0.2
Persistent data on GlusterFS
```

As we can see, now, the web server displays data that's available on the GlusterFS.

We can now verify that data is stored persistently using two different ways:

- On the backend storage
- By recreating the container

Let's verify that the file indeed exists on our `storage.example.com` server:

```
[root@storage ~]# cat /exports/gluster/index.html
Persistent data on GlusterFS
```

Finally, let's try to delete and create the container again:

```
# oc delete pod mywebserverpod
pod "mywebserverpod" deleted
# oc create -f pod-webserver.yaml
pod "mywebserverpod" created
# oc describe pod mywebserverpod | grep IP:
IP: 172.17.0.2
# curl http://172.17.0.2:80
Persistent data on GlusterFS
```

As we can see, the data persists and is available, even after the container has been deleted.

# Managing volumes through oc volume

OpenShift users can attach a volume to any running application by using `oc volume`. In this example, we are going to create a pod with a basic application and attach a persistent volume to it.

First, just deploy a basic Apache web server using `oc new-app`:

```
# oc new-app httpd
...
<output omitted>
...
```

After a little while, all httpd service resources will be available:

```
# oc get pod | egrep "^NAME|httpd"
NAME            READY STATUS    RESTARTS  AGE
httpd-1-qnh5k   1/1   Running   0         49s
```

`oc new-app` created a deployment configuration that controls the application deployment process.

In this example, we are going to attach a PVC named `pvc-data` as a volume to the running container:

```
# oc volume dc/httpd --add --name=demovolume -t pvc --claim-name=pvc-data --mount-path=/var/www/html
deploymentconfig "httpd" updated

# oc get pod | egrep "^NAME|httpd"
NAME READY STATUS RESTARTS AGE
httpd-2-bfbft 1/1 Running 0 40s
```

```
# oc describe pod httpd-2-bfbft | grep -A 4 Volumes:
Volumes:
 demovolume:
 Type: PersistentVolumeClaim (a reference to a PersistentVolumeClaim in the
same namespace)
 ClaimName: pvc-data
 ReadOnly: false
```

We can verify that an NFS share was mounted to the container:

```
# df -h | grep nfsvol1
storage.example.com:/exports/nfsvol1 38G 720M 37G 2%
/var/lib/origin/openshift.local.volumes/pods/12cfe985-482b-11e8-9445-525400
5f9478/volumes/kubernetes.io~nfs/pv-nfsvol1
```

Now, we can create an index.html file on our storage server directly in the export:

```
[root@storage ~]# echo "New NFS data" >/exports/nfsvol1/index.html
```

 The previous command was run on the storage server, not on OpenShift!

Once persistent data is available, we can try to access the web service:

```
# oc describe pod httpd-2-bfbft | grep IP:
IP: 172.17.0.3
```

```
# curl http://172.17.0.3:8080
New NFS data
```

As we can see, attaching a volume to the pod worked fine. Now, we can detach it:

```
# oc volume dc/httpd --remove --name=demovolume
deploymentconfig "httpd" updated
```

 Please be aware that OpenShift rolls new pods out each time you update the corresponding deployment config. This means that the container's IP addresses will be changed. To avoid that, we recommend testing your configuration using the service's IP address.

Once the container is recreated, notice that the persistent data is not available. The `httpd` daemon shows the default page:

```
# oc get pod
NAME READY STATUS RESTARTS AGE
httpd-3-fbq74 1/1 Running 0 1m

# oc describe pod httpd-3-fbq74 | grep IP:
IP: 172.17.0.4

# curl http://172.17.0.4:8080
<!DOCTYPE html PUBLIC "-//W3C//DTD XHTML 1.1//EN"
"http://www.w3.org/TR/xhtml11/DTD/xhtml11.dtd">

<html xmlns="http://www.w3.org/1999/xhtml" xml:lang="en">
 <head>
 <title>Test Page for the Apache HTTP Server on Red Hat Enterprise
Linux</title>
...
<output omitted>
...
```

# Persistent data for a database container

Let's attach an iSCSI-based persistent volume to a MariaDB instance. First, we will have to launch a `mariadb` application as follows:

```
# oc new-app \
-e MYSQL_USER=openshift \
-e MYSQL_PASSWORD=openshift \
-e MYSQL_DATABASE=openshift \
mariadb
Found image a339b72 (10 days old) in image stream "openshift/mariadb" under
tag "10.1" for "mariadb"

MariaDB 10.1
------------
MariaDB is a multi-user, multi-threaded SQL database server. The container
image provides a containerized packaging of the MariaDB mysqld daemon and
client application. The mysqld server daemon accepts connections from
clients and provides access to content from MariaDB databases on behalf of
the clients.

Tags: database, mysql, mariadb, mariadb101, rh-mariadb101, galera

* This image will be deployed in deployment config "mariadb"
```

```
* Port 3306/tcp will be load balanced by service "mariadb"
* Other containers can access this service through the hostname "mariadb"
* This image declares volumes and will default to use non-persistent, host-
local storage.
You can add persistent volumes later by running 'volume dc/mariadb --add
...'

--> Creating resources ...

deploymentconfig "mariadb" created
service "mariadb" created
--> Success
Application is not exposed. You can expose services to the outside world by
executing one or more of the commands below:
'oc expose svc/mariadb'
Run 'oc status' to view your app.
```

Wait a couple of minutes, and check the status of the `mariadb` instance:

```
# oc get pod | egrep "^NAME|mariadb"
NAME              READY STATUS    RESTARTS AGE
mariadb-1-1fmrn 1/1    Running    0         1m
```

We need to know the default location of the database files. This can be gathered using the `oc describe dc` command, as shown in the following code:

```
# oc describe dc mariadb
Name: mariadb
...
<output omitted>
...
 Mounts:
 /var/lib/mysql/data from mariadb-volume-1 (rw)
 Volumes:
 mariadb-volume-1:
 Type: EmptyDir (a temporary directory that shares a pod's lifetime)
 Medium:
...
<output omitted>
...
```

As we can see, by default, that container stores all data at `/var/lib/mysql/data` in the `mariadb-volume-1` volume. This allows us to replace data on it by using the `oc volume` subcommand.

Now, we are going to attach a volume to the `mariadb` container. Please be aware that previously created database structures will be lost, as they are not stored persistently:

```
# oc volume dc/mariadb --add --name=mariadb-volume-1 -t pvc --claim-
name=pvc-db --mount-path=/var/lib/mysql --overwrite
deploymentconfig "mariadb" updated
```

This will automatically redeploy `mariadb` and place database files on the persistent storage.

 The `ext4` file system should be created on the iSCSI target in advance.

Now you see that Openshift integrates easily with the most popular storage protocols and allows you to make containerized applications to be more resilient.

# Summary

Persistent storage usage is a daily activity for OpenShift cluster administrators and OpenShift users in a production environment. In this chapter, we briefly discussed persistent storage OpenShift API objects such as PV and PVC. Both PV and PVC allow you to define and use persistent storage. We showed you how to configure basic underlying storage services such as NFS, GlusterFS, and iSCSI, and how to add them to OpenShift's infrastructure via PV objects. Additionally, we worked on requesting persistent storage via PVC objects. Lastly, we showed you a basic example of persistent storage usage from an application point of view.

# Questions

1. Which would be a good use case for persistent storage?
    1. PostgreSQL database for development
    2. MariaDB database for production
    3. Memcached
    4. JDBC-connector

2. Which of the following OpenShift storage plugins supports the `ReadWriteMany` access mode? choose two:
     1. NFS
     2. iSCSI
     3. Cinder Volume
     4. GlusterFS

3. Which project must PVs belong to?
     1. default
     2. openshift
     3. Any project
     4. openshift-infra

4. Suppose we created a PVC that requests 2 Gi storage. Which PV will be bound to it?
     1. 1950 Mi
     2. 1950 M
     3. 2 Gi
     4. 3 Gi

5. Which OpenShift API objects must be created before using GlusterFS volumes? choose two:
     1. Pod
     2. Service
     3. Endpoint
     4. Route

# Further reading

Here is a list of links for you to take a look at if you are interested in the topics we covered in this chapter:

- https://docs.openshift.org/latest/install_config/persistent_storage/index.html
- http://linux-iscsi.org/wiki/LIO
- https://docs.gluster.org/en/latest/Administrator%20Guide/Setting%20Up%20Volumes/

# 8

# Core OpenShift Concepts

In the previous chapters, we covered Docker and Kubernetes basics and went through the OpenShift architecture. We know how to build the OpenShift lab environment, so now it is time to get our hands dirty and see how we can work with OpenShift's main resources.

This chapter goes over OpenShift core concepts, such as creating new applications with OpenShift pods, services, routes, projects, and users. This will give you foundational skills, which will be enough for you to run and manage your application container infrastructure in OpenShift.

After reading this chapter, you will have learned about the following topics:

- Managing projects and namespaces in OpenShift
- Managing regular users in OpenShift
- Creating new applications in OpenShift
- Managing pods in OpenShift
- Managing services in OpenShift
- Managing routes in OpenShift

## Managing projects in OpenShift

Before we begin, make sure that your OpenShift is up and running. We are going to use MiniShift for this chapter:

```
$ minishift start --openshift-version=v3.9.0 --vm-driver=virtualbox
-- Starting profile 'minishift'
...
<output omitted>
...
```

Once its VM is up, log in as a system admin:

```
$ oc login -u system:admin
...
<output omitted>
...
Using project "myproject".
```

As we covered earlier, Openshift CLI has a lot of similarities with Kubernetes CLI. `oc` is short for OpenShift client, which works similarly to Kubernetes's `kubectl`. You will find a lot of similarities between these two commands as we go.

Before we deep dive into creating our first OpenShift applications and use basic OpenShift resources such as pods, services, and routes, we need to work a little bit with OpenShift's management and other essential features such as OpenShift projects and user accounts. First, let's focus on OpenShift projects.

OpenShift project is a Kubernetes namespace with additional features called annotations that provide user multi-tenancy and role-based access control in OpenShift. Each project has its own set of policies, constraints, and service accounts. You can see that the number of namespaces and projects in OpenShift is the same. The commands we are going to need are `oc get namespaces` and `oc get projects`:

```
$ oc get projects
NAME DISPLAY NAME STATUS
default Active
kube-public Active
kube-system Active
myproject My Project Active
openshift Active
openshift-infra Active
openshift-node Active
```

```
$ oc get namespaces
NAME                STATUS    AGE
default             Active    3d
kube-public         Active    3d
kube-system         Active    3d
myproject           Active    3d
openshift           Active    3d
openshift-infra     Active    3d
openshift-node      Active    3d
```

As we mentioned previously, each namespace, or rather project, is separated from another by a set of rules. This allows different teams to work independently from each other. In order to identify what project we are currently working in, you can use the `oc projects` command. This command gives you a list of OpenShift projects available for you, and it also tells you what projects you are currently working on:

```
$ oc projects
You have access to the following projects and can switch between them with
'oc project <projectname>':
    default
    kube-public
    kube-system
    myproject - My Project
  * new-project1
    openshift
    openshift-infra
    openshift-node
Using project "new-project1" on server "https://127.0.0.1:8443".
```

> The asterisk * also specifies the current project.
>
> We can see that there are a lot of different projects available, though we have not created any because the system admin user has access to everything.

In order to create a new OpenShift project, you must use the `oc new-project` command:

```
$ oc new-project new-project1
Now using project "new-project1" on server "https://127.0.0.1:8443".
...
<output omitted>
...
```

This command creates a new project and automatically switches to it. In our case, it switches to `new-project1`. We can manually switch to another available project by running the `oc project` command. Let's switch to the `default` project:

```
$ oc project default
Now using project "default" on server "https://127.0.0.1:8443".
```

Note that the output of `oc project default` tells you not only that the project is switched to `default`, but it also specifies the OpenShift cluster URL: `https://127.0.0.1:8443`. It is useful when we are dealing with several independently working OpenShift clusters.

In order to delete an OpenShift project, you can use the `oc delete` command:

```
$ oc delete project new-project1
project "new-project1" deleted
```

We are going to work with projects closely in the subsequent chapters.

# Managing users in OpenShift

When we use the `oc` command, it makes an API call to the OpenShift cluster using user credentials.

There are three main user types in OpenShift. Let's quickly talk about each of these three types:

- **Regular users**: A regular OpenShift user. Regular users are usually developers with access to OpenShift projects. Regular OpenShift user examples include user1 and user2.
- **System users**: System OpenShift users are special and most of these users are created when OpenShift is being installed. System user examples are:
    - `system:admin`: OpenShift cluster administrator user
    - `system:node:node1.example.com`: `node1.example.com` node user
    - `system:openshift-registry`: OpenShift registry user
- **Service accounts**: Special system users associated with projects. Some of these users are created when a new OpenShift project is being created.

 We are going to work with system users and service accounts in the next chapter. In this chapter, we are going to work with regular users.

We can get information about the OpenShift user we are currently logged in as by using the `oc whoami` command:

```
$ oc whoami
system:admin
```

In order to create a regular user, you can use the `oc create user` command:

```
$ oc create user user1
user "user1" created
```

> We do not need to set a user password in this lab because our lab environment is set up to accept any password from any user.

By default, the user is going to be created for a project we are currently working on. To get the list of users, use the `oc get users` command:

```
$ oc get users
NAME       UID FULL NAME IDENTITIES
developer 46714e6b-2981-11e8-bae6-025000000001 anypassword:developer
user1 473664ec-299d-11e8-bae6-025000000001
```

We should be able to see two users: `developer` and `user1`.

> Developer users are created as a part of the `oc cluster up` command, as well as the project `myproject`.
>
> The `IDENTITIES` field defines the authentication method. In our lab environment setup, the developer user takes anything as a password. This is what `anypassword:developer` means.

The last essential things we need to learn is how to switch between different users. We can use the `oc login` command to do so:

```
$ oc login -u developer
Logged into "https://127.0.0.1:8443" as "developer" using existing
credentials.
You have one project on this server: "myproject"
Using project "myproject".
```

`user1` does not have any authentication method defined. This is why you won't be able to log in as `user1` if you try to.

We are going to put all of these pieces together and assign a particular user to one or several projects, as well as give users different permissions, in the following chapter.

# Creating new applications in OpenShift

The first and most essential command to run in OpenShift is `oc new-app`. This command is similar to Kubernetes's `kubectl run`, but `oc new-app` is way more powerful and works a little bit differently. We are going to show you how `oc new-app` works in detail later in this chapter.

The best way to test out the `oc new-app` command is to create a new project and then run it over there:

```
$ oc new-project project1
Now using project "project1" on server "https://127.0.0.1:8443".
You can add applications to this project with the 'new-app' command. For
example, try:

    oc new-app centos/ruby-22-
centos7~https://github.com/openshift/ruby-ex.git
to build a new example application in Ruby.
```

The command output tells us to run the `oc new-app centos/ruby-22-centos7~https://github.com/openshift/ruby-ex.git` command. Run the command to see how it works:

```
$ oc new-app centos/ruby-22-
centos7~https://github.com/openshift/ruby-ex.git
--> Found Docker image 1f02469 (8 days old) from Docker Hub for
"centos/ruby-22-centos7"
...
<output omitted>
...
 * An image stream will be created as "ruby-22-centos7:latest" that will
track the source image
 * A source build using source code from
https://github.com/openshift/ruby-ex.git will be created
 * The resulting image will be pushed to image stream "ruby-ex:latest"
 * Every time "ruby-22-centos7:latest" changes a new build will be
```

```
triggered
  * This image will be deployed in deployment config "ruby-ex"
  * Port 8080/tcp will be load balanced by service "ruby-ex"
  * Other containers can access this service through the hostname "ruby-ex"
...
<output omitted>
...
 Run 'oc status' to view your app.
```

We have seen that running `oc new-app` sometimes takes a lot of time or is just stuck for hours.

If this happens to you, try to reinstall the cluster again.

Also, make sure that you have the firewall off on your host.

If all of these options fail for you, you can always run a separate VM and install OpenShift from scratch.

There is going to be a lot of output compared to what we have seen before, but if you read through, you should be able to find out that:

- OpenShift pulls Docker image `centos/ruby-22-centos7`
- OpenShift goes to GitHub and downloads the source code from it
- OpenShift applies GitHub source code to the image and stores it on the internal registry with the name `ruby-ex`
- `ruby-ex` is used to create build and deployment configurations
- The `ruby-ex` service is created to load balance the traffic for pods with `ruby-ex` in their names

The following diagram represents this flow:

oc new-app workflow

We are going to take a closer look at all of these resources in the following chapter.

# Managing pods in OpenShift

OpenShift pods are Kubernetes pods that represent a collection of containers, and each pod serves as a basic management unit. All containers in a pod share the same storage volumes and network. In order to get a list of pods in OpenShift, we can use the `oc get pods` command:

```
$ oc get pods
NAME              READY   STATUS      RESTARTS    AGE
ruby-ex-1-build   0/1     Completed   0           1h
ruby-ex-1-zzhrc   1/1     Running     0           56m
```

It is no different from the Kubernetes pod, which means behind the scenes it is a Docker container running. The only difference is that there are two containers now. One of them is a container (`ruby-ex-1-build`) that is used to build the final image with the source code applied. We can easily verify this by running the `docker ps` command inside the Minishift VM:

```
$ minishift ssh docker ps
CONTAINER ID IMAGE COMMAND CREATED STATUS PORTS NAMES
d07dd7cf63e4 172.30.1.1:5000/myproject/ruby-
ex@sha256:aa86aab41fbf81ce0b09a1209618b67f353b18e5ac2ed00a030e7577bad1ed44
"container-entrypoint"
...
<output omitted>
...
```

We can easily find the right running container by seeing the `myproject/ruby-ex` part of the image's ID. We can do similar actions in Kubernetes, like getting logs, editing or describing, and deleting pods.

Before you start with the next section, try to run `oc delete`.

# Managing services in OpenShift

Similarly to Kubernetes, OpenShift services represent an interface between clients and the actual application running in the pods. A service is an IP:port pair which forwards traffic to backend pods in a round-robin fashion.

By running the `oc new-app` command, OpenShift creates a service automatically. We can verify this by running the `oc get services` command:

```
$ oc get services
NAME CLUSTER-IP        EXTERNAL-IP      PORT(S)      AGE
ruby-ex 172.30.173.195 <none>          8080/TCP     1h
```

The output is similar to what we got with the `kubectl get services` command in Kubernetes. We can delete and recreate this service again by running the `oc delete` and `oc expose` commands. Before we do that, run the `curl` command inside the Minishift VM to verify that the service is up and running:

```
$ minishift ssh "curl -I -m3 172.30.173.195:8080"
...
<output omitted>
...
0 0 0 0 0 0 0 0 --:--:-- --:--:-- 0 HTTP/1.1 200 OK
...
<output omitted>
...
```

The status code is `200`, which means that the web page is available and the service is running properly:

```
$ oc delete svc/ruby-ex
service "ruby-ex" deleted
```

Check that the service is deleted and that the service is no longer available:

```
$ oc get svc
NAME CLUSTER-IP EXTERNAL-IP PORT(S) AGE

$ minishift ssh "curl -I -m3 172.30.173.195:8080"
...
<output omitted>
...
Command failed: exit status 28
```

Now, create a new service with the `oc expose` command:

```
$ oc expose pods/ruby-ex-1-zzhrc
service "ruby-ex-1-zzhrc" exposed
```

 In your case, the container name is going to be different. Rerun `oc get pods` to get the running pod name. There are other methods on how to create a service and we are going to cover them later in this book:

```
$ oc get svc
NAME            CLUSTER-IP EXTERNAL-IP PORT(S) AGE
ruby-ex-1-zzhrc 172.30.79.183 <none> 8080/TCP 1m
```

Finally, check that the service is available again by running the `curl` command on the Minishift VM:

```
$ minishift ssh "curl -I -m3 172.30.79.183:8080"
...
<output omitted>
...
0 0 0 0 0 0 0 0 --:--:-- --:--:-- 0 HTTP/1.1 200 OK
...
<output omitted>
...
```

# Managing routes in OpenShift

OpenShift has an elegant way of exposing a service so that it can be accessed from the outside of an OpenShift cluster. This resource is called a `router` in OpenShift. OpenShift provides an external hostname mapping to a load balancer that distributes traffic among OpenShift services:

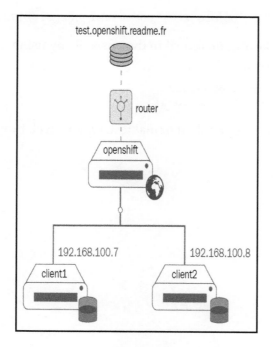

OpenShift router workflow

In order for the OpenShift router to load balance external traffic, it has to use HTTP or HTTPS protocol, and be resolvable by DNS using DNS wildcards.

Let's expose our service outside of the OpenShift cluster by running the `oc expose` command with additional parameters:

```
$ oc expose service/ruby-ex-1-zzhrc --hostname="openshiftdemo.local"
```

Check the list of routes:

```
$ oc get routes
NAME        HOST/PORT PATH SERVICES    PORT  TERMINATION       WILDCARD
ruby-ex-1-zzhrc openshiftdemo.local ruby-ex-1-zzhrc 8080   None
```

If we try to run the `curl openshiftdemo.local` command, it won't work because there is no DNS record for `openshiftdemo.local`. One of the easiest ways is to add a static DNS record to the hosts file. Since we are using the Minishift VM, we need to create a static DNS record pointing to the Minishift VM. The first step is to check the Minishift VM with the `oc status` command:

```
$ oc status
In project My Project (myproject) on server https://192.168.99.109:8443
```

And now we need to make a static record in the hosts file by using minishift VM IP address and our project hostname:

```
$ cat /etc/hosts | grep openshift
192.168.99.109 openshiftdemo.local
```

Everything is ready so that we can do the final test. Open a web browser and open `http://openshiftdemo.local/webpage`:

---

### Welcome to your Ruby application on OpenShift

#### Deploying code changes

The source code for this application is available to be forked from the OpenShift GitHub repository. You can configure a webhook in your repository to make OpenShift automatically start a build whenever you push your code:

1. From the Web Console homepage, navigate to your project
2. Click on Browse > Builds
3. From the view for your Build click on the button to copy your GitHub webhook
4. Navigate to your repository on GitHub and click on repository settings > webhooks
5. Paste your webhook URL provided by OpenShift — that's it!

After you save your webhook, if you refresh your settings page you can see the status of the ping that Github sent to OpenShift to verify it can reach the server.

Note: adding a webhook requires your OpenShift server to be reachable from GitHub.

#### Working in your local Git repository

If you forked the application from the OpenShift GitHub example, you'll need to manually clone the repository to your local system. Copy the application's source code Git URL and then run:

```
$ git clone <git_url> <directory_to_create>

# Within your project directory
# Commit your changes and push to OpenShift

$ git commit -a -m 'Some commit message'
$ git push
```

After pushing changes, you'll need to manually trigger a build if you did not setup a webhook as described above.

#### Managing your application

Documentation on how to manage your application from the Web Console or Command Line is available at the Developer Guide.

#### Web Console

You can use the Web Console to view the state of your application components and launch new builds.

#### Command Line

With the OpenShift command line interface (CLI), you can create applications and manage projects from a terminal.

#### Development Resources

- OpenShift Documentation
- Openshift Origin GitHub
- Source To Image GitHub
- Getting Started with Ruby on OpenShift
- Stack Overflow questions for OpenShift
- Git documentation

Ruby demo application web page

If you somehow do not see a welcome web page, check whether you can ping `openshiftdemo.local` and also try to run the `curl openshiftdemo.local` command.

If you try to open a web page using the IP address of the Minishift VM instead of `openshiftdemo.local`, you will get `Application is not available`. This happens because the OpenShift router is a HAProxy-based container that does load balancing based on a URL. We can easily verify this by running the `oc describe` command with the OpenShift router pod. First, log in as `system:admin` and then check the router pod name in the `default` namespace:

```
$ oc login -u system:admin

...
<output omitted>
...
```

---

```
$ oc get pods -n default
NAME READY STATUS RESTARTS AGE
docker-registry-1-qctp4 1/1 Running 0 22h
persistent-volume-setup-mdmw6 0/1 Completed 0 22h
router-1-s9b7f 1/1 Running 0 22h
```

Finally, run the `oc describe` command, specifying the `router-1-s9b7f pod` and look for the `Image` line:

```
$ oc describe pods router-1-s9b7f -n default | grep Image:
    Image: openshift/origin-haproxy-router:v3.9.0
```

You can replace the HAproxy-based router with other ones, like Nginx or something else, but that is out of the scope of this book.

# Summary

In this chapter, we covered OpenShift core concepts such as pods, services, routes, projects, and users. We are going to work with these topics in detail in the following chapters and work closely with these resources to show you how they are integrated with other OpenShift resources.

In the next chapter, we are going take a look at advanced OpenShift resources, including source to image and image streams, builds and build configs, deployments, and deployment configs, as well as config maps and templates. We are also going to create some of these resources using manual methods with YAML and JSON files.

# Questions

1. What are the two Node types used by OpenShift? choose two:
    1. Node
    2. MiniShift
    3. Vagrant
    4. Master

2. Which of the following is not an Openshift user type? choose two:
    1. Regular users
    2. Admin users
    3. System users
    4. Service accounts

5. Service users

3. In OpenShift, a pod is a minimal unit of deployment which represents a group of containers:
    1. True
    2. False

4. In OpenShift, what resource is responsible for exposing the OpenShift application to the outside? choose one:
    1. Service
    2. Route
    3. Pod
    4. Load balancer

5. What are the two commands that list available pods and routes? choose two:
    1. oc get po
    2. oc list pods
    3. oc get rt
    4. oc get routes

6. In OpenShift, the system admin user account has access to system-related resources only:
    1. True
    2. False

# Further reading

In this chapter, we briefly covered the core concepts of the OpenShift container platform. Here's a list of links that may be helpful to look through so that you can learn more about OpenShift basics:

- **Openshift core concepts**: https://docs.openshift.org/latest/architecture/core_concepts/index.html
- **OpenShift official blog**: https://blog.openshift.com/

# Advanced OpenShift Concepts

**9**

In the previous chapter, we briefly described basic OpenShift objects such as pods, services, and routes. We also gave you an understanding of how to use namespaces for resource isolation and how to manage users in OpenShift.

This chapter deals with advanced OpenShift resources, such as **ImageStreams** and **ConfigMaps**, logically continuing on from the previous chapter on OpenShift core concepts. The OpenShift API provides dozens of varied resources to control different aspects of application deployment, security, and so on. For now, we will focus on some of the most important ones.

After completing this chapter, you will have learned about the following:

- Tracking the version history of images using ImageStreams
- Separating configuration from application code using ConfigMaps
- Controlling resource consumption using LimitRanges and ResourceQuotas
- Autoscaling your application depending on CPU and RAM utilization

## Technical requirements

In this chapter, we will practice with OpenShift deployed on the VM managed by Vagrant. The last section on auto-scaling requires Hawkular metrics to be enabled, so you will have to install OpenShift with `openshift_metrics_install_metrics` Ansible variable. The metrics collector and dashboard are deployed in their own pods, so we will also need to provide the VM with more RAM. Use the following Vagrantfile to deploy the lab:

```
$ cat Vagrantfile
$lab_openshift = <<SCRIPT
yum -y update
yum install -y epel-release git docker httpd-tools java-1.8.0-openjdk-
headless
yum install -y ansible python-passlib
systemctl start docker
```

```
systemctl enable docker
git clone -b release-3.9 https://github.com/openshift/openshift-ansible
/root/openshift-ansible
ssh-keygen -f /root/.ssh/id_rsa -N ''
cp /root/.ssh/id_rsa.pub /root/.ssh/authorized_keys
ssh-keyscan 172.24.0.11 >> .ssh/known_hosts
cp .ssh/known_hosts /root/.ssh/known_hosts
ssh-copy-id -i /root/.ssh/id_rsa root@172.24.0.11
reboot
SCRIPT

Vagrant.configure(2) do |config|
 config.vm.define "openshift" do |conf|
 conf.vm.box = "centos/7"
 conf.vm.hostname = 'openshift.example.com'
 conf.vm.network "private_network", ip: "172.24.0.11"
 conf.vm.provider "virtualbox" do |v|
 v.memory = 6144
 v.cpus = 2
 end
 conf.vm.provision "shell", inline: $lab_openshift
 end
end
```

In order to be able to reach the cluster inside the VM from your host system, make sure file /etc/hosts on your laptop looks like this:

```
$ cat /etc/hosts
127.0.0.1 localhost openshift localhost.localdomain localhost4
localhost4.localdomain4
::1 localhost localhost.localdomain localhost6 localhost6.localdomain6
172.24.0.11 openshift.example.com hawkular-metrics.openshift.example.com
```

Run vagrant up and wait until it finishes all the work. It may take up to 30 mins depending on your internet connectivity and compute resources:

```
$ vagrant up
Bringing machine 'openshift' up with 'virtualbox' provider...
...
<output omitted>
...
```

Once it's done, open SSH session into the VM and become root:

```
$ vagrant ssh
[vagrant@openshift ~]$ sudo -i
[root@openshift ~]#
```

You can use the following inventory for deploying OpenShift:

```
# cat /etc/ansible/hosts
...
<output omitted>
...
[masters]
172.24.0.11

[nodes]
172.24.0.11 openshift_node_labels="{'region': 'infra', 'zone': 'default'}"
openshift_schedulable=true

[etcd]
172.24.0.11

[OSEv3:vars]
openshift_deployment_type=origin
openshift_disable_check=memory_availability,disk_availability
openshift_ip=172.24.0.11
ansible_service_broker_install=false
openshift_master_cluster_hostname=172.24.0.11
openshift_master_cluster_public_hostname=openshift.example.com
openshift_hostname=172.24.0.11
openshift_public_hostname=openshift.example.com
openshift_metrics_install_metrics=true
openshift_metrics_image_version=v3.9
openshift_master_default_subdomain=openshift.example.com

[OSEv3:children]
masters
nodes
etcd
```

Notice that we have specified `openshift_metrics_install_metrics` variable to configure metrics for the section on autoscaling.

As of the time of writing, metrics image hasn't been tagged with the correct version yet, so we had to provide `openshift_metrics_image_version` variable as well to prevent metrics pods going into `ImagePullBackOff` state. More details at https://github.com/openshift/origin/issues/19440.

Now, it's time to install OpenShift:

```
# cd openshift-ansible
# ansible-playbook playbooks/prerequisites.yml
...
<output omitted>
...
# ansible-playbook playbooks/deploy_cluster.yml
...
<output omitted>
..
```

Log in as an unprivileged user:

```
# oc login -u alice
Username: alice
Password: anypassword
Login successful.
```

Remeber that since this time we didn't configure identity provider explicitly, OpenShift defaults to AllowAll, so we can use any password.

Next, create a dedicated project for our lab:

```
# oc new-project advanced
...
<output omitted>
...
```

Log in back as `system:admin`:

```
# oc login -u system:admin
...
<output omitted>
...
```

Next, we will need to run the following command:

```
# oc adm policy add-scc-to-user anyuid -z default
scc "anyuid" added to: ["system:serviceaccount:advanced:default"]
```

We have not discussed the concept behind the command above yet, but at this point it suffices to understand that it relaxes permissions imposed by OpenShift on pods. The concept is known as **Security Context Constraint (SCC)** and is discussed more thoroughly in `Chapter 10`, *Security in OpenShift*, section *Security context constraints*.

Finally, log back in as `alice`:

```
# oc login -u alice
```

# Tracking the version history of images using ImageStreams

Certain OpenShift resources, such as pods, deployments, DeploymentConfigs, ReplicationControllers, and ReplicaSets reference Docker images for deploying containers. Instead of referencing images directly, the common approach is to reference them through image streams, which serve as a layer of indirection between the internal/external repository and client resources, creating a virtual view of available images.

 In the official documentation and some blogs, you may come across comparing image streams to repositories. While it's true in the sense that resources reference images in image streams just like in repositories, this analogy lacks clarity; image streams don't store anything by themselves and are only abstractions for image management. So, in this chapter, we will talk of them as virtual views to give you a more accurate idea of what they actually are.

Using image streams has the following advantages:

- Your application won't break unexpectedly if the upstream image's update introduced errors, because the image stream tags your pod points so that it will still be mapped to the working version of the image, effectively protecting you from outages
- Image-change triggers and periodic reimports of the image can be configured at the image stream's level

You more than likely won't have to create ImageStreams from scratch, but it's important to understand their structure in order to understand their functions.

Minishift and OpenShift, when installed by Ansible, include default image streams for some of the most popular images, such as PostgreSQL, HTTPD, and Python. They reside in the `openshift` project:

```
# oc get is -n openshift
NAME          DOCKER REPO                                              . . .
. . .
<output omitted>
. . .
mongodb       docker-registry.default.svc:5000/openshift/mongodb      . . .
. . .
<output omitted>
. . .
```

In order to see what the words indirection layer from the beginning of this section mean, let's take a closer look at the `mongodb` image stream:

```
# oc describe is/mongodb -n openshift
. . .
<output omitted>
. . .
Unique Images:    3
Tags:             4

3.2 (latest)
  tagged from centos/mongodb-32-centos7:latest

  Provides a MongoDB 3.2 database on CentOS 7. For more information about
using this database image, including OpenShift considerations, see
https://github.com/sclorg/mongodb-container/tree/master/3.2/README.md.
  Tags: mongodb

  * centos/mongodb-32-
centos7@sha256:d4dc006a25db1423caed1dcf0f253f352dbbe0914c20949a6302ccda55af
72b1
      22 hours ago
. . .
<output omitted>
. . .
```

Image streams use a particular notation to reference images in repositories. Let's take a reference from the preceding example and break it down:

```
centos/mongodb-32-
centos7@sha256:d4dc006a25db1423caed1dcf0f253f352dbbe0914c20949a6302ccda55af
72b1
```

The preceding image references have the following structure:

- `centos/mongodb-32-centos7`: Path to the image in the Docker repository
- `sha256`: Indicates that the image identifier is generated using the SHA256 hash algorithm
- `d4dc006a25db1423caed1dcf0f253f352dbbe0914c20949a6302ccda55af72b1`: The image hash/ID itself

ImageStreams are not useful by themselves and only exist to support the life cycle of applications. They are usually created behind the scenes in the following scenarios:

- Creating applications from S2I builds
- Importing images
- Creating applications directly from Docker images
- Manually pushing images into the internal registry

Since S2I builds will be discussed further in this book, we will consider three other methods.

# Importing images

Image streams can be created by importing images from external registries in the internal registry:

```
# oc import-image nginx --confirm
The import completed successfully.

Name: nginx
Namespace: advanced
Created: Less than a second ago
Labels: <none>
Annotations: openshift.io/image.dockerRepositoryCheck=2018-07-18T20:02:07Z
Docker Pull Spec: docker-registry.default.svc:5000/advanced/nginx
Image Lookup: local=false
Unique Images: 1
Tags: 1

latest
  tagged from nginx

  *
nginx@sha256:42e8199b5eb4a9e4896308cabc547740a0c9fc1e1a1719abf31cd444d426fb
c8
```

```
        Less than a second ago

Image Name: nginx:latest
Docker Image:
nginx@sha256:42e8199b5eb4a9e4896308cabc547740a0c9fc1e1a1719abf31cd444d426fb
c8
Name:
sha256:42e8199b5eb4a9e4896308cabc547740a0c9fc1e1a1719abf31cd444d426fbc8
...
<output omitted>
...
```

You can see from the preceding output that the Nginx image was uploaded into the internal registry at

`docker-registry.default.svc:5000/advanced/nginx`. As you will also notice, its name corresponds to the image reference structure we provided earlier.

Let's delete the image stream to provide a clean slate for the next exercise:

```
# oc delete is/nginx
imagestream "nginx" deleted
```

# Creating applications directly from Docker images

Another way to create an image stream is to use the `new-app` command to create an application from a ready-to-use Docker image:

```
# oc new-app gists/lighttpd
--> Found Docker image cd7b707 (11 days old) from Docker Hub for
"gists/lighttpd"

    * An image stream will be created as "lighttpd:latest" that will track
this image
...
<output omitted>
...
```

 Lighttpd is yet another web server, like Nginx or Apache. We used it in this example, because both Nginx and Apache image streams are supplied with OpenShift out-of-the-box.

This creates a number of resources, one of which is an image stream.

If you `describe` the newly created deployment config, you will see that it actually references the image stream, not the image itself:

```
# oc describe dc/lighttpd
...
<output omitted>
...
  Containers:
   lighttpd:
    Image:
gists/lighttpd@sha256:23c7c16d3c294e6595832dccc95c49ed56a5b34e03c8905b6db6f
b8d66b8d950
...
<output omitted>
...
```

In the preceding example, DeploymentConfig references a Lighttpd server image in the image stream according to the following scheme:

- `gists/lighttpd`: Image stream name
- `sha256`: Indicates that the image identifier is generated using the SHA256 hash algorithm
- `23c7c16d3c294e6595832dccc95c49ed56a5b34e03c8905b6db6fb8d66b8d95 0`: The image hash/ID itself

This is how deployment configs and replication controllers usually reference images in OpenShift.

Again, let's clean up the environment:

```
# oc delete all --all
deploymentconfig "lighttpd" deleted
imagestream "lighttpd" deleted
pod "lighttpd-1-hqjfg" deleted
service "lighttpd" deleted
```

# Manually pushing images into the internal registry

The last method of creating image streams we will discuss is pushing images directly into the OpenShift internal registry.

Log in as `alice` unprivileged account, if you haven't already done so:

```
# oc login -u alice
```

Then, run the following command to login to the internal registry:

```
# docker login -u $(oc whoami) -p $(oc whoami -t) docker-
registry.default.svc:5000
Login Succeeded
```

In the preceding command, we used a bash feature called **command expansion**, which allowed us to supply the `login` command with the username, password/token, and registry `IP:port`, from left to right. You can run all these commands (`oc whoami` and `oc whoami -t`) separately to see what output they provide.

Now that we are authenticated in the internal registry, we can push images into it directly, as if it were a general Docker registry. Let's see what we have in our OpenShift internal registry:

```
# docker images
REPOSITORY        TAG      IMAGE ID       CREATED           SIZE
docker.io/cockpit/kubernetes latest 110aeeca4b8c 7 days ago      425 MB
docker.io/centos/nginx-112-centos7 <none> b6923820bf5b 7 days ago       313
MB
docker.io/gists/lighttpd <none>  cd7b7073c0fc  11 days ago    12.1 MB
docker.io/openshift/origin-web-console v3.9.0  aa12a2fc57f7      3 weeks
ago    495 MB
docker.io/openshift/origin-docker-registry v3.9.0  8e6f7a854d66  3 weeks
ago    465 MB
docker.io/openshift/origin-haproxy-router v3.9.0   448cc9658480    3 weeks
ago    1.28 GB
docker.io/openshift/origin-deployer v3.9.0 39ee47797d2e 3 weeks ago 1.26 GB
docker.io/openshift/origin-service-catalog v3.9.0  96cf7dd047cb   3 weeks
ago    296 MB
docker.io/openshift/origin-template-service-broker v3.9.0  be41388b9fcb  3
weeks ago    308 MB
docker.io/openshift/origin-pod v3.9.0  6e08365fbba9  3 weeks ago    223 MB
docker.io/sebp/lighttpd <none>  6b681cc70957  20 months ago  8.53 MB
```

Let's delete the Lighttpd image left over from the previous exercise:

```
# docker rmi cd7b7073c0fc
...
<output omitted>
...
```

Now use the same Lighttpd image, as in the previous subsection:

```
# docker pull gists/lighttpd
...
<output omitted>
...
Status: Downloaded newer image for docker.io/gists/lighttpd:latest
```

Tag it with the registry's address and port included in the tag:

```
# docker tag docker.io/gists/lighttpd docker-
registry.default.svc:5000/advanced/lighttpd
```

 We used the name of the project to create the image stream as part of the path to the image in the registry because the token we used grants developer user permission to create image streams in the `myproject` project only. OpenShift expects us to find images in particular locations so that it can create image streams from images.

Let's see if the image with both tags referencing it is there:

```
# docker images
REPOSITORY      TAG    IMAGE   ID                                    ...
docker-registry.default.svc:5000/advanced/lighttpd latest cd7b7073c0fc ...
docker.io/gists/lighttpd                           latest cd7b7073c0fc ...
...
<output omitted>
...
```

Finally, we need to push the image into the repository:

```
# docker push docker-registry.default.svc:5000/advanced/lighttpd
The push refers to a repository [docker-
registry.default.svc:5000/advanced/lighttpd]
...
<output omitted>
...
```

Now verify that the `lighttpd` image stream was created in OpenShift:

```
# oc get is
NAME        DOCKER REPO                                        TAGS    UPDATED
lighttpd docker-registry.default.svc:5000/advanced/lighttpd latest 15
minutes ago
```

As expected, the image stream was created.

Just as before, we need to delete everything before going on to the next section:

```
$ oc delete is/lighttpd
imagestream "lighttpd" deleted
```

# Separating configuration from application code using ConfigMaps

The ConfigMap resource is used to separate data from a pod running an application. These kinds of resource contain arbitrary data to be injected into a pod as configuration. Injection in this context means that the pod can use it in the following ways:

- Export its key/value pairs as environment variables
- Supply its values as command-line arguments to the application
- Mount it as a volume inside the pod to the location where the application expects to find its configuration file

Before you begin, make sure you are logged in as an unprivileged user for the most representative experience:

```
# oc login -u alice
```

Let's look at the process of exporting ConfigMap as an environment variable into a container. First, we have to create ConfigMap itself from a list of environment variables:

```
# cat example.env
VAR_1=Hello
VAR_2=World

# oc create cm example-config-map --from-env-file=example.env
configmap "example-config-map" created
```

Use the following command to see what the actual resource looks like:

```
# oc describe configmap/example-config-map
Name: example-config-map
Namespace: advanced
Labels: <none>
Annotations: <none>

Data
====
VAR_1:
----
Hello
VAR_2:
----
World
Events: <none>
```

Now we are ready to inject it into a pod. Create a simple Pod definition that references the newly created ConfigMap:

```
# cat example-pod-1.yml
apiVersion: v1
kind: Pod
metadata:
  name: example
spec:
  containers:
    - name: example
      image: cirros
      command: ["/bin/sh", "-c", "env"]
      envFrom:
        - configMapRef:
            name: example-config-map
```

And create the pod using the preceding definition:

```
# oc create -f example-pod-1.yml
pod "example" created
```

As you learned in Chapter 2, *Kubernetes Overview*, OpenShift supports YAML and JSON notations for resource definitions; in this book, we rely primarily on the former. As a reminder of the YAML syntax, you can refer to the link at http://www.yaml.org/start.html.
No matter if you use YAML or JSON, the OpenShift REST API supports very specific fields that vary between resource types and are documented in https://docs.openshift.org/latest/rest_api/api/.

Since the command is a simple Linux command, `env`, not a process or listening server of any kind, the pod exits right after it's completed, but you can still see its logs:

```
# oc logs po/example
. . .
<output omitted>
. . .
VAR_1=Hello
VAR_2=World
```

As you can see, the two environment variables we defined in ConfigMap were successfully injected into the container. If we were to run an application inside our container, it could read them.

The same method can be used to supply these variables as command-line arguments to the container command. First, let's delete the old pod:

```
# oc delete po/example
pod "example" deleted
```

Then, create a new pod definition so that you can use the variables as command-line arguments to echo the command:

```
# cat example-pod-2.yml
apiVersion: v1
kind: Pod
metadata:
  name: example2
spec:
  containers:
    - name: example2
      image: cirros
      command: ["/bin/sh", "-c", "echo ${VAR_1} ${VAR_2}"]
      envFrom:
        - configMapRef:
            name: example-config-map
```

Now, create a container from the updated definition:

```
# oc create -f example-pod-2.yml
pod "example2" created
```

As we mentioned previously, the container will exit right after the command returns, but its logs will contain the output of the command, constructed of two variables from our ConfigMap:

```
# oc logs po/example2
Hello World
```

Lastly, we will walk-through mounting ConfigMap as a configuration file into a pod. Again, let's delete the pod from the previous exercise:

```
# oc delete po/example2
pod "example2" deleted
```

In this example, we will supply the Nginx web server with our custom configuration file, which will make its default virtual host listen on port 8888 instead of 80. Here's the simple configuration to achieve that:

```
# cat nginx_custom_default.conf
server {
    listen        8888;
    server_name  localhost;
    location / {
        root    /usr/share/nginx/html;
        index  index.html index.htm;
    }
}
```

Now, let's go ahead and create a ConfigMap from this configuration:

```
# oc create cm nginx --from-file nginx_custom_default.conf
configmap "nginx" created
```

If we take a look at the raw resource definition of this ConfigMap, we will see the following:

```
# oc export configmap/nginx
apiVersion: v1
data:
  nginx_custom_default.conf: |
    server {
        listen 8888;
        server_name localhost;
        location / {
            root /usr/share/nginx/html;
            index index.html index.htm;
        }
    }
kind: ConfigMap
```

```
metadata:
  creationTimestamp: null
  name: nginx
```

As you can see, the entire contents of the configuration file was inserted as value into the config map definition with the key `nginx_custom_default.conf`, which can be used to reference the configuration in a pod.

Now it's time to create a pod that will use this ConfigMap. Create yet another pod definition with the following structure:

```
# cat example-pod-3.yml
apiVersion: v1
kind: Pod
metadata:
  name: example3
  labels:
    role: web
spec:
  containers:
  - name: example3
    image: nginx
    volumeMounts:
    - name: conf
      mountPath: /etc/nginx/conf.d
  volumes:
  - name: conf
    configMap:
      name: nginx
      items:
      - key: nginx_custom_default.conf
        path: default.conf
```

 You can specify a path parameter in `configMap.items` to provide the name for the file that the configuration will be stored in. Had we not done that in the preceding example, the file name would have been the same as the key from the `configMap-nginx_custom_default.conf`. We must specify the label for our pod in order to be able to create a service for it later on.

Let's create the pod now:

```
# oc create -f example-pod-3.yml
pod "example3" created
```

In order to see whether the server listens on the port specified in the ConfigMap, we could open a bash session inside the pod and see if the configuration file is in place, but let's use a better way that will let us practice with OpenShift resources more.

We will need to create a service for this pod and then expose it. First, create a service:

```
# oc expose po/example3 --port 8888
service "example3" exposed
```

We had to explicitly specify the port in the command because we didn't provide it in the `containerPort` parameter in the pod's definition.

Then expose the service itself through `route`:

```
# oc expose svc/example3
route "example3" exposed
# oc get route
... example3-advanced.openshift.example.com ...
```

Finally, we can use the `curl` command to request a default web page from the server's default virtual host:

```
# curl -H 'Host: example3-advanced.openshift.example.com' 127.0.0.1
...
<output omitted>
...
<title>Welcome to nginx!</title>
...
<output omitted>
...
```

We could have created a separate record for the route above in `/etc/hosts`, pointing to `127.0.0.1`, but in order to keep the environment as clean as possible, it's a good practice to use `Host` HTTP header instead to select a particular application.

The preceding output indicates that Nginx indeed listens on port `8888/tcp`, as specified in the ConfigMap. This concludes our exercise with ConfigMaps, so let's clean up our lab:

```
$ oc delete all --all
route "example3" deleted
pod "example3" deleted
service "example3" deleted

$ oc delete configmap --all
```

```
configmap "example-config-map" deleted
configmap "nginx" deleted
```

 ConfigMaps are not considered similar to other resources such as pods or services and must be deleted separately.

# Controlling resource consumption using ResourceQuotas

One of the main ideas behind OpenShift projects in multi-tenant environments is the need to limit resource consumption at a more granular level than just a whole cluster, providing operations with the ability to scope such limitations to organizations and departments.

OpenShift provides two mechanisms for setting limits on resource consumption in a cluster:

- ResourceQuota
- LimitRanges

This section is dedicated solely to ResourceQuotas. LimitRanges will be discussed in the next section.

ResourceQuota can be used to control the number of API resources that can be created, or the amount of CPU, memory, and storage consumed by pods in the same project the quotas were defined in. Essentially, they determine the capacity of a project. ResourceQuotas allows you to control the following types of resources:

- Pods
- ReplicationControllers
- Services
- Secrets
- ResourceQuotas
- ConfigMaps
- ImageStreams
- PersistentVolumeClaims
- requests.storage
- cpu

- memory
- ephemeral-storage
- limits.ephemeral-storage
- `limits.cpu`
- `limits.memory`

 If CPU/memory or `limits.cpu`/`limits.memory` are managed by quotas, then all pods in the same project must specify requests/limits for the respective computing resources.

In the context of quotas, all pods belong to the following scopes, to which quotas can be applied and that scope a certain set of resources:

| Scope | Description | Managed resources |
|---|---|---|
| `BestEffort` | Applies to all pods running with BestEffort quality of service, which means pods that have equal requests and limits for CPU, memory, or both. These pods can claim any resources they need, but they are most likely to be killed when nodes they run on are low on memory. | • Pods |
| `NotBestEffort` | Applies to all pods running without BestEffort quality of service. | • Pods<br>• CPU<br>• `limits.cpu`<br>• memory<br>• ephemeral-storage<br>• limits.ephemeral-storage<br>• `limits.memory` |
| `Terminating` | Applies to all pods deployed by jobs with `spec.activeDeadlineSeconds >= 0`, which means, for example, build pods that get deployed during S2I builds. | |
| `NotTerminating` | Applies to all pods deployed by jobs with `spec.activeDeadlineSeconds` is nil, which means the usual pods with applications. | |

Now, let's see how to create quotas for a project. Like any other resource, they can be created through an API, but you can also use CLI, which is what we are going to do. Let's switch back to `system:admin` user since managing quotas requires admin privileges:

```
# oc login -u system:admin
```

Then we will be able to create our first quota:

```
# oc create quota my-quota \
--hard=cpu=500m,memory=256Mi,pods=1,resourcequotas=1
resourcequota "my-quota" created
```

As you can see, the quota was successfully created:

```
# oc describe quota/my-quota
Name:              my-quota
Namespace:         advanced
Resource           Used     Hard
--------           ----     ----
cpu                0        500m
memory             0        256Mi
pods               0        1
resourcequotas     1        1
```

 Interestingly enough, the number of quotas itself per project can be controlled by ResourceQuota. Even if you set a limit for quotas to 0, you will still be able to create your first quota, provided there is no other already existing quota that limits this number.

By creating this quota, we have set the limits of 500 CPU millicores (half-core), 256Mi requested RAM, 1 pod, and 1 ResourceQuota on the current project. Let's see if the quota is in effect.

First, create a simple pod definition:

```
$ cat nginx-pod.yml
apiVersion: v1
kind: Pod
metadata:
  name: nginx
  labels:
    role: web
spec:
  containers:
  - name: nginx
    image: nginx
```

Let's try to create a pod from it:

```
# oc create -f nginx-pod.yml
Error from server (Forbidden): error when creating "nginx-pod.yml": pods
"nginx" is forbidden: failed quota: my-quota: must specify cpu,memory
```

As you can see, our definition didn't pass the check by the quota because it explicitly limits the requested amount of CPU and RAM, but we didn't specify them. Let's modify nginx-pod.yml and add resources section:

```
# cat nginx-pod.yml
apiVersion: v1
```

```
kind: Pod
metadata:
  name: nginx
  labels:
    role: web
spec:
  containers:
  - name: nginx
    image: nginx
    resources:
      requests:
        cpu: 100m
        memory: 128Mi
```

Upon creation, the pod will request 1 CPU core and 128 MiB of RAM, which is well within the limits set by the quota. Let's try it again:

```
# oc create -f nginx-pod.yml
pod "nginx" created
```

The pod was created successfully, as expected. At this point, we can take a look at how much of our quota was consumed:

```
# oc describe quota/my-quota
Name:            my-quota
Namespace:       advanced
Resource         Used    Hard
--------         ----    ----
cpu              100m    500m
memory           128Mi   256Mi
pods             1       1
resourcequotas   1       1
```

Now, let's see what happens if we try to create one more pod. Prepare a new pod definition from the one used to create the first pod by replacing nginx with httpd:

```
# cat httpd-pod.yml
apiVersion: v1
kind: Pod
metadata:
  name: httpd
  labels:
    role: web
spec:
  containers:
  - name: httpd
    image: httpd
    resources:
```

```
    requests:
      cpu: 400m
      memory: 128Mi
```

If we try to create the second pod, we will see the following:

```
$ oc create -f httpd-pod.yml
Error from server (Forbidden): error when creating "httpd-pod.yml": pods
"httpd" is forbidden: exceeded quota: my-quota, requested: pods=1, used:
pods=1, limited: pods=1
```

Even though the amount of requested memory wouldn't violate the quota, pod creation was still denied because the quota limits the total number of pods to 1 for the current project.

Edit the quota to allow 2 pods and 2 CPU cores:

```
$ oc edit quota/my-quota
spec:
  hard:
    cpu: 500m
    memory: 256Mi
    pods: "2"
    resourcequotas: "1"
```

Try creating the second pod again:

```
$ oc create -f httpd-pod.yml
pod "httpd" created
```

It worked because the quota was set to allow 2 pods in the current project.

Let's see how many resources are used from the total allowed by the quota again:

```
$ oc describe quota/my-quota
Name:           my-quota
Namespace:      myproject
Resource        Used    Hard
--------        ----    ----
cpu             500m    500m
memory          256Mi   256Mi
pods            2       2
resourcequotas  1       1
```

As you can see, we have exhausted the entire quota and no new pods can be created.

Now that this exercise is over, it's time to prepare for the next one by cleaning up our lab:

```
$ oc delete all --all
pod "httpd" deleted
pod "nginx" deleted

$ oc delete quota/my-quota
resourcequota "my-quota" delete
```

 ConfigMaps and ResourceQuotas are considered separate kinds of resource and must be deleted as such.

# Controlling resource consumption using LimitRanges

This is another way of control resource allocation in OpenShift at the project level, but unlike ResourceQuotas, they are different in certain ways:

- They are applied to individual pods, containers, images, or image streams
- They don't control some resources such as secrets, ConfigMaps, ResourceQuotas, services, and ReplicationControllers
- They can be created from a raw definition only

Depending on the type of resource they are applied to, LimitRanges control various computing resources and objects:

| Resource type | Computing resources/attributes controlled |
|---|---|
| Pod | • CPU<br>• RAM |
| Container | • CPU<br>• RAM |
| Image | Size of an image pushed into an internal registry |
| ImageStream | • Number of unique image tags as per image stream's spec<br>• Number of unique image references as per the image stream's status |
| PersistentVolumeClaim | Amount of storage requested |

Pods and containers can explicitly state the amount of CPU and/or RAM they need and their limits, and LimitRanges takes care that they don't fall outside certain boundaries.

Also, LimitRanges may provide defaults for a requested number of resources and their limits if they are not specified.

Depending on the presence of, and differences between, requests and limits for computing resources declared by pods, they run with different **Quality of Service (QoS)** tiers that serve the purpose of prioritizing running pods when it comes to resource contention. The following table summarizes the available tiers and when they are applied:

| QoS tier | Description |
|---|---|
| BestEffort | This tier is assigned to pods that don't specify requests and limits explicitly. Such pods can consume as much CPU and RAM as they need, but if the node a pod runs on is short on either or both resources, these pods are the first to be terminated. |
| Burstable | Pods that have limits higher than requests get assigned the Burstable QoS tier. They run with a lower priority than BestEffort pods, meaning that they are only terminated when there are no BestEffort pods to terminate. |
| Guaranteed | This tier is applicable to pods that have equal requests and limits for computing resources. Each pod running with this QoS is entitled to the requested amount of resources, but no more. They have the highest priority, which means that they are only killed when there are no BestEffort or Burstable pods. |

Just as in the previous section, setting LimitRanges requires administrative privileges, so make sure you are logged in as system:admin user:

```
# oc login -u system:admin
```

Let's consider an example of creating a LimitRange from scratch:

```
# cat my-limits.yaml
apiVersion: v1
kind: LimitRange
metadata:
  name: my-limits
spec:
  limits:
    - type: Pod
      min:
        cpu: 200m
        memory: 256Mi
      max:
        cpu: 400m
        memory: 512Mi
    - type: Container
      min:
        cpu: 100m
        memory: 128Mi
      max:
```

```
      cpu: 300m
      memory: 256Mi
```

Create limits from the preceding definition:

```
# oc create -f my-limits.yaml
limitrange "my-limits" created
```

Now, let's describe our newly created limits:

```
# oc describe limits/my-limits
Name:         my-limits
Namespace:    advanced
```

| Type | Resource | Min | Max | Default Request | Default Limit | |
|------|----------|-----|-----|-----------------|---------------|---|
| Pod | cpu | 200m | 400m | – | – | ... |
| Pod | memory | 256Mi | 512Mi | – | – | ... |
| Container | cpu | 100m | 300m | 300m | 300m | ... |
| Container | memory | 128Mi | 256Mi | 256Mi | 256Mi | ... |

There are also the `spec.limits[].default` and `spec.limits[].defaultRequest` parameters, which determine the amount of CPU/RAM a container is limited to use and the amount it requests by default, respectively. Since we didn't specify them explicitly, they default to the same maximum value.

The next step is to create a pod that requests a specific amount of computing resources and sets limits on their usage for itself. Prepare the following pod definition:

```
# cat limits-example-pod.yml
apiVersion: v1
kind: Pod
metadata:
  name: limits-example
  labels:
    role: web
spec:
  containers:
  - name: httpd
    image: httpd
    resources:
      requests:
        cpu: 100m
        memory: 256Mi
      limits:
        cpu: 350m
        memory: 256Mi
```

Next, create a pod from the definition:

```
# oc create -f limits-example-pod.yml
Error from server (Forbidden): error when creating "limits-example-
pod.yml": pods "limits-example" is forbidden: [minimum cpu usage per Pod is
200m, but request is 100m., maximum cpu usage per Container is 300m, but
limit is 350m.]
```

As you might expect after looking at the pod's definition, the operation was rejected because the pod's request and limit ranges violate the policy defined earlier.

 Minimum boundaries are also enforced.

Let's edit the pod's definition to comply with the defined LimitRange:

```
# cat limits-example-pod.yml
...
<output omitted>
...
    resources:
      requests:
        cpu: 200m
        memory: 256Mi
      limits:
        cpu: 250m
        memory: 256Mi
```

Try to create it again and observe that it works:

```
# oc create -f limits-example-pod.yml
pod "limits-example" created

# oc get po
NAME            READY   STATUS    RESTARTS   AGE
limits-example  1/1     Running   0          4s
```

Let's clean up the lab to prepare for the next section:

```
# oc delete po/limits-example
pod "limits-example" deleted
```

```
# oc delete limits/my-limits
limitrange "my-limits" delete
```

 LimitRanges are considered a separate kind of resource as well, like templates, ConfigMaps, and ResourceQuotas, so they must be deleted by issuing a separate command.

# Creating complex stacks of applications with templates

Another useful kind of OpenShift resource is a template. Instead of creating resources one-by-one – for example, a pod, service, and route – templates allow you to create multiple objects at once with a single CLI command. More than that —they may include parameters that can be optional, or default to values either static or generated in accordance with specific rules. In a sense, they are similar to Docker Compose or OpenStack Heat—all of these provide the facility to create entire application stacks from the ground up. With templates, the cluster administrator can provide developers with the ability to deploy multi-tier applications with all dependent services.

By default, OpenShift comes installed with quite a few default templates, called **Instant App** and **Quick Start** templates. They can be used to deploy runtime environments based on various languages and frameworks, such as Ruby on Rails (Ruby), Django (Python), and CakePHP (PHP). They also include templates for SQL and NoSQL database engines with persistent storage, which includes `PersistentVolumeClaims` as one of the objects to provide persistence of data.

For this exercise, you will not require admin privileges, so you can login as a regular user:

```
# oc login -u alice
```

Default templates are created in the `openshift` project during installation. You can see them by running the following command:

```
# oc get template -n openshift | cut -d' ' -f1
NAME
3scale-gateway
```

```
amp-apicast-wildcard-router
amp-pvc
cakephp-mysql-example
cakephp-mysql-persistent
dancer-mysql-example
dancer-mysql-persistent
django-psql-example
django-psql-persistent
dotnet-example
dotnet-pgsql-persistent
dotnet-runtime-example
httpd-example
...
<output omitted>
...
```

We used the `cut` command to exclude descriptions and other information for the sake of brevity, but you can run this command without `cut` to see the full output.

Both MiniShift and OpenShift, when installed by the Ansible installer, have default templates installed out-of-the-box but, in the case of containerized quick installation, you may have to create them manually from YAML definitions located in the `roles/openshift_examples/files/examples/` directory of the Ansible installer.

To get a list of parameters that are supported by a particular template, use the `process` command:

```
# oc process --parameters mariadb-persistent -n openshift
NAME                     DESCRIPTION     GENERATOR     VALUE
MEMORY_LIMIT             ...                           512Mi
NAMESPACE                ...                           openshift
DATABASE_SERVICE_NAME    ...                           mariadb
MYSQL_USER               ...             expression    user[A-Z0-9]{3}
MYSQL_PASSWORD           ...             expression    [a-zA-Z0-9]{16}
MYSQL_ROOT_PASSWORD      ...             expression    [a-zA-Z0-9]{16}
MYSQL_DATABASE           ...                           sampledb
MARIADB_VERSION          ...                           10.2
VOLUME_CAPACITY          ...                           1Gi
```

We left out descriptions of the parameters to make the output more readable.

As you may have noticed, some parameters have dynamic default values, generated by expressions loosely based on **Perl Compatible Regular Expressions** (**PCREs**).

The `process` command generates default values from all dynamic expressions, making the template definition ready to be used for creating resources, which is done either by piping its output to the `create` command or by running the `new-app` command—we will get to that in a few moments. For now, let's use that command to see a `List` of objects to be created:

```
# oc process openshift//mariadb-persistent
{
    "kind": "List",
    "apiVersion": "v1",
    "metadata": {},
    "items": [
        {
            "apiVersion": "v1",
            "kind": "Secret",
            ...
            <output omitted>
            ...
            "stringData": {
                "database-name": "sampledb",
                "database-password": "tYuwInpmocV1Q1uy",
                "database-root-password": "icq5jd8bfFPWXbaK",
                "database-user": "userC7A"
            }
        },
        ...
        <output omitted>
        ...
    ]
}
```

 The `process` command allows for an alternate syntax, `<NAMESPACE>//<TEMPLATE>`. We used it here for demonstration purposes, but you are free to use the more familiar `-n <NAMESPACE>` notation.

The list is quite long, so we only provided an excerpt showing the `Secret` resource that contains all generated sensitive values that are to be used for template instantiation.

To make things clearer, let's take a look at the expressions for generating those values in the raw template definition:

```
# oc export template mariadb-persistent -n openshift
```

```
apiVersion: v1
kind: Template
...
<output omitted>
...
objects:
- apiVersion: v1
  kind: Secret
  ...
  <output omitted>
  ...
  stringData:
    database-name: ${MYSQL_DATABASE}
    database-password: ${MYSQL_PASSWORD}
    database-root-password: ${MYSQL_ROOT_PASSWORD}
    database-user: ${MYSQL_USER}
...
<output omitted>
...
parameters:
...
<output omitted>
...
- description: Username for MariaDB user that will be used for accessing
the database.
  displayName: MariaDB Connection Username
  from: user[A-Z0-9]{3}
  generate: expression
  name: MYSQL_USER
  required: true
...
<output omitted>
...
- description: Name of the MariaDB database accessed.
  displayName: MariaDB Database Name
  name: MYSQL_DATABASE
  required: true
  value: sampledb
...
<output omitted>
...
```

You may have noticed, for example, that MYSQL_DATABASE is sampledb, while MYSQL_USER starts with the string user with three alphanumeric characters, just as we saw in the previous listing.

 To learn more about how to construct regular expressions for dynamic parameters, refer to http://perldoc.perl.org/perlre.html.

Now, we will create our own simple template. Create a new template definition with the following contents:

```
# cat example-template.yml
kind: Template
apiVersion: v1
metadata:
  name: example-template
labels:
  role: web
message: You chose to deploy ${WEB_SERVER}
objects:
  - kind: Pod
    apiVersion: v1
    metadata:
      name: example-pod
    spec:
      containers:
        - name: ${WEB_SERVER}
          image: ${WEB_SERVER}
  - kind: Service
    apiVersion: v1
    metadata:
      name: example-svc
    spec:
      ports:
        - port: 80
      selector:
        role: web
  - kind: Route
    apiVersion: v1
    metadata:
      name: example-route
    spec:
      to:
        kind: Service
        name: example-svc
parameters:
```

```
    - name: WEB_SERVER
      displayName: Web Server
      description: Web server image to use
      value: nginx
```

 Though in our case the message parameter is used in quite a rudimentary way, in more complex templates, its purpose is to tell the user how to use the template—what usernames, passwords, URLs, and so on were generated.

This template can be used to create three resources:

- A pod running a web server, which you can choose by supplying the WEB_SERVER parameter. By default, it's nginx.
- A service proxying incoming traffic to the pod.
- A route for external access.

We can process that definition right away and pass the resulting list of resources to the create command, but a common strategy is to create a template from its definition first:

```
# oc create -f example-template.yml
template "example-template" created
```

Let's try to process it:

```
# oc process --parameters example-template
NAME         DESCRIPTION                  GENERATOR        VALUE
WEB_SERVER Web server image to use                        nginx
```

You can see the only parameter with the default value and description that you defined earlier.

Now, it's time to create a stack of resources from our template. This can be done by either piping the output of the process command to the create command, which we mentioned previously, or by using the new-app command. Let's start with the former approach:

```
# oc process example-template | oc create -f -
pod "example-pod" created
service "example-svc" created
route "example-route" created
```

As you can see, the `create` command just takes the list of resources and submits requests for their creation one-by-one to the API, so the output is similar to what you would see if you created three separate resource definitions and created resources from them manually.

But another way to instantiate a template gives you more information about what is going on. Let's delete the created resources first:

```
# oc delete all --all
route "example-route" deleted
pod "example-pod" deleted
service "example-svc" deleted
```

We don't have to delete the template as it's not going to change. Now, we can use the new-app command:

```
# oc new-app --template=example-template
--> Deploying template "myproject/example-template" to project myproject

    example-template
    ---------
    You chose to deploy nginx

    * With parameters:
       * Web Server=nginx

--> Creating resources ...
    pod "example-pod" created
    service "example-svc" created
    route "example-route" created
--> Success
    Access your application via route 'example-route-
advanced.openshift.example.com'
    Run 'oc status' to view your app.
```

```
# oc status
In project advanced on server https://172.24.0.11:8443

http://example-route-advanced.openshift.example.com (svc/example-svc)
  pod/example-pod runs nginx


1 info identified, use 'oc status -v' to see details.
```

As you can see, we created the pod, fronted it with the service, and exposed it through the route in just a single command. Notice that you don't need to run the `oc get route` command to find out what URL your application is accessible through—it all shows in the output.

Let's see if our web server is reachable through `curl`:

```
# curl -IH 'Host: example-route-advanced.openshift.example.com' 127.0.0.1
HTTP/1.1 200 OK
Server: nginx/1.15.1
...
<output omitted>
...
```

 We used the `-I` parameter of the `curl` command to see only response headers, which is enough to check the responsiveness of the server and ensure that it doesn't dump raw HTML into the console. Also, just as before, we used -H option to request a specific application from OpenShift's router.

You can easily delete all of the resources and instantiate the template again, but this time with another web server image, such as Apache:

```
# oc delete all --all
route "example-route" deleted
pod "example-pod" deleted
service "example-svc" deleted

# oc new-app --template=example-template -p WEB_SERVER=httpd
--> Deploying template "myproject/example-template" to project myproject

    example-template
    ---------
    You chose to deploy httpd
...
<output omitted>
...
    Access your application via route 'example-route-
advanced.openshift.example.com'
    Run 'oc status' to view your app.

# curl -H 'Host: example-route-advanced.openshift.example.com' 127.0.0.1
<html><body><h1>It works!</h1></body></html>

# curl -IH 'Host: example-route-advanced.openshift.example.com' 127.0.0.1
HTTP/1.1 200 OK
Date: Thu, 19 Jul 2018 00:59:47 GMT
Server: Apache/2.4.34 (Unix)
...
<output omitted>
...
```

That's it—one parameter and you have a different web server deployed for you in a matter of seconds.

You can also perform a reverse operation—creating a template from existing resources. To do that, use the `export` command:

```
# oc export all --as-template=exported-template > exported-template.yml
```

Let's delete our resources to prevent any conflicts:

```
# oc delete all --all
route "example-route" deleted
pod "example-pod" deleted
service "example-svc" deleted
```

And recreate them from the exported template:

```
# oc new-app -f exported-template.yml
--> Deploying template "advanced/exported-template" for "exported-
template.yml" to project advanced

--> Creating resources ...
    route "example-route" created
    pod "example-pod" created
    service "example-svc" created
--> Success
    Access your application via route 'example-route-
advanced.openshift.example.com'
    Run 'oc status' to view your app.
```

> You might have noticed that the web server was exposed through the same URL as before. This is because the exported template was created from already instantiated resources with all parameters resolved to values, so OpenShift has no way of knowing which fields were parameterized. You can also infer this from the output of the `process` command, which will show you that all the fields are already initialized. So, strictly speaking, this isn't a fully reverse operation, but it can be used for backups.

Now that we are finished, let's do a clean-up:

```
# oc delete all --all
route "example-route" deleted
pod "example-pod" deleted
service "example-svc" deleted

# oc delete template/example-template
template "example-template" deleted
```

# Autoscaling your application depending on CPU and RAM utilization

You can scale pods in your application using the `oc scale` command, but it has two disadvantages:

- It has to be run manually every time you need to scale a pod up or down
- You have to take into account CPU and RAM utilization yourself

This approach doesn't allow businesses to adapt quickly to constantly changing customers demands. There is a better way—`HorizontalPodAutoscaler`.

 At the time of writing, autoscaling can only track CPU and RAM usage. Traffic-based autoscaling, for instance, isn't supported.

Let's login as `system:admin` and see if Hawkular, Cassandra, and Heapster pods are up and running:

```
# oc login -u system:admin
...
<output omitted>
...
# oc get po -n openshift-infra
NAME                         READY STATUS    RESTARTS AGE
hawkular-cassandra-1-ffszl 1/1   Running   0        10m
hawkular-metrics-bl6jh       1/1   Running   0        10m
heapster-brvfd               1/1   Running   0        10m
```

By the time you get to this section, all metrics pods will be ready, but usually it takes 8-10 minutes for them to get started after installation is done.

# CPU-based autoscaling

CPU-based autoscaling also requires limit ranges to be set on CPU requests for the pods being scaled, so we can use the LimitRange definition from one of the previous sections.

```
# cat my-limits.yaml
apiVersion: v1
kind: LimitRange
metadata:
  name: my-limits
spec:
  limits:
    - type: Pod
      min:
        cpu: 50m
        memory: 64Mi
      max:
        cpu: 150m
        memory: 128Mi
    - type: Container
      min:
        cpu: 50m
        memory: 64Mi
      max:
        cpu: 150m
        memory: 128Mi
```

```
# oc create -f my-limits.yaml
limitrange "my-limits" created
```

 Depending on your host machine's CPU, you might have to tweak the values in the file above in order for autoscaling to work, that is why in the listing above they are different than in the beginning of the chapter.

The autoscaling feature can be applied to deployment configs, so the easiest way to create one is to use the already familiar new-app command:

```
# oc new-app httpd
...
```

```
<output omitted>
...
--> Creating resources ...
    deploymentconfig "httpd" created
    service "httpd" created
--> Success
    Application is not exposed. You can expose services to the outside
world by executing one or more of the commands below:
     'oc expose svc/httpd'
    Run 'oc status' to view your app.
```

For demonstration purposes, we used the Apache web server image to create an image stream, which, in turn, is used to create the application. Now that the `deploymentconfig` is ready to manage pods, we can create a `HorizontalPodAutoscaler` to manage the `deploymentconfig` itself:

```
# oc autoscale dc/httpd --min=2 --max=4 --cpu-percent=10
deploymentconfig "httpd" autoscaled
```

 We specified 2 as the minimum number of pods that must be maintained at any time so that you can observe the effect of autoscaling quickly without having to generate CPU load on pods to trigger it. We will do that in a few moments as well.

Let's make sure it was created:

```
# oc get hpa
NAME    REFERENCE              TARGETS     MINPODS MAXPODS REPLICAS  AGE
httpd   DeploymentConfig/httpd 0% / 20%    2       4       2         3m
```

 If you run this command right after creation, you will most likely see unknown instead of `0%` in the preceding output. That is expected because `HorizontalPodAutoscaler` usually needs a few minutes to collect enough metrics.

In a few minutes, you may list running pods and notice that there are two of them now:

```
# oc get po
NAME            READY   STATUS    RESTARTS   AGE
httpd-1-5845b   1/1     Running   0          7s
httpd-1-scq85   1/1     Running   0          2m
```

Now, we have to simulate a large number of user requests to our pods to increase the CPU load so that autoscaling takes effect. But to do that, we need to create a route first:

```
# oc expose svc/httpd
route "httpd" exposed
```

```
# oc get route
... httpd-advanced.openshift.example.com ...
```

At this point, we have everything we need, so let's start simulating CPU load with the `ab` Apache benchmarking utility:

```
# ab -c 100 -n 10000000 -H 'Host: httpd-advanced.openshift.example.com' \
http://127.0.0.1/

This is ApacheBench, Version 2.3 <$Revision: 1430300 $>
Copyright 1996 Adam Twiss, Zeus Technology Ltd, http://www.zeustech.net/
Licensed to The Apache Software Foundation, http://www.apache.org/
...
<output omitted>
...
^C
Percentage of the requests served within a certain time (ms)
  50%  46
  66%  56
  75%  66
  80%  73
  90%  95
  95% 124
  98% 171
  99% 200
 100% 528 (longest request)
```

When `httpd` DeploymentConfig is scaled up, you can just press `Ctrl+C` to stop generating the traffic, as is indicated by `^C` in the output above.

Login in a separate terminal as `system:admin` and at some point you should be able to see that you have 4 pods running :

```
# oc get po
NAME             READY    STATUS     RESTARTS    AGE
httpd-1-5wsb5    1/1      Running    0           6m
httpd-1-gvqg2    1/1      Running    0           4m
httpd-1-n92jp    1/1      Running    0           1m
httpd-1-smqhb    1/1      Running    0           1m
```

Once you press *Ctrl + C* and benchmarking stops, then after a while, the number of pods will go back to normal:

```
# oc get po
NAME             READY    STATUS     RESTARTS    AGE
httpd-1-5wsb5    1/1      Running    0           35m
httpd-1-gvqg2    1/1      Running    0           34m
```

If you are interested, you can see the collected metrics and autoscaling taking place in the web console. Open the web console in a browser at `https://openshift.example.com:8443/`, confirm the security exception for the self-signed certificate, and login with the username `alice` and any password.

As our OpenShift cluster uses self-signed TLS certificates for encrypting HTTP traffic, Hawkular metrics will not be accessible from the **Overview** tab of the web console at first—you will see an error above the list of pods instead. To fix this, click on the provided link to open the Hawkular URL in a separate tab/window in your browser and confirm the security exception for the certificate as well. After that, refresh the **Overview** tab and you will see the calculated metrics for each pod marked with different colors:

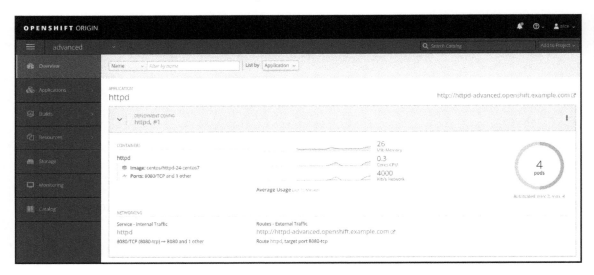

You can also use the **Monitoring** tab to get a more detailed view:

You can clearly see the spikes in CPU load and network traffic that correspond to the `ab` run.

We need to delete CPU-based autoscaler before the next exercise:

```
# oc delete hpa/httpd
horizontalpodautoscaler "httpd" deleted
```

# Memory-based autoscaling

Unlike autoscaling based on CPU utilization, memory-based autoscaling can only be enabled by creating a `HorizontalPodAutoscaler` from a raw YAML/JSON definition:

```
# cat hpa-memory.yml
kind: HorizontalPodAutoscaler
apiVersion: autoscaling/v1
metadata:
  name: hpa-httpd-memory
spec:
  scaleTargetRef:
    apiVersion: v1
```

```
    kind: DeploymentConfig
    name: httpd
  minReplicas: 2
  maxReplicas: 4
  metrics:
  - type: Resource
    resource:
      name: memory
      targetAverageUtilization: 10
```

Let's enable autoscaling now:

```
# oc create -f hpa-memory.yml
horizontalpodautoscaler "hpa-httpd-memory" created
```

Give it a minute or two to pick up the metrics from Heapster and you will be able to see how the current memory utilization is different from the target:

```
# oc get hpa
NAME          REFERENCE     TARGETS    MINPODS MAXPODS      ...
hpa-httpd-memory DeploymentConfig/httpd 7% / 10%  2    4   ...
```

 If you run this command right after creation, you will most likely see unknown instead of 7% in the preceding output. This is expected because HorizontalPodAutoscaler usually needs a few minutes to collect sufficient metrics.

Let's go ahead and generate traffic for the application, just like in the previous section, but establish 1000 concurrent connections this time, instead of 100:

```
# ab -c 1000 -n 10000000 -H 'Host: httpd-advanced.openshift.example.com'
http://127.0.0.1/
This is ApacheBench, Version 2.3 <$Revision: 1430300 $>
Copyright 1996 Adam Twiss, Zeus Technology Ltd, http://www.zeustech.net/
Licensed to The Apache Software Foundation, http://www.apache.org/
...
<output omitted>
...
^C
Percentage of the requests served within a certain time (ms)
  50% 382
  66% 410
  75% 429
  80% 441
```

```
 90% 502
 95% 737
 98% 1439
 99% 3181
100% 38031 (longest request)
```

Laeve  benchmark open for 5-10 minutes, and meanwhile open your browser at `https://hawkular-metrics.openshift.example.com/ hawkular/metrics` to make sure that hawkular metrics are running, and then at `https://openshift.example.com:8443/console/project/ advanced/overview`

You can observe autoscaling taking place from the web console. First it scales our web server to 3 replicas:

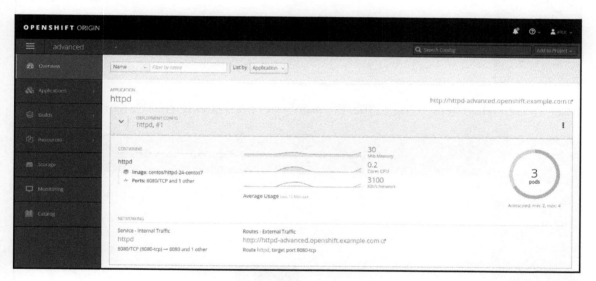

And shortly after, to 4:

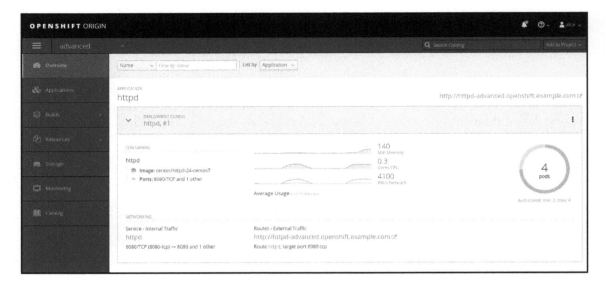

After `ab` is finished generating traffic, the number of pods slowly goes down:

It is possible to observe short bursts in the number of replicas if you put too much load on the service. This is normal and you may see from events that the `deploymentconfig` scales, for example, from 3 to 6 without transient states, then quickly detects the anomaly and corrects it by scaling back to the maximum value.

Due to the specifics of memory utilization by pods, it's common that the `deploymentconfig/replicationcontroller` doesn't fully scale back to the minimum number of replicas.

The exercise is over, so it's time to clean-up:

```
# oc delete all --all
horizontalpodautoscaler "hpa-httpd-memory" deleted
deploymentconfig "httpd" deleted
imagestream "httpd" deleted
route "httpd" deleted
pod "httpd-1-97dnr" deleted
pod "httpd-1-qgl9c" deleted
service "httpd" deleted
```

```
# oc delete limits/my-limits
limitrange "my-limits" deleted
```

 It is not advisable to activate CPU- and RAM-based autoscalers at the same time as they may conflict with each other. Determine what resources your application relies on most of the time and use the appropriate autoscaling.

# Summary

In this chapter, we introduced you to the concept of image streams and methods of creating them, how config maps can be used to manage the configuration of your applications, mechanisms for limiting resource consumption per project using resource quotas and limit ranges, how to use templates to create multiple dependent resources, and how to configure autoscaling for your applications based on CPU or memory utilization.

In the next chapter, we will work on security in OpenShift. We will be giving you an understanding of OpenShift security implementation, which is mandatory for any production environment.

# Questions

1. What are ImageStreams used for? choose 2:

    1. To protect applications from breaking unexpectedly when the image that an ImageStream points to changes.
    2. To implement rolling updates of applications.
    3. To store build images.
    4. To implement automatic build and deployments on image change.

2. What commands can be used to create a ConfigMap? choose 2:

    1. oc create configmap my-configmap --from-file=nginx.conf
    2. oc create cm --from-env-file=environment.env
    3. oc create -f configmap_definition.yaml
    4. oc edit configmap/my-configmap

3. Which of the following valid commands to create a quota? choose 2:

    1. oc create resourcequota example-quota --hard=cpus=2,memory=512Mi
    2. oc create quota example-quota --hard=cpu=4,ram=1Gi
    3. oc create resourcequota my-quota --hard=cpu=4,services=5
    4. oc create quota another-quota --hard=pods=8,secrets=4

4. What resources CAN'T be controlled by a LimitRange? choose 2:

    1. Pod
    2. ConfigMap
    3. ImageStream
    4. Service

5. What is the correct syntax for referencing the VARIABLE parameter in a template?

    1. #{VARIABLE}
    2. <VARIABLE>
    3. ${VARIABLE}
    4. %VARIABLE%

6. What must be specified by pods for CPU-based autoscaling?

   1. Labels
   2. Limits
   3. Requests
   4. Selectors

7. What API version must be used to configure memory-based autoscaling?

   1. v1
   2. v2
   3. v2alpha1
   4. v1beta1

# Further reading

In this chapter, we covered advanced concepts of the OpenShift container platform. Here's a list of links that may be helpful to look through so that you can learn more:

- **OpenShift documentation on ImageStreams**: https://docs.openshift.org/latest/architecture/core_concepts/builds_and_image_streams.html
- **OpenShift documentation on ConfigMaps**: https://docs.openshift.org/latest/dev_guide/configmaps.html
- **OpenShift documentation on ResourceQuotas**: https://docs.openshift.org/latest/admin_guide/quota.html
- **OpenShift documentation on LimitRanges**: https://docs.openshift.org/latest/admin_guide/limits.html
- **OpenShift documentation on templates**: https://docs.openshift.org/latest/dev_guide/templates.html#dev-guide-templates
- **OpenShift documentation on HorizontalPodAutoscaler**: https://docs.openshift.org/latest/dev_guide/pod_autoscaling.html
- **Wikipedia article on YAML notation**: https://en.wikipedia.org/wiki/YAML
- **YAML syntax validator**: http://www.yamllint.com/
- **JSON notation**: http://www.json.org

- **JSON syntax validator**: `https://jsonlint.com/`
- **YAML notation specification**: `http://www.yaml.org/start.html`
- **OpenShift REST API reference**: `https://docs.openshift.org/latest/rest_api/api/`
- **PCRE reference**: `http://perldoc.perl.org/perlre.html`

# 10
# Security in OpenShift

Previously, we worked with advanced OpenShift resources, such as ImageStreams, ConfigMaps, and templates. Those resources allow you to simplify OpenShift resource management and the application delivery process.

In this chapter, we will introduce you to the realm of security in OpenShift. Any business' success depends on many factors, one of which is the company's ability to implement different security strategies for different users, departments, and applications. OpenShift is an enterprise-ready application platform that supports multiple security features, making it possible to integrate it into any corporate security landscape.

This chapter will provide you with an understanding of the following concepts:

- Authentication—users and identities, service accounts, and identity providers
- Authorization and role-based access control
- Admission controllers
- Security context constraints
- Storing sensitive data in OpenShift

## Technical requirements

For this section, we will have to make use of Vagrant to demonstrate the difference between these methods, as we will require two VMs: one for single-node OpenShift cluster, and the other for the FreeIPA server. Use the following Vagrantfile to spin up an environment:

```
$ cat Vagrantfile
$lab_idm = <<SCRIPT
cat <<EOF >> /etc/hosts
172.24.0.11 openshift.example.com openshift
172.24.0.12 idm.example.com idm
EOF
sed -i '/^127.0.0.1.*idm.*$/d' /etc/hosts
yum -y update
```

```
yum -y install ipa-server
systemctl restart dbus
ipa-server-install -r IDM.EXAMPLE.COM -n idm.example.com -p idmsecret -a
idmsecret --unattended
echo idmsecret | kinit admin
echo supersecret | ipa user-add alice --first Alice --last Springs --
password
SCRIPT

$lab_openshift = <<SCRIPT
cat <<EOF >> /etc/hosts
172.24.0.12 idm.example.com idm
EOF
yum -y update
yum install -y epel-release git docker
yum install -y ansible
systemctl start docker
systemctl enable docker
git clone -b release-3.9 https://github.com/openshift/openshift-ansible
/root/openshift-ansible
ssh-keygen -f /root/.ssh/id_rsa -N ''
cp /root/.ssh/id_rsa.pub /root/.ssh/authorized_keys
ssh-keyscan 172.24.0.11 >> .ssh/known_hosts
cp .ssh/known_hosts /root/.ssh/known_hosts
ssh-copy-id -i /root/.ssh/id_rsa root@172.24.0.11
reboot
SCRIPT

Vagrant.configure(2) do |config|
  config.vm.define "openshift" do |conf|
    conf.vm.box = "centos/7"
    conf.vm.hostname = 'openshift.example.com'
    conf.vm.network "private_network", ip: "172.24.0.11"
    conf.vm.provider "virtualbox" do |v|
       v.memory = 4096
       v.cpus = 2
    end
    conf.vm.provision "shell", inline: $lab_openshift
  end

  config.vm.define "idm" do |conf|
    conf.vm.box = "centos/7"
    conf.vm.hostname = 'idm.example.com'
    conf.vm.network "private_network", ip: "172.24.0.12"
    conf.vm.provider "virtualbox" do |v|
```

```
v.memory = 2048
    v.cpus = 1
  end
  conf.vm.provision "shell", inline: $lab_idm
end
end
```

The preceding file may seem complicated compared to the one from the Chapter 6, *OpenShift Installation*, but all it does is automates the steps, performed in that chapter manually, because the purpose of this chapter is to discuss security while building on the knowledge you gained up to this point. Also, it sets up FreeIPA server on another VM and creates a user that will be used later in this chapter.

> The command `systemctl restart dbus` is necessary to prevent installation of FreeIPA from failing during restart of certification manager.
>
> We used the same simple password for both the directory manager and IPA admin for simplicity, but in a production setup, make sure that you use complex and unique passwords!

Run `vagrant up` and wait until it finishes all the work. It may take up to 30 mins depending on your internet connectivity and compute resources:

```
$ vagrant up
Bringing machine 'openshift' up with 'virtualbox' provider...
Bringing machine 'idm' up with 'virtualbox' provider...
...
<output omitted>
...
```

Once it's done, open SSH session into the `openshift` VM and become root:

```
$ vagrant ssh openshift
[vagrant@openshift ~]$ sudo -i
[root@openshift ~]#
```

> Do not be alarmed by some of the output in red produced by the command above. Many CentOS commands, like yum, send warning, errors, and even other information alike to the standard error, which all gets interpreted as errors by Vagrant.

Then use the following Ansible inventory file to install OpenShift on the `openshift` VM. If you went through the `Chapter 6`, *OpenShift Installation,* you will notice that this is the same file with added `openshift_master_identity_providers` variable:

```
# cat /etc/ansible/hosts
...
<output omitted>
...
[masters]
172.24.0.11

[nodes]
172.24.0.11 openshift_node_labels="{'region': 'infra', 'zone': 'default'}"
openshift_schedulable=true

[etcd]
172.24.0.11

[OSEv3:vars]
openshift_deployment_type=origin
openshift_disable_check=memory_availability,disk_availability
openshift_ip=172.24.0.11
ansible_service_broker_install=false
openshift_master_cluster_hostname=172.24.0.11
openshift_master_cluster_public_hostname=172.24.0.11
openshift_hostname=172.24.0.11
openshift_public_hostname=172.24.0.11
openshift_master_identity_providers=[{'name': 'LDAP', 'challenge': 'true',
'login': 'true', 'kind': 'LDAPPasswordIdentityProvider', 'mappingMethod':
'claim', 'attributes': {'id': ['dn'], 'email': ['mail'], 'name': ['cn'],
'preferredUsername': ['uid']}, 'insecure': 'true', 'bindDN':
'uid=admin,cn=users,cn=accounts,dc=idm,dc=example,dc=com', 'bindPassword':
'idmsecret', 'url':
'ldap://idm.example.com/cn=users,cn=accounts,dc=idm,dc=example,dc=com?uid'}
, {'name': 'PASSWORD_FILE', 'challenge': 'true', 'login': 'true', 'kind':
'HTPasswdPasswordIdentityProvider', 'mappingMethod': 'claim', 'filename':
'/etc/origin/master/.users'}]

[OSEv3:children]
masters
nodes
etcd
```

 Even though `openshift_schedulable` variable appears to be on a separate line, it's actually on the previous line. If you just copy this file as it is from the one provided with other materials on this book, it will work.

Run the following playbooks to perform prerequisites check and actual installation, respectively:

```
# cd openshift-ansible
# ansible-playbook playbooks/prerequisites.yml
. . .
<output omitted>
. . .
# ansible-playbook playbooks/deploy_cluster.yml
. . .
<output omitted>
. . .
```

In our exercise, we will be using two identity providers: **LDAP** and **HTPasswd**. We will discuss in more detail in subsequent subsections. Notice that we specified the `claim` mapping method for both of them to demonstrate how it works with multiple providers.

After OpenShift is installed, use the following command provided by the `httpd-tools` package to create an `htpasswd` file with the user `alice` and the hashed password `supersecret`:

```
# htpasswd -c /etc/origin/master/.users alice
New password: redhat123
Re-type new password: redhat123
Adding password for user alice
```

Now we are ready to proceed further.

# Authentication

The term authentication refers to the process of validating one's identity. Usually, users aren't created in OpenShift itself, but provided by an external entity, such as the LDAP server or GitHub. The only part where OpenShift steps in is authorization—determining roles and, therefore, permissions for a user. OpenShift supports integration with various identity management solutions used in corporate environments, such as FreeIPA/Identity Management, Active Directory, GitHub, Gitlab, OpenStack Keystone, and OpenID. For the purpose of brevity, we will only discuss the most commonly used ones, but you can refer to https://docs.openshift.org/latest/install_config/configuring_authentication. html for the complete documentation.

# Users and identities

A user is any human actor that can make requests to the OpenShift API to access resources and perform actions. Users are typically created in an external identity provider, usually a corporate identity management solution such as **Lightweight Directory Access Protocol (LDAP)** or Active Directory.

To support multiple identity providers, OpenShift relies on the concept of identities serving as a bridge between users and identity providers. By default, a new user and identity are created upon the first login. There are four ways to map users to identities:

| Method | Description |
|---|---|
| claim | If a user with the same name already exists and is mapped to another identity, creation of another identity and login will fail. This is useful when you want to maintain a clear separation between identities provided by several providers in the case of identical usernames. A potential use case for this method would be transitioning from one authentication scheme to another. |
| add | If a user with the same name already exists and is mapped to another identity, another identity mapped to the same user is created. This is useful if you need to provide users from separate organizational entities that have their own identity management solutions with the ability to authenticate using mechanisms that are convenient for them. |
| lookup | OpenShift looks up an existing user, identity, and mapping, but doesn't create any of them, so these entities must exist prior to the user being able to log in. |
| generate | If a user with the same name already exists and is mapped to another identity, a separate user mapped to this identity is generated. |

Go to `https://172.24.0.11:8443` in your web browser and you will see the login page where you can choose from available identity providers:

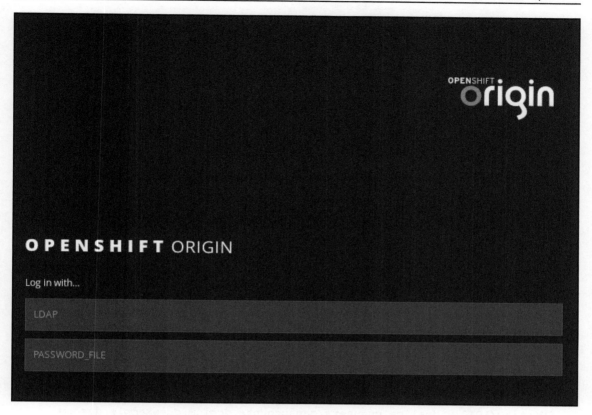

Log in via browser with the LDAP identity provider using the username alice and the password supersecret, and observe that the user was created using CLI:

```
# oc get user
NAME     UID          FULL NAME        IDENTITIES
alice bf11471e-47a8-11e8-8dee-525400daa710   Alice Springs
LDAP:uid=alice,cn=users,cn=accounts,dc=idm,dc=example,dc=com
```

 Notice that identity's name is composed of its type and user locator, delimited by colon. Locator is provider-specific and specifies how to request a particular user from a specific provider.

You can also see that an identity was created as well and mapped to the user:

```
# oc get identity
NAME   IDP NAME   IDP   USER NAME
USER    NAME   USER UID
```

```
LDAP:uid=alice,cn=users,cn=accounts,dc=idm,dc=example,dc=com    LDAP
uid=alice,cn=users,cn=accounts,dc=idm,dc=example,dc=com    alice
bf11471e-47a8-11e8-8dee-525400daa710
```

Let's try to log in with the `PASSWORD_FILE` provider using the same credentials:

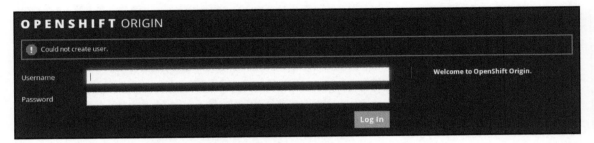

The credentials are correct, but OpenShift was unable to create a new identity and identity mapping to an existing user, as the user was already `claimed` by the LDAP provider. This is exactly what the message **Could not create user** indicates.

Let's delete the user and its identity to provide a clean slate for the upcoming demonstrations:

```
# oc delete user/alice
user "alice" deleted
```

```
# oc delete \
identity/LDAP:uid=alice,cn=users,cn=accounts,dc=idm,dc=example,dc=com

identity "LDAP:uid=alice,cn=users,cn=accounts,dc=idm,dc=example,dc=com"
deleted
```

Change the mapping method for the `PASSWORD_FILE` provider to `add`:

```
# cat /etc/origin/master/master-config.yaml
...
<output omitted>
...
 - challenge: true
 login: true
 mappingMethod: add
 name: PASSWORD_FILE
...
<output omitted>
...
```

And restart the master API service:

```
# systemctl restart origin-master-api
```

Log in with LDAP using alice:supersecret again, just as you did the first time, and then with PASSWORD_FILE using alice:redhat123 . Notice that the second identity was added to the existing one and mapped to the same user:

```
# oc get user
NAME        UID       FULL NAME      IDENTITIES
alice       bf11471e-47a8-11e8-8dee-525400daa710    Alice Springs
LDAP:uid=alice,cn=users,cn=accounts,dc=idm,dc=example,dc=com,
PASSWORD_FILE:alice
```

The order in which you use identity providers to log in is important! As you specified the add method for the PASSWORD_FILE provider only, if you try to log in with it first, you won't be able to log in using **LDAP**, because it is still set up to **claim** non-existing users and return an error if they already exist.

In order to see that we now have two identities mapped to the same user more clearly, run the following command:

```
# oc get identity
NAME IDP       NAME IDP USER NAME
USER   NAME    USER UID
LDAP:uid=alice,cn=users,cn=accounts,dc=idm,dc=example,dc=com    LDAP
uid=alice,cn=users,cn=accounts,dc=idm,dc=example,dc=com    alice
bf11471e-47a8-11e8-8dee-525400daa710
PASSWORD_FILE:alice
PASSWORD_FILE    alice
alice           bf11471e-47a8-11e8-8dee-525400daa7
```

Had the username been different, the second identity would have been mapped to that separate user.

Delete the user and identities before continuing with the next demonstration:

```
# oc delete user/alice
user "alice" deleted
```

```
# oc delete \
identity/LDAP:uid=alice,cn=users,cn=accounts,dc=idm,dc=example,dc=com
identity
```

```
"LDAP:uid=alice,cn=users,cn=accounts,dc=idm,dc=example,dc=com" deleted

# oc delete identity/PASSWORD_FILE:alice
identity "PASSWORD_FILE:alice" deleted
```

Now, change the mapping method for the same provider to `lookup`:

```
# cat /etc/origin/master/master-config.yaml
...
<output omitted>
...
 - challenge: true
 login: true
 mappingMethod: lookup
 name: PASSWORD_FILE
...
<output omitted>
...
```

Restart the master API to apply changes:

```
# systemctl restart origin-master-api
```

Now login with LDAP using `alice:supersecret` first. It should allow you to login. Then try to login with PASSWORD_FILEusing `alice:redhat123`. You should see a new error provided below:

**Could not find user** means that we didn't create an identity in OpenShift for this provider and didn't map it to any user, as `lookup` mapping method requires. Let's rectify this by creating the identity first:

```
# oc create identity PASSWORD_FILE:alice
identity "PASSWORD_FILE:alice" created
```

Then, map it to the pre-existing user:

```
# oc create useridentitymapping PASSWORD_FILE:alice alice
useridentitymapping "PASSWORD_FILE:alice" created
```

After that, the login attempt will be successful.

Once you verified that you can login with `alice:redhat123`, you can delete the user and both identities to proceed further.

```
# oc delete user/alice
user "alice" deleted
# oc delete \
identity/LDAP:uid=alice,cn=users,cn=accounts,dc=idm,dc=example,dc=com

identity "LDAP:uid=alice,cn=users,cn=accounts,dc=idm,dc=example,dc=com"
deleted
# oc delete identity/PASSWORD_FILE:alice
identity "PASSWORD_FILE:alice" deleted
```

 We didn't have to run `oc get identity` command again to get the list of all identities, because you can delete an identity using its name, which depends on the provider's name and the user's locator; since they hadn't changed, we could just use the same command as before.

Lastly, change the mapping method to `generate`:

```
# cat /etc/origin/master/master-config.yaml
...
<output omitted>
...
  - challenge: true
    login: true
    mappingMethod: generate
    name: PASSWORD_FILE
...
<output omitted>
...
```

Restart the master API:

```
# systemctl restart origin-master-api
```

Just as before, log in with LDAP using `alice:supersecret` and then with PASSWORD_FILEusing `alice:redhat123`. Let's see what users were created:

```
# oc get user
NAME       UID       FULL NAME      IDENTITIES
```

```
alice       97bd5ede-47b5-11e8-9f47-525400daa710    Alice Springs
LDAP:uid=alice,cn=users,cn=accounts,dc=idm,dc=example,dc=com
alice2    a145c96e-47b5-11e8-9f47-525400daa710
PASSWORD_FILE:alice
```

As you can see, this method creates a separate user with a generated name using a separate identity mapping if the user with the same name already exists.

You can see that two identities are now mapped to different users:

```
# oc get identity
NAME    IDP NAME IDP USER NAME    USER NAME    USER UID
LDAP:uid=alice,cn=users,cn=accounts,dc=idm,dc=example,dc=com      LDAP
uid=alice,cn=users,cn=accounts,dc=idm,dc=example,dc=com    alice
97bd5ede-47b5-11e8-9f47-525400daa710
PASSWORD_FILE:alice
PASSWORD_FILE    alice
alice2        a145c96e-47b5-11e8-9f47-525400daa710
```

Finally, let's delete the user and identities:

```
# oc delete user/alice
user "alice" deleted

# oc delete user/alice2
user "alice2" deleted

# oc delete \
identity/LDAP:uid=alice,cn=users,cn=accounts,dc=idm,dc=example,dc=com
identity "LDAP:uid=alice,cn=users,cn=accounts,dc=idm,dc=example,dc=com"
deleted
# oc delete identity/PASSWORD_FILE:alice
identity "PASSWORD_FILE:alice" deleted

# exit
$ exit
```

Now that this exercise is over, we can stop our VMs from releasing system resources for MiniShift for the rest of the chapter:

```
$ vagrant halt
==> idm: Attempting graceful shutdown of VM...
==> openshift: Attempting graceful shutdown of VM...
```

 We suggest you to just halt this lab, as it will be used in the section *Admission controllers*.

# Service accounts

Service accounts give us flexibility to control access to API without sharing user's credentials. In order to show you how it works we need to start the MiniShift VM:

```
$ minishift start --openshift-version=v3.9.0 --vm-driver=virtualbox
...
<output omitted>
...
```

Next, `export PATH` to `oc` client:

```
$ export PATH="/home/$USER/.minishift/cache/oc/v3.9.0/linux:$PATH"
```

Now, switch your Docker client to point to the docker daemon inside the MiniShift VM:

```
$ eval $(minishift docker-env)
```

Finally, log in as the privileged user `system:admin` in order to be able to perform privileged operations, such as adding SCCs and roles:

```
$ oc login -u system:admin
```

Now, we are ready to get started.

Another type of user that we will be using is service accounts. They are used by pods and other non-human actors to perform various actions and are a central vehicle by which their access to resources is managed. By default, three service accounts are created in each project:

| Name | Description |
|---|---|
| builder | Used by build pods and assigned the system:image-builder role, which grants push capability into the internal registry to any image stream in the project. |
| deployer | Used by deploy pods and assigned the system:deployer role, which allows modifying replication controllers in the project. |
| default | Used by all other pods by default. |

You can see them by running the following command:

```
$ oc get serviceaccounts
NAME              SECRETS     AGE
builder           2           58s
default           2           58s
deployer          2           58s
```

Each service account is represented by the `ServiceAccount` resource and is associated with two additional secrets—for access to the OpenShift API and the internal registry:

```
$ oc describe serviceaccounts/default
Name: default
Namespace: myproject
Labels: <none>
Annotations: <none>
Image pull secrets:      default-dockercfg-wggrl
Mountable secrets:       default-token-mg64x
                         default-dockercfg-wggrl
Tokens:                  default-token-7cljg
                         default-token-mg64x
Events:                  <none>
```

The service account can be created with a simple command:

```
$ oc create sa myserviceaccount
serviceaccount "myserviceaccount" created
```

Let's delete it for now, as we will be creating it again later on in this chapter:

```
$ oc delete sa/myserviceaccount
serviceaccount "myserviceaccount" deleted
```

Every service account is also a member of two groups:

- `system:serviceaccounts`, which includes all service accounts in the cluster
- `system:serviceaccounts:<project>`, which includes all service accounts in the `project`

You can grant privileges to groups of service accounts, which will effectively grant those privileges to all accounts in the group. For example, to grant view privileges to all service accounts in the cluster in the project `myproject`, type the following command:

```
$ oc adm policy add-role-to-group view system:serviceaccounts -n myproject
role "view" added: "system:serviceaccounts"
```

We specified `-n` only as a demonstration; as your current project is `myproject`, you could have omitted it.

Let's revert our changes and learn how to remove a particular role from a user in the process:

```
$ oc adm policy remove-role-from-group view system:serviceaccounts -n
myproject
role "view" removed: "system:serviceaccounts"
```

# Identity providers

Usually, users aren't created in OpenShift directly, but rather are supplied by an external identity management solution, which can be as complex as LDAP and Active Directory with a trust relationship set up between them, or as simple as a text password file with hashed passwords. Choosing a particular identity provider is influenced by factors such as:

- Your company's existing identity management solution
- How often users are added and deleted
- Whether you need a centralized management

OpenShift implements the following identity providers:

- AllowAll
- DenyAll
- HTPasswd
- LDAP
- Keystone
- BasicAuth
- RequestHeader
- GitLab
- GitHub
- OpenID
- Google

For the sake of brevity, we will limit demonstrations to the first four providers in the preceding list, while you can fill in the gaps by referring to https://docs.openshift.org/ latest/install_config/configuring_authentication.html . These configurations are to be applied to the master configuration file located at /etc/origin/master/master-config.yml.

You will need to bring your vagrant environment up if you want to test out the configuratins below because it won't work with minishift.

# AllowAll

This is the default identity provider for MiniShift and OpenShift Origin, including when the master is started without its configuration file. It allows all users with all passwords, so no authentication is performed. It is only useful for debugging purposes when you integrate your cluster with a corporate identity solution.

A configuration snippet from the master configuration file for this provider is as follows:

```
...
<output omitted>
...
 identityProviders:
  - challenge: true
    login: true
    mappingMethod: claim
    name: anypassword
    provider:
      apiVersion: v1
      kind: AllowAllPasswordIdentityProvider
...
<output omitted>
...
```

# DenyAll

This identity provider is the opposite of AllowAll, that is, it denies access to everyone. It is useful when you want to temporarily lock your cluster from everyone for maintenance or other purposes. This is the default provider for the Red Hat OpenShift Container Platform.

A configuration snippet of the master configuration file for this provider is as follows:

```
...
<output omitted>
...
 identityProviders:
  - challenge: true
    login: true
    mappingMethod: claim
```

```
      name: anypassword
      provider:
        apiVersion: v1
        kind: DenyAllPasswordIdentityProvider
  ...
  <output omitted>
  ...
```

As you can see, all it takes to enable it is changing `Allow` to `Deny`.

# HTPasswd

This provider allows you to create a file with the a of users with hashed passwords, giving you granular access control. While certainly better than having your installation just either accept or deny everyone, this approach still has two disadvantages:

- In the case of HA installation with multiple masters, you will need to synchronize changes to the password file between all masters, which is prone to errors and inefficient. Sure, it can be automated using configuration management and the **version control system** (**VCS**), but there are very few use cases where you wouldn't want to integrate your cluster with the corporate identity management server.
- It doesn't integrate with the corporate identity management solution, which requires you to either create all users in the password file directly, or to set up some sort of synchronization mechanism between your identity management server and OpenShift masters/configuration management server.

To enable this identity provider, we need to create the password file first, which, in turn, requires the `httpd-tools` package to be installed:

```
# sudo yum -y install httpd-tools
...
<output omitted>
...
Complete!
```

Next, create the file and add users to it. Specify the `-c` flag when creating the first user to create the file:

```
# htpasswd -c /etc/origin/master/.htpasswd bob
New password:
Re-type new password:
Adding password for user bob
# htpasswd /etc/origin/master/.htpasswd alice
```

```
New password:
Re-type new password:
Adding password for user alice
```

Now, we can enable this provider by changing AllowAll from the default configuration to `htpasswd` and specifying the location of the password file:

```
...
<output omitted>
...
 identityProviders:
  - challenge: true
    login: true
    mappingMethod: claim
    name: anypassword
    provider:
      apiVersion: v1
      kind: HTPasswdPasswordIdentityProvider
      file: /etc/origin/master/.htpasswd
...
<output omitted>
...
```

Lastly, restart master API service to have it pick up the changes:

```
# systemctl restart origin-master-api
```

# LDAP

This is the identity provider you will most likely use in your organization because of the popularity of LDAP (Lightweight Directory Access Protocol). If you are building your OpenShift lab from scratch, you can use either FreeIPA or IdM—they are very easy to set up. Like other centralized identity management solutions, LDAP spares you the need to synchronize changes to password files between masters in the case of multiple masters setup.

A configuration snippet from the master configuration file for this provider could look like the following:

```
...
<output omitted>
...
  identityProviders:
   - challenge: true
     login: true
     mappingMethod: claim
```

```
        name: ldap
        provider:
          apiVersion: v1
          kind: LDAPPasswordIdentityProvider
          attributes:
            id:
              - dn
            email:
              - mail
            name:
              - cn
            preferredUsername:
              - uid
        insecure: true
        bindDN: 'uid=openshift_admin,cn=users,cn=accounts,dc=example,dc=com'
        bindPassword: 'secretpassword'
        url:
'ldap://idm.example.com/cn=users,cn=accounts,dc=example,dc=com?uid'
...
<output omitted>
...
```

You can set the `insecure` parameter to `false` if your LDAP server supports the LDAPS secure protocol.

# Authorization and role-based access control

Authorization in OpenShift is built around the following concepts:

- **Rules:** Sets of actions allowed to be performed on specific resources.
- **Roles:** Collections of rules that allow them to be applied to a user according to a specific usage profile. Roles can be applied either at the cluster or project level.
- **Role bindings:** Associations between users/groups and roles. A given user or group can be associated with multiple roles.

Let's return to our MiniShift environment. To see a list of all available cluster roles, run the following command:

```
$ oc get clusterrole
NAME
admin
basic-user
cluster-admin
```

```
...
<output omitted>
...
view
```

Use the `describe` command to understand what rules are in a particular role:

```
$ oc describe clusterrole/edit
...
<output omitted>
...
```

You can see from the preceding output that, for example, users with this role can create and delete such resources as pods, configmaps, deploymentconfigs, imagestreams, routes, and services, but cannot do anything with projects, other than view them.

On the other hand, if you describe the view role, you will notice that the only actions allowed on resources are get, list, and watch, which makes it a perfect choice if, for example, you want to grant a development team the ability to view application resources in production, but not to modify any of them or create new resources:

```
$ oc describe clusterrole/view
...
<output omitted>
...
```

# Using built-in roles

Let's see how we can use the `edit` pre-defined role to grant a user access to another user's project. First, login at MiniShift as `alice`:

```
$ oc login -u alice
Authentication required for https://192.168.99.100:8443 (openshift)
Username: alice
Password: <anypassword>
Login successful.
```

 Just as with an OpenShift cluster deployed via Ansible, the default identity provider is AllowAll, which allows you to use any credentials.

Next, create a new project called `alice-project`:

```
$ oc new-project alice-project
Now using project "alice-project" on server "https://192.168.99.100:8443".
...
<output omitted>
...
```

Login as `bob` and observe that they weren't added as a member to any project by default:

```
$ oc login -u bob
Username: bob
Password: <anypassword>
Login successful.

$ oc project alice-project
error: You are not a member of project "alice-project".
You are not a member of any projects. You can request a project to be
created with the 'new-project' command.
To see projects on another server, pass '--server=<server>'.
```

Let's correct this by granting `bob` the privilege to `edit` most of the resources in the `alice-project` project:

```
$ oc login -u alice
...
<output omitted>
...
Using project "alice-project".

$ oc adm policy add-role-to-user edit bob
role "edit" added: "bob"
```

You can use the following command to see the existing `rolebinding` in the current `alice-project` project:

```
$ oc get rolebinding
NAME                      ROLE     USERS GROUPS  SERVICE ACCOUNTS  SUBJECTS
admin                     /admin                 alice
edit                      /edit                  bob
system:deployers          /system:deployer
deployer
system:image-builders     /system:image-builder
builder
system:image-pullers      /system:image-puller
system:serviceaccounts:alice-project
```

Notice that there are always two local bindings for the `deployer` and `builder` service accounts, as well as one binding granting all service accounts in the `alice-project` project the ability to pull images from the internal registry. Another two bindings make `alice` the admin of her project and grant `bob` the privilege of editing most of the resources in the project.

Let's see the details of the `edit` role binding:

```
$ oc describe rolebinding edit
Name:                    edit
Namespace:               alice-project
Created:                 17 hours ago
Labels:                  <none>
Annotations:             <none>
Role:                    /edit
Users:                   bob
...
<output omitted>
...
```

The preceding output tells us that the user `bob` is bound to the `edit` role in the project `alice-project`. The omitted output is the same as in the details of the `edit` role.

Log back in as `bob` and see that now you have access to Alice's project:

```
$ oc login -u bob
Logged into "https://192.168.99.100:8443" as "bob" using existing credentials.

You have one project on this server: "alice-project"

Using project "alice-project".
```

# Creating custom roles

If pre-defined roles aren't sufficient for you, you can always create custom roles with just the specific rules you need. Let's create a custom role that can be used instead of the `edit` role to create and get pods:

```
$ oc login -u system:admin
...
$ oc create clusterrole alice-project-edit --verb=get,list,watch --
```

```
resource=namespace,project
clusterrole "alice-project-edit" created
```

Notice that we had to log in as cluster administrator to create a cluster role. A cluster role is required to make its users members of a particular project.

OpenShift's `create clusterrole` command is limited to creating only one set of resources and verbs, so we couldn't add different verbs for pods. We can work around this limitation by editing the role directly:

```
$ oc edit clusterrole/alice-project-edit
...
<output omitted>
...
- apiGroups:
  - ""   # DO NOT MISS THIS LINE OR IT IS NOT GOING TO WORK
  attributeRestrictions: null
  resources:
  - pods
  verbs:
  - create
  - get
  - list
  - watch

clusterrole "alice-project-edit" edited
```

Next, delete the `edit` role from bob:

```
$ oc adm policy remove-role-from-user edit bob
role "edit" removed: "bob"
```

Assign the new role to bob:

```
$ oc adm policy add-role-to-user alice-project-edit bob
role "alice-project-edit" added: "bob"
```

Login as bob:

```
$ oc login -u bob
...
```

And start a new pod, just as we did before:

```
$ cat nginx-pod.yml
apiVersion: v1
kind: Pod
metadata:
```

```
    name: nginx
    labels:
      role: web
spec:
  containers:
  - name: nginx
    image: nginx
    resources:
      requests:
        cpu: 100m
        memory: 128Mi
```

```
$ oc create -f nginx-pod.yml
pod "nginx" created
```

```
$ oc get po
NAME   READY  STATUS RESTARTS AGE
nginx 0/1    Error  0        2h
```

What happened? Let's take a look into the pod's logs:

```
$ oc logs -f nginx
Error from server (Forbidden): pods "nginx" is forbidden: User "bob" cannot
get pods/log in the namespace "alice-project": User "bob" cannot get
pods/log in project "alice-project"
```

This is expected, because we didn't grant our custom role `alice-project-edit` access to pods' logs. If you look closely, this error message actually contains a suggestion on what we need to do - grant access to `pods/log` resource. Let's fix that by logging as `system:admin` user, adding required section to the role's definition, and log back in as `bob`:

```
$ oc login -u system:admin
...
<output omitted>
...
$ oc edit clusterrole/alice-project-edit
...
<output omitted>
...
- apiGroups:
  - ""
  attributeRestrictions: null
  resources:
  - pods
  - pods/log
  verbs:
  - get
```

```
$ oc login -u bob
...
<output omitted>
...
```

Try listing the pod's logs again:

```
$ oc logs -f nginx
2018/07/18 02:44:31 [warn] 1#1: the "user" directive makes sense only if
the master process runs with super-user privileges, ignored in
/etc/nginx/nginx.conf:2
nginx: [warn] the "user" directive makes sense only if the master process
runs with super-user privileges, ignored in /etc/nginx/nginx.conf:2
2018/07/18 02:44:31 [emerg] 1#1: mkdir() "/var/cache/nginx/client_temp"
failed (13: Permission denied)
nginx: [emerg] mkdir() "/var/cache/nginx/client_temp" failed (13:
Permission denied)
```

This time it works and you are able to see that the container is having problems with permissions. For now, run the following command to correct this, but we will address this problem in more detail in the *Security context constraints* section:

```
$ oc login -u system:admin
...
<output omitted>
...

$ oc delete po/nginx
pod "nginx" deleted

$ oc adm policy add-scc-to-user anyuid -z default
scc "anyuid" added to: ["system:serviceaccount:alice-project:default"]

$ oc login -u bob
...
<output omitted>
...
```

And now it works:

```
$ oc create -f nginx-pod.yml
pod "nginx" created

$ oc get po
NAME    READY   STATUS    RESTARTS  AGE
nginx   1/1     Running   0         2h
```

We just created a custom role that we can use to grant its users the ability to only create pods. It's not very useful as it is, as it won't let you create a service, for example:

```
$ oc expose po/nginx --port=80
Error from server (Forbidden): User "bob" cannot create services in the
namespace "alice-project": User "bob" cannot create services in project
"alice-project" (post services)
```

Now that this exercise is over, let's clean everything up:

```
$ oc login -u system:admin
. . .
<output omitted>
. . .
$ oc delete po/nginx
pod "nginx" deleted
$ oc adm policy remove-role-from-user alice-project-edit bob
role "alice-project-edit" removed: "bob"
$ oc delete clusterrole alice-project-edit
clusterrole "alice-project-edit" deleted
```

 We had to login as system:admin to delete our pod as we didn't grant the alice-project-edit role ability to delete pods, only to create them. This is yet another example of how granular RBAC can be in OpenShift.

# Admission controllers

Due to the specific nature of this section, we won't be using MiniShift, so let's stop it for now:

```
$ minishift stop
. . .
```

Then, start the Vagrant VMs instead:

```
$ vagrant up
. . .
<output omitted>
. . .
```

Finally, open a session in the openshift VM:

```
$ vagrant ssh openshift
$ sudo -i
```

An Admission Controller is a subroutine that's invoked after a request to the API is authenticated and authorized, but before it's persisted to etcd. Admission Controller serve the purpose of mutating and validating resources to be persisted, such as adding various annotations and defaults and making sure that they conform to specific restrictions. All admission controllers are chained, so that mutating controllers are applied first and then validating ones.

The following diagram illustrates the overall resource admission process:

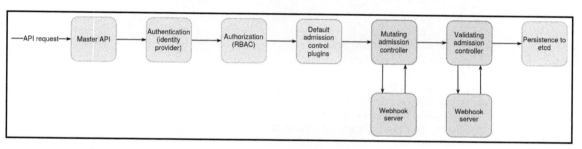

OpenShift resource admission chain

As you can see from the diagram above, the admission chain generally consists of the following types of admission controller:

- Default admission plugins that can be enabled in the `admissionConfig` section of the master configuration file
- Mutating admission webhooks
- Validating admission webhooks

The following are default admission controllers that are present in the master configuration file, unless configured otherwise during installation via the openshift_master_admission_plugin_config variable:

```
# cat /etc/origin/master/master-config.yaml
...
<output omitted>
...
admissionConfig:
  pluginConfig:
    BuildDefaults:
      configuration:
        apiVersion: v1
        env: []
```

```
        kind: BuildDefaultsConfig
        resources:
          limits: {}
          requests: {}
  BuildOverrides:
    configuration:
      apiVersion: v1
      kind: BuildOverridesConfig
  PodPreset:
    configuration:
      apiVersion: v1
      disable: false
      kind: DefaultAdmissionConfig
  openshift.io/ImagePolicy:
    configuration:
      apiVersion: v1
      executionRules:
      - matchImageAnnotations:
        - key: images.openshift.io/deny-execution
          value: 'true'
        name: execution-denied
        onResources:
        - resource: pods
        - resource: builds
        reject: true
        skipOnResolutionFailure: true
      kind: ImagePolicyConfig
...
<output omitted>
...
```

 You won't find those admission plugins in the MiniShift master API configuration, even if you ssh into the MiniShift VM and look at the master configuration file. This is why we use our own installation of OpenShift.

OpenShift supports the following admission control plugins out-of-the-box:

| Admission Control Plugin | Description |
| --- | --- |
| ProjectRequestLimit | Limits the number of self-provisioned projects per user. |
| BuildDefaults | Defines default configuration parameters, such as a git proxy server or node to run builder pods on, for BuildConfigs. |
| BuildOverrides | Can be used to override settings defined in a BuildConfig. |

| RunOnceDuration | Limits the amount of time that builder and deployer pods may run. |
|---|---|
| PodPreset | Enables use of PodPresets to supply pods with such resources as Secrets, ConfigMaps, and volumes. |
| PodNodeConstraints | Confines pods to nodes with particular labels. |
| PodNodeSelector | Confines pods to projects with particular labels. |
| openshift.io/ImagePolicy | Controls which images can be used in the cluster based on their registry and annotations. |
| openshift.io/IngressAdmission | Disables host name collision prevention for routes and ingress objects, allowing users without the `cluster-admin` cluster role to change host names in these objects after they have been created. |

Let's use the `ProjectRequestLimit` admission plugin to demonstrate how admission controllers are configured.

1. Add the `ProjectRequestLimit` section to the end of the admission chain in the master configuration file:

```
admissionConfig:
  pluginConfig:
    ProjectRequestLimit:
      configuration:
        apiVersion: v1
        kind: ProjectRequestLimitConfig
        limits:
        - selector:
            department: ops
          maxProjects: 2
        - maxProjects: 3
...
<output omitted>
...
```

In this particular example we are creating 2 different limits. One is for 'ops' department limiting the maximum number of projects to 2 , and another limitation for everyone esle that limits number of projects to 3.

2. Restart the master API to apply the changes:

```
# systemctl restart origin-master-api
```

3. Log in as `alice` using password `supersecret`, so that the user itself and its identity are created:

```
$ oc login -u alice
Username: alice
Password: supersecret
Login successful
```

4. Log in as the cluster administrator to be able to create labels:

```
$ oc login -u system:admin
```

Now, we need to `label alice` with a key/value pair that matches the selector specified in the admission plugin's configuration:

```
$ oc label user/alice department=ops
user "alice" labeled
```

5. Log back in as `alice`:

```
$ oc login -u alice
```

And try to create several projects:

```
$ oc new-project alice-project-1
. . .
$ oc new-project alice-project-2
. . .
$ oc new-project alice-project-3
Error from server (Forbidden): projectrequests.project.openshift.io
"alice-project-3" is forbidden: user alice cannot create more than
2 project(s).
```

As you can see, the request to create a third project was intercepted by the admission plugin and rejected due to failed validation.

Let's see how a global limit for all users works by creating a new user with no labels associated with it.

1. First, create a new user called bob. You can use the same password `supersecret` for simplicity:

```
$ htpasswd /etc/origin/master/.users bob
New password: supersecret
Re-type new password: supersecret
Adding password for user bob
```

2. Next, log in as the newly created user. This time, we will not associated it with any labels:

```
$ oc login -u bob
Username: bob
Password: supersecret
Login successful
```

Let's try to create projects until we hit the limit:

```
$ oc new-project bob-project-1
...
$ oc new-project bob-project-2
...
$ oc new-project bob-project-3
...
$ oc new-project bob-project-4
Error from server (Forbidden): projectrequests.project.openshift.io
"bob-project-4" is forbidden: user bob cannot create more than 3
project(s).
```

As you can see, bob wasn't able to create more than three projects, just as was specified for unlabeled users in the admission plugin's configuration.

Now that this exercise is over, let's do a clean-up:

```
$ oc delete project bob-project-{1..3}
project "bob-project-1" deleted
project "bob-project-2" deleted
project "bob-project-3" deleted
$ oc login -u alice
...
$ oc delete project alice-project-{1,2}
project "alice-project-1" deleted
project "alice-project-2" deleted
```

Also, delete the admission plugin's section from the master configuration file and restart the master API:

```
# sed -i '/ProjectRequestLimit/,+8d' /etc/origin/master/master-config.yaml
# systemctl restart origin-master-api
# exit
$ exit
```

The first command in the preceding snippet deletes eight lines after the matching string and the string itself.

As we won't need Vagrant for the remainder of this chapter, let's stop its VMs to prepare for the following exercises:

```
$ vagrant halt
. . .
```

 If you are finished experimenting with your Vagrant environment, you can run `vagrant destroy` to wipe it clean.

# Security context constraints

Before we start, let's bring up MiniShift environment again:

```
$ minishift start --openshift-version 3.9.0 --vm-driver virtualbox
. . .
<output omitted>
. . .
```

Another mechanism for controlling the behavior of pods is **security context constraints** (**SCCs**). These cluster-level resources define what resources can be accessed by pods and provide an additional level of control. By default, OpenShift supports seven SCCs:

```
$ oc login -u system:admin
. . .
<output omitted>
. . .
$ oc get scc
anyuid             . . .
hostaccess         . . .
hostmount-anyuid   . . .
hostnetwork        . . .
nonroot            . . .
privileged         . . .
restricted         . . .
```

You may notice `anyuid` SCC we used in the subsection "Creating custom roles" to solve the problem with container's permissions.

By default, all pods, except those for builds and deployments, use a `default` service account assigned by the `restricted` SCC, which doesn't allow privileged containers – that is, those running under the root user and listening on privileged ports (<1024).

Use `docker inspect` to see what user is specified in the `nginx` image metadata:

```
$ docker inspect nginx
[
    {
...
<output omitted>
...
            "User": "",
...
<output omitted>
...
    }
]
```

Coincidentally, the metadata doesn't specify the user, which makes the image run as root. This is exactly what restricted SCC is designed to prevent.

Previously, we just assigned the `anyuid` SCC to a default service account, which means that ALL containers get to run as privileged, and that is a big security risk. A good practice is to create a dedicated service account for our pod/container, so let's do this the right way:

```
$ oc create sa myserviceaccount
serviceaccount "myserviceaccount" created
```

Next, we have to assign the `anyuid` SCC to this account, but to do so we must login as the cluster administrator first:

```
$ oc adm policy add-scc-to-user anyuid -z myserviceaccount
scc "anyuid" added to: ["system:serviceaccount:myproject:myserviceaccount"]
```

Now, add our service account to the pod's definition:

```
$ cat nginx-pod2.yml
apiVersion: v1
kind: Pod
metadata:
  name: nginx
  labels:
    role: web
spec:
  containers:
  - name: nginx
    image: nginx
    resources:
      requests:
        cpu: 100m
        memory: 128Mi
```

```
    serviceAccountName: myserviceaccount
```

Let's try to create the pod again:

```
$ oc create -f nginx-pod2.yml
pod "nginx" created
$ oc get po
NAME      READY     STATUS      RESTARTS    AGE
nginx     1/1       Running     0           15s
```

As you can see, now that we have added the appropriate SCC to the service account used by the pod, it started successfully.

 Instead of allowing your image to run as the root, an even better practice would be to optimize it to run as an arbitrary user by specifying an unprivileged USER, setting the appropriate permissions on files and directories, and configuring your application to listen on unprivileged ports.

Clean up after our exercise, but leave `myserviceaccount` with the `anyuid` SCC assigned in place – we will need it later on to run privileged pods:

```
$ oc delete po/nginx
pod "nginx" deleted
```

# Storing sensitive data in OpenShift

In the modern world, applications are so complex that they are made up of multitudes of services interacting with each other via REST/SOAP APIs, binary protocols, message brokers, integration buses, and so on. An example of this is a backend application in an e-store; managing client orders means that you need to have access to the database with the products' details. Another example includes a payment processing application that must have access to international payment networks, such as SWIFT, in order to verify the card's details and process the payment. These examples are very different in terms of the scope and the technologies that are used, but they have a common trait—all services need some kind of authenticating piece of data to introduce themselves to each other and this data has to be stored somewhere.

An obvious, but the most insecure, strategy would be to pass this data to pods as plain text via config maps, like any other data. With this approach, sensitive data can be viewed by anyone who has view access to project resources, so you cannot implement granular access control.

Being an enterprise-grade PaaS solution, OpenShift incorporates a dedicated security mechanism to secure such data against unwarranted disclosure—Secret.

 While providing an adequate level of protection for sensitive information, OpenShift is not a replacement for a specialized security solution. For example, if you need to store encryption/decryption keys in a secure location, you might want to consider using a **Hardware Security Module (HSM)**.

# What data is considered sensitive?

Generally speaking, any data that must be protected against unauthorized access is treated as sensitive. This includes login credentials, tokens, encryption keys, smart cards, classified documents, and so on. Protection for various types of sensitive data is regulated by many government-approved security information standards and corporate policies, thus being the subject of an entire separate field of Information Security. In the context of applications and microservices, we are mostly interested in a subset of sensitive data, such as:

- Login credentials (username/password)
- API tokens
- Encryption keys
- X.509 certificate/key pairs

# Secrets

Secrets are similar to config maps, which we discussed in the previous chapter, in that they are also used to pass data to pods, but that's where their similarities end. A secret's only use case is to store sensitive data consumed by applications—API tokens, credentials, X.509 certificates/keys, and so on. They are backed by tmpfs (an in-memory temporary filesystem) which prevents them from being stored on persistent storage. Secrets are different from config maps in the following ways:

- Many secrets are created automatically on OpenShift startup (so that pods are able to access the OpenShift API and internal registry, for example)
- Secret values are base64-encoded by default, which makes them impossible to see until they are injected into a container

OpenShift supports three types of secret:

| Type | Description |
|------|-------------|
| generic | Arbitrary data, like the contents of a file, directory, or string. |
| docker-registry | Docker registry credentials stored in the `.dockercfg` file. |
| tls | X.509 certificate and its corresponding key. We will use this type of secret as an example later in this section. |

First, login as `system:admin` user if you haven't already done so:

```
$ oc login -u system:admin
..
<output omitted>
...
```

Use the familiar `get` command to see all secrets in the current project:

```
$ oc get secret
NAME                                   TYPE
DATA          AGE
builder-dockercfg-2bpc7                kubernetes.io/dockercfg                    1
4d
builder-token-2cdj5                    kubernetes.io/service-account-token        4
4d
builder-token-8lhrx                    kubernetes.io/service-account-token        4
4d
default-dockercfg-wggrl                kubernetes.io/dockercfg                    1
4d
default-token-7cljg                    kubernetes.io/service-account-token        4
4d
default-token-mg64x                    kubernetes.io/service-account-token        4
4d
deployer-dockercfg-kd88d               kubernetes.io/dockercfg                    1
4d
deployer-token-5rf6f                   kubernetes.io/service-account-token        4
4d
deployer-token-k8lwh                   kubernetes.io/service-account-token        4
4d
myserviceaccount-dockercfg-n6lg7       kubernetes.io/dockercfg                    1
4d
myserviceaccount-token-fxwpn           kubernetes.io/service-account-token        4
4d
myserviceaccount-token-k4d5g           kubernetes.io/service-account-token        4
4d
```

Notice that there are three secrets for every service account in the project, as was stated in the subsection on service accounts. Let's see what data the `dockercfg` token for the default service account actually has:

```
$ oc edit secret/default-dockercfg-wggrl

# Please edit the object below. Lines beginning with a '#' will be ignored,
# and an empty file will abort the edit. If an error occurs while saving
this file will be
# reopened with the relevant failures.
#
apiVersion: v1
data:
  .dockercfg: ... <output omitted> ...
kind: Secret
...
<output omitted>
...
```

You will see that the `data` attribute contains a long base64-encoded string, representing docker client credentials for accessing the internal registry. Use the following Python one-liner to decode the contents of `.dockercfg`:

```
$ python -c "import base64, json; secret_json =
base64.b64decode('...<base64-encoded value of .dockercfg from the
secret>...'); parsed = json.loads(secret_json); print json.dumps(parsed,
indent=4, sort_keys=True)"
$ {
    "172.30.1.1:5000": {
        "auth": "c2Vydml1j...<output omitted>...ZkFRTEE=",
        "email": "serviceaccount@example.org",
        "password": "eyJhbGci...<output omitted>...wVBfAQLA",
        "username": "serviceaccount"
    },
    "docker-registry.default.svc:5000": {
        "auth": "c2Vydml1j...<output omitted>...ZkFRTEE=",
        "email": "serviceaccount@example.org",
        "password": "eyJhbGci...<output omitted>...wVBfAQLA",
        "username": "serviceaccount"
    }
}
```

Notice that the `auth` and `password` values are the same for the two sections of the document, as they specify credentials for the same registry. Let's drill further down and decode the value of the `auth` field:

```
$ python -c "import base64; print base64.b64decode('c2Vydml1j...<output
```

```
omitted>...ZkFRTEE=')"
$ serviceaccount:eyJhbGci...<output omitted>...wVBfAQLA
```

You may have noticed that the string after the colon is actually the password from the JSON document we decoded earlier. You may use the same one-liner to decode it as well, but we haven't provided the output here, as it contains non-unicode characters.

Now, we get to practice and create our own secret and use it in a pod. One of the most typical use cases for secrets is a web server that's configured with SSL/TLS support, where a secret is used to store a certificate/key pair.

First, we need to create an X.509 certificate and its key:

```
$ openssl req -x509 -nodes -days 365 -newkey rsa:2048 -keyout ssl.key -out
ssl.crt
Generating a 2048 bit RSA private key
.............+++
.............+++
writing new private key to 'ssl.key'
-----
You are about to be asked to enter information that will be incorporated
into your certificate request.
What you are about to enter is what is called a Distinguished Name or a DN.
There are quite a few fields but you can leave some blank
For some fields there will be a default value,
If you enter '.', the field will be left blank.
-----
Country Name (2 letter code) [XX]:US
State or Province Name (full name) []:AZ
Locality Name (eg, city) [Default City]:Phoenix
Organization Name (eg, company) [Default Company Ltd]:ACME
Organizational Unit Name (eg, section) []:IT
Common Name (eg, your name or your server's hostname) []:localhost
Email Address []:
```

It doesn't matter what you specify in the certificate's fields, as it will only be used to demonstrate a working Nginx server with SSL configured.

Next, create a custom Nginx virtual host that's listening on TCP port 443 and configured with the locations of the certificate and key:

```
$ cat nginx_custom_default.conf
server {
    listen      80;
    listen      443 ssl;
```

```
server_name   localhost;
ssl_certificate      ssl/..data/tls.crt;
ssl_certificate_key ssl/..data/tls.key;
location / {
    root   /usr/share/nginx/html;
    index  index.html index.htm;
}
}
```

 TLS secrets are mounted at subdirectory ..data inside the mountPath of the container – that's why the path to both the certificate and the key contains ..data.

Use the preceding configuration file to create a config map that will be used later by the pod:

```
$ oc create cm nginx --from-file nginx_custom_default.conf
configmap "nginx" created
```

The next step is to create the secret using the certificate and key:

```
$ oc create secret tls nginx --cert ssl.crt --key ssl.key
secret "nginx" created
```

Let's take a look at the newly created secret's definition:

```
$ oc export secret/nginx
apiVersion: v1
data:
  tls.crt: ...<base64-encoded certificate>...
  tls.key: ...<base64-encoded key>...
kind: Secret
metadata:
  creationTimestamp: null
  name: nginx
type: kubernetes.io/tls
```

Notice that the secret's keys tls.crt and tls.key store the certificate and key, respectively. When a TLS secret is mounted on the pod, the certificate and key are decrypted and placed in the files with the names of these keys – that's why in the virtual host's configuration we had to specify key names and not the file names as we created them with the openssl command.

The last building block we have to create is the pod itself. Use the appropriate directives to mount the config map and secret as volumes in it:

```
$ cat nginx-pod3.yml
apiVersion: v1
kind: Pod
metadata:
  name: nginx
  labels:
    role: web
spec:
  containers:
  - name: nginx
    image: nginx
    resources:
      requests:
        cpu: 100m
        memory: 128Mi
    volumeMounts:
      - name: conf
        mountPath: /etc/nginx/conf.d
      - name: tls
        mountPath: /etc/nginx/ssl
  volumes:
    - name: conf
      configMap:
        name: nginx
        items:
          - key: nginx_custom_default.conf
            path: default.conf
    - name: tls
      secret:
        secretName: nginx
  serviceAccountName: myserviceaccount
```

Now, it's time to create the pod:

```
$ oc create -f nginx-pod3.yml
pod "nginx" created
```

Observe it being created:

```
$ oc get po
NAME      READY    STATUS           RESTARTS    AGE
```

```
nginx    0/1    ContainerCreating   0        3s
nginx    1/1    Running   0         7s
```

Out of curiosity, let's take a look inside the container to see how the certificate and key are accessible:

```
$ oc rsh nginx ls -l /etc/nginx/ssl
total 0
lrwxrwxrwx 1 root root 14 Apr 25 11:21 tls.crt -> ..data/tls.crt
lrwxrwxrwx 1 root root 14 Apr 25 11:21 tls.key -> ..data/tls.key
```

Use the following command to see that the secret isn't stored on the file system (even though it's ephemeral, in our case), but mounted in memory using `tmpfs`:

```
$ oc rsh nginx df -h
Filesystem Size Used Avail Use% Mounted on
overlay 19G 2.0G 17G 11% /
tmpfs 1000M 0 1000M 0% /dev
tmpfs 1000M 0 1000M 0% /sys/fs/cgroup
/dev/sda1 19G 2.0G 17G 11% /etc/hosts
shm 64M 0 64M 0% /dev/shm
tmpfs 1000M 8.0K 1000M 1% /etc/nginx/ssl
tmpfs 1000M 16K 1000M 1% /run/secrets/kubernetes.io/serviceaccount
tmpfs 1000M 0 1000M 0% /proc/scsi
tmpfs 1000M 0 1000M 0% /sys/firmware
```

Create a service for the pod:

```
$ oc expose po/nginx --port 443
service "nginx" exposed
```

Then, `expose` the service to create an externally available route:

```
$ oc expose svc/nginx
route "nginx" exposed
```

The route was created:

```
$ oc get route
NAME    HOST/PORT    PATH    SERVICES    PORT    TERMINATION   WILDCARD
nginx       nginx-myproject.192.168.42.43.nip.io              nginx     443
None
```

As a final touch, we have to add TLS termination to the route and set its type to `passthrough` so that the OpenShift router accepts encrypted traffic to the service and doesn't alter it in any way. One cannot create a secure route via the `expose` CLI command, so we have to `patch` the route's definition directly:

```
$ oc patch route/nginx -p '{"spec" : {"tls": {"termination":
"passthrough"}}}'
route "nginx" patched
```

To verify that our Nginx server was configured with TLS support correctly, open your favorite web browser, go to the URL representing the route, and confirm the security exception, as we used a self-signed certificate:

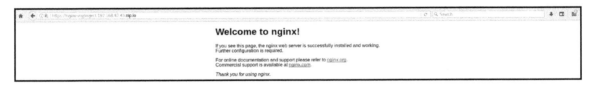

Notice the little lock icon at the left end of the URL, indicating that a secure connection has been established. The warning about invalid certificate, indicated by the yellow triangle (as in Mozilla Firefox), is totally fine in our lab environment.

 In Google Chrome and Chromium web browsers you will see the **Not secure** warning to the left of the URL field, which is the same.

Now that this exercise is over, let's clean up the current project:

```
$ oc delete all --all
route "nginx" deleted
pod "nginx" deleted
service "nginx" deleted

$ oc delete cm/nginx secret/nginx
configmap "nginx" deleted
secret "nginx" deleted
```

 You can specify unencoded data in plain text using the `stringData` section instead of `data`. This can be useful for templates so that you can parameterize various generated secrets, such as webhook keys.

# Summary

In this chapter, you learned about various identity providers that implement authentication in OpenShift, service accounts, and gained an understanding of the connection between users and identities. We also discussed the process of authorization and granting privileges to users, admission controllers, and security context constraints. Lastly, we talked about secrets and learned how they can be used by applications.

In the next chapter, we will deal with networking on the upper level—OpenShift SDN.

# Questions

1. What mapping methods can be used to prevent the mapping of multiple identities to the same user? choose two:
    1. lookup
    2. generate
    3. add
    4. claim

2. What service account is used to run application pods?
    1. all
    2. builder
    3. deployer
    4. default

3. What roles can be assigned to a user to grant the ability to create and delete resources in a particular project? choose two:
    1. create
    2. admin
    3. view
    4. edit

4. What admission control plugin can be used to limit the number of self-provisioned projects per user?
    1. PodPreset
    2. ProjectRequestNumber
    3. ProjectRequestLimit
    4. SelfProvisionedProjects

5.  What SCCs can be used to run containers as root? choose 2:
    1. anyuid
    2. restricted
    3. hostmount-anyuid
    4. privileged
6.  What secret's attribute stores base64-encoded data?
    1. stringData
    2. data
    3. base64
    4. spec

# Further reading

- **Users**: https://docs.openshift.org/latest/admin_guide/manage_users.html
- **Service accounts**: https://docs.openshift.org/latest/admin_guide/service_accounts.html
- **RBAC**: https://docs.openshift.org/latest/admin_guide/manage_rbac.html
- **Identity providers**: https://docs.openshift.org/latest/install_config/configuring_authentication.html
- **Admission Controllers**: https://docs.openshift.org/latest/architecture/additional_concepts/admission_controllers.html
- **Security context constraints**: https://docs.openshift.org/latest/admin_guide/manage_scc.html
- **Secrets**: https://docs.openshift.org/latest/dev_guide/secrets.html

# 11
# Managing OpenShift Networking

In the previous chapter, we introduced you to the realm of security in OpenShift. OpenShift is an enterprise-ready application management platform that supports multiple security features, making it able to integrate into any corporate security landscape.

Like any cloud platform, OpenShift heavily relies on a networking stack on two different layers:

- The underlying network topology, which is directly determined either by physical network equipment or virtual network devices in the case of OpenShift itself deployed in the virtual environment. This level provides connectivity to OpenShift masters and nodes, and is beyond the control of OpenShift itself.
- The virtual network topology, which is determined by the OpenShift SDN plugin being used. This level is concerned with managing connectivity between applications and providing external access to them.

In this chapter, we are going to work with networking on the upper level—OpenShift SDN—and we will cover the following topics:

- Network topology in OpenShift
- SDN plugins
- Egress routers
- Static IPs for external project traffic
- Egress network policies
- DNS

# Technical requirements

For this chapter, we will be using the following configuration of VMs managed via Vagrant using the default VirtualBox provider:

| Name | Role |
|------|------|
| openshift-master | Master |
| openshift-node-1 | Node |
| openshift-node-2 | Node |

 Make sure you have enough RAM on your desktop or laptop you use. The configuration above was tested with 8GB RAM, but it was barely enough, so we recommend running it on a system with 16GB at least.

This configuration corresponds to the following Vagrantfile:

```
$ cat Vagrantfile
$common_provision = <<SCRIPT
cat <<EOF >> /etc/hosts
172.24.0.11 openshift-master.example.com openshift-master
172.24.0.12 openshift-node-1.example.com openshift-node-1
172.24.0.13 openshift-node-2.example.com openshift-node-2
EOF
sed -i '/^127.0.0.1.*openshift.*$/d' /etc/hosts
yum -y update
yum install -y docker
systemctl start docker
systemctl enable docker
SCRIPT

$master_provision = <<SCRIPT
yum -y install git epel-release
yum -y install ansible
git clone -b release-3.9 https://github.com/openshift/openshift-ansible
/root/openshift-ansible
ssh-keygen -f /root/.ssh/id_rsa -N ''
cp /root/.ssh/id_rsa.pub /root/.ssh/authorized_keys
for i in 1 3; do ssh-keyscan 172.24.0.1$i; done >> .ssh/known_hosts
cp .ssh/known_hosts /root/.ssh/known_hosts
for i in 1 2; do sudo ssh-copy-id -o
IdentityFile=/vagrant_private_keys/machines/openshift-node-
$i/virtualbox/private_key -f -i /root/.ssh/id_rsa root@172.24.0.1$((i+1));
done
reboot
SCRIPT
```

```
$node_provision = <<SCRIPT
cp -r /home/vagrant/.ssh /root
reboot
SCRIPT

Vagrant.configure(2) do |config|
  config.vm.define "openshift-node-1" do |conf|
    conf.vm.box = "centos/7"
    conf.vm.hostname = 'openshift-node-1.example.com'
    conf.vm.network "private_network", ip: "172.24.0.12"
    conf.vm.provider "virtualbox" do |v|
       v.memory = 2048
       v.cpus = 2
    end
    conf.vm.provision "shell", inline: $common_provision
    conf.vm.provision "shell", inline: $node_provision
  end

  config.vm.define "openshift-node-2" do |conf|
    conf.vm.box = "centos/7"
    conf.vm.hostname = 'openshift-node-2.example.com'
    conf.vm.network "private_network", ip: "172.24.0.13"
    conf.vm.provider "virtualbox" do |v|
       v.memory = 2048
       v.cpus = 2
    end
    conf.vm.provision "shell", inline: $common_provision
    conf.vm.provision "shell", inline: $node_provision
  end

  config.vm.define "openshift-master" do |conf|
    conf.vm.box = "centos/7"
    conf.vm.hostname = 'openshift-master.example.com'
    conf.vm.network "private_network", ip: "172.24.0.11"
    conf.vm.synced_folder '.vagrant/', '/vagrant_private_keys', type:
'rsync'
    conf.vm.provider "virtualbox" do |v|
       v.memory = 4096
       v.cpus = 2
    end
    conf.vm.provision "shell", inline: $common_provision
    conf.vm.provision "shell", inline: $master_provision
  end
end
```

In order to be able to reach the cluster inside the VM from your host system, make sure
file /etc/hosts on your laptop looks like this:

```
$ cat /etc/hosts
127.0.0.1    localhost openshift localhost.localdomain localhost4
localhost4.localdomain4
::1          localhost localhost.localdomain localhost6
localhost6.localdomain6
172.24.0.11 openshift.example.com
```

Run vagrant up and wait till it finishes all the work. It may take up to 30 mins depending
on your internet connectivity and compute resources:

```
$ vagrant up
Bringing machine 'openshift-node-1' up with 'virtualbox' provider...
Bringing machine 'openshift-node-2' up with 'virtualbox' provider...
Bringing machine 'openshift-master' up with 'virtualbox' provider...
...
<output omitted>
...
```

Once it's done, open SSH session into the master VM and become root:

```
$ vagrant ssh openshift-master
[vagrant@openshift-master ~]$ sudo -i
[root@openshift-master ~]#
```

You can use the following inventory for deploying OpenShift:

```
# cat /etc/ansible/hosts
...
<output omitted>
...
[masters]
172.24.0.11

[nodes]
172.24.0.11 openshift_node_labels="{'region': 'us', 'zone': 'default'}"
openshift_ip=172.24.0.11 openshift_master_cluster_hostname=172.24.0.11
openshift_hostname=172.24.0.11
172.24.0.12 openshift_node_labels="{'region': 'infra', 'zone': 'east'}"
openshift_ip=172.24.0.12 openshift_master_cluster_hostname=172.24.0.12
openshift_hostname=172.24.0.12
172.24.0.13 openshift_node_labels="{'region': 'us', 'zone': 'west'}"
openshift_ip=172.24.0.13 openshift_master_cluster_hostname=172.24.0.13
openshift_hostname=172.24.0.13

[etcd]
```

```
172.24.0.11

[OSEv3:vars]
openshift_deployment_type=origin
openshift_disable_check=memory_availability,disk_availability
ansible_service_broker_install=false
openshift_master_cluster_public_hostname=openshift.example.com
openshift_public_hostname=openshift.example.com
openshift_master_default_subdomain=openshift.example.com
openshift_schedulable=true

[OSEv3:children]
masters
nodes
etcd
```

 Even though variables in the `nodes` group appear to be on separate lines, they are actually on previous ones with hosts they are associated with. If you just copy this file as it is from the one provided with other materials on this book, it will work.

Now, it's time to install OpenShift:

```
# cd openshift-ansible
# ansible-playbook playbooks/prerequisites.yml
...
<output omitted>
...
# ansible-playbook playbooks/deploy_cluster.yml
...
<output omitted>
...
```

# Network topology in OpenShift

In order to provide a common medium for containers to communicate with each other, OpenShift makes use of an overlay network that's implemented via VXLAN. The **Virtual eXtensible Local Area Network** (**VXLAN**) protocol provides a mechanism for transferring Layer 2 (Ethernet) frames across Layer 3 (IP) networks. Depending on the SDN plugin being used, the scope of communication may be limited to pods within the same project or maybe completely unrestricted. No matter which plugin is used, the network topology is still the same.

When a new node is registered in etcd, the master allocates a private /23 subnet from the cluster network. By default, subnets are allocated from 10.128.0.0/14, but can be configured in the networkConfig stanza of the master configuration file. The following is an excerpt from the file containing the relevant parameters:

```
# cat /etc/origin/master/master-config.yaml
...
<output omitted>
...
networkConfig:
  clusterNetworkCIDR: 10.128.0.0/14
  clusterNetworks:
  - cidr: 10.128.0.0/14
    hostSubnetLength: 9
...
<output omitted>
...
```

The hostSubnetLength setting determines how many IP addresses are allocated to every node to be distributed between pods running on a given node. In our default configuration, the size of each subnet is $2^9$=512 addresses, which makes 510 IPs available for pods. Summing up, each pod's IP address will have mask /23 (14+9).

> Please note that the clusterNetworks[].cidr setting can only be changed to a larger subnet that includes the previous setting. For example, it can be set to 10.128.0.0/12, as it contains /14, but not to 10.128.0.0/16, as they don't overlap completely.
> Also, hostSubnetLength cannot be changed once the cluster is created.

The overlay network in OpenShift is built from the following components:

- br0: An OVS bridge that all pods running on a particular node are plugged into via a veth pair. Each node has a single br0 device which serves as a virtual switch.
- tun0: This is an internal port of br0 numbered 2, which is assigned each node subnet's default gateway address and is used for external access. OpenShift also creates routing and netfilter rules to direct traffic to the external network via NAT.
- vxlan_sys_4789: An OVS port 1 of br0 which provides connectivity between pods running on different nodes. It's referred to as vxlan in the OVS rules.

# Tracing connectivity

In this subsection, we will create a `demo` project hosting a single `httpd` pod in order to see first-hand how the overlay network is constructed in OpenShift.

1. First, let's create the project:

   ```
   # oc new-project demo
   ...
   ```

2. Then, create a pod running Apache web server in the project:

   ```
   # cat httpd-pod.yml
   apiVersion: v1
   kind: Pod
   metadata:
     name: httpd
     labels:
       role: web
   spec:
     containers:
     - name: httpd
       image: manageiq/httpd
       resources:
         requests:
           cpu: 400m
           memory: 128Mi
   # oc create -f httpd-pod.yml
   pod "httpd" created
   ```

3. We will need the IP address allocated to the pod, as well as the address of the node it was scheduled to:

   ```
   # oc describe po/httpd | grep '\(Node\|IP\):'
   Node:    172.24.0.13/172.24.0.13
   IP:      10.129.0.20
   ```

4. Another step is to get the name of the pod's network interface, which is actually one end of the `veth` pair that's used to connect the pod to the `br0` bridge:

   ```
   # oc rsh httpd ip a
   ...
   <output omitted>
   ...
   3: eth0@if25: <BROADCAST,MULTICAST,UP,LOWER_UP> mtu 1450 qdisc
   noqueue state UP group default
       link/ether 0a:58:0a:81:00:2c brd ff:ff:ff:ff:ff:ff link-netnsid
   ```

```
    0
        inet 10.129.0.20/23 brd 10.129.1.255 scope global eth0
           valid_lft forever preferred_lft forever
        inet6 fe80::14d1:32ff:fef9:b92c/64 scope link
           valid_lft forever preferred_lft forever
```

Now, let's move on to another project, called `default`. This project is used to host special pods for the router and internal Docker registry. Both pods are deployed on the node labeled `infra`, which is `openshift-node-1` in our case. Let's confirm this and find out the IP address of the registry pod:

```
# oc project default
Now using project "default" on server
"https://openshift-master.example.com:8443".
# oc get po
NAME READY STATUS RESTARTS AGE
docker-registry-1-cplvg 1/1 Running 1 17h
router-1-52xrr 1/1 Running 1 17h
# oc describe po/docker-registry-1-cplvg | grep '\(Node\|IP\):'
Node: 172.24.0.12/172.24.0.12
IP: 10.128.0.5
```

 The reason we picked the registry pod is that the router pod runs in privileged mode to have direct access to the node's networking stack; as such, it wouldn't represent a typical configuration.

Now, launch the following command to get the name of the registry pod's NIC:

```
# oc rsh docker-registry-1-cplvg ip a
...
<output omitted>
...
3: eth0@if12: <BROADCAST,MULTICAST,UP,LOWER_UP> mtu 1450 qdisc noqueue
state UP group default
    link/ether 0a:58:0a:80:00:05 brd ff:ff:ff:ff:ff:ff link-netnsid 0
    inet 10.128.0.5/23 brd 10.128.1.255 scope global eth0
       valid_lft forever preferred_lft forever
    inet6 fe80::948e:9aff:feca:7f61/64 scope link
       valid_lft forever preferred_lft forever
```

The following steps will be performed on the first node—openshift-node-1.

First, let's see what network devices were created on that node after OpenShift was installed:

```
# ip a
...
<output omitted>
...
9: br0: <BROADCAST,MULTICAST> mtu 1450 qdisc noop state DOWN group default
qlen 1000
    link/ether ae:da:68:ed:ac:4c brd ff:ff:ff:ff:ff:ff
10: vxlan_sys_4789: <BROADCAST,MULTICAST,UP,LOWER_UP> mtu 65520 qdisc
noqueue master ovs-system state UNKNOWN group default qlen 1000
    link/ether 0e:fd:50:11:a1:a8 brd ff:ff:ff:ff:ff:ff
11: tun0: <BROADCAST,MULTICAST,UP,LOWER_UP> mtu 1450 qdisc noqueue state
UNKNOWN group default qlen 1000
    link/ether fa:4e:a6:71:84:8e brd ff:ff:ff:ff:ff:ff
    inet 10.128.0.1/23 brd 10.128.1.255 scope global tun0
       valid_lft forever preferred_lft forever
    inet6 fe80::f84e:a6ff:fe71:848e/64 scope link
       valid_lft forever preferred_lft forever
12: veth5d5b06ef@if3: <BROADCAST,MULTICAST,UP,LOWER_UP> mtu 1450 qdisc
noqueue master ovs-system state UP group default
    link/ether be:3e:2d:24:22:42 brd ff:ff:ff:ff:ff:ff link-netnsid 0
    inet6 fe80::bc3e:2dff:fe24:2242/64 scope link
       valid_lft forever preferred_lft forever
```

br0 is the OVS bridge that was mentioned at the beginning of the *Network topology in OpenShift* section. In order to see its active ports, use the ovs-vsctl command, which is provided by the openvswitch package:

```
# ovs-vsctl show
bb215e68-10dc-483f-863c-5cd67927ed6b
    Bridge "br0"
        fail_mode: secure
        Port "vxlan0"
            Interface "vxlan0"
                type: vxlan
                options: {key=flow, remote_ip=flow}
        Port "tun0"
            Interface "tun0"
                type: internal
        Port "veth5d5b06ef"
            Interface "veth5d5b06ef"
        Port "br0"
            Interface "br0"
                type: internal
    ovs_version: "2.6.1"
```

Now, discover the same information about the second node, openshift-node-2:

```
# ip a
...
<output omitted>
...
9: br0: <BROADCAST,MULTICAST> mtu 1450 qdisc noop state DOWN group default
qlen 1000
    link/ether ea:e2:58:58:04:44 brd ff:ff:ff:ff:ff:ff
10: vxlan_sys_4789: <BROADCAST,MULTICAST,UP,LOWER_UP> mtu 65520 qdisc
noqueue master ovs-system state UNKNOWN group default qlen 1000
    link/ether 76:ef:26:5c:61:08 brd ff:ff:ff:ff:ff:ff
11: tun0: <BROADCAST,MULTICAST,UP,LOWER_UP> mtu 1450 qdisc noqueue state
UNKNOWN group default qlen 1000
    link/ether 4a:a7:ab:95:bc:46 brd ff:ff:ff:ff:ff:ff
    inet 10.129.0.1/23 brd 10.129.1.255 scope global tun0
       valid_lft forever preferred_lft forever
    inet6 fe80::48a7:abff:fe95:bc46/64 scope link
       valid_lft forever preferred_lft forever
30: veth7b4d46e7@if3: <BROADCAST,MULTICAST,UP,LOWER_UP> mtu 1450 qdisc
noqueue master ovs-system state UP group default
    link/ether 7e:82:7a:d2:9b:df brd ff:ff:ff:ff:ff:ff link-netnsid 0
    inet6 fe80::7c82:7aff:fed2:9bdf/64 scope link
       valid_lft forever preferred_lft forever
# ovs-vsctl show
3c752e9a-07c9-4b19-9789-a99004f2eaa3
    Bridge "br0"
        fail_mode: secure
        Port "br0"
            Interface "br0"
                type: internal
        Port "vxlan0"
            Interface "vxlan0"
                type: vxlan
                options: {key=flow, remote_ip=flow}
        Port "veth7b4d46e7"
            Interface "veth7b4d46e7"
        Port "tun0"
            Interface "tun0"
                type: internal
    ovs_version: "2.6.1"
```

In order to sum up the preceding code, the following diagram provides a visual representation of what the resulting overlay network looks like in our cluster:

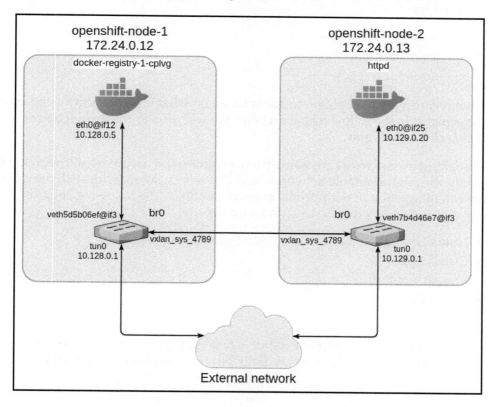

Figure 1 - Overlay network topology

Finally, let's clean up before the next section:

```
# oc delete project demo
project "demo" deleted
```

# SDN plugins

In the previous section, we learned what components the overlay network in OpenShift comprises. Now, it's time to see how it can be configured to suit the requirements of a particular environment.

OpenShift makes its internal SDN plugins available out-of-the-box, as well as plugins for integration with third-party SDN frameworks. The following are three built-in plugins that are available in OpenShift:

- `ovs-subnet`
- `ovs-multitenant`
- `ovs-networkpolicy`

The decision regarding which plugin to use is based on what level of security and control you aim to achieve. In the following subsections, we will discuss the main features and use cases for each of those plugins.

With SDNs taking over networking, third-party vendors have also started to develop their own solutions for programmable networks. Red Hat works closely with such providers to ensure smooth integration of their products into OpenShift. The following solutions have been tested and verified by Red Hat as production-ready:

- Nokia Nuage
- Cisco Contiv
- Juniper Contrail
- Tigera Calico
- VMWare NSX-T

Getting each of those to work with OpenShift is beyond the scope of this book, but you will find detailed instructions by following the links provided at the end of this chapter.

# ovs-subnet plugin

This is the default plugin that's enabled after OpenShift has just been installed. It provides connectivity for pods across the entire cluster with no limitations whatsoever, meaning that traffic can flow freely between all pods. This may be undesirable in large multi-tenant environments that place high importance on security. The SDN plugin being used is determined by the `networkConfig.networkPluginName` setting in the master configuration file:

```
# cat /etc/origin/master/master-config.yaml
...
<output omitted>
...
networkConfig:
  clusterNetworkCIDR: 10.128.0.0/14
  clusterNetworks:
```

```
  - cidr: 10.128.0.0/14
    hostSubnetLength: 9
  externalIPNetworkCIDRs:
  - 0.0.0.0/0
  hostSubnetLength: 9
  networkPluginName: redhat/openshift-ovs-subnet
...
<output omitted>
...
```

The SDN plugin can also be specified explicitly upon installation via the os_sdn_network_plugin_name Ansible variable. By default, it's redhat/openshift-ovs-subnet.

In order to see for yourself what exactly the ovs-subnet plugin does (or, rather, does not do), create two projects with one pod each and try to reach one of them from the other one.

1. First, create a demo-1 project:

   ```
   # oc new-project demo-1
   ...
   ```

2. Next, launch a pod by running the httpd web server using the same YAML definition, like we did in the *Tracing connectivity* subsection:

   ```
   # cat httpd-pod.yml
   apiVersion: v1
   kind: Pod
   metadata:
     name: httpd
     labels:
       role: web
   spec:
     containers:
     - name: httpd
       image: manageiq/httpd
       resources:
         requests:
           cpu: 400m
           memory: 128Mi

   # oc create -f httpd-pod.yml
   pod "httpd" created
   ```

3. Let's find out the IP address assigned to our pod:

```
# oc describe po/httpd | grep IP:
IP: 10.129.0.22
```

4. Move on to creating the second project:

```
# oc new-project demo-2
. . .
```

And create the same pod in that project:

```
# oc create -f httpd-pod.yml
pod "httpd" created
```

5. Now, let's see whether we can `ping` the first pod from the one we have just created:

```
# oc rsh httpd ping 10.129.0.22
PING 10.129.0.22 (10.129.0.22) 56(84) bytes of data.
64 bytes from 10.129.0.22: icmp_seq=1 ttl=64 time=0.345 ms
. . .
<output omitted>
. . .
```

Just to be sure, let's reverse our experiment and try to reach the pod in the demo-2 project from the one deployed in demo-1:

```
# oc project
Using project "demo-2" on server
"https://openshift-master.example.com:8443".
# oc describe po/httpd | grep IP:
IP: 10.129.0.23
# oc project demo-1
Now using project "demo-1" on server
"https://openshift-master.example.com:8443".
# oc rsh httpd ping 10.129.0.23
PING 10.129.0.23 (10.129.0.23) 56(84) bytes of data.
64 bytes from 10.129.0.23: icmp_seq=1 ttl=64 time=0.255 ms
. . .
<output omitted>
. . .
```

As you can see, communication between pods is completely uninhibited, which may be undesirable. In the two following subsections, we will demonstrate how to enforce project isolation using other OpenShift plugins.

# ovs-multitenant plugin

While it's usually not that big of a deal in PoC and sandboxes, security becomes a matter of utmost importance in large enterprises with diverse teams and project portfolios, even more so when the development of certain applications is outsourced to third-party companies. The `ovs-multitenant` plugin is a perfect choice if just having projects separated is enough. Unlike the `ovs-subnet` plugin, which passes all traffic across all pods, this one assigns the same VNID to all pods for each project, keeping them unique across projects, and sets up flow rules on the `br0` bridge to make sure that traffic is only allowed between pods with the same VNID.

There is, however, an exception to that rule—traffic is allowed to flow between the `default` project and each of the other ones. This is because that project is privileged and is assigned VNID, so that all pods in the cluster have access to the router and internal registry. Both of these are integral components of OpenShift.

In order to switch to the new plugin, we will have to perform a series of steps.

1. First, change `networkPluginName` in the master's configuration file:

```
# cat /etc/origin/master/master-config.yaml
...
<output omitted>
...
networkConfig:
  clusterNetworkCIDR: 10.128.0.0/14
  clusterNetworks:
  - cidr: 10.128.0.0/14
    hostSubnetLength: 9
  externalIPNetworkCIDRs:
  - 0.0.0.0/0
  hostSubnetLength: 9
  networkPluginName: redhat/openshift-ovs-multitenant
...
<output omitted>
...
```

Then, on all nodes:

```
# cat /etc/origin/node/node-config.yaml
...
<output omitted>
...
networkPluginName: redhat/openshift-ovs-multitenant
# networkConfig struct introduced in origin 1.0.6 and OSE 3.0.2
which
```

```
# deprecates networkPluginName above. The two should match.
networkConfig:
    mtu: 1450
    networkPluginName: redhat/openshift-ovs-multitenant
...
<output omitted>
...
```

2.  Next, restart the master API and controllers:

    ```
    # systemctl restart origin-master-{api,controllers}
    ```

3.  Stop the node processes on all nodes:

    ```
    # systemctl stop origin-node
    ```

4.  Restart the OpenVSwitch service on all nodes:

    ```
    # systemctl restart openvswitch
    ```

5.  Finally, start the node processes again:

    ```
    # systemctl start origin-node
    ```

 Note that when you restart a node process, pods on that node will get a new IP addresses.

Now, let's see if projects demo-1 and demo-2 are able to reach each other. First, let's get the new IP address of the httpd pod from the demo-1 project:

```
# oc describe po/httpd | grep IP:
IP:    10.129.0.25
```

Now, do the same for the demo-2 project:

```
# oc project demo-2
Now using project "demo-2" on server
"https://openshift-master.example.com:8443".
```

```
# oc describe po/httpd | grep IP:
IP:    10.129.0.24
```

Let's try and ping the pod in the demo-1 project from demo-2:

```
# oc rsh httpd ping 10.129.0.25
PING 10.129.0.25 (10.129.0.25) 56(84) bytes of data.
```

```
^C
--- 10.129.0.25 ping statistics ---
10 packets transmitted, 0 received, 100% packet loss, time 9057ms

command terminated with exit code 1
```

And vice versa:

```
# oc project demo-1
Now using project "demo-1" on server
"https://openshift-master.example.com:8443".
# oc rsh httpd ping 10.129.0.24

PING 10.129.0.24 (10.129.0.24) 56(84) bytes of data.

^C
--- 10.129.0.24 ping statistics ---
5 packets transmitted, 0 received, 100% packet loss, time 4012ms

command terminated with exit code 1
```

We have confirmed that the projects are indeed isolated. But what if in a real-world scenario there is an exception and you need some projects to be able to communicate with each other? An example would be a standard 3-tier application with a database, backend, and frontend residing in different projects for more granular control over resource allocation. For these kinds of use cases, the OpenShift CLI provides a command to `join` projects together, effectively enabling communication between them:

```
# oc adm pod-network join-projects --to=demo-1 demo-2
```

This command provides no output and can be used as a quick way to make exceptions in your security policy.

 It's worth noting that the same result can be achieved by swapping projects: `oc adm pod-network join-projects --to=demo-2 demo-1`.

Now, let's see if it worked. Try to `ping` our pod from the demo-1 project first and then from demo-2:

```
# oc rsh httpd ping 10.129.0.24
PING 10.129.0.24 (10.129.0.24) 56(84) bytes of data.
64 bytes from 10.129.0.24: icmp_seq=1 ttl=64 time=0.323 ms
...
<output omitted>
...
```

```
# oc project demo-2
Now using project "demo-2" on server
"https://openshift-master.example.com:8443".
# oc rsh httpd ping 10.129.0.25
PING 10.129.0.25 (10.129.0.25) 56(84) bytes of data.
64 bytes from 10.129.0.25: icmp_seq=1 ttl=64 time=0.287 ms
...
<output omitted>
...
```

Now that we have tested the plugin's functionality with ordinary projects, let's go ahead and confirm the default project's privileged status. Switch to default and find out the IP address of the registry pod:

```
# oc project default
Now using project "default" on server
"https://openshift-master.example.com:8443".
# oc get po
NAME                      READY   STATUS    RESTARTS  AGE
docker-registry-1-cplvg   1/1     Running   2         22h
router-1-52xrr            1/1     Running   1         22h
# oc describe po/docker-registry-1-cplvg | grep IP:
IP: 10.128.0.6
```

Next, switch back to demo-1 and try to reach the registry pod from there:

```
# oc project demo-1
Now using project "demo-1" on server
"https://openshift-master.example.com:8443".
# oc rsh httpd ping 10.128.0.6
PING 10.128.0.6 (10.128.0.6) 56(84) bytes of data.
64 bytes from 10.128.0.6: icmp_seq=1 ttl=64 time=1.94 ms
...
<output omitted>
...
```

Again, do the same for the demo-2 project:

```
# oc project demo-2
Now using project "demo-2" on server
"https://openshift-master.example.com:8443".
# oc rsh httpd ping 10.128.0.6
PING 10.128.0.6 (10.128.0.6) 56(84) bytes of data.
64 bytes from 10.128.0.6: icmp_seq=1 ttl=64 time=1.72 ms
...
<output omitted>
...
```

Joining projects together is not an irreversible operation—you can isolate a certain project from the rest of the environment just as easily:

```
# oc adm pod-network isolate-projects demo-1
```

The preceding command effectively blocks all traffic to and from all pods in the demo-1 project. Let's confirm that by trying to reach the pod in that project from demo-2, which is where we are right now:

```
# oc rsh httpd ping 10.129.0.25
PING 10.129.0.25 (10.129.0.25) 56(84) bytes of data.

^C
--- 10.129.0.25 ping statistics ---
3 packets transmitted, 0 received, 100% packet loss, time 2014ms

command terminated with exit code 1
```

Just like we did previously, let's do the same from demo-1:

```
# oc project demo-1
Now using project "demo-1" on server
"https://openshift-master.example.com:8443".
```

```
# oc rsh httpd ping 10.129.0.24
PING 10.129.0.24 (10.129.0.24) 56(84) bytes of data.
^C
--- 10.129.0.24 ping statistics ---
4 packets transmitted, 0 received, 100% packet loss, time 3009ms

command terminated with exit code 1
```

As you can see, the project was successfully isolated using just a single command.

Besides joining and isolating projects, OpenShift also provides another feature for managing pod networking—making a project global. This allows traffic to the project from all pods across all projects and vice versa—the same as with the default project. A potential use case for such a configuration is project hosting a messaging bus that's used by all other applications in the cluster.

Let's make the demo-2 project global:

```
# oc adm pod-network make-projects-global demo-2
```

Let's see if it worked:

```
# oc rsh httpd ping 10.129.0.24
PING 10.129.0.24 (10.129.0.24) 56(84) bytes of data.
64 bytes from 10.129.0.24: icmp_seq=1 ttl=64 time=0.276 ms
...
<output omitted>
...
```

Unlike before, where the demo-1 project was isolated, traffic is now allowed.

Now, let's move to the last SDN plugin, which is provided by OpenShift.

# ovs-networkpolicy plugin

While providing a simple to use and mostly adequate mechanism for managing access between projects, the ovs-multitenant plugin lacks the ability to control access at a more granular level. This is where the ovs-networkpolicy plugin steps in—it lets you create custom NetworkPolicy objects that, for example, can apply restrictions to ingress or egress traffic.

In order to migrate from the ovs-multitenant plugin to this one, we have to isolate ordinary projects from each other and allow traffic to and from global projects. Global projects are distinguished by having 0 as their NETID, as seen in the following output:

```
[root@openshift-master book]# oc get netnamespaces
NAME                NETID       EGRESS IPS
default             0           []
demo-1              9793016     []
demo-2              0           []
kube-public         10554334    []
kube-system         8648643     []
logging             11035285    []
management-infra    4781458     []
openshift           13291653    []
openshift-infra     12251614    []
openshift-node      38906       []
```

In our case, the only global projects are default and demo-2.

To spare you the manual effort, a helper script has already been written to create all of the necessary NetworkPolicy objects to allow traffic between pods in the same project and between each project and global ones. This script must be run prior to carrying out the usual steps for migrating from one OpenShift plugin to another.

First, we have to download the script and make it executable:

```
# curl -O
https://raw.githubusercontent.com/openshift/origin/master/contrib/migration
/migrate-network-policy.sh
# chmod +x migrate-network-policy.sh
```

Next, run it and observe what steps are being taken to ensure the presence of correct
network policies across projects:

```
# ./migrate-network-policy.sh

NAMESPACE: default
Namespace is global: adding label legacy-netid=0

NAMESPACE: demo-1
networkpolicy "default-deny" created
networkpolicy "allow-from-self" created
networkpolicy "allow-from-global-namespaces" created

NAMESPACE: demo-2
Namespace is global: adding label legacy-netid=0
...
<output omitted>
...
```

Notice the special treatment that global projects get: they were assigned
the pod.network.openshift.io/legacy-netid=0 label, which is used as a selector by
NetworkPolicy objects to enable access from such projects. To see this for yourself, export
the allow-from-global-namespaces network policy's definition:

```
# oc export networkpolicy/allow-from-global-namespaces
apiVersion: extensions/v1beta1
kind: NetworkPolicy
metadata:
  creationTimestamp: null
  generation: 1
  name: allow-from-global-namespaces
spec:
  ingress:
  - from:
    - namespaceSelector:
        matchLabels:
          pod.network.openshift.io/legacy-netid: "0"
  podSelector: {}
  policyTypes:
  - Ingress
```

Once this is done, the rest of the process is the same as in the previous subsection with the `networkPluginName` set to `redhat/openshift-ovs-networkpolicy`. Refer to the previous section for detailed instructions on how to enable an OpenShift plugin.

Now that this is out of the way, let's remind ourselves what project we are in:

```
# oc project
Using project "demo-1" on server
"https://openshift-master.example.com:8443".
```

Next, find out the new IP address of our Apache pod for future reference:

```
# oc describe po/httpd | grep IP:
IP: 10.129.0.26
```

Do the same for the `demo-2` project:

```
# oc project demo-2
...
# oc describe po/httpd | grep IP:
IP: 10.129.0.27
```

Now, try pinging the pod in `demo-1` from `demo-2`:

```
# oc rsh httpd ping 10.129.0.26
PING 10.129.0.26 (10.129.0.26) 56(84) bytes of data.
64 bytes from 10.129.0.26: icmp_seq=1 ttl=64 time=0.586 ms
...
<output omitted>
...
```

And vice versa, from `demo-1` to `demo-2`:

```
# oc project demo-1
Now using project "demo-1" on server
"https://openshift-master.example.com:8443".
# oc rsh httpd ping 10.129.0.27
PING 10.129.0.27 (10.129.0.27) 56(84) bytes of data.
64 bytes from 10.129.0.27: icmp_seq=1 ttl=64 time=0.346 ms
...
<output omitted>
...
```

Astute readers may recall that `demo-2` is actually a global project, meaning that both ingress and egress traffic is enabled between it and any other project, thanks to the `allow-from-global-namespaces` network policy.

Let's create another project called `demo-3` to host the same `httpd` pod and get the IP address of the pod:

```
# oc new-project demo-3
...

# oc create -f httpd-pod.yml
pod "httpd" created

# oc describe po/httpd | grep IP:
IP: 10.129.0.28
```

Try to reach the pod in the `demo-1` project:

```
# oc rsh httpd ping 10.129.0.26
PING 10.129.0.26 (10.129.0.26) 56(84) bytes of data.
^C
--- 10.129.0.26 ping statistics ---
10 packets transmitted, 0 received, 100% packet loss, time 9063ms

command terminated with exit code 1
```

This time, packets didn't come through because `demo-3` is just a regular project and as such it's subject to network policy restrictions. Let's change that by creating a network policy in the `demo-1` project that will allow traffic from `demo-3`, but before that, we will have to label the `demo-3` project so that the policy can refer to it using a selector:

```
# oc project demo-1
...

# oc label namespace demo-3 name=demo-3
namespace "demo-3" labeled

# cat networkpolicy-demo-3.yml
kind: NetworkPolicy
apiVersion: extensions/v1beta1
metadata:
  name: networkpolicy-demo-3
spec:
  podSelector:
  ingress:
  - from:
    - namespaceSelector:
```

```
        matchLabels:
          name: demo-3
```

```
# oc create -f networkpolicy-demo-3.yml
networkpolicy "networkpolicy-demo-3" created
```

 Notice that `ingress` is on the same level of indentation as `podSelector`—this is not a typo, but an omitted pod selector, because in our example we match namespaces instead of pods.

Let's try accessing `demo-1` again:

```
# oc project demo-3
Now using project "demo-3" on server
"https://openshift-master.example.com:8443".
# oc rsh httpd ping 10.129.0.26
PING 10.129.0.26 (10.129.0.26) 56(84) bytes of data.
64 bytes from 10.129.0.26: icmp_seq=1 ttl=64 time=0.546 ms
...
<output omitted>
...
```

As you can see, the network policy is now in effect.

OpenShift can also be configured to create a default network policy for every project when it's being instantiated. The OpenShift CLI provides a command for bootstrapping a project template:

```
# oc adm create-bootstrap-project-template -o yaml > demo-project-
request.yml
```

Modify the template so that it contains a network policy that blocks all ingress traffic—this is the easiest way to see if it's working or not:

```
# cat demo-project-request.yml
apiVersion: v1
kind: Template
metadata:
  creationTimestamp: null
  name: demo-project-request
objects:
...
<output omitted>
...
- apiVersion: extensions/v1beta1
  kind: NetworkPolicy
```

```
metadata:
  name: default-deny
spec:
  ingress:
...
<output omitted>
...
```

Create the template from its YAML definition:

```
# oc create -f demo-project-request.yml
template "demo-project-request" created
```

 The template was created in the demo-3 project because it's not technically important, but it's recommended to store it in one of the pre-existing projects, such as default or openshift-infra.

To configure OpenShift to pick up the new template, make the following edit to the master's configuration file:

```
# cat /etc/origin/master/master-config.yaml
projectConfig:
  defaultNodeSelector: node-role.kubernetes.io/compute=true
  projectRequestMessage: ''
  projectRequestTemplate: demo-3/demo-project-request
```

Lastly, restart the master API service to activate the changes:

```
# systemctl restart origin-master-api
```

Let's create a new-project and see if the network policy was created:

```
# oc new-project demo-4
...

# oc get networkpolicy
NAME POD-SELECTOR AGE
default-deny <none> 7s
```

Now that the project has been successfully instantiated with the security policy we configured, let's see if the policy itself works. Like we did previously, we will create a pod by running Apache web server and getting its IP address:

```
# cat httpd-pod.yml
apiVersion: v1
kind: Pod
metadata:
  name: httpd
  labels:
    role: web
spec:
  containers:
  - name: httpd
    image: manageiq/httpd
    resources:
      requests:
        cpu: 400m
        memory: 128Mi

# oc create -f httpd-pod.yml
pod "httpd" created

# oc describe po/httpd | grep IP:
IP: 10.129.0.29
```

Next, we will switch the project to demo-3 and see if we can reach our pod from there:

```
# oc project demo-3
Now using project "demo-3" on server
"https://openshift-master.example.com:8443".
# oc rsh httpd ping 10.129.0.29
PING 10.129.0.29 (10.129.0.29) 56(84) bytes of data.
^C
--- 10.129.0.29 ping statistics ---
5 packets transmitted, 0 received, 100% packet loss, time 4019ms

command terminated with exit code 1
```

As expected, all incoming traffic is blocked.

On this note, we conclude the section on OpenShift SDN plugins.

# Egress routers

As you have learned previously, routers in OpenShift direct ingress traffic from external clients to services that, in turn, forward it to pods. OpenShift also offers a reverse type of router intended for forwarding egress traffic from pods to a certain destination in the external network. But unlike ingress routers implemented via HAProxy, egress ones are built on Squid. Egress routers are potentially useful for cases such as:

- Masking different external resources being used by several applications with a single global resource. For example, applications may be developed in such a way that they are built pulling dependencies from different mirrors, and collaboration between their development teams is rather loose. So, instead of getting them to use the same mirror, an operations team can just set up an egress router to intercept all traffic directed to those mirrors and redirect it to the same site.
- To redirect all suspicious requests for specific sites to the audit system for further analysis.

OpenShift supports the following types of egress router:

- *redirect* for redirecting traffic to a certain destination IP
- *http-proxy* for proxying HTTP, HTTPS, and DNS traffic

 Due to limitations regarding `macvlan` interfaces in VirtualBox, an egress router cannot be set up in our virtual lab, nor in AWS. The best platform to use it on is bare-metal.

# Static IPs for external project traffic

The OpenShift scheduler takes all decisions regarding the placement of pods on nodes, taking into account factors such as the even distribution of pods, node affinity, and available resources. The whole point of default scheduling in OpenShift is to use of available resources as efficiently as possible, but it doesn't take into account the project pods that are created in them. The reason for this is that developers shouldn't be concerned with the placement of an applications' pods across the cluster, and that's why they have absolutely no control over where their pods end up. The problem starts to manifest itself in large organizations with multiple applications subject to different policies regarding security and compliance.

For example, an application handling bank account details must be subject to thorough audit, while its development version must have no access to production databases. Since the concept of projects is unknown to the scheduler, pods with different applications may end up on the same node, generating traffic with the same source IP address (the node's IP address), making it impossible to distinguish them from each other on the corporate firewall and to apply the appropriate policies. Technically, one can create a custom scheduling policy which will `pin` pods with specific labels to a specific node or set of nodes, which will provide a consistent pool of source addresses to be permitted through the firewall. However, over time, it will seriously skew the pods' distribution across the cluster, leading to inefficient use of resources and mix operations and the development teams' areas of control, which defeats the purpose of scheduling.

OpenShift provides a solution for exactly this kind of problem—you can assign an externally routable IP address to a particular project and whitelist it on the corporate firewall, at the same time leaving scheduling completely transparent to developers.

 As with egress routers, the virtual environment of VirtualBox places limitations on the possibility of demonstrating this feature.

# Egress network policies

While the idea behind network policies is to control access between pods across projects, egress network policies allow you to restrict access from all pods in a project to certain *external* resources. A typical use case for this feature would be denying pods access to source code from hosting providers and content mirrors to prevent any updates of applications and/or system libraries in those pods. It's important to understand that, unlike egress routers, egress network policies don't perform any redirection of traffic, working on just an *Allow versus Deny* basis instead.

Let's see what level of access pods our demo-1 project has:

```
# oc project demo-1
. . .
# oc rsh httpd ping github.com
PING github.com (192.30.255.113) 56(84) bytes of data.
64 bytes from lb-192-30-255-113-sea.github.com (192.30.255.113): icmp_seq=1
ttl=61 time=61.8 ms
. . .
<output omitted>
. . .
```

```
# oc rsh httpd ping google.com
PING google.com (172.217.14.78) 56(84) bytes of data.
64 bytes from lax17s38-in-f14.1e100.net (172.217.14.78): icmp_seq=1 ttl=61
time=132 ms
...
<output omitted>
...
```

Currently, there are no egress network policies being enforced in the project, so access to external resources is completely unrestricted.

Now, create a custom egress network policy from the YAML definition, which is going to block all traffic to GitHub and permit traffic to all other external resources:

```
# cat demo-egress-policy.yml
kind: EgressNetworkPolicy
apiVersion: v1
metadata:
  name: demo-egress-policy
spec:
  egress:
  - type: Deny
    to:
      dnsName: github.com

# oc create -f demo-egress-policy.yml
egressnetworkpolicy "demo-egress-policy" created
```

Let's try accessing the same resources as in the beginning of this section:

```
# oc rsh httpd ping github.com
PING github.com (192.30.255.113) 56(84) bytes of data.
^C
--- github.com ping statistics ---
20 packets transmitted, 0 received, 100% packet loss, time 19090ms

command terminated with exit code 1
# oc rsh httpd ping google.com
PING google.com (172.217.14.78) 56(84) bytes of data.
64 bytes from lax17s38-in-f14.1e100.net (172.217.14.78): icmp_seq=1 ttl=61
time=35.9 ms
...
<output omitted>
...
```

As you can see, GitHub is now inaccessible, which is exactly what we expected.

In this example, we implemented a *deny all but* type of security policy, but we can also implement a reverse type, granting access to single resources, blocking everything else. Continuing our example with GitHub and Google, edit the policy's specification to resemble the following:

```
# oc edit egressnetworkpolicy/demo-egress-policy
...
<output omitted>
...
spec:
  egress:
  - to:
      dnsName: github.com
    type: Allow
  - to:
      cidrSelector: 0.0.0.0/0
    type: Deny
```

The preceding configuration directs the policy to block traffic to all external resources, except for GitHub and dnsmasq on the node.

Let's test this out:

```
# oc rsh httpd-egress ping github.com
PING github.com (192.30.253.112) 56(84) bytes of data.
64 bytes from lb-192-30-253-112-iad.github.com (192.30.253.112): icmp_seq=1
ttl=61 time=68.4 ms
...
<output omitted>
...
# oc rsh httpd-egress ping google.com
PING google.com (209.85.201.138) 56(84) bytes of data.
^C
--- google.com ping statistics ---
18 packets transmitted, 0 received, 100% packet loss, time 17055ms

command terminated with exit code 1
```

Again, the policy works as expected.

Note that egress rules are evaluated in the order in which they are specified and the first matching rule wins, meaning that, if we had placed the Deny rule first, traffic to GitHub would have been blocked as well, even though it's explicitly permitted in one of the subsequent rules.

# DNS

One of the mechanisms for linking pods together, which has been discussed earlier in this book, relies on environment variables—the same as you would achieve by using plain Docker. When you deploy a multi-container application on OpenShift, pods that provide certain environment variables for pods that consume them must be started first, so that the variables are configured correctly by OpenShift. For example, if you deploy a 3-tier application consisting of a database, backend, and frontend, you will have to deploy the database first so that the backend pod picks up environment variables with the correct address and port for the database.

Pods can access each other's services directly via their IPs, but in a highly dynamic environment, where services may often be re-created, there is a need for a more stable solution. Aside from using environment variables, OpenShift provides its internal DNS, implemented via SkyDNS and dnsmasq for service discovery. This approach doesn't limit your deployment to a certain order and spares you the need to implement additional logic in your deployment strategy. Using OpenShift DNS, all applications can discover each other across the entire cluster via consistent names, which makes it possible for developers to rely on them when migrating to OpenShift. The only thing they need to do is agree with Operations on the names of the services.

DNS in OpenShift gives pods the ability to discover the following resources in OpenShift:

| Name | Domain |
|------|--------|
| Services | `<service>.<project>.svc.cluster.local` |
| Endpoints | `<service>.<project>.endpoints.cluster.local` |

In the following exercise, we will see how two applications that are deployed in different projects can reach each other.

1. First, let's create a project called `demo-1`:

   ```
   # oc new-project demo-1
   ...
   ```

2. Next, create a pod running Apache web server. We will be using the same YAML configuration as before:

   ```
   # oc create -f httpd-pod.yml
   pod "httpd" created
   ```

In order to simulate the way *real* applications interact with each other, we will have to create a service to serve as a sole ingress point for our pod:

```
# oc expose po/httpd --port 80
service "httpd" exposed
```

Now that the first project is ready, let's create another one:

```
# oc new-project demo-2
...
```

Like we did previously, create a pod from the same YAML definition as before:

```
# oc create -f httpd-pod.yml
pod "httpd" created
```

And create a service by exposing the pod:

```
# oc expose po/httpd --port 80
service "httpd" exposed
```

Now, let's open a bash session into the newly created pod and try to reach the pod from the demo-1 project:

```
# oc exec httpd -it bash
bash-4.2$ dig httpd.demo-1.svc.cluster.local
...
<output omitted>
...
;; ANSWER SECTION:
httpd.demo-1.svc.cluster.local. 30 IN A 172.30.35.41
...
<output omitted>
...
```

For the sake of completeness, let's switch the project to demo-1 and try the same from the first pod:

```
# oc project demo-1
Now using project "demo-1" on server
"https://openshift-master.example.com:8443".
# oc exec httpd -it bash
bash-4.2$ dig httpd.demo-2.svc.cluster.local
...
<output omitted>
...
;; ANSWER SECTION:
httpd.demo-2.svc.cluster.local. 30 IN A 172.30.81.86
```

```
...
<output omitted>
...
```

It's even possible to get all endpoints of a particular service, although it's recommended to use services as points of contact:

```
$ dig httpd.demo-2.endpoints.cluster.local
...
<output omitted>
...
;; ANSWER SECTION:
httpd.demo-2.endpoints.cluster.local. 30 IN A 10.129.0.7
...
<output omitted>
...
```

 OpenShift injects cluster-level subdomains into the local resolver's configuration at /etc/resolv.conf, so if you take a look in that file, you will find the line search <project>.svc.cluster.local svc.cluster.local cluster.local. Therefore, FQDNs don't have to be specified in order to reach resources across a project's boundaries and in the same project. For example, you can use httpd.demo-1 to call a service named httpd in the demo-1 project, or just httpd if it's in the same project.

As you can see, both pods can reach each other via their services, which makes it possible not to rely on environment variables. So, in order to migrate their applications to OpenShift, developers will have to configure environment variables of their applications to point to the DNS names of dependent services.

At the beginning of this chapter, we provided diagrams detailing the DNS architecture and DNS request flow in OpenShift. Now, let's see what it looks like on a live cluster.

Run the following command on the master to see what processes are listening on TCP and UDP ports ending with 53 (DNS):

```
# ss -tulpn | grep '53 '
udp UNCONN 0 0 *:8053 *:* users:(("openshift",pid=1492,fd=10))
tcp LISTEN 0 128 *:8053 *:* users:(("openshift",pid=1492,fd=13))
```

The process launched from the openshift binary is no other than the OpenShift Master API, as SkyDNS is embedded into it and uses etcd as a source of authority to keep track of new services and to delete records for deleted ones:

```
# ps auxf | grep openshift
```

```
. . .
root        1492   7.3 10.3 1040996 402668 ?        Ssl  00:41   17:51
/usr/bin/openshift start master api --config=/etc/origin/master/master-
config.yaml --loglevel=2 --listen=https://0.0.0.0:8443 --
master=https://openshift-master.example.com:8443
. . .
```

Now, let's take a look at listening ports on our first node—the setup is completely the same for all nodes in a cluster:

```
# ss -tulpn | grep '53 '
udp UNCONN 0 0 172.24.0.12:53 *:* users:(("dnsmasq",pid=1202,fd=4))
udp UNCONN 0 0 127.0.0.1:53 *:* users:(("openshift",pid=2402,fd=26))
udp UNCONN 0 0 10.128.0.1:53 *:* users:(("dnsmasq",pid=1202,fd=15))
udp UNCONN 0 0 172.17.0.1:53 *:* users:(("dnsmasq",pid=1202,fd=19))
udp UNCONN 0 0 10.0.2.15:53 *:* users:(("dnsmasq",pid=1202,fd=6))
. . .
tcp LISTEN 0 5 172.24.0.12:53 *:* users:(("dnsmasq",pid=1202,fd=5))
tcp LISTEN 0 128 127.0.0.1:53 *:* users:(("openshift",pid=2402,fd=31))
tcp LISTEN 0 5 10.128.0.1:53 *:* users:(("dnsmasq",pid=1202,fd=16))
tcp LISTEN 0 5 172.17.0.1:53 *:* users:(("dnsmasq",pid=1202,fd=20))
tcp LISTEN 0 5 10.0.2.15:53 *:* users:(("dnsmasq",pid=1202,fd=7))
. . .
```

From the preceding output, we can see that SkyDNS is still present on nodes, but there's also `dnsmasq`. The latter actually forwards DNS requests into the `cluster.local` and `in-addr.arpa` zones, while redirecting all others to an upstream DNS server—in our case, its DNS is provided by VirtualBox itself.

Let's take a look at OpenShift processes running on nodes:

```
# ps auxf | grep openshift
. . .
root        2402   9.0  5.4 1067700 102980 ?        Ssl  00:42   22:39
/usr/bin/openshift start node --config=/etc/origin/node/node-config.yaml --
loglevel=2
```

Notice that this is the same OpenShift process as listed in the output of the `ss` command. As with the Master API, SkyDNS is embedded into the Node process as well to serve DNS requests for services of applications that are deployed on OpenShift.

The information we've learned can be represented by the following diagram:

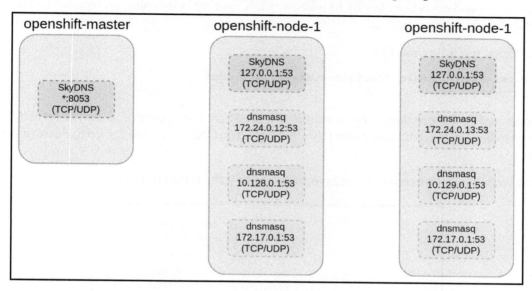

Figure 2 - The DNS architecture in OpenShift

Lastly, let's figure out the actual path DNS queries take before reaching their destinations. For that, we will take a look into various resolver and dnsmasq configuration files.

Our first stop is the configuration of the local DNS resolver for the httpd pod in the demo-2 project:

```
# oc exec httpd -it bash
bash-4.2$ cat /etc/resolv.conf
nameserver 10.0.2.15
search demo-1.svc.cluster.local svc.cluster.local cluster.local example.com
options ndots:5
```

According to the preceding configuration, DNS queries for domains specified in the search directive are to be resolved by the DNS server available at 10.0.2.15, which is the IP of one of the network interfaces dnsmasq is listening to on the node.

Now, let's take a look into the file specifying the DNS forwarding policy for internal zones:

```
# cat /etc/dnsmasq.d/node-dnsmasq.conf
server=/in-addr.arpa/127.0.0.1
server=/cluster.local/127.0.0.1
```

The preceding configuration directs dnsmasq to forward all DNS queries for domains in-addr.arpa and cluster.local to whatever DNS server is listening on localhost, which is SkyDNS.

Next, open the following file:

```
# cat /etc/dnsmasq.d/origin-upstream-dns.conf
server=10.0.2.2
```

As opposed to the previous configuration, this directive configures dnsmasq to forward all other DNS queries to the upstream DNS, which is the DNS provided by VirtualBox in our case.

What we have just discovered can be represented by the following diagram:

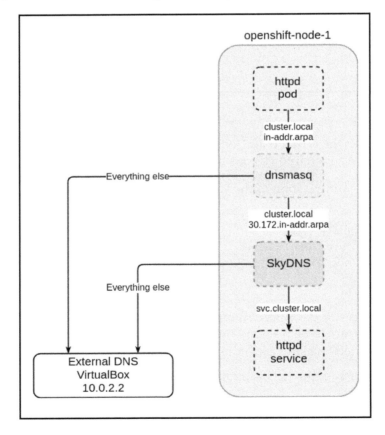

Figure 3 - DNS query flow in OpenShift

This concludes our exploration of OpenShift DNS.

# Summary

In this chapter, you learned about the importance of SDN and the role it plays in OpenShift, the composed network topology diagram for an existing OpenShift cluster, gained knowledge on various OpenShift and third-party plugins, and saw for yourself what features they provide. You also learned about use cases of both egress routers and static IPs for external project traffic, and also created your own egress network policy to restrict access to an external resource.

In the next chapter, we will be working on the deployment of a simple application.

# Questions

1. Which interface of OVS bridge is used to pass traffic from pods running on a particular node to and from pods running on other nodes?
    1. tun0
    2. br0
    3. veth...
    4. vxlan_sys_4789
2. Suppose we have a multi-tenant environment with many applications developed by independent teams and outsource contractors that must be able to collaborate in rare cases, but for the most part must be totally isolated from each other. What is the simplest course of action to achieve that?
    1. Use the ovs-networkpolicy plugin and write custom network policies to enable omni-directional traffic between the projects used by those parties
    2. Use the ovs-subnet plugin
    3. Use the ovs-multitenant plugin and join and isolate projects as needed
    4. Use the plugin for a third-party solution, such as VMWare NSX-T or Tigera Calico

3. What feature is best suited for whitelisting traffic coming from all pods in a specific project?
    1. Egress router in proxy mode
    2. Egress router in redirect mode
    3. Static IP for external traffic from the project
    4. Custom scheduling policy
    5. Custom iptables rules in the OPENSHIFT-ADMIN-OUTPUT-RULES chain of the `filter` table

4. Which of the following is the correct specification of the egress network policy that allows access to `rubygems.org` and `launchpad.net` only, assuming that this is the only egress network policy in the project?

    1.  ```
        - type: Deny
          to:
              cidrSelector: 0.0.0.0/0
        - type: Allow
          to:
             dnsName: rubygems.org
        - type: Allow
          to:
             dnsName: launchpad.net
        ```
    2.  ```
        - type: Allow
          to:
             dnsName: rubygems.org
        - type: Allow
          to:
             dnsName: launchpad.net
        ```
    3.  ```
        - type: Allow
          to:
             dnsName: rubygems.org
        - type: Allow
          to:
             dnsName: launchpad.net
        - type: Deny
          to:
             cidrSelector: 0.0.0.0/0
        ```
    4.  ```
        - type: Allow
          to:
             dnsNames:
        ```
    5.  ```
             - launchpad.net
          - rubygems.org
        ```
        ```

```
- type: Deny
  to:
    cidrSelector: 0.0.0.0/0
```

5. What is the correct DNS name for the service named web in the dev project?
    1. web.dev.cluster.local
    2. web.cluster.local
    3. web.dev.svc.cluster.local
    4. web.dev.endpoints.cluster.local

# Further reading

Please look at the following links for further reading relating to this chapter:

- **OpenShift DNS overview**: https://docs.openshift.org/latest/architecture/networking/networking.html
- **High-level overview of SDN plugins and network topology in OpenShift**: https://docs.openshift.org/latest/architecture/networking/sdn.html
- **A few examples of third-party SDN plugins**: https://docs.openshift.org/latest/architecture/networking/network_plugins.html
- **Optimizing network performance for OpenShift**: https://docs.openshift.org/latest/scaling_performance/network_optimization.html
- **Configuring the SDN in OpenShift and migrating between SDN plugins**: https://docs.openshift.org/latest/install_config/configuring_sdn.html
- **NSX-T Container Plug-in for OpenShift, Installation and Administration Guide**: https://docs.vmware.com/en/VMware-NSX-T/2.1/nsxt_21_ncp_openshift.pdf
- **Installing Red Hat OpenShift Container Platform with Contrail Networking**: https://www.jnpr.net/documentation/en_US/contrail4.0/topics/task/installation/install-redhat-openshift.html
- **Using Contiv with OpenShift**: http://contiv.github.io/documents/openshift/index.html
- **Installing Calico on OpenShift**: https://docs.projectcalico.org/v2.4/getting-started/openshift/installation

- **Configuring Nuage SDN**: `https://docs.openshift.com/container-platform/ 3.9/install_config/configuring_nuagesdn.html`
- **Managing networking in OpenShift via CLI**: `https://docs.openshift.org/latest/admin_guide/managing_networking .html`
- **Red Hat OpenShift Container Platform DNS deep dive**: `https://www.redhat.com/en/blog/red-hat-openshift-container-platf orm-dns-deep-dive-dns-changes-red-hat-openshift-container-platform-36`

# 12
# Deploying Simple Applications in OpenShift

Application deployment is the most important and frequently used feature of OpenShift, as that's what it was built for. All OpenShift users deal with application deployment from Docker images. If there is a well-known application and its image is already available on Docker Hub or any other registries, OpenShift users can deploy it in a simple and reproducible way. In this chapter, we will be working on the deployment of several simple applications from existing Docker images.

After completing this chapter, you will have learned about the following:

- Manual application deployment images, including manual Pod and Service object creation from a YAML file
- How to make use of the `oc new-app` utility to deploy applications from existing Docker images
- Exposing applications via routes

## Technical requirements

This chapter doesn't have strict environmental restrictions; any OpenShift installations and development environments are supported: MinitShift, `oc cluster up`, or standard production-ready deployment based on Ansible. It is up to you which flavor you use. However, this chapter is based on the `oc cluster up` running within vagrant. The following `Vagrantfile` can be used to deploy the lab:

```
$ cat Vagrantfile
Vagrant.configure(2) do |config|
  config.vm.define "openshift" do |conf|
    conf.vm.box = "centos/7"
    conf.vm.network "private_network", ip: "172.24.0.11"
```

```
        conf.vm.hostname = 'openshift.example.com'
        conf.vm.network "forwarded_port", guest: 80, host: 980
        conf.vm.network "forwarded_port", guest: 443, host: 9443
        conf.vm.network "forwarded_port", guest: 8080, host: 8080
        conf.vm.network "forwarded_port", guest: 8443, host: 8443
        conf.vm.provider "virtualbox" do |v|
          v.memory = 4096
          v.cpus = 2
        end
        conf.vm.provision "shell", inline: $lab_main
      end
    end
    $lab_main = <<SCRIPT
    cat <<EOF >> /etc/hosts
    172.24.0.11 openshift.example.com openshift
    172.24.0.12 storage.example.com storage nfs
    EOF
    systemctl disable firewalld
    systemctl stop firewalld
    yum update -y
    yum install -y epel-release
    yum install -y docker
    cat << EOF >/etc/docker/daemon.json
    {
        "insecure-registries": [
          "172.30.0.0/16"
        ]
    }
    EOF
    systemctl restart docker
    systemctl enable docker
    yum -y install centos-release-openshift-origin39
    yum -y install origin-clients
    oc cluster up
    SCRIPT
```

The environment can be deployed as follows:

```
$ vagrant up
```

Once the previously listed vagrant machine is deployed, you may connect to it as follows:

```
$ vagrant ssh
```

Finally, log in as a `developer` user in order to be able to run most commands:

```
$ oc login -u developer
Server [https://localhost:8443]:
The server uses a certificate signed by an unknown authority.
You can bypass the certificate check, but any data you send to the server
could be intercepted by others.
Use insecure connections? (y/n): y

Authentication required for https://localhost:8443 (openshift)
Username: developer
Password: <ANY PASSWORD>
Login successful.

You have one project on this server: "myproject"

Using project "myproject".
Welcome! See 'oc help' to get started.
```

 We can use any password

# Manual application deployment

Among other methods, OpenShift allows for deploying applications directly from existing Docker images. Imagine that your development team has an in-house process of building Docker images from their applications—this way, you can deploy applications in an OpenShift environment by using these images without any modification, which greatly simplifies migration to OpenShift. It takes several steps to create all required OpenShift entities.

First, you have to create a pod, which runs a container deployed from the application's Docker image. Once the pod is up and running, you may need to create a service to have a persistent IP address and internal DNS record associated with it. The service allows your application to be accessible via a consistent **address:port** pair internally inside OpenShift. This may be enough for internal applications that don't require external accesses, like databases or key/value storage.

If your application has to be available from the outside, you need to `expose` it to make it available from an external network, like the internet. This process can be achieved by creating an OpenShift route.

In short, the process looks like this:

1. Create a pod
2. Create a service by exposing the pod
3. Create a route by exposing the service

In this chapter, we will be working with a simple httpd Docker container to demonstrate the application deployment process. We have chosen httpd because it is simple enough and it still allows us to focus on the main goal—the demonstration of OpenShift-related tasks.

# Creating a pod

The `httpd` Docker image is available on Docker Hub. You may want to confirm this by running the following command:

```
$ sudo docker search httpd
INDEX NAME DESCRIPTION STARS OFFICIAL AUTOMATED
docker.io docker.io/httpd The Apache HTTP Server Project 1719 [OK]
<OMITTED>
```

According to the image documentation (https://docs.docker.com/samples/library/httpd/), it listens on TCP port 80. We cannot simply use this container, because it binds to a privileged port. The default security policy in OpenShift doesn't allow applications to bind on ports below 1024. To avoid problems, OpenShift comes with an image stream named `httpd` which points to an OpenShift-ready `httpd` image build. For example, in our version of OpenShift, the `httpd` image stream points to the `docker.io/centos/httpd-24-centos7` Docker container. You may want to verify that by running the following command:

```
$ oc get is -n openshift | egrep "^NAME | ^httpd"
NAME DOCKER REPO TAGS UPDATED
httpd 172.30.1.1:5000/openshift/httpd latest,2.4 3 hours ago


$ oc describe is httpd -n openshift | grep "tagged from"
  tagged from centos/httpd-24-centos7:latest
```

Each time we want to deploy a pod using an `httpd` image, we need to use `centos/httpd-24-centos7` instead.

Let's create a separate project for the lab as follows:

```
$ oc new-project simpleappication
Now using project "simpleappication" on server "https://localhost:8443".
<OMITTED>
```

The simple `httpd` pod can be deployed manually from its definition:

```
$ cat <<EOF > pod_httpd.yml
apiVersion: v1
kind: Pod
metadata:
  name: httpd
  labels:
    name: httpd
spec:
  containers:
    - name: httpd
      image: centos/httpd-24-centos7
      ports:
        - name: web
          containerPort: 8080
EOF
```

 `centos/httpd-24-centos7` binds on port `8080`, which allows for running the container inside OpenShift without tuning its default security policy.

Once the file is created, we can create a pod by running `oc create`:

```
$ oc create -f pod_httpd.yml
pod "httpd" created
```

OpenShift needs some time to download the Docker image and deploy the pod. Once everything is finished, you should be able to have the `httpd` pod in the `Running` state:

```
$ oc get pod
NAME READY STATUS RESTARTS AGE
httpd 1/1 Running 0 2m
```

This pod provides the same functionality as a more complex application would (default `httpd` webpage). We may want to verify that, as shown as follows.

First, get the pod's internal IP address:

```
$ oc describe pod httpd | grep IP:
IP: 172.17.0.2
```

And then use curl to query the IP from the output above:

```
$ curl -s http://172.17.0.2:8080 | head -n 4
<!DOCTYPE html PUBLIC "-//W3C//DTD XHTML 1.1//EN"
"http://www.w3.org/TR/xhtml11/DTD/xhtml11.dtd">
<html xmlns="http://www.w3.org/1999/xhtml" xml:lang="en">
 <head>
```

 Note: This is the beginning of the default Apache welcome page. You may want to replace it for the production installation. This can be achieved by mounting a persistent volume at /var/www/html. For demo purposes, this output indicates that the application itself works and is accessible.

# Creating a service

The service may be created in two different ways:

- Using oc expose
- From the YAML/JSON definition

We will describe both methods. You don't have to use both.

## Creating a service using oc expose

You can create a pod using oc expose in the following way:

```
$ oc get pod
NAME READY STATUS RESTARTS AGE
httpd 1/1 Running 0 13m

$ oc expose pod httpd --name httpd
service "httpd" exposed

$ oc get svc
NAME CLUSTER-IP EXTERNAL-IP PORT(S) AGE
httpd 172.30.128.131 <none> 8080/TCP 3s
```

The preceding command creates a service by exposing the pod, using name=httpd as a selector. You may define a custom service name via the --name option.

The same httpd application will be available from the service IP address, which is 172.30.128.131 in our case, but your output from the previous command most likely will be different:

```
$ curl -s http://172.30.128.131:8080 | head -n4
<!DOCTYPE html PUBLIC "-//W3C//DTD XHTML 1.1//EN"
"http://www.w3.org/TR/xhtml11/DTD/xhtml11.dtd">

<html xmlns="http://www.w3.org/1999/xhtml" xml:lang="en">
  <head>
```

Let's delete the service to recreate it using another method, as shown in the following subsection:

```
$ oc delete svc/httpd
service "httpd" deleted
```

# Creating a service from a YAML definition

The following YAML file allows you to define a `Service` OpenShift object:

```
$ cat <<EOF > svc-httpd.yml
apiVersion: v1
kind: Service
metadata:
  labels:
    name: httpd
  name: httpd
spec:
  ports:
  - port: 8080
    protocol: TCP
    targetPort: 8080
  selector:
    name: httpd
EOF
```

Once the file is in place, you can create the service by running the following command:

```
$ oc create -f svc-httpd.yml
service "httpd" created

$ oc get svc
NAME CLUSTER-IP EXTERNAL-IP PORT(S) AGE
httpd 172.30.112.133 <none> 8080/TCP 2s
```

The service shows the same output as previously described:

```
$ curl -s http://172.30.112.133:8080 | head -n 4
<!DOCTYPE html PUBLIC "-//W3C//DTD XHTML 1.1//EN"
"http://www.w3.org/TR/xhtml11/DTD/xhtml11.dtd">

<html xmlns="http://www.w3.org/1999/xhtml" xml:lang="en">
  <head>
```

# Creating a route

The service allows an application to be accessible internally via a consistent address:port pair. To be able to access it from outside of the cluster, we need to make sure that an OpenShift Route is created. Once the route is created, OpenShift will expose the service to the outside world using the cluster's router, implemented via an HAProxy Docker container by default.

Like services, routes can be created in two ways:

- Using oc expose
- From the YAML/JSON definition

This section shows both methods, but it is enough to use only one.

We assume that previously, you created a service named httpd.

## Creating a route by using oc expose

You can create a route using oc expose in the following way:

```
$ oc expose svc httpd
route "httpd" exposed

$ oc get route
NAME HOST/PORT PATH SERVICES PORT TERMINATION WILDCARD
httpd httpd-simpleappication.127.0.0.1.nip.io httpd 8080 None

$ curl -s http://httpd-simpleappication.127.0.0.1.nip.io | head -n 4
<!DOCTYPE html PUBLIC "-//W3C//DTD XHTML 1.1//EN"
"http://www.w3.org/TR/xhtml11/DTD/xhtml11.dtd">
```

```
<html xmlns="http://www.w3.org/1999/xhtml" xml:lang="en">
   <head>
```

```
$ oc delete route httpd
route "httpd" deleted
```

 The `127.0.0.1.nip.io` DNS zone is used by default by the `oc cluster up` method.

You may want to create a route with an alternate URL, using the `--hostname` option:

```
$ oc expose svc httpd --name httpd1 --hostname httpd.example.com
route "httpd1" exposed
```

```
$ oc get route
NAME HOST/PORT PATH SERVICES PORT TERMINATION WILDCARD
httpd httpd-simpleappication.127.0.0.1.nip.io httpd 8080 None
httpd1 httpd.example.com httpd 8080 None
```

```
$ sudo bash -c  'echo "127.0.0.1 httpd.example.com" >>/etc/hosts'
```

```
$ curl -s http://httpd.example.com | head -n 4
<!DOCTYPE html PUBLIC "-//W3C//DTD XHTML 1.1//EN"
"http://www.w3.org/TR/xhtml11/DTD/xhtml11.dtd">
```

```
<html xmlns="http://www.w3.org/1999/xhtml" xml:lang="en">
   <head>
```

OpenShift allows for creating multiple routes per single application.

 If you are using an alternate name, make sure that the DNS record points to the IP of the OpenShift node that hosts the router pod.

Once the route is created, you may access your application using this external route.

# Creating a route from a YAML definition

Let's create an alternate route for our application named `httpd2`. The route will have the `myhttpd.example.com` URL:

```
$ cat <<EOF > route-httpd2.yml
apiVersion: v1
```

```
kind: Route
metadata:
 labels:
 name: httpd2
 name: httpd2
spec:
 host: myhttpd.example.com
 port:
 targetPort: 8080
 to:
 kind: Service
 name: httpd
 weight: 100
EOF
```

The route may be created by `oc create`:

```
$ oc create -f route-httpd2.yml
route "httpd2" created
$ oc get route
NAME HOST/PORT PATH SERVICES PORT TERMINATION WILDCARD
httpd httpd-simpleappication.127.0.0.1.nip.io httpd 8080 None
httpd1 httpd.example.com httpd 8080 None
httpd2 myhttpd.example.com httpd 8080 None
```

You may see that the new route has been added successfully. Now, if there is a corresponding DNS record, you will be able to access your application using that alternate route.

# Using oc new-app

The `oc` utility allows you to deploy a simple application in a user-friendly way. Generally, you just need to pass one or more options to the `oc new-app` command, which will then create all required resources, including pod(s) and service(s), for your application. Additionally, that command creates `ReplicationController` and `DeploymentConfig` API objects that control how your application is being deployed.

# The oc new-app command

So, `oc new-app` creates the following resources during application deployment from an existing Docker image:

| Resource | Abbreviation | Description |
|---|---|---|
| Pod | pod | Pod representing your container |
| Service | svc | Service containing an internal application endpoint |
| ReplicationController | rc | A replication controller is an OpenShift object that controls the number of replicas for an application |
| DeploymentConfig | dc | Deployment configuration is a definition of your deployment |

`oc new-app` is a very simple utility, yet it's powerful enough to satisfy most simple deployments.

 `oc new-app` doesn't create a route when deploying an application from its Docker image!

The functionality provided by `oc new-app` is also exposed via a web console which is what developers usually are inclined to use.

# Using oc new-app with default options

Let's delete the resources created previously:

```
$ oc delete all --all
route "httpd" deleted
route "httpd1" deleted
route "httpd2" deleted
pod "httpd" deleted
service "httpd" deleted
```

 Another method to delete everything is to delete the project and create it again.

Recently, we showed that OpenShift comes with an image stream that contains the path to the OpenShift-ready `httpd` image. The `oc new-app` utility uses Docker images referenced by image streams by default.

Here is an example of creating a basic `httpd` application:

```
$ oc new-app httpd
--> Found image cc641a9 (5 days old) in image stream "openshift/httpd"
under tag "2.4" for "httpd"

    Apache httpd 2.4
    ----------------
    Apache httpd 2.4 available as container, is a powerful, efficient, and
extensible web server. Apache supports a variety of features, many
implemented as compiled modules which extend the core functionality. These
can range from server-side programming language support to authentication
schemes. Virtual hosting allows one Apache installation to serve many
different Web sites.

    Tags: builder, httpd, httpd24

    * This image will be deployed in deployment config "httpd"
    * Ports 8080/tcp, 8443/tcp will be load balanced by service "httpd"
      * Other containers can access this service through the hostname
"httpd"

--> Creating resources ...
    deploymentconfig "httpd" created
    service "httpd" created
--> Success
    Application is not exposed. You can expose services to the outside
world by executing one or more of the commands below:
     'oc expose svc/httpd'
    Run 'oc status' to view your app.
```

The deployment process takes some time. Once everything is ready, you can check that all resources have been created:

```
$ oc get all
NAME REVISION DESIRED CURRENT TRIGGERED BY
deploymentconfigs/httpd 1 1 1 config,image(httpd:2.4)

NAME READY STATUS RESTARTS AGE
po/httpd-1-n7st4 1/1 Running 0 31s

NAME DESIRED CURRENT READY AGE
rc/httpd-1 1 1 1 32s

NAME CLUSTER-IP EXTERNAL-IP PORT(S) AGE
svc/httpd 172.30.222.179 <none> 8080/TCP,8443/TCP 33s
```

```
$ oc describe pod httpd-1-n7st4 | grep Image:
    Image: centos/httpd-24-
centos7@sha256:6da9085c5e7963efaae3929895b9730d7e76e937a7a0109a23015622f3e7
156b
```

What is left is to expose the service to make the application externally available:

```
$ oc expose svc httpd
route "httpd" exposed

$ curl -s http://httpd-simpleapication.127.0.0.1.nip.io | head -n 4
<!DOCTYPE html PUBLIC "-//W3C//DTD XHTML 1.1//EN"
"http://www.w3.org/TR/xhtml11/DTD/xhtml11.dtd">

<html xmlns="http://www.w3.org/1999/xhtml" xml:lang="en">
  <head>
```

# Advanced deployment

The `oc new-app` command takes a number of parameters, allowing you to modify the deployment process according to your needs. For example, you may need to modify names, specify environment variables, and so on.

Advanced options can always be displayed by using the built-in help function, which can be displayed by `oc new-app --help`:

```
$ oc new-app --help
Create a new application by specifying source code, templates, and/or
images

...
<OMITTED>
...

If you provide source code, a new build will be automatically triggered.
You can use 'oc status' to
check the progress.

Usage:
  oc new-app (IMAGE | IMAGESTREAM | TEMPLATE | PATH | URL ...) [options]

Examples:
  # List all local templates and image streams that can be used to create
an app
```

```
oc new-app --list

# Create an application based on the source code in the current git
repository (with a public
remote)
# and a Docker image
oc new-app . --docker-image=repo/langimage
...
<OMITTED>
...
```

 We are going to work with `oc new-app` a lot in the following chapters. You don't have to learn all options right now.

# Deploying MariaDB

In this section, we will deploy a database container with additional configuration options. The container requires a number of parameters to be passed to `oc new-app`. Let's create a simple `mariadb` container as shown here.

First delete objects created previously:

```
$ oc delete all --all
...
<OUTPUT OMITTED>
...
```

Now we want to create a database container where the database user named `openshift` is allowed to connect to the database named `openshift`. For simplicity reasons, we will use `openshift` as the database password. The following example, shows how to start a MariaDB container:

```
$ oc new-app -e MYSQL_USER=openshift -e MYSQL_PASSWORD=openshift \
-e MYSQL_DATABASE=openshift mariadb

--> Found image 1b0e3a6 (5 days old) in image stream "openshift/mariadb"
under tag "10.2" for "mariadb"

...
<OUTPUT OMITTED>
...

    Run 'oc status' to view your app.
```

Verify mariadb is up and running:

```
$ oc get all
NAME REVISION DESIRED CURRENT TRIGGERED BY
deploymentconfigs/mariadb 1 1 1 config,image(mariadb:10.1)

NAME READY STATUS RESTARTS AGE
po/mariadb-1-54h6x 1/1 Running 0 2m

NAME DESIRED CURRENT READY AGE
rc/mariadb-1 1 1 1 2m

NAME CLUSTER-IP EXTERNAL-IP PORT(S) AGE
svc/mariadb 172.30.233.119 <none> 3306/TCP 2m
```

Now you can access the database using container name, "po/mariadb-1-54h6x" in our case.

Now login to the container using 'oc exec':

```
$ oc exec -it mariadb-1-54h6x /bin/bash
bash-4.2$
```

Connect to mariadb database and verify that database named 'openshift' is created and you have access to it running 'show dababases' command.

```
$ mysql -uopenshift -popenshift -h127.0.0.1 openshift
...
<OUTPUT OMITTED>
...

MariaDB [openshift]> show databases;
+--------------------+
| Database |
+--------------------+
| information_schema |
| openshift |
| test |
+--------------------+
3 rows in set (0.00 sec)
```

The previous output shows that the database service is up and running and ready to be used from the application side. We are going to work more on this topic in the following chapters.

You can exit database and get ready for the next chapter.

```
MariaDB [openshift]> exit
Bye
```

```
bash-4.2$ exit
exit
[vagrant@openshift ~]
```

Clear out your lab environment.

```
$ oc delete all --all
deploymentconfig "mariadb" deleted
imagestream "mariadb" deleted
pod "mariadb-1-9qcsp" deleted
service "mariadb" deleted

$ oc delete project simpleappication
project "simpleappication" deleted

$ oc project myproject
Now using project "myproject" on server "https://localhost:8443".
```

If you are going to continue with the following chapter, you can leave your OpenShift cluster up, otherwise you can shutdown or delete vagrant VM.

# Summary

In this chapter, we showed you how to deploy a number of simple applications from their Docker images, how to create a pod manually, and how to create a service manually. We went through the process of creating a service, and how to create a route manually, as well as how to create a route using `oc expose`. Finally, we showed you how to use the `oc new-app` command to deploy an application from its Docker image.

In the next chapter, we will be working on deployment of multi-tier application using OpenShift templates.

# Questions

1. Which of the following OpenShift entities is not created automatically by `oc new-app`?
    1. Pod
    2. Route
    3. Replication controller
    4. Deployment config

> 5. Service

2. Which of the following entities should be created in order to make an application available externally in a minimal configuration (choose three)?
    1. Pod
    2. Service
    3. Route
    4. Replication controller
    5. Deployment config
    6. Image stream

3. Which command creates a route with the custom URL `myservice.example.com`?
    1. oc expose svc httpd
    2. oc expose svc httpd --host myservice.example.com
    3. oc expose svc httpd --hostname myservice.example.com
    4. oc create svc httpd --hostname myservice.example.com

4. Which commands display all OpenShift routes (choose two)?
    1. oc get all
    2. oc get pod
    3. oc get application
    4. oc get route
    5. docker ps
    6. ip route

# Further reading

We gave you a basic knowledge of application deployment in OpenShift. The following links are useful if you want to read more:

- **Pods and Services**: `https://docs.openshift.org/latest/architecture/core_concepts/pods_and_services.html`
- **Creating applications from images**: `https://docs.openshift.org/latest/dev_guide/application_lifecycle/new_app.html#specifying-an-image`

# 13
# Deploying Multi-Tier Applications Using Templates

Previously, you learned how to run a standalone container in OpenShift. In the real world, almost all applications are composed of multiple interconnected containers. For example, the WordPress container requires access to a database instance. OpenShift provides a facility that lets you pack everything related to your application into a single object, called a *template,* and deploy everything at once by processing that template. The basic template concept was explained in Chapter 9, *Advanced OpenShift Concepts,* and it is very similar to Docker Compose. This chapter will be a hands-on lab experiment, illustrating how to use OpenShift templates to deploy applications. The upcoming labs will show you, in detail, how to create a multi-tier application from scratch.

In this chapter, we will cover the following topics:

- An OpenShift template overview
- Creating a custom template
- Using templates to deploy applications

## Technical requirements

This chapter doesn't have strict environmental restrictions; any OpenShift installations and development environments are supported: MinitShift, oc cluster up, or standard production-ready deployment based on Ansible. It is up to you which flavor you use. However, this chapter is based on the oc cluster up running within vagrant. The following Vagrantfile can be used to deploy the lab:

```
$ cat Vagrantfile
Vagrant.configure(2) do |config|
  config.vm.define "openshift" do |conf|
    conf.vm.box = "centos/7"
```

```
        conf.vm.network "private_network", ip: "172.24.0.11"
        conf.vm.hostname = 'openshift.example.com'
        conf.vm.network "forwarded_port", guest: 80, host: 1080
        conf.vm.network "forwarded_port", guest: 443, host: 9443
        conf.vm.network "forwarded_port", guest: 8080, host: 8080
        conf.vm.network "forwarded_port", guest: 8443, host: 8443
        conf.vm.provider "virtualbox" do |v|
          v.memory = 4096
          v.cpus = 2
        end
        conf.vm.provision "shell", inline: $lab_main
    end
end
$lab_main = <<SCRIPT
cat <<EOF >> /etc/hosts
172.24.0.11 openshift.example.com openshift
172.24.0.12 storage.example.com storage nfs
EOF
systemctl disable firewalld
systemctl stop firewalld
yum update -y
yum install -y epel-release
yum install -y docker
cat << EOF >/etc/docker/daemon.json
{
    "insecure-registries": [
      "172.30.0.0/16"
    ]
}
EOF
systemctl restart docker
systemctl enable docker
yum -y install centos-release-openshift-origin39
yum -y install origin-clients
oc cluster up
SCRIPT
```

The environment can be deployed as follows:

```
$ vagrant up
```

Once the previously listed vagrant machine is deployed, you may connect to it as follows:

```
$ vagrant ssh
$ sudo -i
#
```

Finally, log in as a `developer` user in order to be able to run most commands:

```
# oc login -u developer
Server [https://localhost:8443]:
The server uses a certificate signed by an unknown authority.
You can bypass the certificate check, but any data you send to the server
could be intercepted by others.
Use insecure connections? (y/n): y

Authentication required for https://localhost:8443 (openshift)
Username: developer
Password: <ANY PASSWORD>
Login successful.

You have one project on this server: "myproject"

Using project "myproject".
Welcome! See 'oc help' to get started.
```

 We can use any password, as OpenShift uses the `AllowAll` identity provider by default.

Some of the lab items will require a custom DNS record, which can be simulated by setting a record in `/etc/hosts`. Both methods are acceptable.

It is also assumed that you have a web browser, such as Mozilla Firefox or Google Chrome.

# OpenShift template overview

An OpenShift template is a set of API resources that can be parameterized and processed to produce a list of objects for creation by OpenShift. A template can be processed to create any desired OpenShift objects (such as deployment configurations, build configurations, and so on). A template can also define a set of labels to apply to every object defined in the template. You can apply a template by using the CLI or the web console. For example, a template might contain two pods (an application and a database), a service, and a route. Once the template has been developed, you can reuse it.

# Template syntax

Templates, like any other OpenShift resources, can be created from a raw YAML or JSON definition. An example is as follows:

```
# cat mytemplate.yaml
apiVersion: v1
kind: Template
metadata:
  name: template1
objects:
- apiVersion: v1
  kind: Pod
  metadata:
    name: app1
  spec:
    containers:
    - env:
      - name: SHOW_DATA
        value: ${SHOW_DATA}
      image: example/appimage
      name: app1
      ports:
      - containerPort: 8080
        protocol: TCP
parameters:
- description: Myapp configuration data
  name: SHOW_DATA
  required: true
labels:
  mylabel: app1
```

The preceding example includes only one resource—a pod named `app1`. It also includes a parameter—SHOW_DATA. Parameters can be used to customize application deployment and accommodate all kinds of use cases.

Parameters can also have the following default values:

```
parameters:
- description: Myapp configuration data
  name: SHOW_DATA
  required: true
  value: Example value
```

In some cases, we may want to generate values according to a certain pattern, as shown here:

```
parameters:
  - description: Password used for Redis authentication
    from: '[A-Z0-9]{8}'
    generate: expression
    name: REDIS_PASSWORD
```

In the preceding example, instantiating the template will generate a random password, eight characters long, consisting of all upper and lowercase alphabet letters, as well as numbers. Although that syntax is highly reminiscent of regular expressions, it implements only a small subset of **Perl Compatible Regular Expressions** (**PCRE**), so you can still use the \w, \d, and \a modifiers:

- [w]{10}: This expands to 10 alphabet characters, numbers, and underscores. This follows the PCRE standard and is the same as [a-zA-Z0-9_]{10}.
- [\d]{10}: This expands to 10 numbers. This is the same as [0-9]{10}.
- [\a]{10}: This expands to 10 alphabetical characters. This is the same as [a-zA-Z]{10}.

This capability is very useful for generating random passwords.

 It's important to understand that the process of parameter expansion takes place when resources are being created from the template, not when the template itself is created; so, each generated resource gets its own unique value.

# Adding templates

Once a template is developed, it can be added to OpenShift like any other YAML or JSON-defined objects, using the `oc create` command. It is a common practice to use a separate tenant specifically for templates, which will be shared between multiple projects. A default installation of the Red Hat **OpenShift Container Platform** (**OCP**) provides a number of templates in the `openshift` project. All of an OpenShift cluster's users have read access to the project, but only the cluster admin is able to modify or create templates in the project.

The following example shows how to add a template to your current project:

```
# oc create -f mytemplate.yaml
template "template1" created

# oc get template
NAME            DESCRIPTION       PARAMETERS    OBJECTS
template1                         1 (1 blank)   1
```

You will need to become the `system:admin` user to create a template in the `openshift` tenant:

```
# oc login -u system:admin

# oc create -f mytemplate.json -n openshift
template "template1" created

# oc get template -n openshift|grep temp
template1
```

# Displaying template parameters

The OpenShift community has developed many useful OpenShift templates, to deploy a number of well-known services. Once the template is determined, you will need to understand which parameters it accepts.

There are a couple of ways to list all of the parameters:

- Using the `oc process --parameters` command (this is the easiest one)
- Looking for the `parameters` section in the template's definition

Among many others, the OpenShift default installation comes with the `mariadb-persistent` template, as shown here:

```
# oc get template mariadb-persistent -n openshift
NAME   DESCRIPTION   PARAMETERS OBJECTS
mariadb-persistent MariaDB database service, with persistent storage. For
more information about... 8 (3 generated) 4
```

That template has a number of parameters, listed as follows:

```
# oc process --parameters -n openshift mariadb-persistent
NAME DESCRIPTION GENERATOR VALUE
...
<output omitted>
...
VOLUME_CAPACITY Volume space available for data, e.g. 512Mi, 2Gi. 1Gi
```

If you don't want to import the template into OpenShift, the same method allows you to display the parameters of a locally stored OpenShift template:

```
# oc process --parameters -f mytemplate.yaml
NAME            DESCRIPTION   GENERATOR     VALUE
SHOW_DATA    Myapp configuration data
```

Another method is to use the `oc describe` command:

```
# oc describe template template1
Name:          template1
Namespace:     myproject
...
<output omitted>
...
Parameters:
    Name:          SHOW_DATA
    Description:    Myapp configuration data
    Required:       true
    Value:         <none>
...
<output omitted>
...
```

# Processing a template

The following is a real-life example of deploying an application from a predefined template using `oc new-app` command:

```
# oc new-app jenkins-persistent -p JENKINS_SERVICE_NAME=myjenkins
--> Deploying template "openshift/jenkins-persistent" to project myproject
...
<output omitted>
...
--> Creating resources ...
    route "myjenkins" created
    deploymentconfig "myjenkins" created
    serviceaccount "myjenkins" created
    rolebinding "myjenkins_edit" created
    service "jenkins-jnlp" created
    service "myjenkins" created
--> Success
...
<output omitted>
...
    Access your application via route 'myjenkins-
myproject.127.0.0.1.nip.io'
    Run 'oc status' to view your app
```

In the preceding example, we passed the template's name to the command as a parameter; the `oc` utility can also build an application from the template you specify. The following is the list of objects created by the `oc new-app` command:

```
# oc get all
NAME                         REVISION   DESIRED   CURRENT   TRIGGERED BY
deploymentconfigs/myjenkins  1          1         1
config,image(jenkins:latest)

NAME                HOST/PORT                      PATH       SERVICES PORT
TERMINATION
WILDCARD
routes/myjenkins myjenkins-templates.example.com myjenkins <all>
edge/Redirect
None

NAME                     READY      STATUS     RESTARTS   AGE
po/myjenkins-1-h2mxx     1/1        Running    0          1m

NAME                     DESIRED    CURRENT    READY      AGE
rc/myjenkins-1           1          1          1          1m
```

```
NAME                         CLUSTER-IP      EXTERNAL-IP   PORT(S)     AGE
svc/jenkins-jnlp             172.30.33.180   <none>        50000/TCP   1m
svc/myjenkins                172.30.107.99   <none>        80/TCP      1m
```

This easy you can create a fully functional jenkins CI/CD application running within OpenShift.

Clean out your project before we proceed:

```
# oc delete all --all
deploymentconfig "myjenkins" deleted
route "myjenkins" deleted
pod "myjenkins-1-zg4km" deleted
service "jenkins-jnlp" deleted
service "myjenkins" deleted
```

# Creating a custom template

In most cases, developers use the predefined OpenShift templates that come with the OpenShift installation; however, at times they don't suit a particular case, so a customized template has to be developed. In this section, we will provide you with an overview of how to create your own template.

# Developing YAML/JSON template definitions

If you are familiar with the template layout, you might want to develop a template from scratch, using a standard YAML or JSON-based file. This method will allow you to create a clean template, without any runtime data.

Some of OpenShift's features may speed up the process of template development. For example, oc explain allows you to explore the syntax of all OpenShift API objects, serving as a form of documentation.

If given no parameters, oc explain lists all of the kinds of resources supported by the current version of OpenShift:

```
# oc explain
You must specify the type of resource to explain. Valid resource types
include:

    * all
    * buildconfigs (aka 'bc')
    * builds
```

```
      * certificatesigningrequests (aka 'csr')
      * clusterrolebindings
      * clusterroles
...
<output omitted>
...
      error: Required resource not specified.
See 'oc explain -h' for help and examples.
```

The preceding command accepts the type of a resource as an argument, in order to display its syntax:

```
# oc explain svc
...
<output omitted>
...
FIELDS:
   metadata     <Object>
      Standard object's metadata. More info:
https://git.k8s.io/community/contributors/devel/api-conventions.md#metadata
...
<output omitted>
...
```

Some OpenShift resources have multilevel structures. Use . (the dot) as a level separator, to find out the structure of such an attribute:

```
# oc explain svc.metadata
RESOURCE: metadata <Object>
 ...
 <output omitted>
 ...

FIELDS:
 ...
 <output omitted>
 ...

  uid     <string>
     UID is the unique in time and space value for this object. It is
typically generated by the server on successful creation of a resource and
is not allowed to change on PUT operations. Populated by the system. Read-
only. More info: http://kubernetes.io/docs/user-guide/identifiers#uids
```

And you can go even further in this hierarchy:

```
$ oc explain svc.metadata.uid
FIELD: uid <string>

DESCRIPTION:
     UID is the unique in time and space value for this object. It is
typically generated by the server on successful creation of a resource and
is not allowed to change on PUT operations. Populated by the system. Read-
only. More info: http://kubernetes.io/docs/user-guide/identifiers#uids
```

OpenShift documentation is very good and helpful this way.

# Exporting existing resources as templates

Existing OpenShift resources may be exported as templates by using the `oc export` command. Let's create a running application using `oc new-app` command first.

```
$ oc new-app httpd
--> Found image 9fd201d (10 days old) in image stream "openshift/httpd"
under tag "2.4" for "httpd"
...
<output omitted>
...
--> Success
    Application is not exposed. You can expose services to the outside
world by executing one or more of the commands below:
     'oc expose svc/httpd'
    Run 'oc status' to view your app.
```

```
$ oc get all
NAME                 READY     STATUS      RESTARTS    AGE
httpd-1-dcm2d        1/1       Running     0           2s
httpd-1-deploy       1/1       Running     0           3s
[root@openshift ~]# oc get all
NAME                         REVISION    DESIRED     CURRENT     TRIGGERED BY
deploymentconfigs/httpd      1           1           1
config,image(httpd:2.4)

NAME                     DOCKER REPO                           TAGS      UPDATED
imagestreams/httpd       172.30.1.1:5000/myproject/httpd       2.4

NAME                 READY     STATUS      RESTARTS    AGE
po/httpd-1-dcm2d     1/1       Running     0           15s

NAME             DESIRED     CURRENT     READY       AGE
```

```
rc/httpd-1    1           1           1           17s
```

| NAME AGE | TYPE | CLUSTER-IP | EXTERNAL-IP | PORT(S) |
|---|---|---|---|---|
| svc/httpd 17s | ClusterIP | 172.30.18.224 | <none> | 8080/TCP,8443/TCP |

```
$ oc export dc,svc,route --as-template=myhttpd > myhttpd_template.yaml
```

Once the template is created, you can see its contents:

```
$ cat myhttpd_template.yaml | head -n 20
apiVersion: v1
kind: Template
metadata:
  creationTimestamp: null
  name: myhttpd
objects:
- apiVersion: v1
  kind: DeploymentConfig
  metadata:
    annotations:
      openshift.io/generated-by: OpenShiftNewApp
    creationTimestamp: null
    generation: 1
    labels:
      app: httpd
    name: httpd
  spec:
    replicas: 1
    revisionHistoryLimit: 10
    selector:
```

 This method of creating a template is fast; however, you have to remove all runtime data from the template. For example, all timestamps and status records should be deleted.

# Using the oc new-app -o command

By default, the `oc new-app` command creates all of the resources required for a project. You can modify this behavior and get the utility to create a resource definition file, instead of creating resources:

```
$ oc new-app httpd -o yaml | head -n 20
apiVersion: v1
```

```
items:
- apiVersion: v1
  kind: DeploymentConfig
  metadata:
    annotations:
      openshift.io/generated-by: OpenShiftNewApp
    creationTimestamp: null
    labels:
      app: httpd
    name: httpd
  spec:
    replicas: 1
    selector:
      app: httpd
      deploymentconfig: httpd
    strategy:
      resources: {}
    template:
      metadata:
```

 This doesn't create an OpenShift template, but it can be used to create a skeleton of the template's structure.

Clear out your your project environment, before we proceed.

```
# oc delete all --all
deploymentconfig "httpd" deleted
imagestream "httpd" deleted
pod "httpd-1-dcm2d" deleted
service "httpd" deleted
```

# Using templates to deploy a multi-tier application

During this lab, we will deploy **Gogs** (Git repository management software) with a PostgreSQL backend, using all of the knowledge that we have acquired so far.

# The Gogs application template

We are going to use a template from the OpenShift demos that are available at `https://raw.githubusercontent.com/OpenShiftDemos/gogs-openshift-docker/master/openshift/gogs-template.yaml`:

Let's download this template locally using the following command:

```
# curl -O
https://raw.githubusercontent.com/OpenShiftDemos/gogs-openshift-docker/mast
er/openshift/gogs-template.yaml
```

According to the preceding output, most parameters have a default value (except for the HOSTNAME parameter). If you need to list parameters separately, you can use the following command:

```
# oc process --parameters -f gogs-template.yaml
NAME DESCRIPTION GENERATOR VALUE
APPLICATION_NAME The name for the application. gogs
...
 <output omitted>
...
```

# Creating the Gogs application

Now that we have created the template, it's time to use it:

1. First, we need to create a separate project for this lab:

   ```
   # oc new-project gogs
   Now using project "gogs" on server "https://localhost:8443".
   ```

2. Let's try to deploy Gogs without specifying a mandatory HOSTNAME parameter:

   ```
   # oc new-app -f gogs-template.yaml
   error: error processing template "templats/gogs":
   Template.template.openshift.io "gogs" is invalid:
   template.parameters[1]: Required value: template.parameters[1]:
   parameter HOSTNAME is required and must be specified
   ```

   OpenShift aborted the processing of the template, as the HOSTNAME wasn't provided.

3. Let's try again, with the HOSTNAME set:

```
# oc new-app -f gogs-template.yaml -p HOSTNAME=gogs.example.com
--> Deploying template "gogs/gogs" for "gogs-template.yaml" to
project gogs
...
<output omitted>
...
--> Success
    Access your application via route 'gogs.example.com'
    Run 'oc status' to view your app.
```

The template has been processed by OpenShift. After some time, all of the OpenShift objects specified in the template should be created:

```
# oc get all
NAME DOCKER REPO TAGS          UPDATED
imagestreams/gogs 172.30.1.1:5000/gogs/gogs 0.9.97 About a minute
ago

NAME REVISION DESIRED CURRENT TRIGGERED BY
deploymentconfigs/gogs 1 1 1 config,image(gogs:0.9.97)
deploymentconfigs/gogs-postgresql 1 1 1
config,image(postgresql:9.5)

NAME HOST/PORT PATH SERVICES PORT TERMINATION WILDCARD
routes/gogs gogs.example.com gogs <all> None

NAME READY STATUS RESTARTS AGE
po/gogs-1-vc5g5 1/1 Running 1 1m
po/gogs-postgresql-1-hfxlf 1/1 Running 0 1m

NAME DESIRED CURRENT READY AGE
rc/gogs-1 1 1 1 1m
rc/gogs-postgresql-1 1 1 1 1m

NAME CLUSTER-IP EXTERNAL-IP PORT(S) AGE
svc/gogs 172.30.196.109 <none> 3000/TCP 1m
svc/gogs-postgresql 172.30.196.38 <none> 5432/TCP 1m
```

The route gogs uses the gogs.example.com hostname, which we specified when instantiating the template.

Add gogs.example.com record to your hosts file

```
echo "127.0.0.1 gogs.example.com" >> /etc/hosts
```

Gogs has been successfully deployed. To verify that it works properly, we need to access it through a web browser on `http://gogs.example.com:1080/`

Clear out your environment.

```
$ oc delete all --all
deploymentconfig "mariadb" deleted
imagestream "mariadb" deleted
pod "mariadb-1-9qcsp" deleted
service "mariadb" deleted

$ oc delete project gogs
project "gogs" deleted

$ oc project myproject
Now using project "myproject" on server "https://localhost:8443".
```

If you are going to continue with the following Chapter, you can leave your OpenShift cluster up, otherwise you can shutdown or delete vagrant VM.

# Summary

In this chapter, you learned about OpenShift templates, including how to write your own templates and deploy applications from templates.

In the following chapter, you will learn how OpenShift simplifies Docker image life cycles by providing a Docker build strategy that automates application deployment from the source code, if a Dockerfile is available.

# Questions

1. Which of the following OpenShift projects holds default templates?

    1. default
    2. openshift
    3. openshift-infra
    4. openshift-node
    5. templates

2. Which of the following commands can show you a list of parameters for the `mytemplate` template? choose three:

   1. `oc get template mytemplate -n openshift -o yaml`
   2. `oc process --parameters -f mytemplate.json`
   3. `oc describe template mytemplate -n openshift`
   4. `oc get parameters -t mytemplate`
   5. `oc get template mytemplate -n openshift`
   6. `oc new-app mytrmplate`

3. Which of the following OpenShift entities can be created using templates?

   1. Pod
   2. Service
   3. Route
   4. Deployment config
   5. All of the above

# Further reading

Consider the following links for further reading:

- Templates at `https://docs.openshift.org/latest/dev_guide/templates.html`.
- Loading the Default Image Streams and Templates at `https://docs.openshift.org/latest/install_config/imagestreams_templates.html`.

# 14
# Building Application Images from Dockerfile

In the previous chapter, you learned what OpenShift templates are, along with the concepts of how to write your own templates and deploy applications from templates.

In this chapter, we are going to see how OpenShift simplifies Docker image life cycles by providing a Docker build strategy that automates application deployment from source code. This chapter is a hands-on lab that describes application delivery using the Docker **Source-to-Image (S2I)** strategy.

After completing this chapter, you will have learned how to build and deploy an application from Dockerfile.

We will cover the following topics in this chapter:

- Dockerfile development for OpenShift
- Building applications from Dockerfile
- Dockerfile build customization

## Technical requirements

This chapter doesn't have strict environmental restrictions; any OpenShift installations and development environment is supported—MiniShift, `oc cluster up`, standard Ansible-based production-ready deployment. It is up to you which version you use. However, this chapter is based on the `oc cluster up` method. The following Vagrantfile can be used to deploy development environment:

```
Vagrant.configure(2) do |config|
  config.vm.define "openshift" do |conf|
    conf.vm.box = "centos/7"
    conf.vm.network "private_network", ip: "172.24.0.11"
```

```
      conf.vm.hostname = 'openshift.example.com'
      conf.vm.network "forwarded_port", guest: 80, host: 980
      conf.vm.network "forwarded_port", guest: 443, host: 9443
      conf.vm.network "forwarded_port", guest: 8080, host: 8080
      conf.vm.network "forwarded_port", guest: 8443, host: 8443
      conf.vm.provider "virtualbox" do |v|
        v.memory = 4096
        v.cpus = 2
      end
      conf.vm.provision "shell", inline: $lab_main
    end

$lab_main = <<SCRIPT
cat <<EOF >> /etc/hosts
172.24.0.11 openshift.example.com openshift
172.24.0.12 storage.example.com storage nfs
EOF
systemctl disable firewalld
systemctl stop firewalld
yum update -y
yum install -y epel-release git
yum install -y docker tree
cat << EOF >/etc/docker/daemon.json
{
    "insecure-registries": [
      "172.30.0.0/16"
    ]
}
EOF
systemctl start docker
systemctl enable docker
yum -y install centos-release-openshift-origin39
yum -y install origin-clients
oc cluster up
SCRIPT
```

The environment can be deployed as follows:

```
$ vagrant up
```

Once the previously listed vagrant machine is deployed, you may connect to it as follows:

```
$ vagrant ssh
```

Finally, log in as the developer user in order to be able to perform operations:

```
$ oc login -u developer
Server [https://localhost:8443]:
The server uses a certificate signed by an unknown authority.
You can bypass the certificate check, but any data you send to the server
could be intercepted by others.
Use insecure connections? (y/n): y

Authentication required for https://localhost:8443 (openshift)
Username: developer
Password: <ANY PASSWORD>
Login successful.

You have one project on this server: "myproject"

Using project "myproject".
Welcome! See 'oc help' to get started.

$ sudo -i
#
```

# Dockerfile development for OpenShift

Early in this book, we explained how to containerize applications through Dockerfile development. This involved the `docker build` utility, which creates a ready-to-use container image by following Dockerfile instructions.

Generally speaking, OpenShift supports existing application Dockerfiles, but it has special default security-related requirements that require you to modify/adjust application Dockerfiles to be aligned with OpenShift security standards.

The default security policy runs any containers using a random **User ID** (**UID**) and ignores the USER Dockerfile instruction. The applications are always run under the root user group.

If the application needs read-write access, you need to configure RW access to the root group, which can usually be archived with the following Dockerfile snippet:

```
...
RUN chown -R 1001:0 /var/lib/myaplication /var/log/myapplication &amp;&amp;
\
    chmod -R g=u /var/lib/myaplication /var/log/myapplication
...
USER 1001
```

The preceding example changes the directory and file owner to `1001` and sets the permission for the group to the same as for the owner. This allows applications to have read-write permissions under any UID.

OpenShift doesn't allow applications to bind on ports less than `1024`. So, it may be required to adjust the `EXPOSE` instructions in your Dockerfiles to be able to run applications inside OpenShift infrastructure.

The following Dockerfile snippet provides an example of how to modify the port for the HTTPD image:

```
EXPOSE 8080
```

 It most cases, it will be required to adjust application configuration to listen on a new port. For example, for HTTPD, it is necessary to change `Listen` directive options.

# Building an application from Dockerfile

It is good practice to deploy an application in a separate namespace:

```
$ oc new-project dockerfile
Now using project "dockerfile" on server "https://localhost:8443".
```

For this lab, we are going to use the `redis` container. First, we need a Dockerfile with additional files located at `https://github.com/docker-library/redis.git`. Let's clone this repository locally to understand its structure:

```
$ git clone https://github.com/docker-library/redis.git
Cloning into 'redis'...
remote: Counting objects: 738, done.
remote: Compressing objects: 100% (15/15), done.
remote: Total 738 (delta 7), reused 13 (delta 4), pack-reused 719
Receiving objects: 100% (738/738), 108.56 KiB | 0 bytes/s, done.
Resolving deltas: 100% (323/323), done.
```

The repository contains a number of directories representing a particular version of Redis:

```
$ tree redis/
redis/
├── 3.2
│   ├── 32bit
│   │   ├── docker-entrypoint.sh
│   │   └── Dockerfile
│   ├── alpine
│   │   ├── docker-entrypoint.sh
│   │   └── Dockerfile
│   ├── docker-entrypoint.sh
│   └── Dockerfile
├── 4.0
│   ├── 32bit
│   │   ├── docker-entrypoint.sh
│   │   └── Dockerfile
│   ├── alpine
│   │   ├── docker-entrypoint.sh
│   │   └── Dockerfile
│   ├── docker-entrypoint.sh
│   └── Dockerfile
├── 5.0-rc
│   ├── 32bit
│   │   ├── docker-entrypoint.sh
│   │   └── Dockerfile
│   ├── alpine
│   │   ├── docker-entrypoint.sh
│   │   └── Dockerfile
│   ├── docker-entrypoint.sh
│   └── Dockerfile
├── generate-stackbrew-library.sh
├── LICENSE
├── README.md
└── update.sh
```

The repository structure contains a number of directories representing a particular version. To build the application, we need to specify a directory that contains the required Dockerfile. This can be achieved by using the `--context-dir` option of `oc new-ap`. This will be described later.

# A simple Dockerfile build

Well, we know about directory structure and want to build and deploy a Redis application from the available Dockerfile. Let's focus on version 3.2. The `oc new-app` may initiate a build from source code using a sub-directory. We are ready to initiate a simple Dockerfile build:

```
$ oc new-app https://github.com/docker-library/redis.git --context-dir=3.2
...
<OUTPUT OMITTED>
...
Run 'oc status' to view your app.
```

As we can see, OpenShift created a number of objects such as the following:

- `imagestream` **named** `debian`
- `buildconfig` **named** `redis`
- `deploymentconfig` **named** `redis`
- `service` **named** `redis`

You can run the `oc get all` command to make sure that all objects have been created:

```
$ oc get all
NAME                 TYPE      FROM         LATEST
buildconfigs/redis   Docker    Git          1

NAME                 TYPE    FROM        STATUS    STARTED         DURATION
builds/redis-1       Docker  Git@d24f2be Complete  39 seconds ago  6s

NAME                  DOCKER REPO                              TAGS         UPDATED
imagestreams/debian   172.30.1.1:5000/dockerfile/debian        jessie-slim  39
seconds ago
imagestreams/redis    172.30.1.1:5000/dockerfile/redis         latest       34
seconds ago

NAME                      REVISION DESIRED CURRENT TRIGGERED BY
deploymentconfigs/redis   1        1       1       config,image(redis:latest)

NAME                READY  STATUS      RESTARTS  AGE
po/redis-1-build    0/1    Completed   0         40s
po/redis-1-js789    1/1    Running     0         33s
```

| NAME | DESIRED | CURRENT | READY | AGE |
|------|---------|---------|-------|-----|
| rc/redis-1 | 1 | 1 | 1 | 35s |

| NAME | CLUSTER-IP | EXTERNAL-IP | PORT(S) | AGE |
|------|-----------|-------------|---------|-----|
| svc/redis | 172.30.165.223 | \<none\> | 6379/TCP | 41s |

The previous command initiated a build. OpenShift starts a –build pod which does the build. You may temporarily see that a Pod with –build in the name is in the Running state:

```
$ oc get pod
NAME              READY    STATUS             RESTARTS    AGE
redis-1-build     1/1      Running            0           6s
redis-1-deploy    0/1      ContainerCreating  0           1s
```

Docker build is controlled by a build config object. Build status can be displayed by using the oc logs bc/\<NAME\> command:

```
$ oc logs bc/redis|tail -n10
Successfully built b3b7a77f988a
Pushing image 172.30.1.1:5000/dockerfile/redis:latest ...
Pushed 0/6 layers, 7% complete
Pushed 1/6 layers, 30% complete
Pushed 2/6 layers, 43% complete
Pushed 3/6 layers, 57% complete
Pushed 4/6 layers, 75% complete
Pushed 5/6 layers, 87% complete
Pushed 6/6 layers, 100% complete
Push successful
```

 Another way to work on build process troubleshooting is to use oc status.

OpenShift built the Redis image from Dockerfile and uploaded it to a local registry. Let's make sure that container works:

```
$ oc get pod
NAME             READY    STATUS       RESTARTS    AGE
redis-1-build    0/1      Completed    0           2m
redis-1-js789    1/1      Running      0           1m

$ oc exec redis-1-81f8h /usr/local/bin/redis-cli ping
PONG
```

```
$ oc rsh redis-1-js789 /usr/local/bin/redis-server --version
Redis server v=3.2.11 sha=00000000:0 malloc=jemalloc-4.0.3 bits=64
build=994283e2d09fba41
```

 In this lab, we are using a simple `ping` test to make sure that we have basic reachability. We use the `redis-cli` command delivered by the container.

So, it looks like our Redis application works fine and has version 3.2.11.

# Dockerfile build customization

As we saw before, OpenShift can build an application from Dockerfile. Sometimes, application source code is updated and there is a need to initiate the build process again using the new source code. OpenShift supports this functionality through the `oc start-build` command.

During this section, we will initiate a build process using the new source code of the application using the image stream created recently by the `oc new-app` command.

We built a Redis application from source code using a specific directory 3.0.

The source code contains another Dockerfile, which uses the newer version 4.0:

```
$ tree redis/4.0/
redis/4.0/
├── 32bit
│   ├── docker-entrypoint.sh
│   └── Dockerfile
├── alpine
│   ├── docker-entrypoint.sh
│   └── Dockerfile
├── docker-entrypoint.sh
└── Dockerfile
```

Now, imagine that we need to update the application using new code available in another repository or another context directory in the existing repository. For our particular case, it sounds like we need to change the context directory to `4.0` instead of `3.2`.

The `oc new-app` command created a number of entities that control application build and deployment. The build process is under `build config` object control. We need to display this object to understand what to change to point to another directory in the repository:

```
$ oc get bc
NAME            TYPE        FROM        LATEST
redis           Docker      Git         1

$ oc get bc redis -o yaml
apiVersion: v1
kind: BuildConfig
metadata:
  annotations:
    openshift.io/generated-by: OpenShiftNewApp
  creationTimestamp: 2018-06-04T19:54:26Z
  labels:
    app: redis
  name: redis
  namespace: dockerfile
  resourceVersion: "256886"
  selfLink: /oapi/v1/namespaces/dockerfile/buildconfigs/redis
  uid: 16116413-6831-11e8-91ff-5254005f9478
spec:
  failedBuildsHistoryLimit: 5
  nodeSelector: null
  output:
    to:
      kind: ImageStreamTag
      name: redis:latest
  postCommit: {}
  resources: {}
  runPolicy: Serial
  source:
    contextDir: "3.2"
    git:
      uri: https://github.com/docker-library/redis.git
    type: Git

<OMITTED>
```

We highlighted a source element that specifies which directory to use during the build. Now, if there is a task to point to another context directory, we just need to update the `bc/redis` object by changing `spec.source.contextDir` in the object definition. This can be achieved in several ways:

- Manually using `oc edit`
- In a script using `oc patch`

`oc edit bc/redis` will run a text editor to modify the object. Here is an example of how to use the `oc patch` command to update the object content:

```
$ oc patch bc/redis --patch '{"spec":{"source":{"contextDir":"4.0"}}}'
buildconfig "redis" patched

$ oc get bc/redis -o yaml|grep contextDir:
    contextDir: 4.0
```

Well, we updated our build configuration but nothing happened. Our pod has not been changed. This indicates that the build process was not triggered. You may verify that by displaying pods through `oc get pod`.

If there is a need to initiate the application rebuild process, `oc start-build` must be run. This command starts a new build from the available build configuration.

Let's list all current builds:

```
$ oc get build
NAME       TYPE     FROM         STATUS     STARTED          DURATION
redis-1    Docker   Git@d24f2be  Complete   12 minutes ago   6s
```

So, recently, we initiated a build, which was completed some time ago. Let's try to run the build again:

```
$ oc start-build bc/redis
build "redis-2" started
```

The build creates a number of new pods representing the new version (version 2). After some time, the pod statuses will be changed:

```
$ oc get pod
NAME             READY    STATUS             RESTARTS    AGE
redis-1-build    0/1      Completed          0           13m
redis-1-js789    1/1      Running            0           12m
redis-2-build    0/1      Completed          0           8s
redis-2-deploy   1/1      Running            0           2s
redis-2-16bb1    0/1      ContainerCreating  0           0s
```

You can see that `redis` is now going through Build and Deploy stages before the new version of `redis` container is up and running. If you wait for a minute or so, you should see the following:

```
$ oc get pod
NAME             READY    STATUS             RESTARTS    AGE
```

```
redis-1-build      0/1        Completed        0          14m
redis-2-build      0/1        Completed        0          1m
redis-2-l6bbl      1/1        Running          0          57s
```

Well, it looks like that build has been completed:

```
$ oc get build
NAME        TYPE      FROM            STATUS     STARTED          DURATION
redis-1     Docker    Git@d24f2be     Complete   15 minutes ago   6s
redis-2     Docker    Git@d24f2be     Complete   2 minutes ago    6s
```

Now we can check the version of our application:

```
$ oc rsh redis-2-l6bbl /usr/local/bin/redis-server --version
Redis server v=4.0.9 sha=00000000:0 malloc=jemalloc-4.0.3 bits=64
build=40ca48d6a92db598
```

Finally, let's make sure that the application is up and running:

```
$ oc rsh redis-2-l6bbl /usr/local/bin/redis-cli ping
PONG
```

We were able to initiate the build from the updated source code.

Clear out your lab environment.

```
$ oc delete all --all
deploymentconfig "redis" deleted
buildconfig "redis" deleted
imagestream "debian" deleted
imagestream "redis" deleted
pod "redis-2-vw92x" deleted
service "redis" deleted

$ oc delete project dockerfile
project "dockerfile" deleted

$ oc project myproject
Now using project "myproject" on server "https://localhost:8443".
```

If you are going to continue with the following Chapter, you can leave your OpenShift cluster up, otherwise you can shutdown or delete vagrant VM.

# Summary

In this chapter, you have learned how to adjust Dockerfile to be able to run in OpenShift. We also explained how to build applications from Dockerfile, how to use `oc new-app` to initiate a Docker build, and finally how to use `oc start-build` to start the new build from the existing build config.

In the following chapter, we are going to talk about the most frequently used application images that are already available on Docker Hub. But every now and then it is required to build a custom image that contains custom software or is aligned with company security policies/standards. We are going to learn how OpenShift automates the build process through the S2I build strategy, which is one of the main advantages of OpenShift, and how it allows you to build an image from your application's source code and then run it as a container.

# Questions

1. Which of the following OpenShift commands can update existing API objects? choose two:

    1. `oc edit bc/redis`
    2. `oc get bc redis`
    3. `oc patch bc/redis --patch ...`
    4. `oc update bc/redis`
    5. `oc build bc/redis`

2. Which of the following commands start a new build? (choose one):

    1. `oc new-app`
    2. `oc new build`
    3. `oc start-build`
    4. `oc get build`

3. Which file must exist in the repository to perform docker build (choose one)?

     1. `Jenkinsfile`
     2. `Dockerfile`
     3. `README.md`
     4. `index.php`
     5. `docker.info`

# Further reading

Here is a list of topics with links related to this chapter that you might want to deep dive into:

- **Creating New Applications at** `https://docs.openshift.com/container-platform/3.9/dev_guide/application_lifecycle/new_app.html`
- **How Builds Work at** `https://docs.openshift.org/latest/dev_guide/builds/index.html`

# 15
# Building PHP Applications from Source Code

In the previous chapter, you learned how to build applications from Dockerfile, how to use `oc new-app` to initiate a Docker build, and finally, how to use `oc start-build` to start a new build from an existing build config.

In this chapter, we will discuss the most frequently used application images that are already available on Docker Hub. Every now and then, it is required to build a custom image that contains custom software or is aligned with company security policy/standards. You will learn how OpenShift automates the build process through a **Source-to-Image (S2I)** build strategy, which is one of its main advantages. You will also learn how it allows you to build an image from your application's source code and then run it as a container.

We will cover the following topics in this chapter:

- PHP S2I
- Building a simple PHP application
- Understanding the PHP build process

# Technical requirements

This chapter doesn't have strict requirements when it comes to the lab environment, so any OpenShift installation and development environment is supported—Minishift, `oc cluster up`, or a standard production-ready deployment based on Ansible. It is up to you which flavor to use. However, this chapter will focus on the `oc cluster up` method. The following Vagrantfile can be used to deploy our virtual lab:

```
Vagrant.configure(2) do |config|
  config.vm.define "openshift" do |conf|
    conf.vm.box = "centos/7"
```

```
      conf.vm.network "private_network", ip: "172.24.0.11"
      conf.vm.hostname = 'openshift.example.com'
      conf.vm.network "forwarded_port", guest: 80, host: 980
      conf.vm.network "forwarded_port", guest: 443, host: 9443
      conf.vm.network "forwarded_port", guest: 8080, host: 8080
      conf.vm.network "forwarded_port", guest: 8443, host: 8443
      conf.vm.provider "virtualbox" do |v|
        v.memory = 4096
        v.cpus = 2
      end
      conf.vm.provision "shell", inline: $lab_main
    end

$lab_main = <<SCRIPT
cat <<EOF >> /etc/hosts
172.24.0.11 openshift.example.com openshift
172.24.0.12 storage.example.com storage nfs
EOF
systemctl disable firewalld
systemctl stop firewalld
yum update -y
yum install -y epel-release git
yum install -y docker
cat << EOF >/etc/docker/daemon.json
{
    "insecure-registries": [
      "172.30.0.0/16"
    ]
}
EOF
systemctl start docker
systemctl enable docker
yum -y install centos-release-openshift-origin39
yum -y install origin-clients
oc cluster up
SCRIPT
```

The environment can be deployed by running a single command:

```
$ vagrant up
```

Once the virtual machine is deployed, you can connect to it as follows:

```
$ vagrant ssh
```

Finally, log in as the developer, to be able to perform unprivileged operations:

```
$ oc login -u developer
```

```
Server [https://localhost:8443]:
The server uses a certificate signed by an unknown authority.
You can bypass the certificate check, but any data you send to the server
could be intercepted by others.
Use insecure connections? (y/n): y

Authentication required for https://localhost:8443 (openshift)
Username: developer
Password: <ANY PASSWORD>
Login successful.

You have one project on this server: "myproject"

Using project "myproject".
Welcome! See 'oc help' to get started.
```

# PHP S2I

OpenShift supports S2I builds for PHP, and also for many other runtimes. The S2I process produces a ready-to-run image by combining the source code of an application with a base builder image, which prepares the application. The builder is a special image that is able to handle application installation and configuration for a particular programming language/framework. For example, the PHP builder can only handle PHP source code, and it doesn't support Java by default. Most of the frequently used programming languages, like Python, Ruby, Java, and Node.js, are already covered by OpenShift built-in builders. The S2I process involves the following steps:

1. Determining the correct base builder image. This process relies on complex heuristics and primarily involves looking for specific files and file extensions, like `Gemfile` for Ruby on Rails, or `requirements.txt` for Python. The runtime environment that the builder image is determined by can also be overriden by the user from CLI

2. Creating a `BuildConfig` pointing to the application source code's repository and to the ImageStream for the builder image

3. Starting a `build` pod from the builder image

4. Downloading the application's source code

5. Streaming the scripts and the application's source code into the builder image container, using the `tar` utility for images that support it

6. Running the `assemble` script (the one provided by the builder image has the highest priority)

7. Saving the final image to the internal registry

8. Creating resources necessary to support the application. They include, but not limited to, `DeploymentConfig`, `Service`, and `Pod`.

The PHP builder supports changing the default PHP configuration by using a number of environment variables. They are described on the web page for each particular builder.

The build process can be initiated by running the `oc new-app`. This command takes the repository URL/local path as an argument, and creates all required OpenShift entities to support the S2I build and application deployment at the same time.

The following OpenShift entities are created by default:

| Type | Name | Description |
|---|---|---|
| Pod | `<application name>-<build sequential number>-build` | Builder pod that builds your application, producing the application image and possibly some artifacts to be used in future builds along the way |
| Pod | `<name>-<build sequential number>-<id>` | Application pod produced by the build process |
| Service | `<name>` | Application service |
| Replication controller | `<name>-<build sequential number>` | Application replication controller, maintaining only one replica by default |
| Deployment config | `<name>` | Deployment configuration containing all information on how to deploy the application |
| Image stream | `<name>` | Path to the image built |
| Build config | `<name>` | Build configuration containing all required information on how to build the application |
| Build | `<name>-<build sequential number>` | Particular build; can be run multiple times |

 OpenShift doesn't create a route automatically. If you need to expose your application, a route should be created by running `oc expose svc <name>`.

# Building a simple PHP application

The first S2I lab will use a very simple PHP application that displays the PHP configuration using a standard PHP function—phpinfo(). It's composed of a single index.php file, with the following content:

```
$ cat index.php
<?php
phpinfo();
?>
```

This application is enough to demonstrate a basic S2I build. We have already prepared a Git repository on GitHub, which contains the code of our application. The repository is located at https://github.com/neoncyrex/phpinfo.git, and is going to be used in this lab.

First, we need to create a separate project for our new lab, as follows:

```
$ oc new-project phpinfo
Now using project "phpinfo" on server "https://localhost:8443".
<OMITTED>
```

The oc new-app command can build an application from its source code, using either a local or remote Git repository.

Let's clone the repository locally, to be able to make changes to it. This will create the phpinfo directory, with repository files:

```
$ git clone https://github.com/neoncyrex/phpinfo.git
Cloning into 'phpinfo'...
remote: Counting objects: 6, done.
remote: Compressing objects: 100% (3/3), done.
remote: Total 6 (delta 0), reused 3 (delta 0), pack-reused 0
Unpacking objects: 100% (6/6), done.
```

The build and application deployment processes can be initiated by running the oc new-app command. This basic S2I strategy can be triggered as follows:

```
$ oc new-app phpinfo
--> Found image 23e49b6 (17 hours old) in image stream "openshift/php"
under tag "7.0" for "php"
...
<output omitted>
...
--> Success
    Build scheduled, use 'oc logs -f bc/phpinfo' to track its progress.
```

```
        Application is not exposed. You can expose services to the outside
world by executing one or more of the commands below:
        'oc expose svc/phpinfo'
    Run 'oc status' to view your app.
```

The preceding command does the following:

- Uses phpinfo as a path to the application's source code
- Automatically detects the programming language—PHP
- Initiates the build process
- Creates a number of OpenShift resources

The build process takes some time. During the first phase, you can see a container with -build in its name. This container is deployed from the PHP builder image and is responsible for build operations:

```
$ oc get pod
NAME                READY   STATUS    RESTARTS   AGE
phpinfo-1-build     1/1     Running   0          23s
```

After some time, the application will be available. That means that the application's pod should be in a Running state:

```
$ oc get pod
NAME                READY   STATUS      RESTARTS   AGE
phpinfo-1-build     0/1     Completed   0          39s
phpinfo-1-h9xt5     1/1     Running     0          4s
```

OpenShift built and deployed the phpinfo application, which is now available by using its service IP. Let's try to access our application using the curl command:

```
$ oc get svc
NAME     CLUSTER-IP      EXTERNAL-IP  PORT(S)            AGE
phpinfo 172.30.54.195   <none>       8080/TCP,8443/TCP  1h

$ curl -s http://172.30.54.195:8080 | head -n 10
<!DOCTYPE html PUBLIC "-//W3C//DTD XHTML 1.0 Transitional//EN" "DTD/xhtml1-
transitional.dtd">
<html xmlns="http://www.w3.org/1999/xhtml"><head>
<style type="text/css">
body {background-color: #fff; color: #222; font-family: sans-serif;}
pre {margin: 0; font-family: monospace;}
a:link {color: #009; text-decoration: none; background-color: #fff;}
a:hover {text-decoration: underline;}
table {border-collapse: collapse; border: 0; width: 934px; box-shadow: 1px
2px 3px #ccc;}
```

```
.center {text-align: center;}
.center table {margin: 1em auto; text-align: left;}
```

 The `phpinfo()` function displays the PHP configuration as an HTML table.

A summary of the build process can be displayed by running the `oc status` or `oc status -v` commands:

```
$ oc status -v
In project phpinfo on server https://localhost:8443

svc/phpinfo - 172.30.54.195 ports 8080, 8443
  dc/phpinfo deploys istag/phpinfo:latest <-
    bc/phpinfo source builds
https://github.com/neoncyrex/phpinfo.git#master on openshift/php:7.0
    deployment #1 deployed about an hour ago - 1 pod

Info:
  * pod/phpinfo-1-build has no liveness probe to verify pods are still
running.
    try: oc set probe pod/phpinfo-1-build --liveness ...
  * dc/phpinfo has no readiness probe to verify pods are ready to accept
traffic or ensure deployment is successful.
    try: oc set probe dc/phpinfo --readiness ...
  * dc/phpinfo has no liveness probe to verify pods are still running.
    try: oc set probe dc/phpinfo --liveness ...
View details with 'oc describe <resource>/<name>' or list everything with
'oc get all'.
```

The preceding command shows that deployment #1 has been rolled out. It can also contain some useful information for troubleshooting the build, in case something goes wrong.

There is another way to display build logs with low-level details—using the `oc logs` command. We need to show the log for the `buildconfig` (or just `bc`) entity, which can be displayed, as follows, by using the `oc logs bc/phpinfo` command:

```
$ oc logs bc/phpinfo
Cloning "https://github.com/neoncyrex/phpinfo.git" ...
  Commit: 638030df45052ad1d9300248babe0b141cf5dbed (initial commit)
  Author: vagrant <vagrant@openshift.example.com>
  Date: Sat Jun 2 04:22:59 2018 +0000
---> Installing application source...
=> sourcing 20-copy-config.sh ...
---> 05:00:11 Processing additional arbitrary httpd configuration provided
```

```
by s2i ...
=> sourcing 00-documentroot.conf ...
=> sourcing 50-mpm-tuning.conf ...
=> sourcing 40-ssl-certs.sh ...
Pushing image 172.30.1.1:5000/phpinfo/phpinfo:latest ...
Pushed 0/10 layers, 23% complete
Pushed 1/10 layers, 30% complete
Pushed 2/10 layers, 21% complete
Pushed 3/10 layers, 30% complete
Pushed 4/10 layers, 40% complete
Pushed 5/10 layers, 51% complete
Pushed 6/10 layers, 60% complete
Pushed 7/10 layers, 76% complete
Pushed 8/10 layers, 87% complete
Pushed 9/10 layers, 95% complete
Pushed 10/10 layers, 100% complete
Push successful
```

The preceding output gives us some insight into how builds work.

# Understanding the PHP build process

Now that we know that the phpinfo application works as expected, let's focus on the low-level details that are required to understand the build process. OpenShift created a number of API resources to make the build possible. Some of them are related to the deployment process, which we learned about in previous chapters. We can display all entities as follows:

```
$ oc get all
NAME                 TYPE    FROM       LATEST
buildconfigs/phpinfo Source  Git@master 1

NAME              TYPE    FROM         STATUS    STARTED           DURATION
builds/phpinfo-1  Source  Git@638030d  Complete  About an hour ago 34s

NAME                   DOCKER REPO                        TAGS
UPDATED
imagestreams/phpinfo 172.30.1.1:5000/phpinfo/phpinfo latest
About an hour ago

NAME                       REVISION DESIRED CURRENT TRIGGERED BY
deploymentconfigs/phpinfo 1        1       1 config,image(phpinfo:latest)

NAME                 READY  STATUS     RESTARTS  AGE
po/phpinfo-1-build   0/1    Completed  0         1h
```

```
po/phpinfo-1-h9xt5  1/1    Running    0         1h

NAME          DESIRED  CURRENT READY  AGE
rc/phpinfo-1 1         1       1      1h

NAME          CLUSTER-IP    EXTERNAL-IP PORT(S)        AGE
svc/phpinfo 172.30.54.195 <none>      8080/TCP,8443/TCP 1h
```

Most of the entities (the pod, service, replication controller, and deployment configuration) in the preceding output are already familiar to you, from previous chapters.

The S2I build strategy uses the following additional entities—**build configuration, build, and image stream**. The build config has all of the information necessary to build the application. As with the rest of the OpenShift API resources, its configuration can be gathered using the oc get command:

```
$ oc get bc phpinfo -o yaml
apiVersion: v1
kind: BuildConfig
...
<output omitted>
...
spec:
...
<output omitted>
...
  source:
    git:
      ref: master
      uri: https://github.com/neoncyrex/phpinfo.git
    type: Git
  strategy:
    sourceStrategy:
      from:
        kind: ImageStreamTag
        name: php:7.0
        namespace: openshift
    type: Source
  successfulBuildsHistoryLimit: 5
  triggers:
  - github:
      secret: 5qFv8z-J1me1Mj7Q27rY
    type: GitHub
  - generic:
      secret: -g6nTMasd6TRCMxBvKWz
    type: Generic
  - type: ConfigChange
```

```
  - imageChange:
      lastTriggeredImageID: centos/php-70-
centos7@sha256:eb2631e76762e7c489561488ac1eee966bf55601b6ab31d4fbf60315d99d
c740
    type: ImageChange
status:
  lastVersion: 1
```

The following fields are especially important:

- `spec.source.git`: Repository URL for the application source code
- `spec.strategy.sourceStrategy`: Contains information on which builder will be used.

In our case, OpenShift uses a built-in builder from image stream `php:7.0`, in the `openshift` namespace. Let's look at its configuration:

```
$ oc get is php -o yaml -n openshift
apiVersion: v1
kind: ImageStream
<OMITTED>
spec:
  lookupPolicy:
    local: false
  tags:
<OMITTED>
  - annotations:
<OMITTED>
      openshift.io/display-name: PHP 7.0
      openshift.io/provider-display-name: Red Hat, Inc.
      sampleRepo: https://github.com/openshift/cakephp-ex.git
      supports: php:7.0,php
      tags: builder,php
      version: "7.0"
    from:
      kind: DockerImage
      name: centos/php-70-centos7:latest
<OMITTED>
```

The PHP builder image used to build our application is `centos/php-70-centos7:latest`.

We now have all the information on how to build an application from source code. OpenShift puts together all the information (provided by you and inferred from the source code) and starts a new build. Each build has a sequential number, starting from 1. You can display all builds by running the following command:

```
$ oc get build
NAME        TYPE    FROM          STATUS    STARTED       DURATION
phpinfo-1 Source Git@638030d Complete 2 hours ago 34s
```

This build is reported as `Complete`, as our application is already up and running.

# Starting a new build

If an application's source code was updated, you can trigger the rebuild process by running the `oc start-build` command. The build itself is managed by the build configuration.

First, we need to gather information on all available build configurations:

```
$ oc get bc
NAME     TYPE    FROM        LATEST
phpinfo Source Git@master 1
```

As you can see, we only have one build, `phpinfo`, and it was deployed only once; hence, the number 1.

Let's start a new build, as follows:

```
$ oc start-build phpinfo
build "phpinfo-2" started

$ oc get pod
NAME              READY  STATUS       RESTARTS AGE
phpinfo-1-build   0/1    Completed 0          2h
phpinfo-1-h9xt5   1/1    Running   0          2h
phpinfo-2-build   0/1    Init:0/2  0          3s
```

OpenShift started a new build, versioned as 2, which is present in the names of the pods spawned by the new build. Once everything is complete, your application will be redeployed:

```
$ oc get pod
NAME              READY  STATUS       RESTARTS AGE
phpinfo-1-build   0/1    Completed 0          2h
phpinfo-2-build   0/1    Completed 0          32s
phpinfo-2-zqtj6   1/1    Running   0          23s
```

The latest version of the build is now 2:

```
$ oc get bc
NAME     TYPE   FROM        LATEST
phpinfo  Source Git@master  2
```

A list of all builds is kept by OpenShift for future inspection:

```
$ oc get build
NAME       TYPE   FROM         STATUS   STARTED             DURATION
phpinfo-1  Source Git@638030d  Complete 2 hours ago         34s
phpinfo-2  Source Git@638030d  Complete About a minute ago  7s
```

This example is not close to production, as the build was triggered manually, not by changes to the source code. However, it gives you a general idea of how to use builds.

Use the following code to clean everything up for the next lab:

```
$ oc delete all --all
deploymentconfig "phpinfo" deleted
buildconfig "phpinfo" deleted
imagestream "phpinfo" deleted
pod "phpinfo-2-fbd81" deleted
service "phpinfo" deleted

$ oc delete project phpinfo
project "phpinfo" deleted

$ oc project myproject
Now using project "myproject" on server "https://127.0.0.1:8443".
```

# Summary

In this chapter, you learned about the build entities created by OpenShift, and how to deploy a simple PHP application from source code. We showed you how to start a new build and how to customize a build process.

In the following chapter, you will build and deploy a WordPress application from a custom template. You will also learn how to create and deploy OpenShift templates, and how to deploy applications from OpenShift templates.

# Questions

1. Which of the following OpenShift entities controls how to build a particular application from source code? choose two:

    1. Pod
    2. Route
    3. Replication controller
    4. Build config
    5. Build
    6. Deployment config

2. Which of the following commands starts a new build? choose one:

    1. `oc new-app`
    2. `oc new build`
    3. `oc start-build`
    4. `oc get build`

3. Which of the following commands display information on a build? choose three:

    1. `oc status -v`
    2. `oc status`
    3. `oc logs build/phpdemo-2`
    4. `oc show logs`

# Further reading

S2I is one of the most important features of OpenShift. You may want to have more deep knowledge of this process. The following links provide additional information:

- Builds and Image Streams at `https://docs.openshift.org/latest/architecture/core_concepts/builds_and_image_streams.html#builds`.
- PHP at `https://docs.openshift.com/online/using_images/s2i_images/php.html/`.

# 16
# Building a Multi-Tier Application from Source Code

In the previous chapter, we learned what build entities are—created by OpenShift—and how to deploy a simple PHP application from source code. We showed you how to start a new build and how to customize a build process.

In this chapter, you are going to build and deploy a WordPress application from a custom template. You are also going to work with OpenShift templates, learn how to create and deploy OpenShift templates, and deploy applications from OpenShift templates.

We are going to cover the topic that is building a multi-tier application.

## Technical requirements

This chapter relies on a working installation of OpenShift. We assume that OpenShift master's address is openshift.example.com and the default subdomain is example.com.

Some of the lab items require a custom DNS record, which can be simulated by setting a record in /etc/hosts. Both methods are acceptable.

You will be required to run minishift in this Chapter, to avoid certain errors and reconfiguration you might be required to do with other openshift deployment methods.

```
$ minishift start --openshift-version=v3.9.0 --vm-driver=virtualbox --
memory 4GB


...
output truncated for brevity
...
-- Minishift VM will be configured with ...
   Memory: 4 GB
   vCPUs : 2
```

```
   Disk size: 20 GB
...
output truncated for brevity
...
OpenShift server started.

The server is accessible via web console at:
    https://192.168.99.110:8443

You are logged in as:
    User: developer
    Password: <any value>

To login as administrator:
    oc login -u system:admin
```

# Building a multi-tier application

We explained to you previously how to use templates to deploy simple and multi-tier applications. This allows for deploying complex applications by creating deployment configs and deploying a number of pods, services, and routes. This approach is limited since most of the multi-tier applications need to be built from source code. OpenShift templates allow building applications from source code. The combination of building an application from source code and using templates to deploy and build a multi-tier application is described in this chapter. This is a hands-on chapter that gives you real examples of leveraging OpenShift templates to deploy applications in a production environment. Now it is time to see how to build a WordPress application from source code using MariaDB as a database.

# WordPress template

WordPress is a free and open-source **Content Management System** (**CMS**) based on PHP and MySQL. We want to demonstrate the **Source-to-Image** (**S2I**) build process for WordPress using templates prepared at `https://github.com/openshift-evangelists/wordpress-quickstart`. This repository contains ready-to-use templates for deploying WordPress on an OpenShift cluster. There are two example templates available in the repository. Let's clone the repository first:

```
$ git clone
https://github.com/openshift-evangelists/wordpress-quickstart.git
Cloning into 'wordpress-quickstart'...
remote: Counting objects: 331, done.
```

```
remote: Total 331 (delta 0), reused 0 (delta 0), pack-reused 331
Receiving objects: 100% (331/331), 1.07 MiB | 1.96 MiB/s, done.
Resolving deltas: 100% (119/119), done.
```

We are going to apply the `wordpress-quickstart/templates/classic-standalone.json` WordPress template. For simplicity, we converted the template from JSON to YAML and removed persistent storage-related entities. We also removed a default value for the `APPLICATION_NAME` parameter.

# Building a WordPress application

First, we want to place the application into a separate namespace:

```
$ oc new-project wp
Now using project "wp" on server "https://openshift.example.com:8443".
```

First, since it is a new template for us, we want to gather some information regarding available parameters. As was previously described, `oc process --parameters` can be helpful:

```
$ oc process --parameters -f wordpress-quickstart/templates/classic-standalone.json

NAME DESCRIPTION GENERATOR VALUE
APPLICATION_NAME The name of the WordPress instance.
QUICKSTART_REPOSITORY_URL The URL of the quickstart Git repository.
https://github.com/openshift-evangelists/wordpress-quickstart
WORDPRESS_DEPLOYMENT_STRATEGY Type of the deployment strategy for
Wordpress. Recreate
WORDPRESS_MEMORY_LIMIT Amount of memory available to WordPress. 512Mi
DATABASE_MEMORY_LIMIT Amount of memory available to the database. 512Mi
DATABASE_USERNAME The name of the database user. expression user[a-f0-9]{8}
DATABASE_PASSWORD The password for the database user. expression [a-zA-
Z0-9]{12}
MYSQL_VERSION The version of the MySQL database. 5.7
PHP_VERSION The version of the PHP builder. 7.0
```

Notice that only `APPLICATION_NAME` doesn't have a default value.

Let's build the application from source code by instantiating that template with its
`APPLICATION_NAME=wordpress`:

```
$ oc new-app -f wordpress-quickstart/templates/classic-standalone.json -p
APPLICATION_NAME=wordpress
--> Deploying template "wp/wordpress-classic-standalone" for
"wordpress.yaml" to project wp
...
<output omitted>
...
--> Success
    Build scheduled, use 'oc logs -f bc/wordpress' to track its progress.
    Access your application via route 'wordpress-wp.apps.kropachev.pro'
    Run 'oc status' to view your app.
```

You may want to check the build logs for wordpress application:

```
$ oc logs bc/wordpress -f
Cloning "https://github.com/openshift-evangelists/wordpress-quickstart" ...
  Commit: 0f5076fbb3c898b77b820571fa30d1293c3ac33b (Update README with
details on how to enable WebDav access.)
...
<output omitted>
...
Pushed 9/10 layers, 96% complete
Pushed 10/10 layers, 100% complete
Push successful
```

After some time, all WordPress pods will be up and running, as shown as follows:

```
$ oc get pod
NAME READY STATUS RESTARTS AGE
wordpress-1-build 0/1 Completed 0 2m
wordpress-1-zjfs2 1/1 Running 0 51s
wordpress-db-1-9mxgb 1/1 Running 0 2m
```

This indicates that our application should work now. Let's see what URL it was exposed
through and try to access it via a web browser:

```
$ oc get route
NAME HOST/PORT PATH SERVICES PORT TERMINATION WILDCARD
wordpress wordpress-wp.127.0.0.1.nip.io wordpress 8080 edge/Allow None
```

Once you open your browser and go to `http://wordpress-wp.127.0.0.1.nip.io/`, the
WordPress application should display a configuration page. Choose you favorite language
and press `continue` On the next page, just fill in the fields, as shown here, and click on
`Install WordPress`.

# Welcome

Welcome to the famous five-minute WordPress installation process! Just fill in the information below and you'll be on your way to using the most extendable and powerful personal publishing platform in the world.

## Information needed

Please provide the following information. Don't worry, you can always change these settings later.

| | |
|---|---|
| **Site Title** | My Example WordPress |
| **Username** | admin |
| | Usernames can have only alphanumeric characters, spaces, underscores, hyphens, periods, and the @ symbol. |
| **Password** | openshift     👁 Hide |
| | Very weak |
| | **Important:** You will need this password to log in. Please store it in a secure location. |
| **Confirm Password** | ☑ Confirm use of weak password |
| **Your Email** | openshift@example.com |
| | Double-check your email address before continuing. |
| **Search Engine Visibility** | ☐ Discourage search engines from indexing this site |
| | It is up to search engines to honor this request. |

Install WordPress

The next window displays the installation status:

Once you click on the **Log In** button, the following page is displayed:

You just need to type in the **username** and **password** provided during the setup phase. At this point, you should see the WordPress workspace:

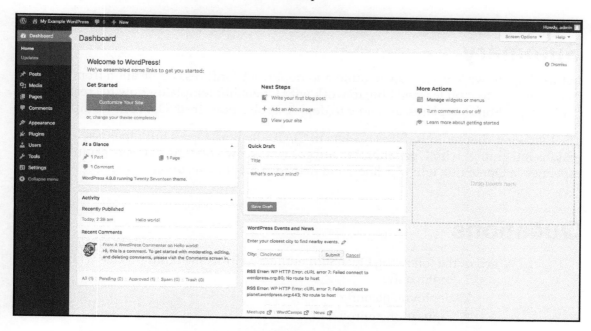

This indicates that everything was configured properly.

Use the following code to clean everything up for the next lab:

```
$ oc delete all --all
deploymentconfig "wordpress" deleted
deploymentconfig "wordpress-db" deleted
buildconfig "wordpress" deleted
imagestream "wordpress-img" deleted
route "wordpress" deleted
pod "wordpress-1-tnvhl" deleted
pod "wordpress-db-1-pdsbb" deleted
service "wordpress" deleted
service "wordpress-db" deleted

$ oc delete project wp
project "wp" deleted

$ oc project myproject
Now using project "myproject" on server "https://127.0.0.1:8443".
```

You may also delete your minishift VM running `minishift destroy` command, if you are done for today. Or just keep minishift up and proceed with the next chapter.

# Summary

In this chapter, we learned how to build and deploy a WordPress application from a custom template. You learned how to work with OpenShift templates, how to create and deploy OpenShift templates, and how to deploy applications from OpenShift templates.

The following chapter introduces readers to CI/CD, Jenkins, OpenShift pipelines, and Jenkins integration with OpenShift. We are going to show you how to create sample CI/CD pipelines in OpenShift, edit pipelines, and manage pipeline execution.

# Questions

1. Which of the following OpenShift entities controls the build process (choose one):
   1. buildconfig
   2. deploymentconfig
   3. replicationctonroller
   4. service
   5. pod
   6. route

2. Which of the following OpenShift entities can be created using templates (choose one):
   1. pod
   2. service
   3. route
   4. deployment config
   5. buildconfig
   6. All of above

# 17
# CI/CD Pipelines in OpenShift

In the previous chapter, you learned how to build and deploy a WordPress application from a custom template. You also learned how to create and deploy OpenShift templates, and how to deploy applications from OpenShift templates.

This chapter will introduce the reader to **Continuous Integration/Continuous Delivery (CI/CD)**, Jenkins, OpenShift pipelines, and Jenkins integration with OpenShift. We will discuss CI/CD, pipelines, and Jenkins as CI/CD, following by how Jenkins works in OpenShift. We will also show you how to create a sample CI/CD pipeline in OpenShift, how to edit pipelines, and how to manage pipeline execution.

After reading this chapter, you will understand the following topics:

- CI/CD and CI/CD pipelines
- Jenkins as CI/CD
- Jenkins in OpenShift

# Technical requirements

In this chapter, we will use the following technologies and software:

- The command-line interface
- Minishift
- GitHub
- Web browsers

The Vagrant installation, and all of the code that we will use in this chapter, are located on GitHub, at `https://github.com/PacktPublishing/Learn-OpenShift`.

You can use Firefox or any other browser to navigate through Docker Hub.

As a prerequisite, you will need a stable internet connection from your laptop.

We will use Minishift as our lab environment in this chapter. Before you start, please delete your existing Minishift VM (if there is one), because we will need to create a new VM, with non-standard parameters:

```
$ minishift start --openshift-version=v3.9.0 --vm-driver=virtualbox --
memory 4GB
...
output truncated for brevity
...
-- Minishift VM will be configured with ...
    Memory: 4 GB
    vCPUs : 2
    Disk size: 20 GB
...
output truncated for brevity
...
OpenShift server started.

The server is accessible via web console at:
    https://192.168.99.110:8443

You are logged in as:
    User: developer
    Password: <any value>

To login as administrator:
    oc login -u system:admin
```

Make sure that the Memory shows 4 GB at least; otherwise, you might not have enough memory for your lab. You can also adjust the amount of memory by stopping the Minishift VM and changing it via the VirtualBox console. But, the safest method is to delete the Minishift VM and create a new one.

# CI/CD and CI/CD pipelines

You may have already heard the term **CI/CD**. It comprises the two main acronyms people use when talking about modern application deployment. While CI stands for **Continuous Integration**, CD has two meanings; one of them is **Continuous Deployment,** and another one is **Continuous Delivery**. All three terms are easy to understand, and are described as follows:

- **Continuous Integration**: Emphasizes creating and building automation tests against application builds, as well as merging updates into a single branch as often as possible. It helps to catch bugs early on and to avoid the integration difficulties that developers usually encounter when developing new code and merging changes into different branches.

- **Continuous Delivery**: Helps to extend Continuous Integration processes, to push new code from the development to the production stage in a reproducible fashion. If, with Continuous Integration, you automate builds and tests, then Continuous Delivery automates application release processes, usually using approval procedures.

- **Continuous Deployment**: Extends Continuous Delivery even further, by providing a seamless and uninterrupted application delivery process, without any human intervention. This application deployment method requires quite a lot of effort to make sure that, when you run the code, it won't break anything and will work as expected.

The CI and CD processes are put into a series of steps and procedures to form a **pipeline**, often referred to as the CI/CD pipeline. Continuous Integration is shown with both Continuous Delivery and Continuous Deployment in the following diagram:

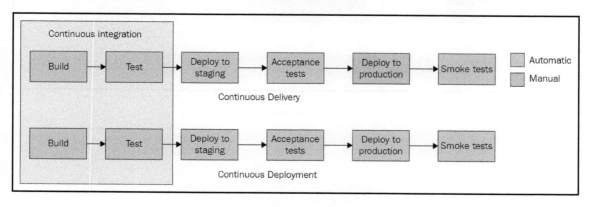

CI/CD pipeline example

The pipeline stages are not strict, but following best practices will help you to make your CI/CD pipeline stable and repeatable.

There are many CI/CD tools that can help you to automate the application delivery process, but one of the most popular ones in the industry is called Jenkins. It just so happens that OpenShift has built in integration with Jenkins, which we will discuss in the following sections.

# Jenkins as CI/CD

Jenkins is an open source automation tool that can be used to accelerate the application development process using CI/CD pipelines. Jenkins controls and manages application development life cycle processes, including the build, test, publish, stage, deploy, and smoke test processes, among others.

The standard Jenkins architecture is shown in the following diagram:

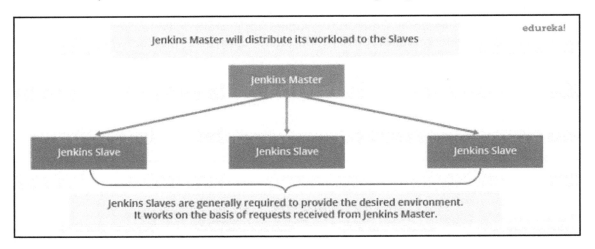

Jenkins architecture

There are two main components in the Jenkins architecture:

- **Jenkins Master**: Your CI/CD controller, handling various tasks, such as:
    - Job scheduling
    - Distributing the workload among Jenkins Slaves
    - Jenkins Slave monitoring
    - Logging and representing job results
- **Jenkins Slaves**: A set of Java-based programs that run on the remote host. Jenkins Slaves mainly execute instructions from Jenkins Masters.

Jenkins Masters and Jenkins Slaves are functionalities, which basically means that both can coexist on the same host. In small or lab environments, there are usually no issues with running both a Jenkins Master and Jenkins Slaves on the same host, but if you have hundreds (or thousands) of jobs running in your environment, it makes sense to run the Jenkins Master and Jenkins Slaves on different nodes, and to have several Jenkins Slaves, to distribute the load among them.

# Jenkins in OpenShift

OpenShift leverages the Jenkins CI/CD model, and extends it by using a combination of the following components:

- **OpenShift Domain Specific Language (DSL)**: DSL is provided by the OpenShift Jenkins client plugin that runs on the Jenkins Master pod and interacts with the OpenShift API server. The OpenShift DSL provides a method for controlling your application life cycle.
- **Jenkins Pipeline Build Strategy**: Similar to other OpenShift build strategies, it defines the build's workflow. Jenkins Pipeline Build Strategy allows a developer to create a Jenkins pipeline that is monitored and controlled by OpenShift.
- **Jenkinsfile**: Defines CI/CD pipelines through a series of steps during application deployment in OpenShift, using the Apache Groovy programming language.

# Creating Jenkins pipelines in OpenShift

Once the Minishift cluster is up, open your favorite web browser and open OpenShift, using the URL given from the output of the `minishift start` command. It is accessible via `https://192.168.99.110:8443`, in our case:

OpenShift login page

Use the **developer** user, with any password, to log in on the welcome page:

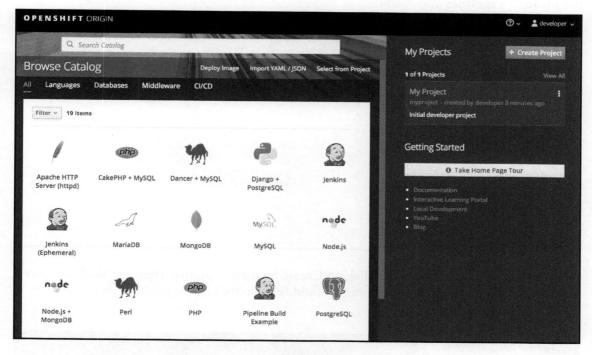

OpenShift welcome page

Click on **My Project** to access the OpenShift **Project Overview** page. From there, click on the **Builds | Pipelines** sub-menu:

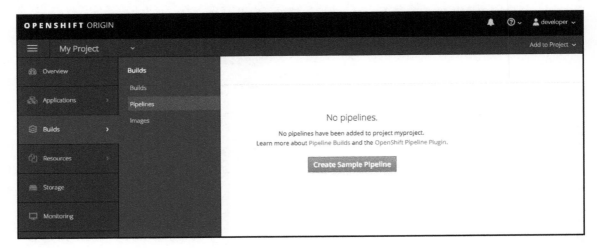

From here, you should be able to click on **Create Sample Pipeline**. Then, scroll all the way down and click on the **Create** button. It should tell you that the `Pipeline Build Example` has been created:

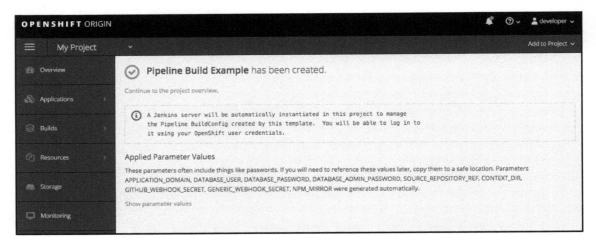

OpenShift creates a set of pods including Jenkins, mongodb and nodejs, with further integration with OpenShift. And all of that with just one click. This is just a demo, but isn't that cool? Now go back to the **Overview** menu to check the overall progress:

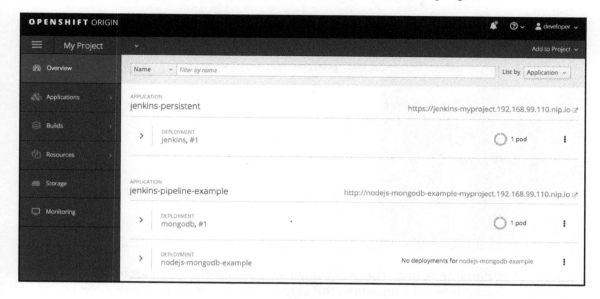

OpenShift project menu

You should be able to see a few applications, with pods. The first one is a Jenkins application, and the second one is MongoDB, as a part of our test application. There should be **No deployments** for `nodejs-mongodb-example`, because it will be controlled by Jenkins pipelines.

Depending on your internet connection, it will take time to pull all of the images and start all of the pods, especially for Jenkins, as it is roughly 2.5 GB. You can go to the **Monitoring** tab and click on **View details** to check the current status of the overall process. If the last message from Jenkins is **pulling image openshift/jenkins-2-centos7**, then just wait patiently, or go and make some coffee.

# Starting a Jenkins pipeline

Once both the Jenkins and MongoDB pods are running, go back to the **Builds** | **Pipelines** sub-menu:

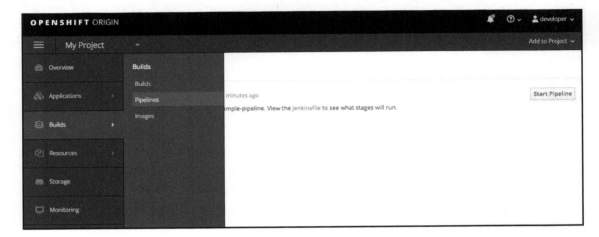

Click the **Start Pipeline** button. This will trigger a CI/CD pipeline, to start building. Depending on your internet connection, this step will take some time to complete; by the end of it, you should be able to see that two stages were completed successfully:

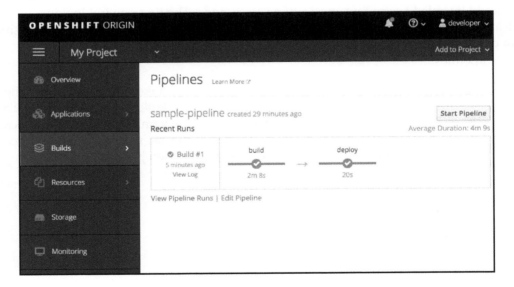

Clicking on **View Log** should open a new tab with the Jenkins console output from the Jenkins login page:

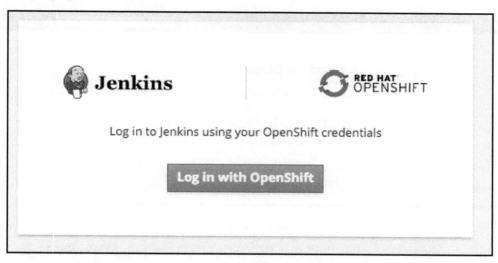

Jenkins login page

Click on **Log in with OpenShift** and use the same credentials that you used to authenticate in OpenShift (use the **developer** user, with any password):

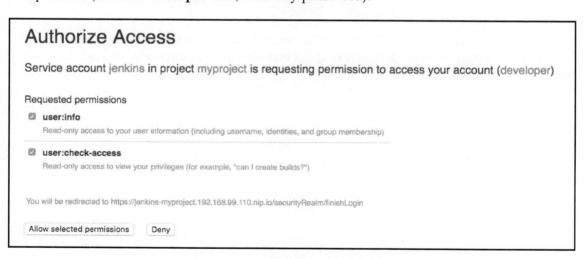

Jenkins user authorization

You will need to authorize the **developer** user to access Jenkins, by clicking on **Allow selected permissions**. This will get you to the Jenkins **Console Output**:

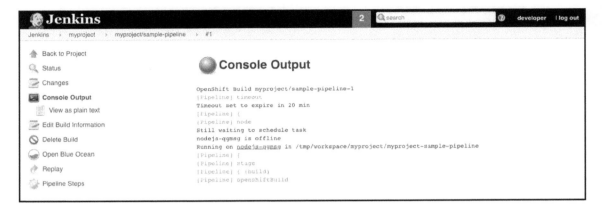

Jenkins Console Output

Scroll down to see the complete log, close the lab, and go back to the OpenShift tab.

If you are interested in how Jenkins works in detail and want to learn more, just follow the links in the *Further reading* section of this chapter.

We mentioned previously that there is a difference between the Continuous Delivery and Continuous Deployment models; one of them includes human intervention, and the other one does not.

What we are going to do next is modify our test pipeline and add an approval step. Go back to the **pipeline** sub-menu:

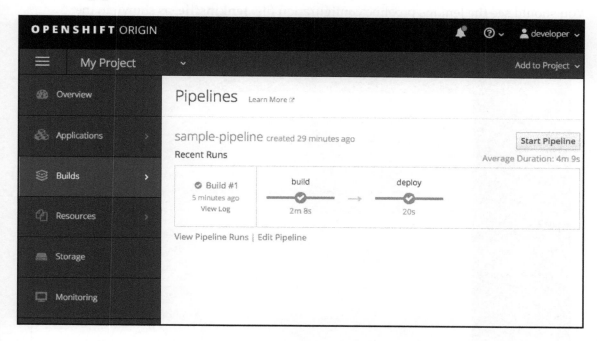

Clicking on **Edit Pipeline** should redirect us to editing our first pipeline.

# Editing Jenkinsfile

You should see the Jenkins pipeline configuration file, **Jenkinsfile**, as shown in the following screenshot:

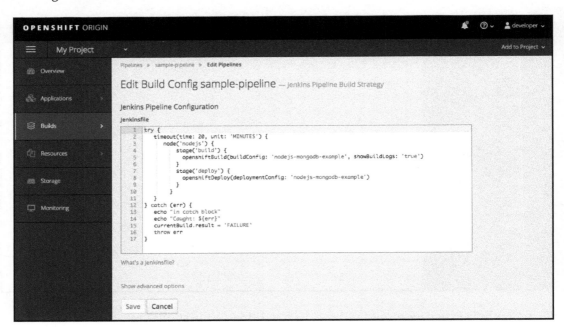

Editing pipelines

 Jenkins uses the Apache Groovy Programming Language. It is pretty easy to learn, and we are not going to delve too deeply into the details; rather, we will give you some basic skills. You can find more information regarding Groovy in the *Further reading* section.

We simply need to add a new stage with an arbitrary name; let's call it the `approval` stage, in between the `build` and `deploy` stages. This new `approval` stage will put the deployment stage on hold, until you manually approve it:

```
...
node('nodejs') {
 stage('build') {
 openshiftBuild(buildConfig: 'nodejs-mongodb-example', showBuildLogs:
'true')
 }
 stage('approval') {
 input "Approve moving to deploy stage?"
```

```
}
stage('deploy') {
openshiftDeploy(deploymentConfig: 'nodejs-mongodb-example')
}
}
...
```

Click on **Save** and start the pipeline.

# Managing pipeline execution

Adding one more stage called *approval* triggers the second build to start, and eventually you should be able to see the new **approval** stage, with **Input Required**:

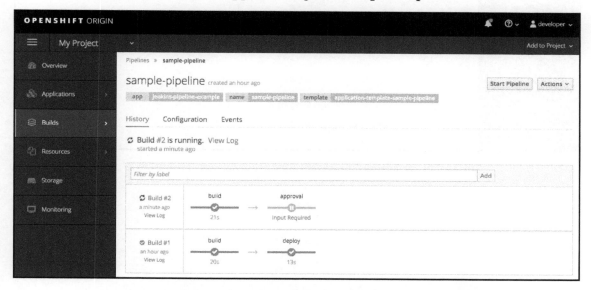

Clicking on **Input Required** will open a new tab and redirect you to the Jenkins approval stage, asking: **Approve moving to deploy stage?** Shown as follows:

The result will be different depending on what you answer. In our case, we are going to press the **Proceed** button. This will redirect us to the Jenkins Console Output, but we can just close it and go back to the OpenShift pipeline tab. From the following screenshot, we can see that the CI/CD pipeline has completed the deploy stage and now we have three stages instead of two as in `Build #1`.

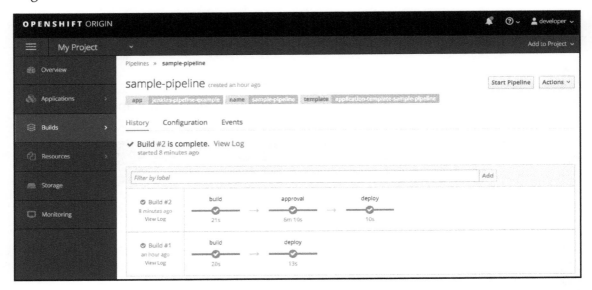

As a result, you should see a `nodejs-mongodb-example,` `#2` pod running in the
**Overview** menu. The `#2` means that it is build number two:

Jenkins is a lot more complicated than that, but this should have provided you with a good
overview of CI/CD in OpenShift, and how easy it is to get started with Jenkins in OpenShift

You are save know to stop and delete your minishift VM running `minishift delete`
command, unless you are going to do more practice.

# Summary

In this chapter, we introduced you to CI/CD, Jenkins, OpenShift pipelines, and Jenkins
integration with OpenShift. We showed you how to create a sample CI/CD pipeline in
OpenShift, how to edit pipelines, and how to manage pipeline execution.

In the next chapter, we will briefly touch on HA in general, and will then focus on
OpenShift HA. We will discuss how OpenShift provides redundancy in the event of a
failure, and how you can prevent this from happening by properly designing your
OpenShift cluster. At the end of the chapter, we will discuss how to back up and restore
OpenShift cluster data, in case something goes wrong.

# Questions

1. What CI/CD method allows you to automate the application delivery process without any human intervention? choose one:
    1. Continuous delivery
    2. Continuous deployment
    3. Continuous integration
    4. Continuous automation

2. Which three CI/CD pipeline components does OpenShift use? choose three:
    1. OpenShift Domain Specific Language
    2. Jenkins Pipeline Build Strategy
    3. Jenkins Java Connector
    4. Jenkinsfile
    5. Jenkins Build Strategy

3. You have to manually configure OpenShift authentication for OpenShift pipelines with Jenkins:
    1. True
    2. False

4. What command in Jenkinsfile allows you to implement a manual approval procedure? choose one:
    1. Input
    2. Hold
    3. Approve
    4. Accept

5. Which menu in the OpenShift GUI brings you to the OpenShift pipelines page? choose one:
    1. Build | Pipelines
    2. Jenkins | Pipelines
    3. Build | Jenkins
    4. Overview

6. The CI/CD pipeline stages in Jenkinsfile are predefined, and cannot be changed:
    1. True
    2. False

# Further reading

We briefly covered a lot of different topics regarding CI/CD in this chapter. The following links can help you delve into a topic you might be interested in:

- **CI/CD overview**: https://www.atlassian.com/continuous-delivery/ci-vs-ci-vs-cd
- **Apache Groovy documentation**: http://groovy-lang.org/syntax.html
- **OpenShift pipelines**: https://docs.openshift.com/container-platform/latest/dev_guide/openshift_pipeline.html
- **OpenShift Jenkins DSL plugin documentation**: https://github.com/openshift/jenkins-client-plugin
- **Jenkinsfile documentation**: https://jenkins.io/doc/book/pipeline/jenkinsfile/

# 18
# OpenShift HA Architecture Overview

In the previous chapter, we introduced you to CI/CD, Jenkins, OpenShift pipelines, and Jenkins integration with OpenShift. We also illustrated how to create a sample CI/CD pipeline in OpenShift, how to edit pipelines, and how to manage pipeline execution.

In this chapter, we will briefly touch on **high availability** (**HA**) in general, and will then focus on OpenShift HA. We will discuss how OpenShift provides redundancy in the case of a failure, and how you can prevent this from happening by properly designing your OpenShift cluster. At the end of this chapter, we will discuss how to back up and restore OpenShift cluster data in case something goes wrong.

In this chapter, we will cover the following topics:

- What is high availability?
- HA in OpenShift
- OpenShift backup and restore

## What is high availability?

HA is a very important topic when it comes to real customers and real money. We all work for different businesses, and the last thing that any business wants is to have an outage. This is a problem that can cause people to lose their jobs and companies to go bankrupt. It has happened, and it will continue to happen. But if you plan your HA design properly and implement it in the right way, you will have a better chance of keeping your job and maintaining your company's good reputation.

HA usually refers to a concept or strategy to keep a system up and running for a long time. That's where the terms *high* and *availability* come together. When people ask, *Does it support HA?*, they are usually asking whether the system is redundant, and whether it stays up and running if something goes wrong. In order to provide HA, each and every component of the system needs to be fault tolerant, and all of the lower- and upper-level components and protocols must be highly available. For example, if you have OpenShift designed and implemented in HA mode, but your network has a single point of failure, your application will stop working. So, it is critical to plan properly, and to make sure that your application stays up and running, no matter where a failure occurs.

# HA in OpenShift

In the previous chapters, we ran our applications on a single node, or sometimes, two nodes. Some might say that if there is more than one OpenShift node in the cluster, it is considered a redundant configuration, but that is far from true.

If we compare standard OpenShift architecture and OpenShift HA, you will see some differences between them:

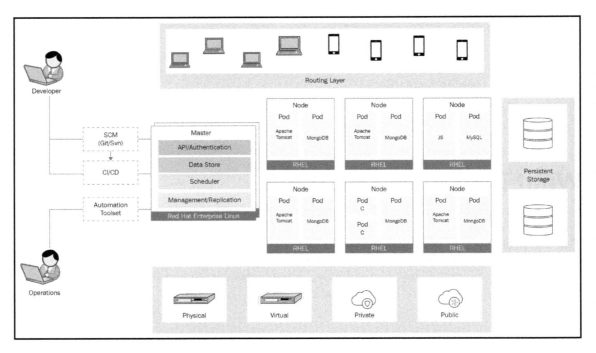

OpenShift classic architecture

Here we have nodes, masters, storage, and a routing layer consisting of infra nodes. OpenShift HA architecture is quite similar but has one distinct difference—in the routing layer we have load balances that make the overall solution always accessible. All other components are redundant by nature:

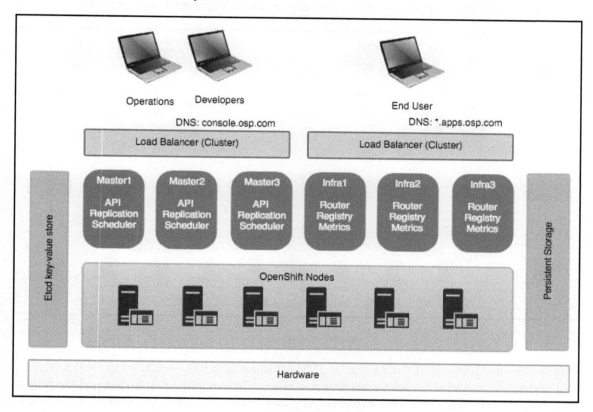

OpenShift HA architecture

# Virtual IPs

We can see that in OpenShift HA, we have what's called an enterprise load balancer, with two **Virtual IPs** (**VIPs**). We need one VIP for traffic to master nodes, and another VIP for traffic to actual OpenShift applications, running on OpenShift nodes within pods:

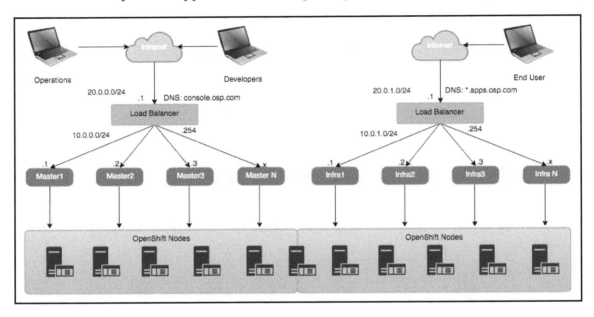

OpenShift with external load balancers

Why can't we just use DNS load balancing? The reason is, if we use DNS load balancing and one of the masters or nodes goes down, some traffic will still keep flowing to the failed node. Load balancing allows for implementing health checks and stops routing the traffic to the failed endpoint. For example, if one of the infra nodes fails, the load balancer will detect the failure, remove that node from the server pool, and stop sending traffic to the node. When the node comes back up, the load balancer will detect that, and will start load balancing traffic to the node. So, having VIPs is essential for OpenShift to be highly available from the outside.

| Node name | Physical IP address | Virtual IP address | DNS |
|-----------|---------------------|---------------------|-----|
| Infra1 | 10.0.0.1/24 | 10.0.0.11 | *.apps.osp.com |
| Infra2 | 10.0.0.2/24 | 10.0.0.11 | *.apps.osp.com |
| Infra3 | 10.0.0.3/24 | 10.0.0.11 | *.apps.osp.com |
| Master1 | 10.0.1.4/24 | 10.0.0.14 | console.osp.com |

| Master2 | 10.0.1.5/24 | 10.0.0.14 | console.osp.com |
| Master3 | 10.0.1.6/24 | 10.0.0.14 | console.osp.com |

Using an external load balancer is an ideal option when building OpenShift HA, because an external load balancer automatically detects a failure of any OpenShift infra or master node and distributes the load among the other nodes available.

Let's suppose that we have three infra nodes, all serving the traffic at a speed of 50 Mbps. If the Infra1 node fails, then the external load balancer automatically detects the failure and stops serving traffic to the Infra1 node. So, there will be no downtime for both end users and applications, and the load balancer will automatically distribute the load between Infra2 and Infra3, so both nodes will end up serving the traffic at a speed of 75 Mbps.

The downside of this scenario is that we have to use external load balancers, take care of their HA, implement additional health checks, and employ further configurations. And, if we are using commercial load balancer appliances from F5 or A10, they are going to be very expensive, as well. However, this is the most scalable solution that makes sure that OpenShift cluster is always accessible from the outside.

# IP failover

Another way to ensure that your OpenShift applications are always available from the outside is to implement IP failover mechanisms. This method is useful when you do not have an external load balancer, but still want OpenShift to always be accessible from the outside. The OpenShift IP failover design primarily relies on two different technologies:

- **Keepalived**: Provides high availability of VIPs across OpenShift infra nodes.

- **DNS**: Manages external traffic load balancing.

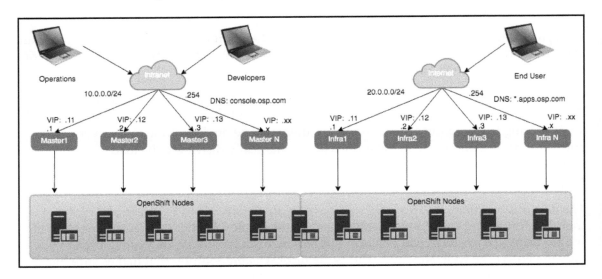

OpenShift DNS and keepalived

In our example, keepalived separately manages several VIPs on master and infrastructure nodes. Two DNS mappings are used to load balance the traffic between the VIPs of the OpenShift infra and master nodes:

| Node name | Physical IP address | Virtual IP address | DNS |
|-----------|---------------------|---------------------|------------------|
| Infra1 | 10.0.0.1/24 | 10.0.0.11 | *.apps.osp.com |
| Infra2 | 10.0.0.2/24 | 10.0.0.12 | *.apps.osp.com |
| Infra3 | 10.0.0.3/24 | 10.0.0.13 | *.apps.osp.com |
| Master1 | 20.0.0.1/24 | 20.0.0.11 | console.osp.com |
| Master2 | 20.0.0.2/24 | 20.0.0.12 | console.osp.com |
| Master3 | 20.0.0.3/24 | 20.0.0.13 | console.osp.com |

In the preceding example, we do not need an external load balancer, and, if one of the OpenShift nodes goes down, the Virtual IP will automatically be moved to another node. Depending on how we configure preemptive options, the Virtual IP may come back to an infra node if a failed info node recovers.

There is a downside to this solution, which may or may not be critical for your particular case. Let's suppose that we have three infra nodes, all serving the traffic at a speed of 50 Mbps. If one of the nodes fails, then the VIP from Infra1 will be moved to Infra2. There will be no interruption for end users or applications, but Infra2 will now serve the traffic at a speed of 100 Mbps, while Infra3 is still doing it at 50 Mbps.

This is OK when the workload is not too high, but if there is too much traffic, it may cause issues by overloading Infra2. So, you have to vet out all possible scenarios; by solving one particular failure scenario, you may create a new one.

 There are other methods for making your OpenShift cluster available externally. Discussing methods like DNS LB, GSLB, custom scripts, or even manual switchover, could easily extend this book by a thousand pages. We have focused on the methods that are proven to work and are supported by OpenShift.

# OpenShift infrastructure nodes

OpenShift infrastructure nodes are labeled with infra, by default. They run on two main OpenShift components:

- OpenShift internal registry
- OpenShift router

An Openshift infrastructure node is the easiest to install, operate, and troubleshoot, because the structure of an OpenShift infra node is simple, stable, and predictable. Infra nodes are usually installed in HA mode as a part of the initial OpenShift installation; they are rarely modified. The only time you might work with infra nodes directly is when you have a lot of traffic going through infra nodes and they can't handle it.

But, by the time you run into a situation like that, you will have much bigger problems than just scaling the number of infra nodes:

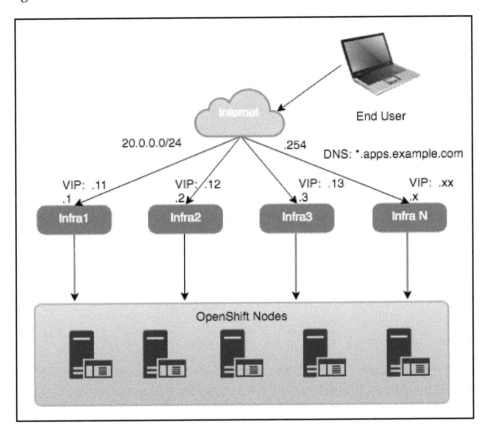

OpenShift infra nodes

The best practice is to have a minimum of three infra nodes installed, with the pod anti-affinity feature enabled for both the registry and router. You need to have anti-affinity enabled, because you can run into a situation where you lose one infrastructure node and the new router pod start a on the node that is already running an OpenShift router. So if you have only two infra nodes, without the pod anti-affinity feature enabled, in the case of a failure, you will have two routers and two registries running on the same infra node, listening on the same ports. The pod anti-affinity rule prevents one pod from running with another pod on the same host, thus preventing two registries (or two routers) from running on the same OpenShift infra node.

# OpenShift masters

OpenShift masters are control plane nodes and the central control points for OpenShift solutions. In earlier releases, you had to install an OpenShift master using Pacemaker (to provide failover), but in recent releases, this is taken care of by keepalived and external storage. If you ever have an OpenShift master fail completely, you can just delete the node and reinstall it.

In order to remove a node from your OpenShift cluster, you can use the `oc delete node` command, and then run `scaleup.yml` from the `openshift-ansible` Git project.

> The `openshift-ansible` project is available at `https://github.com/openshift/openshift-ansible`.

> The `scaleup.yml` file is located in `openshift-ansible/playbooks/byo/openshift-node/scaleup.yml`, once you have downloaded the `openshift-ansible` project.

> You will be required to adjust your Ansible inventory file and add a new node under the `[new_masters]` section.

If, at some point, you lose all OpenShift masters, it will not impact your end users, and customer-to-application traffic will keep flowing; however, you won't be able to make any new changes to the OpenShift cluster. At that point, there is not much that you can do, other than restore OpenShift masters from the last backup. We will discuss OpenShift backup and restore later in this chapter.

# OpenShift etcd

The OpenShift etcd key-value store is the most critical and sensitive OpenShift component, because all OpenShift master persistent data is kept in the etcd cluster. The good news is that etcd itself works in active/active configuration, and is installed during the initial installation. You will need to properly design your etcd cluster, so that you do not run into a situation where you are required to reinstall your etcd in order to handle a greater load. There is a general recommendation to install and configure your etcd cluster on dedicated nodes, separate from OpenShift masters, in a quantity of three, five, or seven members.

OpenShift keeps all configuration data in the etcd key-value store, so it is very important to regularly back up your etcd—at some point you will be required to restore it.

# OpenShift nodes

OpenShift nodes are the easiest to work with, when it comes to HA. Since OpenShift pods are stateless by nature, we do not need to directly take care of high availability of OpenShift nodes; we just need to make sure that the application pods are running on different OpenShift nodes, so that if an OpenShift node goes down, there is no downtime for the end user and a new application pod is brought up by the replication controller. If you ever have an OpenShift node fail completely, you can just delete that node and reinstall it.

In order to remove a node from your OpenShift cluster, you can use the `oc delete node` command, and then run `scaleup.yml` from the `openshift-ansible` Git project.

The `openshift-ansible` project is available at `https://github.com/ openshift/openshift-ansible`.

The `scaleup.yml` file is located in `openshift- ansible/playbooks/byo/openshift-node/scaleup.yml`, once you have downloaded the `openshift-ansible` project.

You will be required to adjust your Ansible inventory file and add a new node, under the `[new_nodes]` section.

There is no need to back up any data on an OpenShift node since there is no stateful data located on a node. In most cases, you will want to delete an OpenShift node from an OpenShift cluster, reinstall it, and bring it back, new and fresh.

# External storage for OpenShift persistent data

The external storage configuration and design for OpenShift persistent data is out of the scope of this book, but some general advice is to make sure that you have your external storage available in a redundant and scalable fashion, meaning that if one or several components fail, it will not affect overall storage performance and will always be accessible by OpenShift.

You will need to take care of regular external storage back up and restore procedures separately, and you will need to have a tested and verified procedure for if you lose persistent storage data.

# OpenShift backup and restore

No matter what you do, there will be times when something goes wrong with your OpenShift cluster, and some (or all) data is lost. That's why you need to know when and how to make OpenShift backups and how to bring OpenShift back to an operational state. The OpenShift installation procedure includes the following components that you will need to back up:

- Etcd key-value store data
- Master configuration data
- Ansible host installation playbooks
- Pod data
- Registry data
- Project configuration data
- Additionally installed software

Depending on the failure situation, you may need to either reinstall the whole OpenShift cluster or reinstall some components separately. In most cases, you will be required to completely reinstall the OpenShift cluster.

# Etcd key-value store backup

The etcd backup procedure can be performed on any etcd node, and consists of the following steps:

1. Stop the etcd service: `systemctl stop etcd`
2. Create an etcd backup: `etcdctl backup --data-dir /var/lib/etcd --backup-dir ~/etcd.back`
3. Copy the etcd db file: `cp /var/lib/etcd/member/snap/db ~/etcd/member/snap/db`
4. Start the etcd service: `systemtl start etcd`

The etcd key-value store recovery procedure is performed on etcd nodes and consists of the following steps:

1. Create a single node cluster
2. Restore data to `/var/lib/etcd/`, from backup, while etcd is not running
3. Restore `/etc/etcd/etcd.conf`, from backup

4. Restart etcd

5. Add new nodes to the etcd cluster

# OpenShift masters

The OpenShift master node backup procedure can be performed on all master nodes, and consists of the following steps:

1. **Back up master certs and keys**: `cd /etc/origin/master; tar cf /tmp/certs-and-keys-$(hostname).tar *.key *.crt`

2. **Back up registry certificates**: `cd /etc/docker/certs.d/; tar cf /tmp/docker-registry-certs-$(hostname).tar *`

The master node recovery procedure can be performed on all master nodes and consists of the following step:

1. Restore the previously saved data on every master node to `/etc/sysconfig/`, `/etc/origin/`, and `/etc/docker/` directories.

2. Restart OpenShift all services

# OpenShift nodes

There is no specific need to save any data on an OpenShift node, since there is no stateful data; you can easily reinstall all of the nodes one by one, or while reinstalling the OpenShift cluster.

# Persistent storage

In many cases, OpenShift pod persistent data can be saved and restored with the `oc rsync` command, but it is not the most reliable and efficient method. Persistent storage backup procedures are very different for every storage type, and must be considered separately.

# Summary

In this chapter, we briefly touched on OpenShift HA and on HA in general. We discussed how OpenShift provides redundancy in the case of a failure and how you can prevent this from happening by properly designing your OpenShift cluster. We finished the chapter with the backup and restore methods and procedures in OpenShift.

In the next chapter, we will discuss OpenShift DC in single and multiple data centers. OpenShift multi-DC is one of the most difficult topics when it comes to OpenShift design and implementation in a scalable and distributed environment. The next chapter will illustrate how to properly design OpenShift, in order to work in a distributed and redundant configuration across one or more data centers.

# Questions

1. Which of these HA methods provides external access to the OpenShift cluster using an external load balancer? choose one:
     1. Virtual IP
     2. IP failover
     3. GSLB
     4. DNS load balancing
2. What are the two valid HA methods to provide access to OpenShift from the outside? choose two:
     1. Virtual IP
     2. IP failover
     3. GSLB
     4. DNS load balancing

3. Etcd is a key-value store that is used to store the system's configuration and state in OpenShift:
    1. True
    2. False

4. What command can be used to back up and restore application data in OpenShift? choose one:
    1. `oc rsync`
    2. `oc backup`
    3. `oc save`
    4. `oc load`

5. There is no need to restore any data in the OpenShift master disaster recovery procedure:
    1. True
    2. False

# Further reading

The following links will help you to dive deeper into some of this chapter's topics:

- **OpenShift HA design**: `http://v1.uncontained.io/playbooks/installation/`
- **OpenShift High Availability**: `https://docs.openshift.com/enterprise/latest/admin_guide/high_availability.html`
- **Infrastructure nodes and pod anti-affinity**: `https://docs.openshift.com/container-platform/3.7/admin_guide/manage_nodes.html#infrastructure-nodes`
- **OpenShift backup and restore**: `https://docs.openshift.com/container-platform/3.4/admin_guide/backup_restore.html`
- **OpenShift scaling and performance guide**: `https://docs.openshift.com/container-platform/3.7/scaling_performance/index.html`
- **Etcd optimal cluster size**: `https://coreos.com/etcd/docs/latest/v2/admin_guide.html#optimal-cluster-size`
- **Adding hosts to an OpenShift cluster**: `https://docs.openshift.com/container-platform/latest/install_config/adding_hosts_to_existing_cluster.html`

# 19

# OpenShift HA Design for Single and Multiple DCs

In the previous chapter, we briefly touched upon OpenShift HA and **high availability (HA)** in general. We discussed how OpenShift provides redundancy in case of a failure and how you can prevent this from happening by designing your OpenShift cluster properly. Finally, we finished the chapter with backup and restore methods and procedures in OpenShift.

In this chapter, we are going to talk about OpenShift scenarios in single and multiple data centers. This chapter will also explain how to properly design OpenShift in a distributed and redundant configuration across one or more data centers.

After reading this chapter, you will have an understanding of the following topics:

- OpenShift single-DC HA design
- OpenShift multi-DC HA design

# OpenShift single-DC HA design

In the previous chapter, we briefly covered HA and OpenShift HA in general, but we did'nt discuss how to practically design OpenShift in your data center environment.

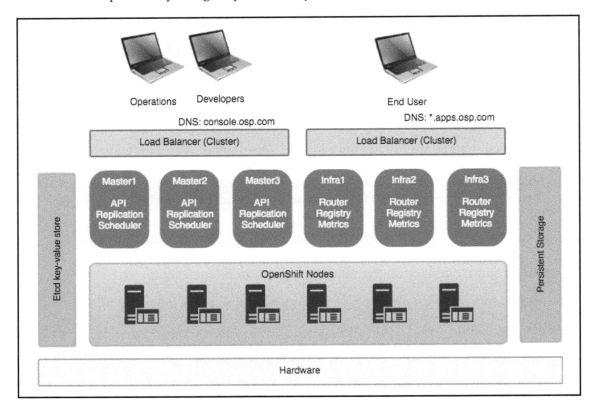

Let's recall what main OpenShift components we have and how they provide redundancy:

- Openshift infrastructure nodes
- OpenShift master nodes
- OpenShift nodes
- Etcd key-value store
- Persistent storage

# OpenShift infrastructure nodes

OpenShift infrastructure nodes are essential components that provide access from the outside of an OpenShift cluster. OpenShift infrastructure nodes scale horizontally, which means that we can add as many nodes as we need in order to add network throughput. If you recall from the previous chapter, we need to consider which VIP method to use. We have two main VIP methods:

- **VIP using an external load balancer**:

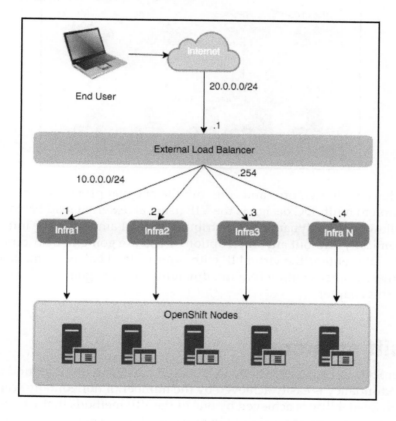

- **IP failover using keepalived**:

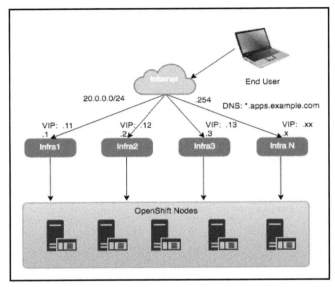

Both methods have their own pros and cons, but the one that provides better scalability and smooth migration to multi-DC design is the VIP using an external load balancer method. This method allows you to dynamically distribute the load among all the infra nodes and add them dynamically without any interruption. If you are going to distribute the load across multiple data centers, the virtual IP with external load balancers method allows you to implement these changes with minimum downtime. We are going to discuss multi-DC design later in this chapter.

# OpenShift masters

Similar to OpenShift infrastructure nodes, OpenShift masters require redundancy and high availability. Redundancy is easily achieved by the number of horizontally scalable master nodes, and high availability is achieved by one of the VIP methods that we discussed previously. For the same reason, using an external load balancer is a way better and scalable solution compared to the keepalived and DNS method.

# OpenShift nodes

OpenShift nodes do not have any specific HA requirements since they are running stateless pods in a redundant fashion. The only HA and redundancy consideration is to have enough OpenShift nodes to handle additional workload when a failure happens in your data center, whether a server, a rack, or a whole row of racks goes down. You need to distribute the workload and make sure that no matter what fails, you have redundant components and pods up and running.

# Etcd key-value store

OpenShift etcd is a highly distributed key-value store where all critical OpenShift cluster-related data is kept. Etcd works in active/active configuration by default, which means it provides both redundancy and high availability by default. There is a general recommendation to install and configure your etcd cluster on dedicated nodes separately from OpenShift masters in a quantity of three, five, or seven members.

# Persistent storage

External storage configuration and design for OpenShift persistent data is out of the scope of this book, but general advice is to make sure that you have your external storage available in a redundant and scalable fashion, meaning that if one or several components fails, it does not affect overall storage performance and is always accessible by OpenShift.

# Physical placement consideration

Considering that our OpenShift cluster is going to be up and running within a single data center, we need to take extra caution and make sure that we follow some simple rules:

- The same OpenShift components need to be connected to different switches and power circuits, and located in different racks or server rooms if possible
- All hardware should be running on OpenShift components connected to physical networking using interface teaming with LACP and MC-LAG on networking switches
- An external storage cluster for persistent data should follow the same rules and should be connected to different switches and power circuits, and located in different racks or server rooms if possible

- Use different load balancer clusters that work independently from each other and do not form a single point of failure
- If you want to provide additional reliability for an OpenShift solution, you can also use the server hardware RAID for OpenShift OS, ECC-enabled RAM, multiple networking cards, dual-socket motherboards, and SSD disks

# Design considerations

Considering a design like this, you have to ask yourself several questions:

- What happens if any critical component (OpenStack, network, or storage) goes down?
- What do I do if the OpenShift cluster upgrades?
- What do I do if external storage for OpenShift persistent data becomes unavailable?
- How much time does it take to recover an OpenShift cluster if the whole thing goes down?

There are other questions, of course, that you have to ask yourself, but if you are able to answer these questions without any hesitation, then you are on the right track.

# OpenShift multi-DC HA design

OpenShift multi-DC is one of the most difficult topics when it comes to OpenShift design and implementation in a scalable and distributed environment. This happens mainly because there are not that many deployments and best practices developed around this topic. It may be relatively easy to deploy an OpenShift cluster in a single data center environment, but when it comes to a multi-DC design, this is where things will get complicated. The reason is that now we have to consider all OpenShift and adjacent components, like networking and storage, to be scalable and highly available across multiple data centers as well. There are two main HA strategies for a design that involves more than one data center:

- Single OpenShift cluster across all data centers (for example, one cluster per three DCs)
- One OpenShift cluster per data center (for example, three clusters per three DCs)

For all of these strategies, we need to use active/active scenarios because an active/passive scenario is a waste of resources and money. And although there are still many companies utilizing active/passive scenarios, they usually have plans to migrate to active/active scenarios.

# One OpenShift cluster across all data centers

This particular design option is the most natural and the easiest to operate, but the most dangerous among all the other options. One data center environment brings one set of problems, and if you add another data center, it will give you twice as many problems. If you have an unreliable data center interconnect link, it will add up alongside the failure risks as well. Some of you may disagree, but this is what usually happens if you do not plan and design your solution properly:

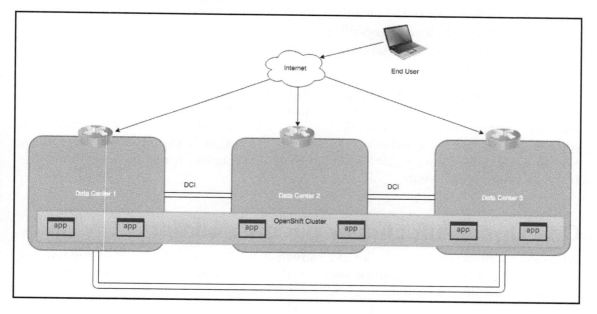

Considering a design like the preceding, you will have the following challenges:

- How do I load balance the traffic across all of these data centers from the internet?
- How do I distribute each and every OpenShift component across these data centers so that, in case of a failure, OpenShift is still able to handle all the load?
- How does my storage solution work across all three data centers?
- Do I need to extend the same network subnet across all data centers?
- How do I solve asymmetric routing problems?
- What happens with the OpenShift cluster if there is a split brain scenario?
- What happens if any critical component (OpenStack, network, or storage) goes down in one of the data centers?
- How much time does it take if the whole OpenShift cluster goes down?
- How do I scale out this solution, for example, if a new data center comes out?
- What do I do if an OpenShift cluster upgrades?
- What do I do if external storage for OpenShift persistent data becomes unavailable?

So, as you can see, having just a single OpenShift cluster across all your data centers adds a lot more questions and problems compared to a single cluster in one data center. This solution has one main benefit—having one single OpenShift cluster is easier to operate. But you need to ask yourself whether you are building a solution that will be easy to operate or a reliable and stable solution that is going to be up and running during the most difficult and even catastrophic events.

# One OpenShift cluster per data center

While the previous solution has a lot of disadvantages, there is another, not so popular, but very stable, predictable, and scalable solution. That solution is where you have as many clusters as there are data centers:

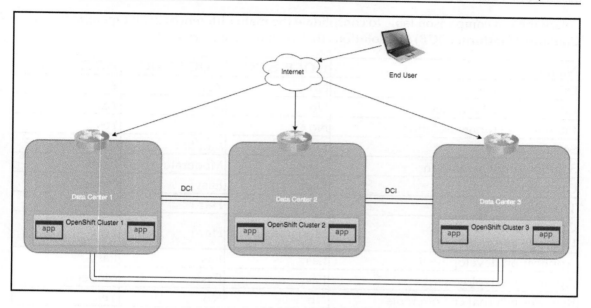

The main benefit of this solution is that all of your OpenShift clusters are going to be independent of each other and won't affect other OpenShift clusters if something goes wrong. You will still have challenges, but they are a bit different from single Openshift clusters across all DCs and easier to solve. Besides, this solution scales much better than the other ones. However, you should answer these questions before implementing this solution:

- How do I load balance the traffic across all of these data centers from the internet?
- What happens with the OpenShift cluster if there is a split brain scenario?
- How does my storage data work across all three data centers?
- Do I need database replication across all the data center? If yes, how will it work?
- What happens if any critical component (OpenStack, network, or storage) goes down in one of the data centers?
- How much time does it take if the whole OpenShift cluster goes down?
- How do I scale out this solution, for example, if a new data center comes out?
- What do I do regarding OpenShift cluster upgrades?
- What do I do if external storage for OpenShift persistent data becomes unavailable?

Following is a comparison table to consolidate the main differences in all **OpenShift Container Platform** (**OCP**) HA solutions that we have just discussed:

| Name | 1xOCP-1xDC | 1xOCP-3xDC | 3xOCP-3xDC |
|---|---|---|---|
| DC redundancy | No | Yes | Yes |
| Intercluster redundancy | No | No | Yes |
| Intercluster storage isolation | No | No | Yes |
| Scalability | Limited | Limited | Unlimited |
| Solution implementation | Easy | Moderate | Hard |
| Operations | Easy | Easy | Moderate |
| Troubleshooting | Easy | Hard | Moderate |
| Cluster seamless Upgrade and recovery | Moderate | Hard | Easy |
| Application development | Easy | Easy | Easy |
| Application deployment | Easy | Easy | Moderate |
| Requires external custom tools | No | No | Yes |

As you can see, each and every HA solution has their own pros and cons:

- **1xOCP-1xDC**: This is easiest to implement, operate, and troubleshoot, but suffers from data center or OpenShift cluster failures and has limited scalability.
- **1xOCP-3xDC**: In addition to all the benefits of the previous solution, it has better redundancy but adds a lot of troubleshooting effort if something goes wrong. This solution is also difficult to perform seamless upgrades and recoveries on.
- **3xOCP-3xDC**: This is a next level solution architecture that is much harder to implement, operate, and troubleshoot, but is the most stable, scalable solution ever. This solution requires extensive experience and expertise, but ensures that you will always have your application up and running.

In order to successfully implement the last solution where we have one OpenShift cluster per data center, we are required to take a closer look at the following topics:

- Networking
- Storage
- Application deployment

# Networking

The main problem in networking when you are building a solution like this is how to properly load balance the traffic, and when failure happens, how to re-route the traffic to other OpenShift clusters. The main technologies we can use here are the following:

- **Anycast IP addresses**: In order to effectively load balance the traffic across all our data centers, we can use an anycast IP address. This will help not only load balance the traffic but also provide IP failover if an application becomes unavailable in one of the data centers.
- **Application health checks**: Application health checks are a must have in this solution. They will help you to identify the failure and reroute the traffic to other data centers.
- **Dynamic routing protocols**: Make sure that you have IGP/BGP connectivity between load balancers and network HW. When failure happens, IGP/BGP will withdraw its IP anycast address so that the traffic goes to other data centers.
- **SSL Offloading**: Depending on the implementation, you might need to configure SSL offloading on load balancers. This will take traffic decryption off the OpenShift cluster:

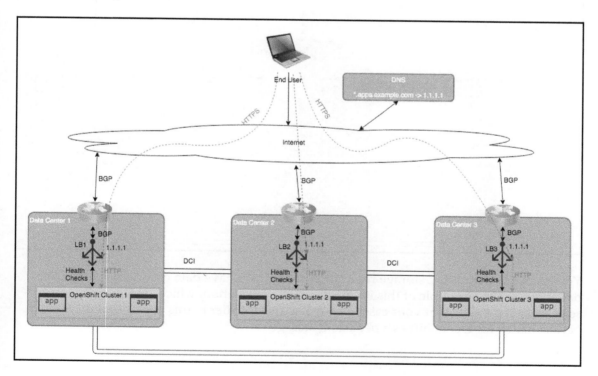

# Storage

Storage has always from a problem when it comes to geographically distributed application deployment across several platforms. Even major cloud providers have not solved it yet. This is the prime reason why application instances must be able to work independently from each other and be stateless. However, we can suggest a few architectures that will point you in the right direction and help solve the problem:

**Storage geo-replication**:

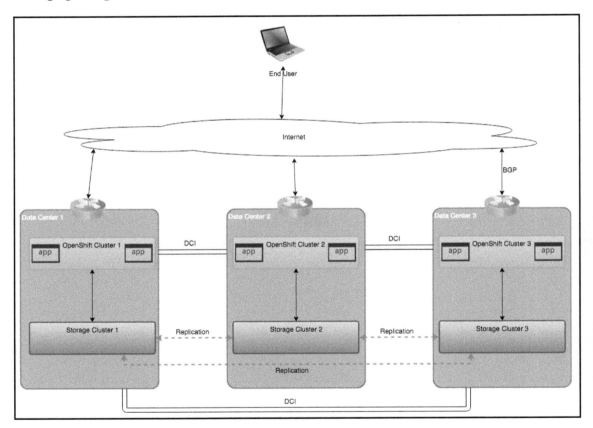

You can set up Multi-DC storage replication so that you have data consistency across all data centers. One example of this is GlusterFS geo-replication, which supports different scenarios that should suit your case. As we discussed earlier in this book, GlusterFS is a perfect match for OpenShift as a persistent storage.

**Database geo-replication**:

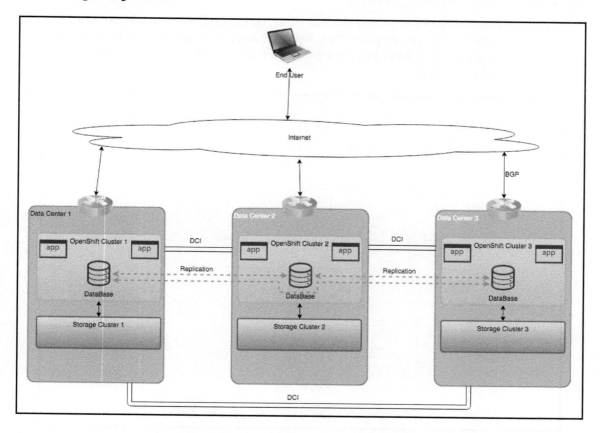

In most cases, the only stateful information you have in OpenShift will be kept in databases. Modern databases support multi-site, multi-DC, and multi-region replication architectures, such as Cassandra, MongoDB, Kafka, and Hazelcast.

 You will still need to take care of backup and restore procedures if the database gets corrupted.

## Application deployment

Once you are done with network and storage designs, the final step should be taken towards application deployment processes. Since we have several clusters, there must be a process regarding how to deliver your applications consistently across all OpenShift clusters and all data centers:

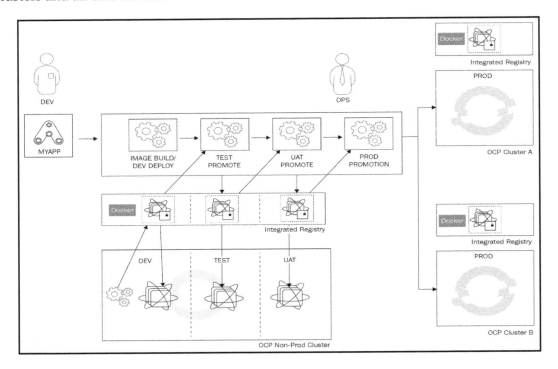

This is where external tools come into the picture. We can use external CI/CD software to automate the application deployment process across all OpenShift clusters, or we can build a separate OpenShift cluster with CI/CD to develop, build, test, and release applications to production OpenShift clusters.

# Summary

In this chapter, we talked about OpenShift scenarios in single and multiple data centers. This chapter also explained how to properly design OpenShift in a distributed and redundant configuration across one or more data centers.

In the next chapter, we are going to cover main network aspects while designing an OpenShift cluster in one or across multiple data centers. We will also cover commonly made mistakes, solutions, and overall guidance from a networking point of view.

# Questions

1. Which OpenShift component has built-in HA and works in active/active mode? choose one:
    1. OpenShift Etcd key-value store
    2. OpenShift Masters
    3. OpenShift infrastructure nodes
    4. OpenShift nodes

2. Which OpenShift HA solution out of the ones listed supports unlimited scalability? choose one:
    1. 1xOSP - 3xDC
    2. 3xOSP - 1xDC
    3. 3xOSP - 3xDC
    4. 1xOSP - 1xDC

3. Anycast IP addresses ensure that application traffic is load balanced across several data centers:
    1. True
    2. False

4. What are the two options to ensure application data consistency in geo-replicated OpenShift deployments? choose two:
    1. Persistent storage replication
    2. Application database replication
    3. Openshift cluster replication
    4. Openshift etcd key-value store replication

# Further reading

Here are a list of topics with links related to this chapter that you might want to deep dive into:

- **OpeShift HA design**: http://v1.uncontained.io/playbooks/installation/
- **OpenShift high availability**: https://docs.openshift.com/enterprise/latest/admin_guide/high_availability.html
- **Openshift for single and multiple DCs**: https://blog.openshift.com/deploying-openshift-applications-multiple-datacenters/
- **GlusterFS geo-replication**: https://docs.gluster.org/en/latest/Administrator%20Guide/Geo%20Replication/

# Network Design for OpenShift HA **20**

In the previous chapter, we talked about OpenShift scenarios in single and multiple data centers and explained how to properly design OpenShift in a distributed and redundant configuration across one or more data centers.

In this chapter, we are going to cover the main network aspects while designing OpenShift clusters in one or across multiple data centers. We will also cover commonly made mistakes, solutions, and overall guidance from a networking point of view.

After reading this chapter, you will have an understanding of the following topics:

- Common network topologies for OpenShift deployments
- Commonly made mistakes while designing networks for OpenShift
- General network requirements and design guidelines for OpenShift deployments

## Common network topologies for OpenShift deployments

Though each and every network infrastructure is unique in one way or other, all of these networks have a lot in common and can be split into two different types:

- Physical or data center networks
- Virtual or cloud networks

# Data center networks

Most of the physical and data center networks have a similar structures and components, such as the following:

- **Core/spine layer switches**: To interconnect different parts of the network, including aggregation/leaf switches, as well as, edge of the network and/or even Data Center Interconnect links
- **Access/leaf switches**: To connect physical servers to the revenue-generating network
- **Edge firewalls**: To filter the external traffic to the inside of the network
- **Border routers**: To connect to the internet or any other external network
- **Load balancers**: To load balance the incoming traffic between groups of application servers

This is depicted on the following diagram:

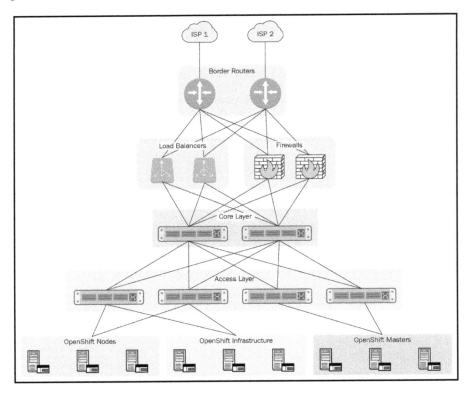

Some of these components can be collapsed, such as firewalls and border routers. Some components are optional, such as load balancers. There may be additional components, but these are the essential building blocks for every data center.

# Access layer switches

The Network Access Layer is an essential but critical network component that usually has several features configured, such as:

- **Multi-Chassis Link Aggregation (MC-LAG)**: Allows server links to be connected to different access layer switches with bonding enabled in active/active mode
- **Virtual LAN (VLAN)**: A very old but solid technology that separates one broadcast domain from another
- **L3 gateway**: An IP Gateway to allow VLAN traffic in and out
- **Dynamic routing protocol: Interior Gateway Protocol (IGP)/Border Gateway Protocol (BGP)** allows server IP addresses/subnets to be exchanged dynamically and failover from one transit link to another without any downtime
- **Control Plane Policing (CoPP)**: This is a common way to protect management access to/from the equipment

# Core layer switches

The network core layer is the heart of the network of all other data center components and has a very limited number of features configured, such as the following:

- **Dynamic routing protocol**: IGP/BGP allows server IP addresses/subnets to be exchanged dynamically and failover from one transit link to another without any downtime
- **CoPP**: This is a common way to protect management access to/from the equipment

# Edge firewalls

Edge firewalls are a first-level defense against attacks from the internet. Edge firewalls also logically separate different network segments from one another and usually have the following features enabled:

- **Stateful inspection**: Keeps track of the traffic coming in and out, dynamically opening and closing requested ports to the servers inside the data center
- **Application firewall**: Allows you to dynamically identify the application by checking application signatures and take a proper action, such as permit or deny
- **Distributed denial-of-service (DDoS) protection**: Identifies and blocks malicious traffic while enabling legitimate traffic to be processed and reached out to by the applications running inside the data center
- **Intrusion Prevention System (IPS) and Intrusion Detection System (IDS)**: These provide protection techniques against exploit attacks regarding data center applications, using their vulnerabilities
- **Network Address Translation (NAT)**: NAT allows hosts inside the data center network to access the internet by changing the source IP address to a publicly available IP address
- **CoPP**: This is a common way to protect management access to/from the equipment

# Load balancers

Load balancers are one of the optional network components that have additional features that keep track of application availability and dynamically load balance the requests from the internet across the servers inside the data center. Load balancers have a specific set of features configured, such as the following:

- **Destination Network Address Translation (DNAT)**: DNAT allows hosts from the outside of the data center network to access the servers inside the data center network by changing the destination IP address from a publicly available IP address to a private IP address of an appropriate server from the pool
- **Load balancing**: Works in conjunction with DNAT to dynamically track application availability and dynamically remove servers from the server groups

- **SSL offloading**: Takes care of web traffic encryption/decryption going to/from unsecured networks by terminating SSL traffic on the load balancer
- **CoPP**: This is a common way to protect management access to/from the equipment

# Border routers

A border router is a point of communication between the data center network and the internet, and has a very limited number of features configured, such as the following:

- **Dynamic Routing Protocol**: BGP holds the whole internet-routing table to calculate the optimal path to the final destination as well as advertise the data center public IP address pool to the internet
- **CoPP**: This is a common way to protect management access to/from the equipment

# Cloud networks

Similar to physical and data center networks, cloud networks have their own structure and components, such as the following:

- **Software-Defined Networking (SDN)**: SDN replaces traditional network architectures by implementing networks on demand by using popular SDN transport and encapsulation protocols
- **Security groups**: Flexible and programmable firewall filters that allow traffic control at scale, avoiding a single point of failure
- **NAT gateways**: To efficiently route traffic in and out of the cloud network, providing NAT services when necessary
- **Load balancers**: To load balance the incoming traffic between groups of application servers

Though different cloud providers use different protocols and implementations of one or another component, the main functionality stays the same and works similarly from one cloud provider to another:

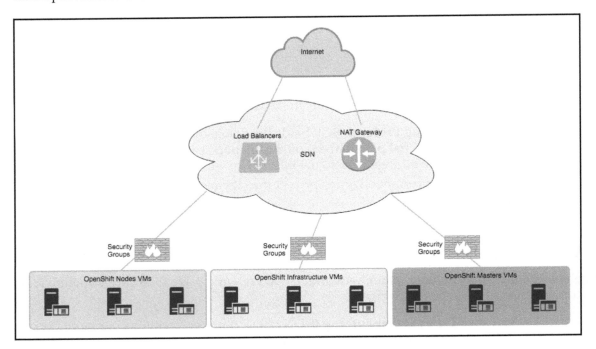

## SDN

SDN allows applications to be abstracted and completely independent of underlying network implementations by using modern and popular communication and transport protocols, such as the following:

- **OpenFlow**: This is a protocol that allows access to the forwarding plane of a network switch or router over the network. OpenFlow allows network controllers to calculate a packet path across the network. Many products and companies are using OpenFlow to build their SDN networks, including OpenStack. OpenFlow is supported by leading network manufacturers, including Cisco Systems, Juniper Networks, Alcatel-Lucent, Dell, Arista, and others.

- **Virtual Extensible LAN (VXLAN)**: This is an encapsulation protocol that allows running an overlay network on existing routing networks. VXLAN is one of the most popular protocols that is being used to interconnect different network segments of SDN into a single solution.

# Security groups

Security groups are the main security method for controlling the traffic going in and out of **Virtual Machines** (**VMs**) that are running applications, and they have one main function—**stateful inspection**. This keeps track of the traffic going in and out, dynamically opening and closing requested ports to the applications inside the VMs.

# Load balancers

If data center networks quite often use physical load balancers, then cloud networks tend to use software load balancers, providing the same functionaly at a high level, including DNAT, load balancing, and even SSL offloading.

So, the power of cloud networks must not be underestimated.

# Network Address Translation (NAT) gateways

A NAT gateway is a point of communication between applications inside a cloud provider and the internet, and has a very limited number of features configured, such as—NAT. This allows hosts inside the data center network to access the internet by changing the source IP address to a publicly available IP address.

# Commonly made mistakes while designing networks for OpenShift

While network design is generally simple, there are many ways to make a mistake that will make the whole network a single point of failure. The most commonly made mistakes are as follows:

- On access and core network layers, people often use static **Link Aggregation (LAG)** methods instead of dynamic link control, such as **Link Aggregation Control Protocol (LACP)** 802.3ad. MTU values are not properly set throughout the network and CoPP filters block protocol communication between networking equipment, which causes failover not to work in case of a failure.
- When using load balancers, quite often active/passive deployments cannot failover properly from one node to the other. This is usually caused by inconsistent configuration between load balancer cluster nodes.
- Firewalls and security groups are quite often a bottleneck, and a single firewall cluster consisting of two and more nodes can be a single point of failure if a single control plane is used. We have seen stateless filters used instead of stateful filters, which causes bidirectional traffic to be blocked. And finally, when failover preemption is used, it causes the firewall cluster to flap indefinitely.
- On border routers, having one of several full internet-routing tables takes a lot of time for BGP to reconverge, which often causes traffic to be blackholed. The only default gateway causes BGP to not take the most optimal route and the **Equal-Cost Multi-Path (ECMP)** causes asymmetric routing and packet loss.

# General network requirements and design guidelines for OpenShift deployments

The network is a critical component for OpenShift because every piece of OpenShift solution is dependent on network availability, performance, scalability, and stability. Both control and data plane traffic uses different parts of the network to talk to one another. In order to make OpenShift solutions available most of the time and to avoid unplanned network outages, several things have to be considered:

- All the physical hosts running OpenShift require having redundant physical connectivity to access-level switches using MC-LAG or a similar technology

- A set of load balancers implemented in a redundant fashion with separate data and control planes
- A set of firewalls implemented in a redundant fashion with separate data and control planes
- A dedicated management network to be used where applicable for security reasons
- VIP with **keepalived** is implemented if no external load balancer is used on both infrastructure nodes and the upstream network has no single point of failure
- AnyCast IPs if several Data Centers
- Network convergence is taken care of by additional mechanisms such as **Bidirectional Forwarding Detection** (**BFD**), additional tuning settings such as PortFast in the case of the **Spanning Tree Protocol** (**STP**), and tuning protocol timers in routing protocols
- The MTU parameter is properly set on OpenShift nodes and aligned with the network to make sure that no packet fragmentation is happening
- Proper ports are opened for the communication to and from any OpenShift component if isolated with a firewall or any type of **Access Control List** (**ACL**) on a network device

Taking in mind all of the preceding considerations will help you avoid 99% of all the issues that you may face while designing your OpenShift cluster.

# Summary

In this chapter, we covered the main network aspects while designing an OpenShift cluster in one or across multiple data centers. We also discussed commonly made mistakes, solutions, and overall guidance from a networking point of view.

In the next chapter, we are going to give a brief overview of new OpenShift 3.9 features that we have and have not covered in this book. We are going to briefly discuss what to expect from the following OpenShift releases later this year (2018).

# Questions

1. Which network component in the standard data center deployment is optional? choose one:

    1. Firewall

2. Load balancer
3. Core switch
4. Border router

2. What are the two commonly made mistakes on a firewall? choose two:

    1. Failover preemption
    2. Stateless filters
    3. Stateful filters
    4. Having one or several full internet tables

3. Physical data center and cloud networks have exactly the same components:

    1. True
    2. False

4. What command can be used to backup and restore application data in OpenShift? choose one:

    1. `oc rsync`
    2. `oc backup`
    3. `oc save`
    4. `oc load`

5. Which network component is responsible for letting the application out to the internet in cloud networks? choose one:

    1. Load balancer
    2. NAT gateway
    3. Border router
    4. Edge Firewall

# Further reading

Here is a list of topics with links related to this chapter that you might want to deep dive into:

- **Network Design and Architecture Center: Data Center Networks at** https://www.juniper.net/documentation/en_US/design-and-architecture/data-center/.
- **AWS Single VPC Design at** https://aws.amazon.com/answers/networking/aws-single-vpc-design/.

# What is New in OpenShift 3.9? 21

In the previous chapter, we covered the main network aspects while designing OpenShift clusters in one or across multiple data centers. We also discussed commonly made mistakes, solutions, and overall guidance from a networking point of view.

In this chapter, we are going to give a brief overview of the new OpenShift 3.9 features that we have and have not covered in this book. We are going to briefly discuss what to expect from the following OpenShift releases later in 2018.

In this chapter, we will cover the following topics:

- Major changes in OpenShift 3.9
- What to expect from the following OpenShift releases

## Major changes in OpenShift 3.9

At the time of writing this book, **OpenShift Container Platform** (**OCP**) 3.9 has been just released. OCP 3.9 is significantly different from the other releases, in that the earlier versions of OpenShift were one step behind a version of Kubernetes, meaning that OpenShift 3.5 was using Kubernetes 1.6, and OpenShift 3.7 was using Kubernetes 1.8. This is the main reason why Red Hat skipped version 3.8 and jumped right to 3.9, syncing up with Kubernetes 1.9. This does not mean that OpenShift 3.8 has been renamed 3.9, in fact, it is quite the opposite. OpenShift 3.9 includes all the new features from both 3.8 and 3.9, which includes the following:

- **CRI-O**: A lightweight **Container Runtime Interface** (**CRI**) that natively works with Kubernetes. It is designed to bring additional features into Kubernetes, such as the following:
    - Enhanced security

- Better scalability and performance over traditional container runtime interfaces
- Compatibility with any compliant **Open Container Initiative (OCI)**, including Docker

- **Red Hat CloudForms Management Engine 4.6 Container Management**: This is easy to use and to configure integration with Red Hat CloudForms through Ansible playbook installation, which includes following new features, updates, and older version enhancements:
    - OpenShift template provisioning
    - Alert management
    - Enhancements for UX
    - Enhancements for chargeback
    - Provider updates
- **End-to-end online expansion and resize for containerized GlusterFS PV**: This feature allows an OpenShift user to expand **persistent volume (PV)** claims online. Originally, this was only possible from the CLI.
- **Automated container native storage deployment with OpenShift container platform advances installation**: This allows integration with file and block storage devices that are provided by the most popular cloud providers, including Amazon AWS, Google GCE, and Microsoft Azure.
- **Device plugins**: A special plugin that allows you to use special devices in the OCP without the need to write any custom code. A device plugin is a portable solution to consume hardware resources across OpenShift clusters.
- **Support our own HAProxy RPM for consumption by the router**: The capability of upgrading HAProxy routers under heavy load without causing any outages. OpenShift 3.9 allows you to perform seamless updates and upgrades.
- **Quick installation**: This is now being deprecated. You will be able to install a new cluster using this method, but won't be able to perform any updates or upgrades. This method will be removed in the future version. Advanced installation should be used instead.
- **Automated 3.7 to 3.9 control plane upgrade**: Using the advanced OpenShift installer through Ansible, it is possible to perform automated upgrades from 3.7 to 3.8 to 3.9. This includes the following:
    - API, controllers, and nodes on the control plane that host seamless 1 hop upgrades
    - Router, registry, service catalog, and brokers direct upgrade

- Node, Docker, **Open vSwitch** (**OVS**) direct upgrade
- Logging and metrics direct upgrade

- **Prometheus**: This is a new product suite and a replacement for standard logging and metrics in OpenShift in the near future.
- **CLI plugins**: A new feature that allows you to extend `oc` command capabilities with the new functionalities.

# What to expect from the following OpenShift releases

While it is still hard to predict what to expect from future OpenShift versions, we can derive some of this information from the technology preview features that you can find in the OCP 3.9 release notes as well as in the latest Red Hat events such as Red Hat Summit 2018, which took place from May 7 to May 11 in 2018. The good part is that the OCP software release cycle is every 3 months, which means that by the time you read this book, there is a chance that we will already have a new version of OpenShift coming out. The following table shows the difference between the versions of OCP in terms of **Tech Preview** (**TP**) and **General Availability** (**GA**):

| Features | OCP 3.7 | OCP 3.9 | OCP 3.10, OCP 3.11 |
|---|---|---|---|
| Prometheus cluster monitoring | TP | TP | GA* |
| CRI-O | | TP | GA* |
| CLI plugins | TP | TP | GA* |
| Device plugins | | TP | GA |
| CPU manager | | TP | TP* |
| Huge pages | | TP | GA* |
| PV resize | | TP | TP* |
| Local storage PVs | TP | TP | GA* |

*Data is given based on our predictions.
Besides all of the preceding data given here, we are going to see other OpenShift enhancements, such as the following:

- Prometheus cluster monitoring in conjunction with the Admin Web Console and operator **lifecycle manager** (**LCM**) features is going to make life easier for a *lazy* OpenShift admin, giving them a nice, easy to use and configured web console, functional enough to complete most of the tasks from a web interface. This is just one of the features that these projects are going to add together, but there is going to be so much more than that.

- Istio and OpenShift service mesh products are going to bring OpenShift hybrid meshing to the next level by using on-demand service connections. Therefore, there will no longer be a need to provision such things manually.

- One of the greatest things we are going to see in the future releases is seamless and easy to perform cluster upgrades and cluster scaling. What this means is that currently, we can only remove OpenShift nodes from the cluster without rebooting or restarting master nodes, but this is not the case with adding a new node. The process of adding a new node is not that fast nor always easy. So, what we are going to see in the upcoming releases is an ability to use *golden* images and the ability to add them to the cluster on the fly.

- Integration with the OpenStack **Infrastructure as a service** (**IaaS**) platform is going to be closer to reality. We are going to see how OpenShift on OpenStack deployments can leverage this type of deployment by utilizing underlying OpenStack platform services like **Load Balancer as a Service** (**LBaaS**), **Firewall as a Service** (**FWaaS**), **DNS as a Service** (**DNSaaS**), and so on, alongside further integration with tested and certified Neutron plugins, as well as bare metal servers provisioning and management through Ironic.

- Another huge enhancement we are going to see in the future is OpenShift integration with CoreOS products such as CoreOS, Quay, and Tectonic. All of these products are very unique and useful when it comes to questioning how it is going to work with an OCP:

    - **CoreOS**: This is an OS that is designed and built to run containers at scale. CoreOS has a really small footprint, it's lightweight, and has minimum functionality, which is enough to run containers and container orchestration platforms like Kubernetes.

- **Quay**: This is a highly distributed and reliable container registry for containers and Kubernetes, which allows you to run several instances of Quay to ensure redundancy out of the box. Quay also has a geo-replication feature available that allows seamless synchronization of your container images between different data centers. One of the other most important features of Quay is automatic container scanning for security vulnerabilities. This is one of the most requested security features in the container industry. Quay also has a continuous integration feature, which allows you to build and push images when developers commit the code, automatically.
- **Tectonic**: This is a container orchestration platform by CoreOS, which works similarly to the OCP, but has a lot less functionality compared to OpenShift. The uniqueness of Tectonic is that its control plane services are running inside the Kubernetes service that Tectonic is managing. This is a classic chicken or the egg situation that CoreOS managed to solve.

We are going to see most of these functionalities or the most requested features one way or the other migrated to or merged with the OCP. The whole of 2018 is probably going to be a little bit hectic for the OCP development team due to the recent acquisition of CoreOS. These teams are going to work together to decide which features to move forward with and which of them to let go forever. But no matter what, it is all going to benefit OpenShift and make it the most successful container management platform of all time.

# Summary

In this chapter, we gave a brief overview of new OpenShift 3.9 features that we have and have not covered in this book. We also briefly discussed what to expect from the following OpenShift releases later in 2018.

This was the last chapter of the book, so we thank you for reading it and we hope that you gained useful knowledge of concepts behind OpenShift, as well as obtained some hands-on skills installing OpenShift and managing its resources.

# Questions

1. Which one of the following is not designed to bring additional features into Kubernetes in CRI-O? choose one:

    1. Docker replacement
    2. Enhanced security
    3. Better scalability and performance
    4. Compatibility with any compliant OCI

2. What are the main two products that have been brought by the recent CoreOS acquisition and need to be integrated into OpenShift in the future? choose two:

    1. Quay
    2. Mesos
    3. Tectonik
    4. Kubernetes

3. CoreOS is an OS that is designed and built to run containers at scale:

    1. True
    2. False

4. Which of the following OpenShift features allows expanding OpenShift `oc` command capabilities ? choose one:

    1. CLI plugins
    2. OCI plugins
    3. Device plugins
    4. CLI enhancement

# Further reading

Here is a list of topics with links related to this chapter that you might want to deep dive into:

- **OpenShift Container Platform 3.9 Release Notes at** `https://docs.openshift.com/container-platform/3.9/release_notes/ocp_3_9_release_notes.html`.
- **OpenShift roadmap from Red Hat Summit 2018 at** `https://www.youtube.com/watch?v=1AelNjx6BB4`.
- **OpenShift Container Platform Tested Integrations at** `https://access.redhat.com/articles/2176281`.

# Assessments

## Chapter 1

1. Answer is 1 (Docker Container, Docker Image, Docker Registry)
2. Answer is 2 and 3 (Private Registry and Public registry)
3. Answer is True.
4. Answer is 1 (Cgroups)
5. Answer is 1 and 4 (`docker build -t new_httpd_image .` and `docker build -t new_httpd_image ./`)
6. Answer is False

## Chapter 2

1. Answer is 1 and 4 (Node and Master)
2. Answer is 1 and 3 (Docker and Rkt)
3. Answer is True
4. Answer is 2 and 3 (kubelet and kube-proxy)
5. Answer is 1 and 5 (JSON and YAML)
6. Answer is False

## Chapter 3

1. Answer is 2 (CRI)
2. Answer is 1 and 3 (Docker and Rkt)
3. Answer is True
4. Answer is 1 (kubectl describe pods/httpd)
5. Answer is 2 and 3 (CRI-O talks directly to Container Runtime and CRI-O is OCI-compliant)
6. Answer is True

# Chapter 4

1. Answer is PaaS
2. Answer is 1 and 3 (OpenShift Origin and OpenShift Enterprise)
3. Answer is False
4. Answer is 4 (Persistent storage)
5. Answer is 1 and 2(Router as an ingress traffic control and OpenShift Internal Registry)
6. Answer is True

# Chapter 5

1. Answer is 1 (Docker)
2. Answer is 1 (8443)
3. Answer is False
4. Answer is 2 (oc login -u system:admin)
5. Answer is 1 and 3 (oc login -u system:admin and oc cluster down)
6. Answer is True

# Chapter 6

1. Answer is 1 and 4 (masters and ectd)
2. Answer is 3 (infra)
3. Answer is 2 (playbooks/byo/config.yml)

# Chapter 7

1. Answer is 2 (MariaDB database for production)
2. Answer is 1 and 4 (NFS and GlusterFS)
3. Answer is 3 (Any project)
4. Answer is 2 (1950 M)
5. Answer is 2 and 3 (Service and Endpoint)

# Chapter 8

1. Answer is 1 and 4 (Node and Master)
2. Answer is 2 and 5 (Admin users and Service users)
3. Answer is True
4. Answer is 2 (Route)
5. Answer is 1 and 4 (oc get po and oc get routes)
6. Answer is False

# Chapter 9

1. Answer is 1 and 4 (To protect applications from breaking unexpectedly when the image that an ImageStream points to changes and To implement automatic build and deployments on image change.)
2. Answer is 1 and 3 (`oc create configmap my-configmap --from-file=nginx.conf` and `oc create -f configmap_definition.yaml`)
3. Answer is 3 and 4 (`oc create resourcequota my-quota --hard=cpu=4,services=5` and `oc create quota another-quota --hard=pods=8,secrets=4`)
4. Answer is 2 and 4 (ConfigMap and Service)
5. Answer is 3 (${VARIABLE})
6. Answer is 3 (Requests)
7. Answer is 3 (v2alpha1)

# Chapter 10

1. Answer is 2 and 4 (generate and claim)
2. Answer is 4 (default)
3. Answer is 2 and 4 (admin and edit)
4. Answer is 3 (ProjectRequestLimit)
5. Answer is 1 and 4 (anyuid and privileged)
6. Answer is 2 (data)

# Chapter 11

1. Answer is 4 (`vxlan_sys_4789`)
2. Answer is 3 (Use the ovs-multitenant plugin and join and isolate projects as needed)
3. Answer is 3 (Static IP for external traffic from the project)
4. Answer is 3:

```
- type: Allow
  to:
      dnsName: rubygems.org
- type: Allow
  to:
      dnsName: launchpad.net
- type: Deny
  to:
      cidrSelector: 0.0.0.0/0
```

5. Answer is 5 (`web.dev.svc.cluster.local`)

# Chapter 12

1. Answer is 2 (**Route**)
2. Answer is 1,2,3 (Pod, Service, Route)
3. Answer is 3 (`oc expose svc httpd --hostname myservice.example.com`)
4. Answer is 1 and 4 (oc get all, oc get route)

# Chapter 13

1. Answer is 2 (openshift)
2. Answer is 1,2,3:

    1. `oc get template mytemplate -n openshift -o yaml`
    2. `oc process --parameters -f mytemplate.json`
    3. `oc describe template mytemplate -n openshift`

3. Answer is 5 (All of the above)

# Chapter 14

1. Answer is 1, 3 (`oc edit bc/redis`, `oc patch bc/redis --patch ...`)
2. Answer is 3 `oc start-build`
3. Answer is 2 `Dockerfile`

# Chapter 15

1. Answer is 3, 4 (Replication controller, Build config)
2. Answer is 3 (`oc start-build`)
3. Answer is 1,2,3:
    1. `oc status -v`
    2. `oc status`
    3. `oc logs build/phpdemo-2`

# Chapter 16

1. Answer is 1 (buildconfig)
2. Answer is 6 (All of above)

# Chapter 17

1. Answer is 2 (Continuous deployment)
2. Answer is 1,2 4 (OpenShift Domain Specific Language, Jenkins Pipeline Build Strategy, Jenkinsfile )
3. Answer is False
4. Answer is 1 (Input)
5. Answer is 1 (Build | Pipelines)
6. Answer is False

# Chapter 18

1. Answer is 1 (Virtual IP)
2. Answer is 1, 2 (Virtual IP, IP failover)
3. Answer is True
4. Answer is 1 (oc rsync)
5. Answer is False

# Chapter 19

1. Answer is 1 (`OpenShift Etcd key-value store`)
2. Answer is 3 (3xOSP - 3xDC)
3. Answer is True
4. Answer is 1, 2 (Persistent storage replication, Application database replication)

# Chapter 20

1. Answer is 2 (Load balancer)
2. Answer is 1, 2 (Failover preemption, Stateless filters)
3. Answer is False
4. Answer is `oc rsync`
5. Answer is 2 (NAT gateway)

# Chapter 21

1. Answer is 1 (Docker replacement)
2. Answer is 1, 3 (Quay, Tectonik)
3. Answer is True
4. Answer is 1 (CLI plugins)

# Other Books You May Enjoy

If you enjoyed this book, you may be interested in these other books by Packt:

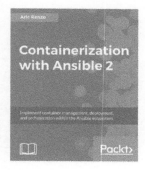

**Containerization with Ansible 2**
Aric Renzo

ISBN: 978-1-78829-191-0

- Increase your productivity by using Ansible roles to define and build images
- Learn how to work with Ansible Container to manage, test, and deploy your containerized applications.
- Increase the flexibility and portability of your applications by learning to use Ansible
- Discover how you can apply your existing Ansible roles to the image build process
- Get you up and running from building a simple container image to deploying a complex, multi-container app in the cloud.
- Take an indepth look at the architecture of Ansible Container, and learn how to build re-usable container images, reliably and efficiently.

**OpenStack for Architects - Second Edition**
Ben Silverman, Michael Solberg

ISBN: 978-1-78862-451-0

- Learn the overall structure of an OpenStack deployment
- Craft an OpenStack deployment process which fits within your organization
- Apply Agile Development methodologies to engineer and operate OpenStack clouds
- Build a product roadmap for Infrastructure as a Service based on OpenStack
- Make use of containers to increase the manageability and resiliency of applications running in and on OpenStack.
- Use enterprise security guidelines for your OpenStack deployment

# Leave a review - let other readers know what you think

Please share your thoughts on this book with others by leaving a review on the site that you bought it from. If you purchased the book from Amazon, please leave us an honest review on this book's Amazon page. This is vital so that other potential readers can see and use your unbiased opinion to make purchasing decisions, we can understand what our customers think about our products, and our authors can see your feedback on the title that they have worked with Packt to create. It will only take a few minutes of your time, but is valuable to other potential customers, our authors, and Packt. Thank you!

# Index

## A

Access Control List (ACL) 457
access layer switches
 Control Plane Policing (CoPP) 451
 dynamic routing protocol 451
 L3 gateway 451
 Multi-Chassis Link Aggregation (MC-LAG) 451
 Virtual LAN (VLAN) 451
Admission Control Plugin
 BuildDefaults 270
 BuildOverrides 270
 openshift.io/ImagePolicy 271
 openshift.io/IngressAdmission 271
 PodNodeConstraints 271
 PodNodeSelector 271
 PodPreset 271
 ProjectRequestLimit 270
 RunOnceDuration 271
Admission Controller 268, 270, 271, 272, 274
advanced deployment 339
Amazon Web Services (AWS) 95
Ansible inventory
 about 132
 etcd 133
 glusterfs 133
 glusterfs_registry 133
 lb 133
 masters 132
 new_masters 132
 new_nodes 133
 nfs 133
 nodes 133
Ansible variables
 ansible_ssh_user 134
 deployment_type 134
 openshift_clock_enabled 135

openshift_disable_check 135
openshift_master_identity_providers 134
openshift_node_labels 134
openshift_schedulable 134
openshit_master_default_subdomain 134
reference 134
application
 autoscaling, based on CPU utilization 230
 autoscaling, based on RAM utilization 230
 building, from Dockerfile 366
 creating 184
architecture, Docker
 about 14
 Docker client 14
 Docker server 14
authentication
 about 247
 identities 247, 248, 249, 250, 252, 254
 identity providers 257
 reference 257
 service accounts 255, 256
 users 247, 248, 249, 250, 252, 254
authorization 261, 262

## B

Bidirectional Forwarding Detection (BFD) 457
Border Gateway Protocol (BGP) 451
border router
 about 453
 CoPP 453
 Dynamic Routing Protocol 453
brew
 reference 109

## C

CentOS 7
 oc cluster up, deployment process 104, 105,

106, 107
Ceph
  reference 150
CI/CD
  about 401
  Jenkins, using as 402
client-side verification
  about 158
  GlusterFS, verification 159
  iSCSI, verification 159
  NFS, verification 158
cloud networks
  about 453
  load balancers 453, 455
  Network Address Translation (NAT) gateways
    453, 455
  security groups 453, 455
  software-defined networking (SDN) 453, 454
cloud technology 91
complex stacks, application
  creating, with templates 221, 223, 227, 230
components, Docker
  Docker containers 15
  Docker images 15
  Docker registry 15
ConfigMaps
  used, for separating configuration from
    application code 206, 209, 211
container filesystem 16
container image layers 17
container management systems
  Docker Swarm 55
  Kubernetes 55
  overview 54
Container Network Interface (CNI) 85
Container Runtime 82, 83
Container Runtime Interface (CRI) 82, 83
Container-as-a-Service (CaaS) 21
containers
  advantages 11, 12, 13
  features 11
  inspecting 35
  managing, with Docker CLI 32
  overview 11
  removing 36

  starting 35
  stopping 35
Content Management System (CMS) 392
Continuous Delivery 401
Continuous Deployment 401
Continuous Integration 401
control groups (cgroups) 15
core layer switches
  about 451
  CoPP 451
  dynamic routing protocol 451
CoreOS 464
CPU-based autoscaling 231, 234, 235
CRI-O
  about 83
  installing 85, 86, 87
  virtual environment, stopping 87
  with Kubernetes 84
  working with 85, 86, 87
custom Docker image
  creating 43
  creating, with Dockerfile build 46
  customizing, with docker commit 44, 46
  Docker history, using 47
  Dockerfile instructions, using 48, 49, 50
custom template
  creating 353

D

data center networks
  about 450
  access layer switches 451
  access/leaf switches 450
  border routers 450, 453
  core layer switches 451
  core/spine layer switches 450
  edge firewalls 450, 452
  load balancers 450, 452
deployment variants 103
development environment
  benefits 102
  need for 102
DNS 319, 320, 322
DNS as a Service (DNSaaS) 464
DNS

about 317
Docker CLI
  commands, executing inside container 34
  containers, inspecting 35
  containers, managing 32
  containers, starting 34
  containers, stopping 34
  Docker help, using 24
  Docker info, using 24
  docker logs command 33, 34
  Docker man, using 24
  Docker port, mapping 35
  docker ps command 33, 34
  images, loading 29, 30
  images, managing 24, 25, 27
  images, saving 29, 30
  images, uploading to Docker registry 30, 31
  images, working with 27, 28
  using 23
Docker Community Edition (CE) 21
Docker containers
  architecture 13
  Linux containers 15
Docker Enterprise Edition (EE) 21
Docker for macOS
  reference 108
Docker for Windows
  reference 110
Docker Hub
  features 20
  overview 20
  reference 20
Docker images
  about 16
  applications, creating 202
  container filesystem 16
  container image layers 17, 18
  layers 16
  storage drivers 17
Docker registry
  about 18
  accessing 19
  images, uploading 30, 31
  private registry 19
  public registry 19

Docker Swarm
  about 55
  versus Kubernetes 55
Docker
  architecture 14
  configuration 21, 23
  installation 21
  reference 21
Dockerfile
  application, building from 366
  build customization 370, 371, 372
  development, for OpenShift 365, 366
  simple Dockerfile build 368, 369
Domain Specific Language (DSL) 118

## E

edge firewalls
  application firewall 452
  CoPP 452
  distributed denial-of-service (DDoS) protection 452
  Intrusion Detection System (IDS) 452
  Intrusion Prevention System (IPS) 452
  Network Address Translation (NAT) 452
  stateful inspection 452
egress network policies 314, 315, 316
egress routers 313
environment variables
  containers, linking 38, 39, 40
  passing, to container 36, 38
  using 36
ephemeral storage
  versus persistent storage 146
equal-cost multi-path (ECMP) 456

## F

Firewall as a Service (FWaaS) 464

## G

General Availability (GA) 463
GlusterFS shares
  packages, installing 155
GlusterFS
  brick, configuring 156
  configuring 154

packages, installing 155
verification 159
volume, configuring 156
Gogs application
creating 358, 359, 360
template 358

# H

HA, in OpenShift
IP failover 423, 425
OpenShift etcd 427
OpenShift infrastructure nodes 425, 426
OpenShift masters 427
OpenShift nodes 428
virtual IPs 422, 423
high availability (HA) 11, 419, 420, 433

# I

identity providers
AllowAll 258
DenyAll 258
HTPasswd 259, 260
LDAP 260
selecting 257
ImageStreams
applications, creating from Docker images 202
images, importing 201
used, for tracking version history of images 199
Infrastructure as a service (IaaS) 464
Interior Gateway Protocol (IGP) 451
internet Small Computer Systems Interface (iSCSI)
configuring 156
verification 159
Interprocess Communication (IPC) 15

# J

Jenkins architecture
about 402
components 403
Jenkins Master 403
Jenkins Pipeline Build Strategy 403
Jenkins pipeline
creating, in OpenShift 400, 405, 406, 407
execution, managing 413, 414, 415
starting 408, 409, 410

Jenkins Slaves 403
Jenkins
as CI/CD 402
in OpenShift 403
Jenkinsfile
about 403
editing 412
JSON files
kubernetes services, creating 74
JSON template definitions
developing 353, 354

# K

kubectl
about 63
get command, using 65, 66
help options 64, 65
Kubernetes advanced resources 72, 73, 74
Kubernetes labels, using 70
Kubernetes pods, executing 66, 67
Kubernetes resources 68
Kubernetes resources, deleting 71
Kubernetes resources, editing 69
kubernetes services, creating with YAML and JSON files 74
Kubernetes services, exposing 69
Kuberentes API
reference 75
Kubernetes labels
reference 71
Kubernetes, resources
Labels 58
Namespaces 57
Persistent Volume Claims (PVC) 58
Persistent Volumes (PV) 58
Pods 58
Replication Controllers (RC) 58
Secrets 58
Services 58
Kubernetes
about 55
configuration 61, 62, 63
installation 61, 62, 63
key concepts 56, 59, 60
limitations 76, 77

masters 56
nodes 57
reference 61
using, with CRI-O 84, 85
versus Docker Swarm 55

# L

lifecycle manager (LCM) 464
LimitRanges
  used, for controlling resource consumption 217,
    219, 221
Link Aggregation (LAG) 456
Link Aggregation Control Protocol (LACP) 456
Linux containers
  control groups (cgroups) 15
  features 15
  Linux namespaces 15
  Security Enhanced Linux (SELinux) 16
Load Balancer as a Service (LBaaS) 464
load balancers
  about 452, 455
  CoPP 453
  Destination Network Address Translation (DNAT)
    452
  load balancing 452
  SSL offloading 453
local area networks (LANs) 156

# M

macOS
  oc cluster up, deployment process 107, 109,
    110
mandatory access control (MAC) 16
manual application deployment
  about 329
  pod, creating 330, 331
  route, creating 334
  service, creating 332
MariaDB image
  reference 38
MariaDB
  deploying 340, 341
memory-based autoscaling 238, 239
MiniShift
  about 115

prerequisites 116
reference 115
starting 117
stopping 117
Mount (mnt) 15
multi-tier application
  building 392
  deploying, templates used 357

# N

National Security Agency (NSA) 16
Network (net) 15
Network Address Translation (NAT) gateways 455
network design
  guidelines 456
  mistakes 456
Network File System (NFS)
  exports, configuring on server 152, 153
  packages, installing on server and clients 152
  service, enabling 154
  service, starting 154
  setting up 151, 152
  verification 154, 158
network topologies
  about 449
  cloud networks 453
  data center networks 450
network topology, OpenShift
  about 291, 292
  connectivity, tracing 293, 295, 297

# O

oc cluster up
  for CentOS 7 104, 105, 106, 107
  for macOS 107, 109, 110
  for Windows 110, 111
  OpenShift, accessing through web browser 112
  prerequisites 103
  system requisites 103
  working with 103
oc expose
  used, for creating route 334
  used, for creating service 332
oc new-app -o command
  using 356

oc new-app command
 using 336, 337
 using, with default options 337, 338
OCI-compliant Container Runtime Interface 83
one OpenShift cluster per Data Center
 application deployment 446
 implementing 441, 442
 networking 443
 storage 444, 445
Open Container Initiative (OCI) 83
OpenFlow 454
OpenShift 3.9
 features 461, 463
OpenShift Container Platform (OCP) 3.9 461
OpenShift Domain Specific Language (DSL) 403
OpenShift HA 420, 421
OpenShift installation procedure, components
 etcd key-value store backup 429
 OpenShift masters 430
 OpenShift nodes 430
 persistent storage 430
OpenShift multi-DC HA design
 about 438
 one OpenShift cluster across all data centers
  439, 440
 one OpenShift cluster per data center 440, 441
 one OpenShift cluster per Data Center 442
OpenShift Origin
 about 95
 reference 95
OpenShift persistent data
 external storage 428
OpenShift persistent storage
 about 146
 Persistent Volume (PV) 147
 Persistent Volume Claims (PVC) 148
OpenShift single-DC HA design
 about 434
 considerations 438
 etcd key-value store 437
 OpenShift infrastructure nodes 435, 436
 OpenShift Masters 436
 OpenShift nodes 437
 persistent storage 437
 physical placement consideration 437

OpenShift, advanced installation
 Ansible inventory 132, 135
 Ansible playbooks 136
 Ansible playbooks, installation 137
 methods 132
OpenShift, installation methods
 containerized installation 125
 deployment scenarios 126, 127, 128
 overview 125
 RPM installation 125
openshift-ansible project
 reference 427, 428
OpenShift
 about 93
 additional Kubernetes resource extensions 98
 architecture 96
 authentication 97
 backup 429
 business value 94
 capabilities 97
 CI/CD integration 98
 Dockerfile development 365, 366
 features 93, 97
 flavors 95
 future enhancements 463, 465
 GUI 98
 hardware requisites 124
 image builders 98
 installing, with Vagrant box 121
 internal image registry 98
 Jenkins pipelines, creating 400, 405, 406, 407
 multi-tenancy 97
 network topology 291, 292
 prerequisites 124
 REST API 98
 restore 429
 SCM integration 98
 storage life cycle 148, 149
 template, overview 347
 wen console 98
OpenStack Cinder
 reference 151
ovs-multitenant plugin 301, 302, 303, 305, 306
ovs-networkpolicy plugin 306, 307, 309, 310, 311
ovs-subnet plugin 298, 300

# P

Perl Compatible Regular Expressions (PCRE) 349
persistent storage
  claims, using as volumes in pod definition 170,
    171
  persistent data, for database container 174, 175,
    176
  persistent volume, requesting 167
  PVC, building to particular PV 168
  PVC, building to PV 169
  using 41, 43
  using, in pods 167
  versus ephemeral storage 146
  volumes, managing via oc volume 172, 173,
    174
Persistent Volume (PV) 146, 147
Persistent Volume Claim (PVC) 146, 148, 149,
  167
PHP build process 385, 386
PHP build
  process 384
  starting 387
PHP S2I 379, 380
Physical Volumes (PV)
  configuring 160
  creating, for GlusterFS volume 163, 164, 165
  creating, for iSCSI 166
  creating, for NFS shares 161, 162, 163
Platform as a Service (PaaS) 91
pods
  creating 330
  managing 186
private registry 19
Process ID (PID) 15
projects
  managing 179, 182
public registry 19

# Q

Quay 465

# R

Red Hat OpenShift Container Platform 95
Red Hat OpenShift Dedicated 95

Red Hat OpenShift Online 95
ResourceQuotas
  used, for controlling resource consumption 212,
    215, 217
resources
  exporting, as templates 355, 356
role-based access control
  about 261
  built-in roles, using 262, 264
  custom roles, creating 264, 265, 268
route
  creating, from YAML definition 335
  creating, oc expose used 334
  managing 189, 192
RPM installation method
  Ansible, installation 130
  Docker, activating 129
  environment preparation 128
  SELinux, enabling 130
  SSH access, ensuring 131

# S

SDN plugins
  about 297
  ovs-multitenant plugin 301, 302, 303, 305, 306
  ovs-networkpolicy plugin 306, 307, 309, 310,
    311
  ovs-subnet plugin 298, 300
secrets, types
  docker-registry 278
  generic 278
  tls 278
security context constraints (SCCs) 267, 274
  about 276
Security Enhanced Linux (SELinux) 16
security groups 455
sensitive data
  considerations 277
  secrets 277, 279, 280, 282, 283, 284
  storing 276
service
  creating, from YAML definition 333
  creating, oc expose used 332
  managing 187
simple PHP application

building 381, 382, 383
software-defined networking (SDN)
  about 454
  OpenFlow 454
  Virtual Extensible LAN (VXLAN) 455
Source-to-Image (S2I) 9, 76, 392
Spanning Tree Protocol (STP) 457
stateful inspection 455
static IPs
  for external project traffic 313
storage area network (SAN) 156
storage backends
  comparison 149, 150
storage drivers 17
storage infrastructure
  client-side verification 158
  GlusterFS, configuring 154
  internet Small Computer Systems Interface
   (iSCSI), configuring 156
  Network File System (NFS), setting up 151, 152
  setting up 150

# T

Tech Preview (TP) 463
Tectonic 465
template parameters
  displaying 350, 351
templates
  adding 350
  processing 352
  resources, exporting as 355, 356
  syntax 348, 349
  used, for creating complex stacks of application
   221, 223, 227, 230
  used, for deploying multi-tier application 357

# U

User IDs (UIDs) 15, 152
users
  managing 182, 184

# V

Vagrant box
  OpenShift, installing 121
Vagrant, components
  Box 118
  Provider 118
  Vagrant software 118
  Vagrantfile 118
Vagrant
  about 117
  installation 119
  reference 22, 119
version history, images
  tracking, with ImageStreams 199
virtual environment
  deleting 75
  stopping 87
Virtual eXtensible Local Area Network (VXLAN)
  291, 455
virtual machine (VM) 21, 455
VirtualBox
  reference 119

# W

web browser
  OpenShift, accessing 112
wide area networks (WANs) 156
Windows
  oc cluster up, deployment process 110, 111
WordPress application
  building 393, 394, 396
  creating 396, 397
WordPress template 392

# Y

YAML application
  service, creating 333
YAML definition
  route, creating 335
YAML files
  kubernetes services, creating 74
YAML template definitions
  developing 353, 354

Lightning Source UK Ltd.
Milton Keynes UK
UKHW031933280519
343477UK00004B/296/P